W9-BCP-045

A HOLISTIC APPROACH TO RIGHTS

Affirmative Action, Reproductive Rights, Censorship, and Future Generations

Eugene Schlossberger

University Press of America,® Inc.
Lanham · Boulder · New York · Toronto · Plymouth, UK

Copyright © 2008 by
University Press of America®, Inc.
4501 Forbes Boulevard
Suite 200
Lanham, Maryland 20706
UPA Acquisitions Department (301) 459-3366

Estover Road
Plymouth PL6 7PY
United Kingdom

Library of Congress Control Number: 2007937973
ISBN-13: 978-0-7618-3936-1 (clothbound : alk. paper)
ISBN-10: 0-7618-3936-4 (clothbound : alk. paper)
ISBN-13: 978-0-7618-3937-8 (paperback : alk. paper)
ISBN-10: 0-7618-3937-2 (paperback : alk. paper)

For my wife, Maricar, and my children, Aaron, Noah, and Rachel.

Contents

Preface   vii

Chapter 1:   Introduction and Overview   1

Part I: Theory of Rights

Chapter 2:   The Many Flavors of Rights: Entitlements, Liberties,   55
Permissions, and the Right to Die

Chapter 3:   Rights as Warrants   67

Chapter 4:   Why the Correlation Thesis Should Be Discarded   109

Chapter 5:   A New Theory of Natural Rights   127

Part II: Particular Rights and Applications

Chapter 6:   The Right to Speech: Regulating Violence and   161
Pornography in the Media

Chapter 7:   Moral Rights and the Right to the Truth   193

Chapter 8:   Rights of and Obligations to Future Generations   213

Chapter 9:   The Right to Reproduce   239

Chapter 10: Group Rights, Loyalty, and Affirmative Action   277

Index   351

About the Author   355

Preface

This book, whose roots stretch back more than twenty years, is about the nature of rights and the various particular rights that enliven our social, political, and legal discourse, from broad rights of central importance, such as the right to free speech, to very specific rights, such as the right to call oneself a poet. The Holistic approach, with its emphasis on balancing diverse factors to achieve a livable total picture, may seem less than gratifying to many in this polarized society of ours, yet it reflects, it seems to me, the nuanced, complex, and messy nature of moral reality. Ethics, as Aristotle said, is not an exact science: the world of ethics is neither the purified, perfect domain of absolutes Kant envisioned nor a Newtonian theatre of diverse phenomena regulated by law-like principles. Rather, ethics is the realm of unhappy compromise in which flawed and diverse human beings struggle to lead some semblance of a good human life. In this struggle there are guidelines rather than rules, and cogency plays a larger role than validity. This volume is an attempt to work out some part of the conceptual structure of one aspect of the landscape of ethics, ranging from a theoretical analysis of what rights are to a practical proposal for regulating violence and pornography in the media.

In the course of thinking about these matters I have profited from conversations with many individuals, including Joel Feinberg, Joan Callahan, Judith Andre, Hugh LaFollette, John Rowan, David Detmer, Peter Markie, Rachel Cohon, my students, and others too numerous to name. I would like to express my thanks to all who have sharpened and clarified my thinking.

An earlier version of parts of Chapter 2 was presented at the Central Division Meetings of the American Philosophical Association, Minneapolis, May 2000, under the title "Three Flavors of Rights and Human Cloning," and, further revised, published as "Entitlements, Liberties, Permissions, and the Presumption of Permissibility," *Journal of Social Philosophy* 24:4, Winter 2003, pp. 537-544. An earlier version of parts of Chapter 4 was presented at the Central Division Meeting of the American Philosophical Association in April 2002. A modified version of much of Chapter 7 appeared as "Losing the Right to the Truth," *Journal of Value Inquiry* 33, 1999, pp. 389-403.

Chapter 1:
Introduction and Overview

Rights are like hankies—anyone who is unhappy about something tends to ask for one. "We now find," wrote Iredell Jenkins, "the most exaggerated hopes and extravagant claims advanced as rights."[1] At the other extreme, Alasdair MacIntyre claimed there are no such things as universal rights for exactly the same reason that we don't believe in witches or unicorns, namely, that "every attempt to give good reasons for believing there are such rights has failed."[2] The rights claims deemed self-evident truths by the United States Declaration of Independence were anything but self-evident to Jeremy Bentham, Thomas Hobbes, Mao Zedong, or the Ayatollah Khomeini. Bentham famously dismissed talk of rights as nonsense and talk of natural rights as "nonsense on stilts," and it must be admitted that some of the rights claimed by persons of some repute strain credulity. Does in vitro fertilization really violate, as one United States Senator has claimed, a baby's right to be a surprise? Does a baby, as Paul Ramsey insisted, have a right to be born with a unique genotype?[3] Other right claims provoke heated controversy, personal and political. Do African-Americans have a right to affirmative action? Do the Kurdish people have a right to a homeland? Does everyone have a right not to be differentially treated on the basis of race or gender? Do we have a right to reproduce at will? Do we have what some call a "right to our emotions," a right to feel whatever we happen to feel, unfair or not? Do we always have a right to be told the truth? Do we have a right to be given the means for basic sustenance even if we are able to work and choose not to? Do we have a right to self-esteem? Do we have a right to be loved? Controversy about which rights exist is matched by equal controversy about the application and extent of those rights. The United States Supreme Court controversially held that the U.S. Constitution protects such "penumbral rights" as the right to privacy, that is, "shadow rights" not explicitly mentioned in the document,[4] and, equally controversially, that the right to privacy includes the right to an abortion.[5] Before 1937, the same court held that minimal wage laws violated the right to freedom of contract.[6]

Rights claims are not only highly controverted but very strong claims indeed. The right to life, as generally understood, entails that you are obligated not to kill me, even at the price of great personal suffering. If you and I are remote cousins, the only remaining relatives of our rich, distant cousin, Joe, who is lying, intestate, on his death bed, your right to life entails that I am obligated not to kill you, even though your remaining alive means I must lead a life of poverty instead of wealth. It might also mean that my brilliant medical research program that will save countless lives, or my philanthropic plans that would bring about enormous good, must remain unrealized while you squander away cousin Joe's legacy gambling at casinos. In some cases, your right to life might require me to give up my own, as when you have the only histocompatible heart and I need a heart transplant or when you are occupying the last seat in a lifeboat. When one demands that someone else endure a lifetime of poverty, refrain from saving countless lives, or even forego her life, one had better be able to produce a very strong reason. Yet in the welter of claims about rights, many writers pay scant attention to what might justify rights claims, what a right is, and what kind of right is being claimed. One aim of this volume is to justify and clarify natural rights, as well a variety of other important rights, and to answer the questions "what is a right, which rights do we have, what do they entail, and why do we have them?"

The answer to these questions is more complex than is usually acknowledged. The language of rights is complex, richly nuanced, and open-ended. There are many different sorts of rights deriving from different sources. Rights enter in a wide variety of ways, directly and indirectly, into legal, moral, and social deliberation. Rights are complex and open-ended networks of interconnected legal, moral, and social demands on moral thinking that must be weighed and balanced against each other and against other legal, moral, and social considerations.

In short, there is more to rights than is dreamt of in most philosophies. Another aim of this volume is to pursue a holistic approach to rights that is sensitive to and illuminates this complexity. The holistic approach is not a grand theory of rights. Rather, it combines several general tendencies in looking at rights. Some of these tendencies may be found to some extent in other theories of rights, but the holistic approach tends to go further and to combine these features. The holistic approach is pluralistic in that it recognizes diverse sources, flavors, and types of rights. Many theories of rights attempt to identify a single source of rights, such as utility or autonomy. The holistic approach identifies a broad spectrum of sources of rights, including duties of team loyalty to fellow members of the moral community. Most theories of rights acknowledge more than one type of right (e.g., legal and moral). The holistic approach recognizes a wider variety of rights, including social rights, presumptive rights, and proclamative rights. The holistic approach tends to think of rights as making adequate provision for certain things, all things considered. The holistic approach tends to focus on global aims rather than upon drawing particular lines in the sand and prefers solutions that create adequate provision overall without, when feasible, mandating particular choices. Thus, in deciding whether a given statute or action violates rights, the holistic approach engages in a reasoned weighing of a broad variety of factors, including the circumstances of a society and the whole of a society's laws and legal mechanisms, to an extent generally not found in more traditional discussions of rights. The results tend to be more nuanced and flexible. Some writers advocate a broad right of self-determination for peoples, a broad right not to be discriminated against that undermines affirmative action or a broad right to compensation that requires affirmative action, and a broad right to reproduce that proscribes population control laws. The holistic approach yields a more careful, balanced, and complex view of these and other issues.

The holistic approach is thus not a theory of rights, but a global set of tendencies. The cumulative effect of these tendencies is significant. Understanding the complexity of rights changes the way we look at particular issues. The great hope of philosophers is that theory informs practice. This book begins with several particular theories about rights that reflect a holistic approach to understanding rights. Those theoretical analyses are used to clarify the nature of some important rights, such as the rights of future generations, in ways that guide public policy. The results include a practical proposal for regulating violence and pornography in the media as well as recommendations concerning population control policies, the use of new reproductive technologies, affirmative action, the right of a people to self-determination, and when to lie.

This book, then, applies new theories about rights to pressing social issues, offering a more nuanced and satisfactory understanding of a wide variety of topics including affirmative action, group rights, the rights of future generations, regulation of violence and pornography in the media, the right to the truth, the right to one's emotions, and the right to privacy. As with most theories, whether in philosophy or science, the resulting conclusions are sometimes "just common sense" with a theoretical underpinning and, other times, quite surprising. Some traditional and widely-held views and assumptions are overturned while others are maintained and illuminated.

This chapter contains a brief synopsis of the volume followed by introductory remarks about the nature of rights. Chapter 1 functions somewhat like the overture of an opera, introducing a variety of themes, some of which are explored in detail later in the work while others merely round out, by their brief appearance, the overall terrain in which the body of the work resides. Although some key points are made, some of the discussions in Chapter 1 must remain cursory. Chapter 2 introduces some important distinctions. Detailed analysis begins with Chapter 3.

A. Synopsis

Chapter 1: Introduction and Overview

Chapter 1 offers an overview of issues and distinctions in rights theory. Topics discussed include: negative and positive rights; procedural and end-state rights; *prima facie* or vector rights versus actual rights or resultant rights; the will, interest, and warrant theories of rights; rights *in rem* and rights *in personam*; natural rights, presumptive rights, legal rights (which may be explicit or implicit, redressable or non-redressable, discretionary or non-discretionary), moral rights, social rights, and rights stemming from regulative ideals; entitlements, liberties, permissions, powers, and immunities; rights based on self-oriented interests and rights based on world-oriented interests; autonomy, interest, need, and contract theories of rights; the claim that rights are morally basic; criticisms of John Rawls and Alan Gewirth; and several criticisms of the very idea of rights.

Part I: Theory of Rights

Chapter 2: The Many Flavors of Rights: Entitlements, Liberties, Permissions, and the Right to Die

Chapter 2 details various flavors of rights, namely three domains of rights (legal, moral, and social), five sources of rights (natural rights, presumptive rights, moral rights, positive rights, and rights ensconced in a society's regulative ideals), and, in particular, three species of rights: entitlements, liberties, and permissions. Entitlements are claims to something, such as a claim to being given a free public education or a claim to others' forbearance from blocking the entrance to the voting booth. A permission, as Hohfeld[7] notes, is merely the absence of a duty to refrain. Liberties are permissions the exercise of which law or morals is committed to supporting, even at the cost of some sacrifice on the part of others. When a particular form of support is enacted into law, it generally becomes a positive legal entitlement, but the relevant liberty remains the ground or rationale for that positive legal entitlement and may be appealed to in legal reasoning when deciding which specific entitlements the law recognizes or resolving disputes about the nature and scope of a positive legal entitlement. For example, the liberty of speech prompted the U. S. Supreme Court in *Sullivan*[8] to hold that public figures and the general public must bear the costs of non-maliciously published falsehoods in order to support the press' exercise of its permission right to comment on public figures. Most *in rem* rights, whether "positive" or "negative," include more than one species of right. Speech rights, for example, include an entitlement that the state refrain from criminalizing the publication of political views, a permission to use purple ink in writing, and the liberties mentioned above. The right to vote, in the United States, includes the permission to walk to the polls, the entitlement that the state refrain from imposing poll taxes, and various forms of public support such as transportation to the polls for disabled voters and mechanisms for casting absentee ballots. Chapter 2 explores briefly the logic of these sorts of rights and argues for a presumption in favor of permissions—neither law nor morality should impose an obligation to refrain from something without being able to show a good reason for doing so. The onus of proof, thus, rests on those who deny a permission. In the case of liberties and entitlements, however, the burden of proof shifts to those who advocate them. The usefulness of these distinctions in clarifying the range of pos-

sible positions concerning a right, as well as the nature of the arguments needed
to support each position, is illustrated by a brief discussion of the right to die.

Chapter 3: Rights as Warrants

What is a right? Two views have dominated the literature. According to the
will theory, "x has right to y" means that, in some particular respects, x's will
has sovereignty over y. The interest or beneficiary theory holds that to have a
right is to be the beneficiary of a duty. Chapter 3 proposes a third view. Rights
are networks of warrants: x's having a right to y consists in the fact that x has a
network of warrants (usually of different sorts) concerning y under various sets
of shifting circumstances. A warrant, on this view, is a publicly recognized sanction (grounding, justification) for a person, partial person, or constructive person
(e.g., a corporation) to do, say, demand, believe, feel, receive, or think something as his, her, or its due. When Z is my due, my claimed relation to Z is merited or earned, in the sense that it is called for, mete, because of something about
me, and to do or say otherwise is to deny an important truth about my status,
since Z's being my due is a form of public recognition of my status. When a
right claim is *descriptive*, the claim is that the relevant sanction is in fact part of
the public framework of discourse. When a right claim is *prescriptive*, the claim
is that the relevant sanction should be part of the public framework of discourse.
One has a *vector warrant* when the warrant has some weight, for example, when
there is some legitimate, publicly sanctioned justification for one's demanding
something as one's due. One has a *resultant warrant* for that demand when one
is overall (all things considered) justified in making that demand as one's due.

The conflict between the will, interest, and warrant theories is not over the
use of the word "right": each theory makes a substantial claim about the nature
of rights. In a wide variety of cases in which we generally employ the language
of rights, x (a person, partial person, or constructive person) has a particular kind
of socially or legally recognized special status and x's having that status, in tan-
dem with other facts, confers a particular kind of recognized status on x's relation to y. In those cases, x possess a network of publicly recognized protections
(a social *imprimatur*) as x's due, in the circumstances, enabling x to do, to some
extent, some or all of the following: fend off certain criticisms or challenges
regarding y, justify certain kinds of actions regarding y, demand certain actions
of others regarding y, fend off certain challenges to making that demand, take
certain actions to insure those demands are met, influence others' deliberations,
etc. The ways in which x's special relation to y may enter into legal and moral
reasoning are diverse and open-ended. This claim is perspicuously made by saying that rights are networks of warrants. While it is possible to capture the same
facts by defining rights as opportunities for the exercise of sovereign will and
supplementing rights with several other kinds of special relationships to y (e.g.,
justified moral expectation), convenience will require the use of some term covering all of these special relationships, e.g., "shrights." An examination of
shrights will reveal them to be various forms of warrant. A parallel point applies
to solutions to cases problematic for the will and interest theories. Thus, Chapter

3 argues, any tenable forms of the will or interest theory, when properly fleshed out, will turn out to be versions of the warrant theory using different terms.

The bulk of Chapter 3 consists of a comprehensive articulation of the warrant theory, answers to objections (e.g., that the warrant theory creates too many rights), a detailed examination of cases problematic for the will and interest theories (such as third-party beneficiaries of a duty, non-waivable rights, and rights of small children and others unable to exercise sovereign will), arguments that responses to these problematic cases by, among others, Kramer, Steiner, and Hart are not fully satisfactory, and an indication of how the warrant theory satisfactorily accommodates these cases. Finally, rights as warrants reflects a conception of the law as moral discourse in action. Law, on this view, is an intelligible system proclaiming the public morality as it is realized in a lived community. This conception, it is argued, accords well with the manner in which legal reasoning actually proceeds. Similarly, viewing moral rights as warrants reflects a conception of moral thinking as giving case-specific reasons for adopting a particular balance between potentially conflicting moral considerations.

Chapter 4: Why the Correlation Thesis Should Be Discarded

Chapter 4 distinguishes between 192 versions of the thesis that all rights correlate to duties (and/or vice versa) and argues that each version of the correlation thesis is weak enough to have no substantial import, an unhelpful stipulation, or, if not false, at most materially true. In sum, it is not incoherent to posit legal or moral requirements usefully called "duties" that correspond in no strong and straightforward way to rights, and it is not incoherent to posit warrants usefully called "rights" that correspond in no strong and straightforward way to duties. Examples examined in Chapter 4 include duties to ideals, epistemological rights, the right claimed by some ethical egoists to pursue one's own welfare, rights creating standards of appropriateness that fall short of duty, and proclamative rights. Creating duties may be the most important role rights play in moral and legal reasoning, but the correlation thesis overlooks the richness and complexity of the numerous other ways rights enter into legal and moral reasoning. While calling all of the warrants discussed "rights" captures the richness of rights talk, restricting the term "rights" to those that correlate appropriately with duties forces the introduction of other terms to cover the entire range of warrants invoked in legal and moral discourse. It is not clear what advantage is gained by insisting that the right to call oneself a poet is not a "right" but a "shright."

Chapter 5: A New Theory of Natural Rights

Chapter 5 presents a new theory of natural rights, called "T" for convenience. Answering those who deny the existence of natural rights, Chapter 5 shows that either there are natural rights or there are no moral constraints at all on using force against persons. However, most theories of natural rights are mistaken about the character of those natural rights. Natural rights, it emerges, are not limits on law but claims on societies to make adequate overall provision for certain things within their boundaries. Chapter 5 also provides a framework for resolving disputes about which natural rights exist.

The basic idea of T may be briefly summarized. Any enduring human society needs some methods of enforcing its rules or mechanisms for settling disputes within its borders, whether formal or *de facto*, that rely, ultimately, upon force or the threat of force. What makes morally permissible a society's use of force against its inhabitants? The answer lies in the difference between persons and dandelions. It is perfectly acceptable to destroy a dandelion marring the beauty of one's lawn and quite unacceptable to kill a tall person in a movie theater blocking one's view of the screen. What is it about persons that gives them a moral status different from dandelions? Let us dub "P" the feature of persons that makes morally questionable the use of force against them. Since all legal systems, it is argued, must take an implicit stand on the nature of P, the question "what is P" cannot be avoided. Governments, it is argued, are justified in using force against persons exactly when that force is necessary to preserve P. Thus, any government that does not make adequate provision for P is not legitimate (its use of force is not justifiable). Hence every inhabitant of any region has a claim against his or her government to adequate provision for P. Thus there is a natural right to adequate provision for P (and appropriate conditions necessary for P). More specifically:

1. If the use of force against persons does not require justification then there are no genuine moral constraints on conduct concerning persons.
2. If the use of force against persons requires justification then it is by virtue of some feature P of persons.
3. Thus, either there is some feature of persons, P, that requires the use of force against persons to be justified or there are no genuine moral constraints on conduct concerning persons.
4. There are genuine moral constraints on conduct concerning persons.
5. Thus, there is some feature of persons, P, that requires the use of force against persons to be justified.
6. Every government must, ultimately, rely upon the use of force against persons. More specifically, without (continuing) government use of force, the reasonable pursuit of P is ineluctably unfeasible.
7. No use of force is wrong when the reasonable pursuit of P is ineluctably unfeasible (since it is P that requires the use of force to be justified).
8. Therefore governmental use of force is not wrong when the reasonable pursuit of P is ineluctably unfeasible.
9. Thus, continuing governmental use of force necessary to make feasible the reasonable pursuit of P is not wrong.
10. Governmental use of force is not justified if it is not necessary to preserve P (make feasible the reasonable pursuit of P within its borders).
11. Thus, governmental use of force against persons is justified exactly when that force is necessary to preserve P and reasonably successful overall, given the prevailing circumstances, in making the reasonable pursuit of P feasible.

12. Thus, governmental use of force against persons is not justified unless that government makes adequate provision for P within its boundaries.
13. Thus, no government is legitimate unless it makes adequate provision for P within its boundaries.
14. Thus, for any person, A, and every government or society, B, that is willing to use force against A to enforce its dispute settlement mechanisms, A has a moral claim against B to make adequate provision for P within the domain affected by B's mechanisms.
15. Thus, there is a natural right to adequate provision for P.

Defining the nature of P and what counts as "adequate provision" yields a detailed theory of natural rights. Thus T has three levels. Theorists who adopt the basic framework (level I) may disagree about what P is (level II) or about what constitutes adequate provision (level III). In this way, T provides a general framework able to accommodate widely divergent views, providing a way of formulating, focusing, and perhaps resolving major disputes about natural rights. In the case of human beings, it is suggested, P should be understood as the ability to take feasible rational steps toward formulating, pursuing, and instantiating (individually and collectively) a morally defensible conception of a good human life. (For non-human, partial, or constructive persons, the definition must be appropriately modified.)

If T is correct, some views generally regarded as antagonistic to natural rights, such as Marxism, are in fact committed to natural rights, although the rights to which those theories are committed differ from those celebrated by traditional natural rights theorists. Neither T itself nor, it is argued, the principle of equality before the law requires that natural rights must be equal rights. However, T places the burden of proof on those who argue natural rights need not apply substantially to all. That is, T justifies the use of force of a government or society that makes adequate provision for P for every citizen. T is silent, however, about whether force against Jones is justifiable in order to make the rational pursuit of P feasible for Smith. Thus, if a government wishes to claim that it is justified in using force against Jones to make P feasible for Smith, it must show why such a trade-off is permissible. Finally, T views the natural right to free speech not as a shield against governmental regulation of speech, but as a claim each person has upon his or her government or social system to *adequate provision* for speech and advocacy within its domain. What counts as "adequate provision" depends on the circumstances of a society and the totality of its laws. Thus, when inquiring whether a society or government violates natural rights, one must examine not just a particular law or custom but the laws and practices of the society as a whole. Consider the oft-ridiculed claim made by the United Nation's *Universal Declaration of Human Rights* that everyone has a natural right to paid vacations. It is at least arguable that some degree of time apart from labor is a necessary condition for human flourishing, and so perhaps there is a natural right for some degree of leisure, broadly understood. But societies may employ numerous methods of providing for leisure. Rather than demand a specific form of leisure, such as paid holidays, draw a line in the sand that no government may cross in restricting leisure, or establish a minimal baseline of leisure to which everyone throughout history is entitled, T more plausibly suggests that a natural right to leisure would be a requirement on societies to insure, within their domain, overall opportunities for leisure that are, under the circumstances, adequate. Similarly, T replaces the implausible claim that a law restricting the use of a particular profane word on network television violates natural rights with the more plausible claim that societies must provide overall opportunities for free debate and discussion that, given the particular circumstances of the society, are adequate for P. Conversely, on traditional accounts of rights, natural rights are not violated when a government systematically undercuts individuals' ability to debate freely by instituting a series of restrictions, none of which goes quite so far as to cross the imaginary line in the sand drawn by natural rights. T eliminates both these undesirable results.

The details of this theory, answers to objections, and T's implications for the rights of privacy and property are explored.

Part II: Particular Rights and Applications

Chapter 6: The Right to Speech: Regulating Violence and Pornography in the Media

Does the right to speech protect pornography and violence in the media from government regulation? Chapter 6 begins with an analysis of speech rights and the nature of pornography and concludes with a practical proposal for regulating violence and sex in the media, a proposal that illustrates the holistic approach to balancing rights and public goals that should inform our thinking not only about pornography, but also about such pressing issues as privacy versus security.

An adequate discussion of speech rights must incorporate a conception of the role of speech. Six conceptions of the role of speech are enumerated: 1) as an instance of general autonomy, 2) as a precondition of general autonomy, 3) as free debate and discussion, 4) as a personal good, 5) as an important social condition, and 6) as a precondition for political equality and/or an implicit condition or value of democracy. Several of these roles played by speech contribute to speech's being a necessary condition for P. Speech as rational debate and advocacy is crucial to P as an essential way of fixing belief, refining attitudes and other elements of one's worldview, and making good decisions, both individually and as a community, as well as an essential aspect of salubrious interaction with others. But self-realization, it is argued, both individually and collectively as a community, also contributes to P in a significant way, as does belonging to a good community, a precondition for which is healthy public discourse. Thus the natural right to free speech focuses primarily on speech as rational debate and advocacy and secondarily on speech as self-realization and speech as conducive to communal good. Moreover, each of the six conceptions of speech provides some support for various presumptive rights regarding speech. For example, while repeating the names of the planets in one's backyard is not a crucial condition for P, the presumption in favor of permissibility suggests that doing so should not be outlawed without a strong reason. Hence speech as autonomy is a relevant concern in formulating presumptive rights. Finally, both 6) and 1) are embedded in the regulative ideals of our society. Each conception of free expression gives rise to different arguments concerning the protection of pornography. Chapter 6 looks closely at each of the six aspects, what each involves, and what scope it offers for speech protection.

A careful look at one particular kind of speech, threats, helps illustrate that speech protection is a matter of balancing diverse factors rather than a line drawn in the sand by some principle. Indeed, the account of rights advocated by this volume suggests that speech rights are holistic in several ways. Policies regarding speech rights should: A. focus on broad global aims, for example, affecting the overall attitudes toward violence predominating in the media rather than proscribing particular programs or images, B. conceive of rights in terms of adequate provision rather than as lines in the sand that should not be crossed, C. resolve conflicts through the reasoned balancing of a wide range of considerations for a particular situation, through an open-ended process of justification drawing upon an open-ended list of analyses, moral principles and values, some theoretical and some practical, and D. prefer solutions that have a broad effect on the bigger picture without mandating particular, individual choices.

Applying speech rights to pornography requires an account of pornography. The literature contains at least four distinct criteria. The content test deems as pornographic materials that explicitly depict human sexuality. The affect test classifies as pornographic materials that appeal to prurient interests (are sexually arousing). The offense test regards as pornographic materials that offend the sensibilities, with regard to sexuality, of a majority of the relevant community. The attitude test defines as pornographic materials that convey with implicit approval certain kinds of attitudes about human sexuality, e.g., that people are mere objects of sexual desire, that the degradation of people is acceptable, and/or that sex is a good to be consumed for the purpose of experiencing "highs." It is argued that the attitude test is the appropriate test for identifying pornography for the purpose of regulation.

Previous discussions of regulating pornography have tended to focus on the wrong questions. Traditional forms of regulation, which proscribe or regulate individual programs or images, do not directly address the real problem, namely the preponderance and general tenor of media messages. A society must exert some influence over the overall tone of its public life without unduly restricting individuals' ability to advocate their views and without heavy-handed control of public forums like television. A new approach to regulating violence and pornography in the media, consistent with the earlier analysis of speech rights and pornography, is proposed.

The proposal calls for the establishment of a committee, reasonably free of political interference but ultimately answerable to the public (like the Federal Reserve or the EPA), which employs a "constructive attitude" standard in assigning rating points to each television program to the extent to which the program appears to present with explicit or tacit approval either the use of violence, the suggestion that violence is something to be enjoyed, or the notion that sex is a commodity to be imbibed like root beer. Four levels of point use are outlined. The lowest level sufficient to achieve a reasonably satisfactory outcome should be employed. Level I merely requires broadcasters to post the committee's rating at the beginning of the broadcast. Level II uses a station's average monthly point total as one consideration, among others, in granting licenses. Level III creates tax and other incentives for broadcasters who maintain a low point total. Level IV requires broadcasters not to exceed a particular (fairly liberal) yearly point total. It is argued that levels I, II, and III are not radical departures from current practice in other areas of public policy (e.g., requiring warning labels on drugs). All four levels exert some influence upon the general tenor of television broadcasts without directly mandating or prohibiting any particular broadcasting choices. Equally important, they mitigate the effect of particular decisions by program raters: even should a benighted committee assign a high point rating to, for example, *Macbeth*, networks remain free to air *Macbeth*. They must merely either balance the program with lower rated programs or pay some form of higher cost, e.g., lose a tax incentive.

It is argued that this proposal does not violate natural rights and can plausibly be held consistent with U. S. Constitutional law. Three further objections to the proposal are addressed: the argument that the proposal is prone to abuse, the slippery slope argument (that the proposal would lead to an erosion of speech rights), and the argument that it is inherently objectionable for a society to exercise some control over the general tenor of its social milieu.

The holistic approach requires a change in our legal thinking, which is historically rooted in decisions about individual cases. But in a world that is increasingly global, a change is long overdue.

Chapter 7: Moral Rights and the Right to the Truth

"The right to the truth" may mean a legal or moral right to a specific truth (e.g., a patient has a right to be informed of her medical condition by medical providers), based on one's relation to the fact in question or the other party. "The right to the truth" may also mean a general moral right, in the sense of a legitimate moral expectation, as one's due, not to be subject to dishonesty. Chapter 7 focuses on the general moral right to the truth. Three grounds for the warrants comprised by the general moral right to the truth are examined. Two are familiar: lying violates others' autonomy and lying violates Kant's principle of universality. The third is somewhat novel. Many moral rights, including a general right to the truth, derive from duties of team loyalty: much as teammates on a baseball team have duties of loyalty to one another based on the common enterprise of the team, it is argued that those who are actively engaged in the moral enterprise, in the joint project of building a good world, have duties of team loyalty to one another.

Can one lose the right to the truth by asking an improper question? Williams, the Chair of a Department of Philosophy of a public university, is a prominent member of a group calling for the criminalization of same-sex relationships and the removal of gays from schools, government, and the media. Her previous decisions about raises, tenure, and promotion give faculty members ample reason to believe that her personal politics strongly affect her actions. Moreover, Williams is suspicious, prone to grilling subordinates, and quick to jump to conclusions. Finally, tenure at her university cannot be achieved without the vigorous support of the Chair. Williams, in idle conversation, asks an untenured junior philosophy faculty member, Perez, where he spent his break. Answering the question honestly would suggest that Perez is a closet gay. Does Williams retain a general right to a truthful reply, or is Perez entitled to lie?

Chapter 7 argues that people lose the general right to the truth by asking certain kinds of inappropriate questions, namely those that undermine morality, abuse the institution of truth-telling, or impose an illicit choice. We are entitled to lie in response to such a question, although the lie should be as small as possible, providing that the moral fault of the hearer is directly productive of the motivation to lie and the lie does not significantly impede the asker in performing legitimate tasks, violate specific rights to the truth, or cause incommensurate harm. (Moreover, the benefit of the doubt goes to truth-telling: when in doubt about any of these conditions, tell the truth.) Such lies, it is argued, do not violate respect for autonomy, since, in fact, they restore the autonomy of the speaker improperly undermined by the questioner. In general, we are morally entitled to use commensurate methods of freeing ourselves from an improperly imposed choice situation, even if those methods would ordinarily be unacceptable. In *Sophie's Choice*, for example, Sophie would be morally justified in shooting the Nazi officer who demands that Sophie pick one child to die or he will kill both of her children. Similarly, Williams, by asking her question, threatens Perez' autonomy by imposing a choice she is not entitled to impose. By lying, Perez regains some part of the autonomy to which he is entitled. Moreover, it is argued, such lies do not violate the principle of universality, properly understood. As Kant's analysis of capital punishment reveals, the principle of universality is a principle of reciprocity. It is the questioner, Williams, who abuses the institution of truth-telling, and hence lying in such a case is not an instance of acquiring an advantage by requiring others to adhere to a standard to which does not oneself adhere. Finally, those who are not active members of the moral community, it is argued, lose the right to such loyalty, just as baseball players who throw a game are not entitled to the loyalty of their teammates. It is for this reason, it is argued, that a burglar who demands to know where the family jewels are kept loses the right to a truthful reply. (It is not just that burglar's right to the truth is overridden, not just that his vector right fails to be a resultant right, for in that case one would still owe the burglar something. Rather, the burglar loses altogether the right to a truthful response to his question.) By asking a morally improper question, Williams removes herself, in that respect, from "team morality," and hence, it is argued, the duties of team loyalty do not apply to answering Williams' question.

The above arguments and restrictions indicate that while Williams has lost the right to a truthful reply to her question, Williams retains whatever specific rights to the truth she might have, including those she has as Chair. Perez should not mislead the Chair in a manner that affects the Chair's legitimate decisions or causes harm to Williams incommensurate with the harm caused by her question. It would be inappropriate, for instance, for Perez to say that he attended a professional conference he did not attend. Similarly, Perez should restrict himself to a lie whose foreseeable consequences are of only minor importance, and the lie's divergence from the truth should be no greater than needed. Perez should not say that he went to France or Madagascar.

Further examples, such as inappropriate questions during a job interview, are analyzed by way of illustration. Some meet the criteria for losing the right to the truth while others do not. In some instances, at least, telling a lie to an improper question does not violate the hearer's general right to the truth. In at least this respect, morality does not require martyrdom: morality and ordinary common sense are not conflicting guides to conduct.

Chapter 8: Rights of and Obligations to Future Generations

Many of our decisions are significantly shaped by what we owe to posterity, a factor that figures prominently in discussions of environmental and political policy. The commonsense view is that we have discounted obligations to future generations and that future generations have discounted rights. (Discounting, in this context, differs importantly from discounting in economics, since dollars, unlike happiness, are fungible, durable, and have virtually unlimited future earning power.) For instance, we should generally strive to ensure, as much as is feasible, that what we pass on to future generations is not grossly worse, all things considered, than what we received from previous generations. Similarly, we should do our best to take reasonable steps to avoid acting in ways that will cause great hardship for large numbers of person in the future. More generally, we should do our best to insure that conditions are reasonably favorable for the continued flourishing of human life and of what is good, noble, and significant about human accomplishment as a common enterprise. Thus, for instance, we have a discounted obligation to future generations not to deplete the world's oil supply and future generations have a discounted right that we not indulge in certain forms of environmental irresponsibility. But how can future generations have rights, and how can we bear obligations toward them, since they do not (yet) exist? Several interesting puzzles about the rights of future generations have been raised, including, among others, conundrums about giving moral consideration to merely possible persons, Macklin's objection that the class of future persons is indeterminate, and Parfit's and Schwartz's argument that future generations cannot be harmed by irresponsible actions on our part unless they result in a fate worse than nonexistence, since, without those actions, different people would have been born, and so future generations owe their very existence to those irresponsible actions of ours. Answering these objections raises several interesting issues, such as whether it is possible to harm the dead and whether a prediction about a future event is true or false at the time the prediction is made. Chapter 8 addresses in detail several objections to the claim that we have discounted obligations toward future generations, explaining how it is possible for future generations to have some, if lesser, rights and offering a suggestion about the nature of those rights. It is argued that while Mary Anne Warren is correct that only actual persons (past, present, or future) command genuine moral consideration, R. I. Sikora is correct that the welfare of merely possible persons enters into moral deliberation: population planning compares the moral desirability of the possible situation in which it is A who actually commands moral consideration versus the possible situation in which it is B who actually commands moral consideration.

In particular, Chapter 8 defends three key theses:

P1) It is *prima facie* wrong (unjust) to do something now that clearly and foreseeably poses a clear and present danger of later resulting in an actual person's rights' being violated (that is, in an actual violation of an actual person's rights).

P6) The following can serve as the basis for A's violating an obligation to B: A's doing something, X, that A is not entitled to do, such that A's doing X guarantees that B will not receive some good, G, when A is not entitled to guarantee that whoever occupies B's position will not receive G.

P7) Each of us has a (collective) *prima facie* obligation to strive to insure that there will be future generations.

P1) and P7) together mean that we have a *prima facie* collective duty to strive to insure that there is a future generation and that the rights they will in fact have, in the future, will not be violated by what we do now. This seems to be enough to yield many of the results environmentalists seek when they speak of the rights of future generations, yet neither P1) nor P7) requires assigning rights now to potential persons who have not yet existed, much less to potential persons who will never in fact exist. P6), it is argued, is not subject to the Parfit-Schwartz argument. P6) and P7), together with reasonable background assumptions (e.g., about what constitutes a fair share), seem adequate to establish that we bear significant obligations to future generations, such as not depleting the earth's oil reserves. Some reason is also given for holding the stronger claim that future generations do have rights now.

Chapter 9: The Right to Reproduce

Is there a natural or objective moral right to reproduce, that is, do we have a right to create, in some fashion, children who carry some portion of our individual genetic code? If so, are our reproductive rights violated either by legal restrictions on new reproductive technologies such as human cloning or by restrictions on reproduction for the purpose of population control? Does it violate rights to restrict unsupported births or pregnancies predictably resulting in severe birth defects?

Chapter 9 argues that while there is no natural right to reproduce, eight reasons for having an interest in genetic reproduction (e.g., an interest in participat-

ing in the process of evolution) are sufficient to justify a weak liberty to reproduce. Because, it is argued at length, the rationales proposed for singling out for
restriction the appropriate usage of new reproductive technologies are untenable,
the presumption in favor of permissibility suggests that new reproductive technologies as such should not be banned when appropriately used. (Of course,
more general bans or restrictions, such as a ban on all animal experimentation or
limiting all couples to two children, would apply as well to the use of cloning or
GIFT.) While the eight reasons for having an interest in genetic reproduction
provide some reason for societies to support the use of such technologies (e.g.
via government subsidy or requiring insurance companies to cover the procedures), they are not jointly strong enough, it is argued, to require others to make
sacrifices. Thus it is a matter of legitimate social choice whether to support (as
opposed to refrain from criminalizing) the use of new reproductive technologies.
However, strong reasons, both social and environmental, support limiting overall population size, regardless of the method of procreation employed. It is argued that, at present, overpopulation should be addressed regionally rather than
globally. A definition of "overpopulated region" is offered and reasons are given
for thinking overpopulated regions have strong reason to limit their populations.
In overpopulated regions, then, the presumption in favor of permissibility regarding reproduction does not apply. Nonetheless, restricting reproduction for
the purpose of population control might be held to violate either a liberty to reproduce or an entitlement not to be interfered with in reproducing. However, it
is suggested, encouraging (by insisting on a right to reproduce at will) the bearing of infants and then allowing them to starve is not a licit choice. Thus, when
Jones lacks the means of supporting a child, Jones' reproducing requires a sacrifice on Smith's part. That is, for Jones to reproduce, Smith (among others) must
pay for the support of Jones' child and/or the costs of procreation itself, which
means, given finite resources, Smith must give up something she could otherwise have had. Thus, either people do not possess an entitlement or strong liberty to reproduce at will or Jones' desire to reproduce imposes upon Smith an
obligation to make sacrifices to support Jones' child. As noted above, the weak
liberty to reproduce is not strong enough to impose a duty on others to make
sacrifices to enable one to reproduce. Moreover, reasons for thinking people
have an entitlement to reproduce at will (e.g., a woman's rights over her body)
are shown to be untenable. Thus it is within the legitimate discretion of societies
to restrict reproduction in appropriate ways for certain reasons, such as reducing
the number of unsupported pregnancies or reducing the number of pregnancies
in overpopulated regions. In each region, the value of reproductive freedom
must be weighed against the legitimate reasons for restricting reproduction in
that region.

   Chapter 9 concludes that the use of new reproductive technologies for the
purpose of creating offspring who will be reared by at least one of the persons
who provided the DNA (the egg, the sperm, or the cloned cell) should be permitted, subject to the same safety controls and standards used for all medical technologies. Although a society that legally proscribes some such technologies does

not rise to the level of violating natural rights, it acts wrongly in so doing. Societies in overpopulated regions that institute equitable and humane mechanisms for controlling their populations do not violate natural or (objective) moral rights and are responding legitimately to pressing environmental and standard of living concerns. Population control programs should be holistic and tailored to the particular region. While restricting unsupported births and/or pregnancies predictably resulting in severe birth defects does not, *per se*, violate natural or moral rights, it is argued that no legislation restricting unsupported births or pregnancies predictably resulting in severe birth defects should be passed in the United States at the present time. Educational and advertising initiatives to foster responsible reproduction may play a useful role when implemented carefully and thoughtfully and supported by broader, non-governmental initiatives.

Chapter 10: Group Rights, Loyalty, and Affirmative Action

Group Rights have spawned controversy both in their own right and through their relevance to hotly debated and deeply divisive issues such as affirmative action, self-determination for ethnic groups, and cultural rights of minorities. Moreover, group rights raise issues about the nature of loyalty and group identification that bear on patriotism, standing by one's mate, and identity politics. Chapter 10 contains a detailed analysis of the nature of group rights, substantive conclusions about loyalty and affirmative action, and a look at related issues such as the right of self-determination.

One major controversy regarding group rights centers on the individualist thesis that all rights are rights of individuals, and so, if there are any group rights, they are merely aggregates of the individual rights held by members of the group. We may, accordingly, distinguish between three positions. 1) There are rights that belong to groups, that is, a group as such is the possessor of the right. On this view, the right (if it exists) of the Quebecois to street signs in French is a right possessed by Quebecois as a group, as a collective entity. 2) Rights belong only to individuals as individuals—a "group right" is just shorthand for the aggregate of rights of the individual members of the group. 3) Some rights are possessed by individuals as members of a group because of their interest in the group as such (a group-oriented interest). X is a group-oriented interest of A when x is in A's interest only because it benefits a group and x benefits A specifically because A has an interest in the group as a group, and not merely because the groups' benefiting helps bring about some benefit to A whose value does not include within its content the group's flourishing as a group. Chapter 10 argues at length for view 3) and against view 1). For instance, it is generally and incorrectly held that the rights of corporations and states are rights of type 1). Corporations and states, however, are not groups, but organizations. The widely prevalent mistake of identifying organizations as groups significantly distorts many discussions of group rights. Chapter 10 spells out clearly the difference between groups and organizations, e.g., a group of farmers and an organization whose membership consists of those same farmers. An analysis of the nature of organizational rights as virtual rights shows that groups lack the required features to possess rights in the same way that organizations may. Other purported group rights are shown to be actually either distributed or derivative rights of individuals. Several additional reasons for holding view 1), including the argument that some rights can be enjoyed only collectively, are examined and found wanting.

Group rights, then, are rights that individuals have by virtue of a particular loyalty pertaining to their group, that is, because they have particular warrants regarding their legitimate interests in and commitments to a group as such. Not all group loyalties create rights—warrants, after all, are based on warranting features, and loyalties can be morally evaluated. This raises the second major objection, that group rights violate universalism and equality: group rights, it is sometimes held, deny that everyone has the same rights and that everyone should be treated equally. Answering this objection requires determining which sorts of bonds of special concern (particularist bonds) are morally justifiable. Seven sorts of overlapping particularist bond are enumerated: 1) Typological bonds (feeling a particularist bond and hence giving preferential treatment to others who share a common characteristic, such as race or gender, solely because it is a shared characteristic), 2) Bonds of legitimate social responsibilities, 3) Bonds of team loyalty to those engaged in a common project, 4) Bonds of commitment to a shared way of life or shared set of values, 5) Bonds of commitment to a shared history, 6) Frontier bonds, and 7) Bonds resulting from acts of commitment. It is argued at length that while some bonds of types 2), 3), 4), 6), and 7) can justify loyalty, typological bonds are not morally justifiable: sharing a common characteristic creates a morally compelling interest only when (and only because) sharing that characteristic falls under one of the other categories. George Fletcher's claim that loyalty arises from bonds of shared history is examined at length. Fletcher argues that Jones' history and culture are part of what he is, part of what makes him the person he is, and so for Jones to deny them is for Jones to deny his very self. Fletcher also argues that loyalty is not an autonomous choice. Others support this latter claim by insisting that loyalty is an emotion, not a rationally considered choice. Close scrutiny of these arguments and of the nature of loyalty (e.g., sports loyalty, loyalty to one's children, and spousal loyalty) suggest that shared history alone cannot morally ground loyalty and that true loyalty always involves moral choice. Thus bonds of special concern based solely on shared history or shared typology, *per se*, do not create legitimate warrants.

If typological bonds do not create morally justified loyalties, is there a right not to be discriminated against? It is argued that there is no such natural right, but there exists a presumptive right that governments not discriminate on the basis of gender, race, ethnicity, etc. In the public sphere, then, there is a presumptive but not a natural right not to be discriminated against. Is the private sphere different? The question is complicated by the fact that the private/public distinction is problematic: much of what Judith Jarvis Thomson calls "purely private benefits" are not purely private. In any case, an argument is given that you are morally warranted in demanding, as your due, that others not treat you adversely merely because of your ethnic origin or unfairly assign negative traits to you based only on your ethnic origin, except in special circumstances that might justify such actions or thoughts:

1. People are obligated to participate, in some manner and to some reasonable degree, in the moral enterprise, that is, in the joint project of making this a morally good world.

2. A wrongs B when they are teammates in the moral enterprise and A treats B in a manner inconsistent with the manner in which teammates in an enterprise should treat each other, all things considered.

3. Absent other overriding circumstances or concerns, treating a teammate in a manner that ultimately undermines or is in blatant opposition to the goals of the team is treating a teammate in a manner inconsistent with the manner in which teammates in an enterprise should treat each other.

4. Therefore A wrongs B when they are teammates in the moral enterprise and, absent other overriding circumstances or concerns, A treats B in a manner that ultimately undermines or is in blatant opposition to the goals of the team.

5. Treating someone adversely merely because of her ethnic origin, race, gender, etc., or unfairly assigning negative traits to her based only on her ethnic origin, race, gender, etc., except in special circumstances that might justify such actions or thoughts, is treating someone in a manner that ultimately undermines or is in blatant opposition to the goals of the moral enterprise.

6. Thus A wrongs B when they are teammates in the moral enterprise and A treats B adversely merely because of her ethnic origin, race, gender, etc., or unfairly assigns negative traits to B based only on her ethnic origin, race, gender, etc., except in special circumstances that might justify such actions or thoughts.

7. When someone, C, is obligated to do x and, were C to do x, C would owe you y, C wrongs you if C denies you y.

8. Therefore A wrongs B when A treats B adversely merely because of her ethnic origin, race, gender, etc., or unfairly assigns negative traits to B based only on her ethnic origin, race, gender, etc., except in special circumstances that might justify such actions or thoughts.

However, in many cases, the wrong done you by such discrimination is non-redressable: it is within the sphere of choice of others to wrong you in this way.

The results of this analysis are applied to affirmative action and the right of self-determination. In many ways, the conclusions to be drawn from the preceding discussion will please no one. Magic bullets that decide social issues involving group rights do not exist. Instead, each claim must be individually weighed. Arguments about affirmative action (or, rather, five very different types of affirmative action) focus on a) the compensatory justice argument (that, e.g., because women have been unfairly discriminated against, women are due compensation in the form of preferential treatment), b) the non-discrimination argument (affirmative action discriminates and hence violates rights), or c) weighing the consequences (benefits and harms) of affirmative action programs (a brief and partial list of which is provided). An analysis of compensation, coupled with the earlier conclusions about loyalty, shows that the compensatory justice argument is inconclusive. While the earlier discussion shows that there is reason for opposition to discrimination to be part of public policy, and hence some justification for a liberty from discrimination, there is also a presumption in favor of permissibility for individuals to dispose of private goods as they see fit. Hence, to the chagrin of both liberals and conservatives, law regarding the disposal of private goods should result from weighing, in particular instances, whether the legitimate policy goal of opposing such discrimination is strong enough to outweigh the presumption in favor of permissibility. Conversely, to the extent that affirmative action discriminates, particular affirmative action measures should be evaluated by weighing the particular benefits and rationale for the measure against the general public policy goal of opposing discrimination. Hence the argument from non-discrimination is inconclusive. No general principle, in other words, either restricts or demands, across the board, affirmative action or permitting the discriminatory disposal of private goods: each case must be carefully weighed. Affirmative action should be used carefully as a tool in particular situations in which it is likely to have beneficial consequences. Too often affirmative action programs are broadscale, heavy-handed, and ill-conceived. But while many affirmative action programs are justly subject to criticism, blanket condemnation of affirmative action ignores the important good that narrowly focused and thoughtfully conceived affirmative action programs accomplish.

The discussion of group rights also suggests that while there is no general right of self-determination every group possesses, members of particular groups can successfully argue for resultant rights to a particular homeland. Each case must be weighed and argued individually, and, although some general factors can be articulated in advance, such as the importance and value of joint practices that would be difficult to realize within a larger state, the relevant factors, circumstantial, historical, moral, and legal, will differ from case to case. The price of this complexity is that it rules out simple solutions. The virtue is that it promotes understanding, helping to de-villify opponents. Moreover, because overridden vector rights still retain some force, something is still due those who are the losers of the moral weighing.

Finally, while diverse bonds such as family, local community, culture, and so forth are of deep importance in human life, so is the broader, universalist bond of all moral agents, and, beyond that, the interconnectedness of all that exists.

B. Introductory Remarks

Since rights fall into a variety of categories, it is important to draw a number of distinctions marking different sorts of rights. Some of the traditional distinctions regarding rights, I will argue in the course of the volume, are misguided and some others are incomplete. What follows is a brief overview of some important distinctions, some of which will be examined in detail in later chapters.

One traditional distinction is often expressed by contrasting *prima facie* with actual rights or operative rights with overridden rights.[9] The distinction is clearly important and necessary. Normally, I might have a right that you keep your promise to me. Normally, you act wrongly if you break your promise to me. But circumstances may void the promise or circumstances may override the promise. You may be justified in breaking your promise, in certain instances, if the promise was obtained by force (the promise may be void). You are generally justified in missing my dinner party in order to save a life, even though you promised me you would attend the party (the promise may be overridden). In general, it often happens that someone is justified in doing x even though someone else would normally have a right that she not do x (or things like x). However, there is considerable dispute about how to describe such situations. Suppose Jones' government appropriates his boat, over his objection, because taking Jones' boat is the only way to save a crew of drowning sailors. Ordinarily, Jones has a property right in his boat and the boat may not be used against Jones' express prohibition. Nonetheless, the government is justified in appropriating Jones' boat in that instance. There are several rival ways of understanding this situation. One possibility is that Jones' property right in the boat is expressly defined to exclude this situation, and hence his property right to the boat was not violated. For instance, Jones might be said to have the right to deny use of the boat to others except in non-emergency situations. Since this was an emergency situation, Jones' right did not come into play. Some hold rights to be both absolute, in the sense that there are no degrees of rightholding (either one has a right or one doesn't), and inviolable, in the sense that if one has a right to x then one is overall entitled to x. Benditt, for instance, asks how I may be said to have a right to enter my house if, when a terrorist in my house threatens to shoot a hostage if anyone enters, I am justly forbidden from doing so and would act wrongly and perhaps actionably if I did so.[10] If rights are absolute and inviolate, Jones must simply have no right at all to the boat in this situation. However, although Jones' objection to the government's use of the boat to rescue the crew is in some sense inappropriate, surely it is less inappropriate than is Jones' objecting to the use of someone else's boat: the fact that it is Jones' boat gives at least some small measure of justification to Jones' objection, a fact difficult to explain if Jones has no color of right at all to the boat in that situation. Jones may also be due notice or compensation, which appears to indicate that some sort of right of Jones was violated, although an alternate explanation is that Jones' property right to the boat consists solely in control over the boat in non-emergency situations plus compensation for its use in emergency situations or that the emergency situation generates additional, separate rights, such as a right to notification or compensation. However this construal, while consistent, leaves unexplained why compensation is due when the boat is used in emergency situations. The reason cannot be the obvious one, namely that Jones' right was violated, since, *ex hypothesi*, it wasn't.

Others hold that rights are absolute but not inviolable, that is, rights can be overridden by other considerations. More commonly, philosophers distinguish between *prima facie* and actual rights, where "*prima facie*" means, roughly, "ordinarily, other things being equal": I have a *prima facie* right to your keeping your promise to attend my dinner, but, if you must miss my dinner in order to save a child's life, then I don't have an actual right to your attending. It may seem that this is equivalent to saying that I have an actual right to your attending that is overridden by the need to save the child, but these formulations are not precisely the same. If the latter is true, then my rights have been (justifiably) violated, and so I am due some sort of compensation (even if just an apology), even though you acted rightly in violating my rights by missing my dinner. Does Jones have merely a *prima facie* right to deny the use of the boat but not an actual right to do so? If so, it is unclear why Jones' *prima facie* right would give some small degree of justification to Jones' objection to the use of his boat and why violation of a *prima facie* but not actual right requires compensation. Ordinarily, houses have roofs, and hence someone who is inside the house when it rains does not get wet. Yet remaining inside a roofless house when it rains keeps one no drier. The house's appearing, at first glance, to have a roof likewise fails to keep one dry. Only an actual roof keeps one from getting wet.[11] One could insist that the emergency situation's rendering Jones' *prima facie* right non-actual generates additional, separate rights, such as a right to notification or compensation, but, as noted above, the rationale for these additional rights remains obscure unless some actual right of Jones' was violated. After all, if the boat turns out to be stolen property, a fact known to Jones, Jones had an apparent right that was not, in the circumstances actual, but no compensation is due Jones. It is hard to imagine a plausible explanation of the difference that does not, directly or indirectly, attribute to Jones some actual sort of right. A similar point pertains to calling Jones' property right to the boat a defeasible right (that is, saying that Jones has a property right to the boat unless one of an open-ended set of conditions obtains).

As Chapter 3 will indicate, I prefer to speak of vector and resultant rights: a vector right is a warrant for x you possess that carries some weight, even though, when all factors are considered, you may not be, overall, warranted in x, and hence not have a resultant right for x. In physics, a vector force is a genuine force that contributes, along with other forces, to the resulting overall motion of an object. Similarly, a vector right is a genuine right that contributes, along with other moral considerations, to the resulting set of overall entitlements. Jones has a vector right to deny the use of the boat but not a resultant right, and so, since Jones does have some warrant to deny its use, Jones' objection has some small degree of justification, although Jones' is not overall warranted in denying the use of the boat because the government has a greater warrant to appropriate it. Vector rights provide a plausible response to Benditt: one has a vector right to enter the house, a right that must, since it is a genuine right, be appropriately acknowledged (possibly in the form of compensation), but that vector right is overridden, and hence, because one lacks the resultant right to enter, one may be liable if one does. In one sense, then, Benditt is correct that one does not have the right to enter the house: one lacks the resultant right to do so. In another sense, one retains the vector right to enter the house, and the retention of that right is not vacuous, since it entitles one to various things to which one would not be entitled otherwise. In general, describing the situation in terms of vector rights facilitates marking the difference between an overridden vector right (a condition that defeats Jones' resultant right but not his vector right), a voided right (a condition that voids Jones' having a vector property right in the boat, e.g., the boat is stolen property), and the absence of any right at all. As noted, an overridden right retains some force. Additionally, a voided right may give others rights that would not exist otherwise. For instance, if I use fraud to obtain a promissory note from you, and I use that promissory note to obtain a loan from a third party who acted in good faith and who was not negligent in placing credence in the promissory note, the third party can demand redress from me, redress that would not be due had you never signed the promissory note. Thus a voided promise is different from the absence of a promise. A middle case exists when I obtain the promise by unintentionally misleading Jones, for example, because I was sincerely mistaken about the date of the dinner party. Vector rights permit any number of complex categories.

Of course, vagueness is sometimes useful. I will employ the term "*prima facie* right" simply to indicate that one normally has a right or obligation of that general sort, without specifying further the precise nature of the situation.

It is also traditional to distinguish between rights *in rem* and rights *in personam*. Rights *in rem* are, roughly speaking, broad general rights such as the right of contract. Saying "I have a right to free speech," a right *in rem*, does not indicate exactly what I am entitled to do or who else is required to do what. Rights *in personam* are particular rights against particular persons, such as the right to be repaid $15 by Tom before noon on Monday. Some writers have argued that rights *in rem* are meaningless until spelled out in terms of rights *in personam*. Others have argued that a right *in rem* is exhausted by, can be reduced to, a set of rights *in personam*: rights *in rem* are just loose ways of referring to a bundle of rights *in personam*. Yet others have held that rights *in rem* provide grounds for arguing for rights *in personam*. Arguments and examples in Chapters 3 and 4 make clear that Carl Wellman[12] is correct that it is misleading to think of rights as coming in two levels—broad and specific. Rather, rights do not come singly, but in complex networks of levels of specificity. The right to be repaid $15 by Tom before noon on Monday may appear to be a right *in personam*, but it includes various rights of remedy (e.g., filing suit in small claims court), various immunities for invoking those rights of remedy (e.g., immunity from a lawsuit filed by the other party for abuse of process, and hence a warrant for demanding that Tom refrain from filing a suit for abuse of process), various claims against others not to interfere in various ways with pursuing those remedies (and hence a warrant to take appropriate legal action if someone does attempt to interfere), various claims against others not to interfere in various ways with Tom's repaying the money, immunity to or mitigation of criticism for demanding repayment at an inopportune time, etc. Different warrants come into play if Tom files for bankruptcy. One might attempt to spell out the right to be paid $15 by Tom as a large complex of conditional more specific rights. However, given the complex, shifting, and open-ended nature of legal and moral reasoning, it is virtually impossible to spell out in advance all the ramifications, partial and indirect, of the possession of a right. One may be tempted to say that such related rights are not part of the right to be repaid $15 by Tom before noon on Monday but are somehow external, different rights one may also posses. However, if we both have a right to be repaid $15 by Tom before noon on Monday but I have a right to sue for specific performance while your only right of remedy is pleading with Tom, then, in a key sense, you and I have a different right. It is unclear that there is some rigorously isolable element, robust enough to capture what is being claimed by claiming a right, that we identically possess. For example, what your will has sovereignty over and what my will has sovereignty over are quite different. Thus, if the will theory is correct that to have a right to x is for one's will to have sovereignty over x, then you and I possess different rights. Strictly speaking, then, all rights are rights *in rem*, an open-ended network of linked warrants in shifting circumstances. Nonetheless, it is sometimes useful to contrast broad rights *in rem*, like the right to life, with more specific rights *in personam* they entail (or which constitute them), as long as it is understood that the distinction is relative rather than absolute, just as it is sometimes useful to say we both have the right to be repaid $15 by Tom before noon on Monday, ignoring the differences between our respective rights.

Tradition next distinguishes between three different realms or arenas in which persons may have rights, whether *in rem* or *in personam*: there are natural rights, legal rights, and moral rights. Legal rights are the rights that a legal system confers. United States citizens have the legal rights recognized by United States law.[13] Natural rights are the rights people have, regardless of the particular legal system in which they live, which serve as constraints upon the legitimacy of legal systems. In some sense, natural rights are prior to legal rights, and the set of legal rights any given legal system recognizes should be consistent with and incorporate natural rights: if there is a natural right to x, and the laws of Freedonia do not recognize, explicitly or *de facto*, a right to x, then something is wrong with the laws of Freedonia.

Moral rights are the things to which one is morally entitled. What this means is subject to considerable debate. Chapter 7 suggests moral rights are legitimate moral expectations as one's due: "I have a right to the truth" means that I am morally entitled to expect you to tell me the truth, as my due. If you're a habitual liar, I would not be epistemologically entitled to expect you to tell me the truth, that is, I would be foolish if I were surprised when you lied to me, but I might still be morally entitled to expect you to tell me the truth.

It is sometimes held that "I have a moral right to your doing x" just means "you (morally) ought to do x." However, there are many things you morally

ought to do without my having a moral right that you do them. Consider the
following examples:

1) You ought to be kind to your grandmother, but I have no right that you
   be kind to your grandmother. My moral rights, as this example brings
   out, pertain to things that apply in some special way to me.

2) If you can give me a significant, morally acceptable benefit at virtually
   no cost to yourself, you ought to do so. Even more strongly, you ought,
   other things being equal, not act for the sole purpose of denying another
   person a morally acceptable benefit. But I may have no right to your
   doing so, even when it directly concerns me. Suppose, for example, that
   I love the sight of the apple tree in your yard. You enjoy the apple tree,
   but you cut it down, at some expense, just to spite me. You ought, morally, not to have done that, but you do not violate my moral rights in
   doing so. The lesson taught by this example is that a necessary condition for "you ought to do x" implying "I have a right to do x" is that x
   is my due.

3) Judith Jarvis Thomson, in her justly famous paper on abortion,[14] argues
   that the (moral) right to life does not include the right to be given what
   one needs to live. While it may be morally heinous to refuse to throw a
   life preserver to someone who is drowning, she claims, refusing to toss
   the life preserver does not violate his rights. Others hold that there is a
   right to be rescued, while a third group recognizes a duty to rescue (to
   be a good Samaritan) but no corresponding right to be rescued. Notice,
   however, that by contributing a dollar a day, or $30 a month, one can
   save someone from dying of starvation. Presumably, most readers of
   this volume can afford to donate $30 a month, which is roughly the cost
   of a pair of jeans, without significant hardship. If there is a duty to rescue, it seems to follow that we have a duty to give that $30 to charity
   instead of spending it on a monthly movie, a weekly can of soda, etc.
   As Fishkin[15] points out, the logic of this argument appears to require
   that any personal expenditure is immoral unless it is either necessary
   for one's survival or produces a greater sum available for donation to
   hunger relief (e.g., buying work tools). If there is a right to be rescued,
   we violate someone's rights by going to a movie. Of course, there may
   be conditions on the duty to rescue that limit its application. For instance, one might hold that one has a duty to rescue only when no one
   else is in a position to do so. Since others are in as good a position as
   you are to contribute the $30, the duty to rescue does not require donat-
   ing your movie money to charity. However, it is not clear why, if there
   is a duty to rescue, it does not apply when others could perform the rescue but do not do so. Adding such conditions to the duty to rescue or
   the right to be rescued would appear to entail, for instance, that a
   drowning person has a right to be thrown a life preserver if one person
   is standing next to it, but no right at all if two people are standing next
   to the life preserver, each of whom could equally toss the preserver.

Thus, if you are drowning, you should hope that only one and not two people are present to assist you. It would appear, then, that while A morally ought to rescue a stranger, B, if A can do so without significant hardship, B does not have a (moral) right to be rescued by A.

4) You are a private individual with no institutional connection to the Annual Hobart Painting Exhibition (or the art world generally). You decide to give $10 of your own money to the painter of the biggest painting at a particular exhibition. You say this aloud after the exhibition has gotten underway (so that no one can say she acted in reliance upon your announcement). Your announcement has no official standing—you merely stated your intention aloud so that everyone hears you. Jones has painted the biggest painting, but, because you don't like Jones, you give the $10 to Smith, who painted the second biggest painting. Morally, you ought to have given the money to Jones—if nothing else, giving the money to Smith means you lied. The money is, in some sense, Jones' due, and it does pertain specifically to Jones. Thus the three conditions so far mentioned appear to be met. Have you violated Jones' rights?

In any case, whatever the precise definition of a moral right may be, natural and legal rights concern laws and political systems, while moral rights concern moral obligations. If I am your spouse and ask you if you are having an affair with our neighbor, I might have a moral right to a truthful answer, that is, I may have a legitimate moral expectation that, as my due, you answer my question truthfully. In most jurisdictions I do not have a legal right to a truthful answer (I can't sue you or put you in jail for lying to me), and most theorists would agree that I do not have a natural right to a truthful answer. Clearly, some moral rights should not be legal rights—there are aspects of ethical conduct that are not the law's business. On the other hand, moral rights often play an important role in legal reasoning. In *Prince*,[16] for instance, the court based its decision concerning the *mens rea* requirement for 24 & 25, Vict. c. 100 # 55 on a purported moral right corresponding to no legal duty (see Chapter 4). Conversely, legal rights can create moral rights. First, if there is a *prima facie* general moral obligation to obey the law, then the passage of a law requiring me to do something creates a *prima facie* moral obligation for me to do it. Second, there are areas where morality permits any of several possible arrangements. The law can then determine which of those arrangements should be instantiated. (To take a non-moral example, it doesn't matter, from the standpoint of safety, whether everyone drives on the left or everyone drives on the right, as long as everyone drives on the same side. The law arbitrarily picks a side. Once U.S. law opts for driving on the right, it becomes unsafe to drive in the U.S. on the left, just as it is unsafe to drive on the right in London.) Laws regarding fiduciary relationships provide a strong example. In short, the relationship between moral and legal rights is complex.

These distinctions, it will become clear, do not go far enough. First, social rights constitute a fourth arena to complement natural, moral, and legal rights:

social rights are those warrants and entitlements conferred by social understandings, such as the right to a response to an RSVP invitation. Social rights will be scarcely mentioned in this volume, but debates about social rights frequently enter into personal conflicts, so it is worth mentioning that much of what is said about rights in this volume applies as well to social rights.

Second, there are importantly different kinds of legal rights. Some legal rights are nondiscretionary rights, that is, rights one simply may not violate, while others are discretionary rights, rights one may violate at a price. Consider the following three legal rights: the right not to be killed, the right to have you fulfill your contract to sell me your house, and the contractual right that you ship my goods before June 3. The right not to be killed, within our legal system, entitles me to take action to prevent you from doing it—it carries with it a right of self-defense, a right to avert. Moreover, you may be incarcerated if you kill me—it is a right backed by criminal sanctions. [17] In short, my right not to be killed is a strong nondiscretionary right. The second example is a partially nondiscretionary right. It is not a crime to refuse to honor your contract to sell me your house, nor may I use force to make you do so. Thus, in a sense, the law permits you to violate my right. However, the law allows me to ask the courts to force you to sell me your house (one remedy is specific performance). So it is a partially nondiscretionary right. The last right is discretionary—it is not a crime (in most instances) to break a shipping contract and I may not use force to prevent you from breaking such a contract. My only remedy, in many cases, is to collect damages from you. Thus, you may, at your discretion, violate my right, though you will pay for doing so. Of course, one could deny this distinction by insisting that it is also within your discretion to rob a bank, though you will pay for it with jail time. Undoubtedly many criminals do regard jail time as part of the price of doing business. Saying so, however, overlooks an important difference between criminal and civil wrongs. Criminal wrongs are forbidden, while civil wrongs are, generally, merely grounds for remedy. As a result, the state has a duty, other things being equal, to penalize those who do criminal wrongs, and, although district attorneys have some discretion about which cases to prosecute, they betray their office if they use that discretion arbitrarily, while persons who have been libeled have no duty of any sort to bring suit.

The rights listed above, both discretionary and non-discretionary, are redressable. Other rights violations are non-redressable. Suppose you borrow ten dollars from me, interest free, which you repay. Morally, you owe me a debt of gratitude and reciprocity. In quite similar circumstances, I later ask you to lend me ten dollars. You refuse. In some sense you have wronged me. I am morally justified in demanding, as my due, that you reciprocate. But, if you do not, I am not warranted in demanding some form of redress. Unless some sort of promise of reciprocity was made, it is within your purview to decide whether to honor your debt of gratitude and reciprocity or not. You act wrongly if you do not. You wrong me, in the sense that you deny me something you owe me. But that is your choice, and while I am justified in judging harshly your choice, no redress is appropriate. (Unless one counts, as a form of redress, refusing to aid you in the future when I have no specific duty to do so.) Similarly, we owe one another normal courtesy, absent special circumstances, and so someone wrongs you by ostentatiously turning his back on you when you greet him, given that you have done him no wrong, the situation is appropriate for exchanging greetings, and so forth. He has a social obligation to refrain from such behavior, such behavior denies you your due as a social being in good standing, and it is wrong for him to do so. However, no redress for this wrong is appropriate because it is within the purview of people to decide whether to wrong people in that way: he has the right to be gratuitously rude, in the sense that doing wrong in that way is within his discretion (that is, it is his due as a social being to have dominion over whether or not he is gratuitously rude).

Of course, he will pay in various ways for being gratuitously rude to you. Your respect for him may diminish or you may fail to be courteous to him in the future. But this is a consequence of his rudeness rather than a punishment or form of redress. The difference is significant. If a parent catches his child lying to him, he is less trustful of the child in future. But this lessened trust is not a punishment in the way grounding the child would be. No parent would say "since I will trust you less in future, I don't need to ground you." The former is a consequence of the lie, the latter a punishment for it. You may, legitimately, judge someone who is rude to you adversely, morally or otherwise, for his rudeness, eschew his company, deny him courtesy, or deny him many non-obligatory benefits. All of these are negative effects of his rudeness. They may all be deliberate responses to his rudeness, but they are not punishments. Punishment would not a licit response to his rudeness, since it is within his purview to be rude.

It is tempting to say that nondressable rights have no meaning (and, hence, are perhaps not rights at all), but a violation of a nonredressable right may enter in various ways into legal, moral, and social reasoning. You may avert to his act of rudeness as justification for your own, e.g., when you refuse to invite him to a party to which it would otherwise be improper not to invite him. A defendants' disdainful demeanor in court, violating the court's right to respect as its due, may stop short of the redressable wrong of contempt of court but, in some jurisdictions, may nonetheless be cited as a factor in sentencing.

Thus there are at least three importantly different categories of rights violations: those that are preventable and redressable, those that are redressable and not preventable, and those that are neither preventable nor redressable.

Legal rights may also be implicit or recognized. When the Supreme Court held that the Constitution contained a penumbral right of privacy, it did not claim that it was creating a new set of rights. Rather, the Supreme Court held that the Constitutional right to privacy existed all along in American law, though the courts previously had not recognized it in their findings. By an "implicit" legal right I mean a right implicit in the law of a society but not yet recognized by its legal system. Implicit rights differ from newly created rights in several important ways, the most important of which is that they are retroactive in their application. A new right takes effect now (most jurisdictions proscribe, for obvious reasons, *post facto* legal requirements). When the courts recognize an implicit right, the court is claiming that the right has existed all along, and, hence, that previous court decisions failing to recognize the right were in error and can be reversed. The difference, thus, is legally significant. Conversely, the courts may find that a legal right previously recognized by courts does not, in fact, exist. Such findings differ from the loss of a right, since the court avers that there never was such a legal right, and thus court decisions upholding the right were in error. (Of course, fairness sometimes limits the extent to which the court will backtrack an implicit right. Timeliness is a restriction on some suits, for instance.) The status of implicit rights is a subject of some controversy. A legal realist, who believes that there is a fact of the matter about what the law is, holds that implicit rights are genuinely existing legal rights, and courts that do not recognize those rights make a straightforward mistake of law. For those positivists who hold that the law in a jurisdiction is whatever is in fact enforced in that jurisdiction, the idea of an implicit right is a legal fiction. Thus the status of implicit rights invokes the battle between legal positivists and legal realists. Both, however, need to mark the difference between a revision of previous findings that may be retroactive and a change in current law. The term "implicit right" affords a useful way to do so.

Next, I would argue that when some people speak of natural rights they are conflating two quite different things. "Natural rights," Chapter 5 urges, are those rights that must be adequately respected by a legal system on pain of illegitimacy. That is, if I have a natural right to free speech, any legal or social system that does not respect my right to free speech is not, in that respect, a legitimate legal or social system—it does not possess political authority, or at least its authority is suspect until it changes. (It may, of course, possess *de facto* authority in the sense that I will pay dearly if I defy its dictates—in that sense, the Mafia in Chicago in the 1920's had *de facto* authority when demanding protection money. But there is no *prima facie* moral duty to obey the Mafia or respect its institutions.) Natural rights are thus very strong. In addition, there is a set of what I call "presumptive rights." Presumptive rights are those rights that, by and large, legal systems generally ought to recognize. Legal systems that do not respect a presumptive right are generally, in that respect, flawed, but they do not thereby lose legitimacy. So presumptive rights can be used to criticize positive systems of law and can be appealed to in debates about what the law ought to be, but they have rather a different status from natural rights. I would argue that some principle of equal rights is a presumptive but not a natural right. A legal system that gives adequate opportunity for free debate and discussion but even more opportunity to others does not violate anyone's natural rights, but it does, in most cases, violate a presumptive right to equal treatment, and thus there are general grounds for criticizing the system and advocating change.

Natural and presumptive rights are, in some sense, universal, that is, they are not specific to a culture or society; they are general rights individuals can claim against all societies, although it will become clear in Chapter 5 that the specific content of these rights is very responsive to the particular circumstances and culture of a society. Positive rights, on the other hand, are the particular legal, moral, and social rights that a given society recognizes in its laws, shared moral views, and social understandings. Since human societies across the globe and across time are quite diverse, positive rights vary greatly from one society to another and from one era to another. When a society's set of positive rights is not fully consistent with natural and presumptive rights, that society's set of positive rights should be modified.

Standing between the poles of universal natural and presumptive rights and society-specific positive rights are regulative ideals and the rights they generate. Regulative ideals are part of a society's self-conception as a society. A legal system is not just a collection of rules and procedures, but a public vision. Different regulative ideals can licitly link natural rights to a society. There is, for example, as I would argue, a natural right to adequate participation in shaping one's destiny. Full human lives are not bovine, and what is of distinctive moral importance about human beings involves working toward a vision of a good future with some degree of thought.

However, contrary to countless endlessly repeated bromides, the right to vote is not a natural right, if the argument of Chapter 5 is correct. The natural right to adequate participation in shaping one's destiny does not require elections: many different political arrangements make adequate provision for this crucial aspect of the moral life. While the United States defines itself as a nation, in part, by observing the natural right to participation via a commitment to equality and representative democracy, a good meritocratic society lacks these commitments as such. Although significant arbitrary discrimination and pervasive lack of opportunity for significant forms of self-determination may be severe evils, neither trait is found in a beneficent and well-governed meritocratic society without universal elections and with inequalities appropriately based on relevant merit. As long as that society provides ample opportunities to citizens to participate in social decisions, that society observes the natural right to participation, even though it does not recognize a right to vote. Communal meetings devoted to finding consensus and a system of rotating offices with checks and balances observe the natural right to participation in yet other ways. A tribal council of elders that is not unduly restrictive, arbitrary or unreasonable in its mandates and decisions, permits anyone to address the council freely and is committed to giving due consideration to such addresses may not be an ideal form of government, but such a system can also make adequate provision for shaping one's own destiny.

Each of these systems of governance, while respecting the natural right to adequate participation, encapsulates a different regulative ideal, and each regulative ideal emphasizes a different set of virtues. Communal meetings and rotating offices, for instance, emphasize the virtue of universal direct participation in community decisions, a virtue not found in a system of elected representatives. Each regulative ideal also gives rise to different rights. The right to vote is a right embedded in the regulative ideals of the United States. Citizens of a meritocracy may lack the right to vote but possess a right to dedication on the part of public servants, that is, to public servants being honorable fiduciaries to the best of their abilities, a right that United States citizens, who chose their leaders, lack. In the United States, a politician who proclaims he is running for office for his own benefit, is elected, and, once elected, keeps all campaign promises and obeys the law scrupulously while using his office to benefit himself violates no one's rights, however unsavory we might find such a politician.

Some regulative ideals may be illicit in that they violate natural rights. Some licit regulative ideals are arguably better, overall, than others. But societies may legitimately choose from a range of legitimate regulative ideals.

A society's regulative ideals differ from other elements of its positive law or morality because a society's positive law and morality can be criticized for failing to conform perspicuously to that society's regulative system. Regulative ideals may be appealed to either when arguing that a right as yet unrecognized by the courts is implicit in a given legal system or when criticizing existing legal rights and arguing for change. The right to vote may not be a natural or even a presumptive right, but neither is it an ordinary positive right, like the right to municipal garbage collection—it is a right that is partly definitive of the United States as a society. A municipality that decides no longer to provide free garbage collection acts within its legitimate discretion. Withdrawing the right to vote, in the United States, violates the defining spirit of the nation. Thus there is a significant moral and political difference between the two that is worth demarcating. Similarly, the right to public dedication in a meritocracy is not a natural or presumptive right, but neither is it an ordinary positive right. It is a right endemic to a meritocracy as part of its self-conception. Thus, while rights grounded in defining ideals may legitimately vary from society to society, their status and justification is significantly different from other positive rights, and, hence, it is useful to place them in a separate category.

Because politicians and theorists so often conflate democracy with a system of individual rights, it is worth repeating that the two are separate. As de Tocqueville famously noted, democratically governed societies need not recognize most traditional individual rights other than, perhaps, the right to vote. No paradox or inconsistency would ensue, for example, if United States voters, through their duly elected representatives, repealed the First Amendment and made the practice of any religion except Roman Catholicism a criminal offense. The United States would then be a representative democracy without freedom of religion, although such an occurrence would violate the regulative ideals that have historically defined American society. Conversely, an hereditary monarch's power to criminalize behavior, raise taxes, and set foreign policy may be limited by an extensive list of strong individual rights, such as freedom of religion (though not a right to vote), perhaps subject to review by an independent (non-elected) judiciary. Thus George W. Bush is mistaken in broadly identifying "freedom" with the right to vote.

There are other rights that do not fall into any of these categories. An adequate theory of rights must take account of them. Consider the right to be called a poet. Smith, let us suppose, has written, in the course of his entire life, only the following two line verse:

Roses are red, violets are blue.
You stink like an old gym shoe.

Jones, on the other hand, has published 13 books of poetry, won a Nobel Prize and two Pulitzer Prizes, has been anthologized in every collection of contemporary poetry published by a major publisher, etc. While both Jones and Smith may have the speech right to call themselves poets, someone might correctly say that Jones has earned the right to call herself a poet and Smith has not. What kind of right is this? It is not a natural right, a legal right, a legitimate moral expectation, or a social right. Epistemological rights also resist classification. "I have the right to believe X" can mean simply that I am entitled not to be punished for or interfered with in holding my belief in X. However, it can also mean that I am epistemologically warranted in believing X, that is, that the evidence, as far as I know it, makes it reasonable to believe X. This latter right claim plays an important role in many sorts of deliberations but does not fall readily into the categories mentioned earlier. (See Chapters 3 and 4 for a fuller discussion of epistemological rights and the right to call oneself a poet.)

In general, I will argue that rights are warrants. Since there are many kinds of warrants, there are many kinds of rights. If my arguments are correct, several categories of rights exist: natural, presumptive, regulative ideal, several kinds of legal rights (e.g., implicit and explicit, discretionary and non-discretionary), moral rights, epistemological rights, social rights, and so forth.

Rights from all of these categories come in different flavors. Wesley Newcomb Hohfeld[18] distinguished between four different flavors of rights. Although Hohfeld was specifically discussing legal rights, similar points can be made about natural rights, presumptive rights, moral rights, and so forth. Various examples and arguments in this volume indicate that Hohfeld's categories are not exhaustive, but, since Hohfeld's taxonomy has been extremely influential, it is worth describing. Strictly speaking, each kind of Hohfeldian right pertains to something in a particular respect against a certain individual. For instance, I may have an immunity with regard to x in respect y against you, but not against Smith (or, similarly, not in respect z).

Claim-rights (entitlements) are claims upon someone or something. The correlate of a claim-right is a duty. If I have a claim-right on you to ten dollars, you have a duty to pay me ten dollars. Permission rights (privileges) are those things I have no duty to refrain from doing. My having a privilege (permission right) to do x with respect to you is equivalent to your having no claim-right on me not do to x. The correlate of a privilege Hohfeld calls a no-right. For instance, if you have a privilege to do x, I have a no-right to your not doing x. Powers are the abilities to change someone's rights. Using Judith Jarvis Thomson's example, when I release you from a promise, I cause myself to lose a claim-right and you to gain a privilege. Immunities are freedoms from the powers of others. I have an immunity concerning x when you have no power concerning x. Chapter 2 adds liberties to Hohfeld's list of four. Liberties, as I use the term, are permissions whose exercise is due public support of some kind [19].

In addition, many philosophers distinguish between negative rights and positive rights. Negative rights are rights of non-interference. A negative right to an education means that you may not prevent me from pursuing an education. A positive right to an education means that I must be provided with an education. If I lend you ten dollars, I have a positive claim-right and you have a duty to give me ten dollars. If I have a right to speak, I have a negative claim-right— you have a duty not to interfere with my speaking. This distinction has been impressed to do major theoretical work. Some have argued that negative rights always outweigh positive rights, others that all basic political rights are negative rights. However, positive rights are closely related to negative rights and can generally be recast as a complex of negative rights. Intuitively, it seems just a matter of phrasing whether one says one has the right to be provided free instruction about history, a positive right, or the negative rights not to be interfered with when walking into a history class one has not paid for, sitting down, taking notes, etc.: in practice, the negative and positive rights amount to the same thing. Of course, the positive right appears to entail that, say, the state must mount history classes, while the negative right merely permits anyone to attend whatever history classes, if any, the state may decide to fund. However, this difference disappears in practice if the state owes a duty to the Federal Government to mount history classes. Similar points can be made about any practical difference that might be raised; some set of circumstances render the positive and negative rights equivalent in practice. More technically, the positive duty to do x is equivalent to the negative duty to refrain from all sets of actions, s, such that the members of s collectively amount to not doing x. The duty to go to my party at time t is equivalent to the duty to refrain from all of the following at time t: staying home, going to the beach, going to Cleveland, etc. where the list articulates everything you could do that does not entail or include going to my party. Thus a purely formal distinction between positive and negative rights will not do. Moreover, the distinction between negative and positive rights typically depends upon theoretical and circumstantial background assumptions. Suppose, for the purpose of discussion, that a simple Lockean theory of property is correct: we own whatever we mix with our labor, provided we leave as much and as good for others. That is, if you take some clay from the riverbank and shape it into a pot, you own the pot absolutely, provided there is still plenty of equally good clay left for anyone who wants some. As long as there remain copious quantities of equally good free land and other resources, it is clear that a right to welfare payments is a positive right. But the situation changes dramatically if all available land is already claimed and we add to the theory that, when all natural resources are already claimed, that is, when there is not as much and as good left for others, people can justly own whatever they mix with their labor only if they provide a welfare system for those who were excluded from ownership. In that case, since I have a negative right not to be interfered with in using your land unless you and other landowners institute a system of welfare, your duty to contribute to welfare for me does not correlate to any positive right I possess but rather constitutes a precondition for your negative right that I forbear from trespassing on your land. Put another way, my right to welfare amounts to the fact that I am at liberty to use your land unless I waive (perhaps involuntarily) that liberty in exchange for a welfare system that supports me. This is not a "positive" right. It is a privilege (the absence of a duty). Different theories of property yield different analyses. So our ordinary common sense intuitions about which rights are negative and which are positive reflect basic assumptions about the relevant underlying theory justifying those rights. Finally, as Chapters 3 and 4 make clear, most *in rem* rights involve complex mixtures of positive claims and claims of non-interference. In short, when used as a convenient shorthand, the distinction between negative and positive rights is often useful. But the distinction cannot be used to do rigorous theoretical work, because making the distinction rigorous requires that the relevant theoretical work already be done.[20]

Some have also sought to distinguish between right claims based on self-regarding (self-oriented) interests and right claims based on other-regarding (world-oriented) interests. Some liberals have suggested that the criminal law may legitimately aim only at protecting the former. I've argued elsewhere that world-oriented interests may be more significant and deserving of legal protection than self-oriented interests.[21] Our world-oriented interests may be more important to us than our self-oriented interests. Gandhi, for instance, was willing to lay down his life to promote an end not only to violence between Sikhs and Moslems in Calcutta but also to hatred in their hearts. World-oriented interests may also be of more moral importance and more directly constitutive of our moral identity and life projects than self-oriented interests. Some of the reasons proposed for granting state protection or support only to self-oriented interests, such as Dworkin's egalitarian argument, are discussed elsewhere in the volume. The discussion of obligations to the dead in Chapter 8 indicates that world-oriented interests can create obligations. Here it is sufficient to indicate briefly a reason for thinking that the distinction cannot be rigorously maintained. If Jones regards masturbation as a kind of moral pollution, his interest in Smith's refraining from masturbating, an "other-oriented" interest, can be recast as the self-oriented interest in living in a masturbation-free world. We do, after all, regard Jones' interest in living in an unpolluted or quiet (noise-free) neighborhood as a self-oriented interest: when Jones asks his neighbor to turn down his blasting stereo, we view him as pursuing his self-oriented interest in relative quiet, not his other-oriented interest that his neighbor not play his stereo. Smith's interest may be considerably more important to him than Jones' is to her. If there is a significant difference between demanding that Smith turn down his stereo and that Smith refrain from masturbating, it is not a purely formal distinction, but a moral judgment about the relative importance to well-being of being in a place free of loud noise and being in a place free of masturbation.

The negative/positive right distinction and the self-regarding/other-regarding distinctions are often broached in the service of a broader liberal agenda, a key element of which is the doctrine of state neutrality. Joseph Raz describes modern political liberalism as committed to state neutrality in the justification and consequences of state action in the sense that the state refrain from deliberately fostering particular life plans over others and excluding particular ideals.[22] Dworkin suggests "the state must be neutral on what might be called the question of the good life."[23] If this view is correct about political rights, political rights must not be grounded in particular conceptions of the good. If this view is correct in the broad terms often urged, pertaining to all state action, then all state-supported rights are affected. For instance, inheritance rights deriving from public policy considerations are illicit, unless the content of public policy is itself neutral with respect to differing conceptions of the good. Setting aside provisions of wills that are conditional upon the legatee's refraining from marrying a particular person, on the grounds that public policy is to promote marriage, for instance, would appear to violate the broad demand for neutrality. The requirement of state neutrality has been challenged on several grounds in addition to those that appear elsewhere in this volume. Anthony Langlois, for instance, argues that this restriction of state neutrality is actually not neutral in that it discriminates against traditionalist, communitarian visions of the good. "To educate and inform people such that they have the choice to leave is to undermine the meaning of being Amish": what remains is a community that is not Amish, but "a liberal community with an Amish gloss."[24] Lord Devlin objects to state neutrality because (among other reasons) a society is entitled to protect its survival and doing so violates the neutrality requirement.[25] A common morality, suggests Devlin, is a prerequisite for and partially constitutive of the social cohesion that permits a society to endure as a society. Since societies are entitled to protect their existence, societies are entitled to protect the common morality without which the society cannot survive as a society. If Devlin is correct, there is no clear line limiting the state's power to limit rights or take stands on questions of the good. Protecting the common morality is a holistic process, not merely a matter of stamping out threats that, individually, threaten to undermine the society's existence. John Rowan, for instance, discussing the impact of Devlin's argument on the regulation of pornography, writes that "the likelihood of such a collapse as a result of private pornography usage is almost nil."[26] But one cannot protect social cohesion on a piecemeal basis, as if the test were simply whether any one activity, single-handedly, destroys or severely harms social cohesion. To do so is to commit a covert form of slippery slope fallacy. Although the loss of no single hair, by itself, makes one bald, one may not conclude that losing hair does not make one bald. Similarly, assume that it is a licit legislative goal to reduce America's dependence on foreign oil. No single activity, such as setting one's thermostat to 80 degrees in the winter, makes America dependent on foreign oil. It does not follow that proscribing any one of those activities is unjustifiable and that hence no laws designed to eliminate America's dependence on foreign oil are licit. Similarly, social cohesion is the result of the totality of a society's life. Devlin's argument suggests that society is entitled to erect a network of policies that, jointly and globally, protect social cohesion. Second, an argument can be made in support of Devlin that the laws of a society voice its public morality, and so the absence of a prohibition of x amounts to a public statement that x is tolerable, even if disapproved. While the absence of a prohibition against x does not betoken approval of x, it does generally indicate that the community either considers x sufficiently rare not to warrant consideration or does not find it intolerable. Even when scant public consideration has been given to a commonly encountered behavior, the absence of a prohibition generally indicates a judgment that the behavior is not intolerable. The fact that I have not heretofore considered whether wearing a brown hat and purple socks is intolerable counts as evidence that either I don't regard the possibility of someone doing so very likely or that I don't find the prospect intolerable. When something of a public nature is commonly encountered but has not grabbed our collective attention sufficiently for us to consider whether it is tolerable, that generally (though not necessarily) indicates we do not consider it not bad enough to be intolerable. If it were both commonly encountered and so bad that we would, upon consideration, judge it to be intolerable, we would (normally) have paid more attention to it. While a detailed discussion of the principle of state neutrality is beyond the scope of this volume, it should be noted that the holistic view of rights advocated in this volume, which requires neither state neutrality nor drawing strict lines in the sand, avoids these and other criticisms.

Next, traditional discussions of rights distinguish between two views of what rights claims are: the interest or benefit theory of rights and the will theory of rights. This volume proposes an alternative theory of the nature of rights. Rights, it will be argued, are warrants.

The interest or benefit theory says that to have a right is to be the beneficiary of someone's duty, or, alternatively, to possess an interest compelling enough to place another under a duty. As Joseph Raz puts it, "X has a right if and only if X can have rights, and, other things being equal, an aspect of X's well-being (his or her interest) is a sufficient reason for holding some other person(s) to be under a duty."[27] For example, my interest in living is sufficient to obligate you not to kill me. If you lend me ten dollars, you are the beneficiary of a duty I have to pay you ten dollars. Hence you have a right to be paid ten dollars. The will theory of rights says that to have a right to is to be entitled to impose your will in some fashion—to have a right is to be a small-scale sovereign about some domain. When I loan you ten dollars, I at am liberty to require you to pay me the ten dollars or waive the repayment. If I have a right to wear a funny hat while cleaning house, then whether or not I wear a funny hat while cleaning house is properly governed by my will. It may sometimes appear that this distinction is of merely theoretical interest, but the two views yield different results.[28] For instance, the notion of an inalienable right, a right you cannot lose or waive, is intelligible on the benefit theory but not on the will theory. My right to be paid ten dollars when I loan you ten dollars is alienable—I can execute a document as a result of which you no longer owe me ten dollars. So that is a right I can waive or lose. Some people have argued that the right to life is inalienable—I cannot lose or waive my right to life. It is on these grounds that they argue, for example, that physician-assisted suicide is wrong or should be legally prohibited. Now, whether or not there are any inalienable rights, the concept of an inalienable right makes sense on the benefit theory. If someone has an absolute and unwaivable duty to do something and I am the beneficiary of that duty, then I have an inalienable right. If you have an absolute duty not to kill me, whether I want you to or not, and I am the beneficiary of that duty, then I have an inalienable right not to be killed by you. On the will theory, however, a right is the ability to impose one's will. To assert that you may not kill me even if I ask you to do so is to refuse to allow me to impose my will on whether I live, and hence, by definition, to deny that I have a right. Thus, on the will theory the very notion of an inalienable right is self-contradictory. If the will theory is correct, then, one reason often given for objecting to physician-assisted suicide is simply incorrect. So the difference between these two theories is of some practical importance.

The will and interest theories have dominated the literature on the nature of rights claims. Chapter 3 proposes a third option. Rights, Chapter 3 argues, are networks of warrants, publicly recognized sanctions to do, say, demand, believe, feel, receive, or think something as one's due, in the sense that it is merited by one's relevant status. Ramifications of viewing rights as warrants will emerge throughout the course of the volume.

Another distinction, typified by Robert Nozick's criticism of John Rawls, is between procedural rights and end-state (outcome) rights.[29] In a criminal trial, opposing attorneys present evidence to the jury in accordance with a set of rules, such as the rules of discovery, the rules for introducing evidence, and the rules for examining witnesses. If all of those rules are reasonable rules and were followed properly and conscientiously, the trial was procedurally fair and just. A procedurally fair trial may result in an unjust outcome: an innocent person might be found guilty or a guilty person found innocent. Conversely, a procedurally unfair trial might still have a fair outcome: the jury might reach a fair and true verdict despite the procedural improprieties. The same distinction applies to rights. The right of the defendant to cross-examine witnesses is a procedural right. The right to a just verdict is an end-state right. Nozick believes that political rights are essentially procedural rights, because, he argues, the results of a just process are just. Rawls, according to Nozick, sees a just society as a society with fair outcomes, and so political rights center not so much on the fairness of the procedure but on the fairness of the outcome. There is an obvious connection between the distinction between procedural and end-state rights and the distinction between negative and positive rights. It is not surprising that Nozick views political rights as negative rights. If rights center on the fairness of the procedure and ignore the outcome, then it seems plausible that rights are primarily rights of non-interference. Negative rights alone generally do not guarantee any particular outcome, but they do help define the conditions under which processes occur. If, for example, educational rights are purely negative rights, they merely require the state not to interfere with people in pursuing an education. Such rights guarantee nothing about the outcome, that is, about how educated people will actually be. Conversely, if educational rights center on outcomes, on how educated people end up becoming, negative educational rights are inadequate (they do not guarantee the appropriate outcomes). Of course, there are intermediate positions.

Suppose, for example, that the right to an education requires only that the state fund and make available to all a public educational facility in which people can learn as much as they are able and willing to learn. This right goes beyond a negative right, since the state must fund the school and allow everyone to attend, but it is not a purely outcome-oriented right, since how long people choose to remain in school and how much they learn in school is affected by their economic situations, their aptitudes, and their individual choices and preferences.

Viewing rights as warrants permits both kinds of rights: it is coherent to say that one is warranted in demanding a certain kind of process and also coherent to say one is warranted in demanding a certain kind of outcome. Nozick and Rawls are discussing basic political rights, but, more generally, at least some examples of each kind of warrant seem justified. Pinkham knowingly and freely chooses to gamble 10 dollars on the outcome of a toss of the dice, Pinkham is able to sustain the loss without dire effect, Pinkham is not driven to making the bet as a result of dire circumstances that leave him no other method of avoiding disastrous harm, and so forth. The dice are fairly tossed. If Pinkham loses, no unfairness or right violation has occurred. Pinkham has the right to a fair toss and, perhaps, rights that ensure his bet is made freely and not coerced, but he has no rights regarding the outcome of the toss. However, if Gorgas has lead a blameless life, never committing any crime or other form of wrongdoing, and, through no negligence or other fault of hers, Gorgas is imprisoned for 40 years as a result of a mistaken verdict, is it really the case that no rights of Gorgas whatsoever were violated, so long as the trial followed fair rules and the jury voted in good faith? While there is not space to do justice to this issue, it should be noted that Nozick's much discussed "Wilt Chamberlain" argument, in which he purports to demonstrate that end-state rights require continual interference with freedom, at most shows that end-claim states impose a cost to be balanced against the reasons for making any end-state right claim. Vector rights, conceived as warrants, must always be balanced against other factors when deciding which resultant rights apply to a given case. Thus Nozick's argument, even if successful, does not show that there are no end-state vector rights, nor even that there are no end-state resultant rights, if, in a given case, the cost of interference is outweighed by other factors. Hence this volume will assume claims of end-state and procedural rights are both legitimate candidates for rights and must be weighed on their merits: no right claim will automatically be deemed illegitimate or mistaken merely because the right claimed is an end-state or a procedural right.

Finally, there are various theories about the source or justification of rights. Some writers suggest that it is the importance of respecting individuals' autonomy that generates rights. Others have argued that rights are needed or beneficial or useful, and so what justifies rights is the benefit they convey. The distinction between autonomy-grounded and utility-grounded theories of rights bears some connection to the will and interest theories of rights. There is no contradiction in maintaining both that autonomy is the source of rights and that to have a right is to be the beneficiary of a duty or that to have a right is to be entitled to exercise one's will and that what grounds or justifies such realms of sovereignty is utility. Nonetheless, if what grounds rights is the importance of autonomy, it seems natural to think of rights as providing an area of autonomy, an area in which one can exercise one's will. Autonomy-based theories of rights and the will theory are natural allies. Similarly, if what grounds rights is the benefit they convey, it seems natural to think of having a right as receiving the benefit of an obligation. Utility-based theories of rights and the interest theory have a natural mutual affinity.

Space does not permit a detailed criticism of autonomy-based and utility-based theories of rights. The issues involved are complex and so treating them fairly would require an additional lengthy volume. However, a few criticisms that have or might be raised may be briefly mentioned. The somewhat cursory arguments mentioned are meant only to suggest that a problem exists, not to demonstrate that the problem is insoluble.

Autonomy can be thinly defined, for example, as the mere ability to make choices. Some authors instead offer a rich definition of autonomy. For Thomas Hill Jr., for instance, being autonomous requires having distinctly human values, actually making decisions by a process of rational reflection, considering all relevant considerations, being free from manipulations or threats by others, and having ample opportunity to realize these choices in one's life.[30] Rich notions of autonomy face two basic problems. First, the more richly autonomy is defined, the narrower grows the realm of autonomous beings. Even ignoring the external components of Hill's definition (e.g., that others respect autonomy rights), we must acknowledge that the majority of living adults do not routinely (and are not routinely disposed to) make decisions by reflecting rationally on all relevant considerations in a manner free of manipulation by others. If such a rich conception of autonomy is the basis of rights, then it appears that most adults do not merit rights. Obviously, there are several possible responses to this objection. For example, it might be claimed that every adult has the capacity for this sort of rich autonomy. If "capacity" means "born physically able to acquire" it is difficult to evaluate this hypothesis. Moreover, it is not clear why one merits rights simply because one was born with an ability to become something one has not become and that may be unattainable at this point in one's life. If "capacity" means "functionally able to exercise these capacities at this point in one's life," it is empirically false that all or even most living adults possess this capacity, as any teacher of mediocre students can attest. Space does not permit a detailed treatment of this issue. The claim made here, in any case, is simply that there are problems for autonomy based theories of rights, not that those problems are insoluble. Second, the more richly one defines autonomy, the more controversial one's claims become. Hill's definition denies autonomy to those lacking distinctly human values. Could organisms with a distinctly different set of values nonetheless possess the sort of autonomy that justifies rights? In the absence of a compelling argument, Hill's definition appears arbitrary, but compelling arguments of this sort have been notoriously difficult to discover. (A parallel difficulty besets, as we shall see, contract or agreement theories.) Thin theories of autonomy thus have an obvious advantage. However, the more thinly one defines autonomy, the less clear it is that autonomy, so defined, can justify rights. A tempting thin theory of autonomy is that autonomy is the ability to make free choices, where "free" just means either uncaused or self-initiated. However, as the following passage from *Moral Responsibility and Persons* suggests, this thin conception of autonomy is inadequate to ground rights:

> Suppose we encounter an organism, the Wanter, that sometimes desires light and sometimes desires shade. It has no convictions, judgments, or general values; it simply feels a yen for light or a yen for shade. In other words, the Wanter has desires, not aspirations. So it is not committed to the world's meeting some moral standard. It does not have a general desire, for example, that the autonomy of organisms be respected. For if it did, the Wanter would have a moral value (it would believe that autonomy is valuable for its own sake). And *ex hypothesi*, the Wanter has no general values or moral views. It merely wants to be in the light. In addition, let the Wanter's choice of shade or light be as free as you like. The Wanter has no general values, and so its choice will not be a principled choice. But it is free to choose shade or light as its whimsy suggests.
>
> Now to the extent that it is, other things being equal, bad to cause pain, we do not want the Wanter to feel pain or frustration. But suppose it is convenient to fool the Wanter, or to anaesthetize it, so that although its desires are not met it feels no pain or frustration. There is no reason not to do so. No one would think it immoral to fool the Wanter into thinking its desires are met. By way of contrast, it is at least plausible to say that fooling a person into thinking that her desires are met in order to gain some advantage for oneself is an immoral form of manipulation.
>
> Of course, the Wanter has some minimal rights; it has a right, perhaps, not to be wantonly tortured. (That is, only a powerful benefit would permit Wanters to be tortured.) But this is because the Wanter *cares* about not feeling pain…. What the Wanter lacks is not free will or desires, but the kinds of values and attitudes that would make its choices and desires morally significant.
>
> Thus the aims of the Wanter do not command respect the way that the aims of persons do. For persons, unlike Wanters, have standards they wish the world to met.[31]

Thus very thin conceptions of autonomy will not serve to justify rights while rich conceptions of autonomy are controversial and may appear to exclude obvious rightholders.

Utility-based theories of rights suffer from two broad categories of difficulties. First, the literature contains a host of arguments that something besides utility, such as autonomy or justice, must play a fundamental role in moral reasoning. The infamous pleasure machine-argument, for instance, shows that no purely subjective state can be the overriding consideration in moral thought. Second, if utility is the reason for introducing rights, it would appear that rights should be discarded when they conflict with utility. Yet one of the basic functions of rights is to counter utility. Even if rights do not, as Dworkin holds, trump utility, they do often function as a counterbalancing moral consideration.

Some have thought that rule-utilitarianism, the view that morality requires choosing the set of rules that produce the most overall utility, avoids this problem. Perhaps the strongest of several oft-raised objections to rule utilitarianism is the accusation that rule utilitarianism is guilty of "rule-worship": when one knows, in a particular case, without having to calculate, that violating a right will produce more overall utility and that the possibility of error is scant, when the public consequences of violating the rule in this case are nugatory, and so forth, there is no reason to adhere to the rule unless, e.g., justice *per se* is an independent moral *desideratum*. But if justice *per se* is an independent moral *desideratum*, then why doesn't justice *per se* ground at least some rights?

It should be noted that most of these (and other) difficulties stem from the demand that utility or autonomy alone ground rights. Rights as warrants and, more generally, the holistic account of rights urged in this volume, permit and even encourage multiple grounds of rights. If, as I have suggested in *The Ethical Engineer*,[32] moral reasoning consists in balancing, for each particular case, a variety of diverse ethical considerations, then it seems reasonable that a variety of diverse ethical considerations, including utilitarian concerns and the importance of autonomy, might ground or justify warrants. Similarly, individuals attain a diverse variety of statuses as a result of which something might be their due. An epistemological warrant might be grounded in what it is rational to believe, reflecting the right holder's status as a rational enquirer. Other rights might be grounded in a person's status as an autonomous agent and correspondingly be warranted by the importance of autonomy. These ethical considerations may be mutually supporting—one's status as a rational enquirer may be closely related to one's status as an autonomous agent. Having a good of one's own may be a precondition for being richly autonomous. But rights as warrants does not require that these considerations can be reduced to a single ethical parameter, and the history of ethics provides some reason for skepticism that they can or should be. Indeed, some of the rights argued for in this volume do not seem primarily to protect autonomy while others do not seem to be primarily directed toward advancing utility. At the very least, recognizing multiple grounds for warrants permits a more direct and plausible explanation of such rights.

Thus rights as warrants sidesteps many of the objections raised above. If act-utilitarian considerations provide merely one type of warrant or aspect of warrants among others, the apparent fact that utility can best be served by violating rights in some cases poses no problem, since there are or may be other reasons for not violating the relevant right. The fact that autonomy theorists disagree about whether engaging in a process of rational scrutiny is a necessary condition for a definition of autonomy intended to ground all rights is not a reason for holding that Chang's ability to engage in rational scrutiny cannot provide one (among possibly several) grounds warranting Chang in claiming as his due that the law not punish him for reasoning about public policy. Since, intuitively, autonomy and utility are both significant moral considerations, a view that accommodates both has obvious appeal.

Another set of theories of rights might be called contract theories: rights arise, on these views, because people agree to them. Since such theories are influential, a few brief words seem indicated. It should be stressed, however, that the cursory remarks below are meant only to indicate the presence of some difficulties with justifying rights entirely by agreement. The warrant theory of rights, which permits contractual arguments to ground some rights, in whole or part, without being limited to contractual arguments, avoids these difficulties.

Contract theories can be actual or hypothethical: rights might be held to arise either from actual agreements between people or from what people would agree to under certain ideal conditions. Actual contract theories suffer from four major problems. First, it is difficult to show that people actually agreed to whatever set of rights is claimed. In response, it is sometimes argued that remaining within in a society's borders constitutes tacit agreement to living by the set of rights that society recognizes, legally and morally. This answer, however, raises the second problem, the problem of the dissenter. Suppose Jones does not agree. Then Jones is not bound by the set of rights (or afforded their protection). How can Jones effectively refuse the contract? He could leave. Unfortunately, however, there is no place for him to go, since there is virtually no place on the globe entirely free of some government's strictures or supervision. Moreover, that form of dissent is unduly costly. Consider Klaus, who insists that anyone who dissents to his becoming absolute monarch should signal disagreement by cutting off his or her hand. When no hands are cut off, Klaus cannot insist that everyone has given tacit consent to Klaus' becoming absolute monarch. The appeal of contract justifications is that the moral force of rights is imposed not from without but by ourselves, since people are morally bound by only those rights they themselves freely chose to recognize. In other words, people bind themselves. But when there is no way not to choose without unduly harming oneself, people cannot be said freely to choose. The third, related problem is that the conditions under which the contract was reached might not be fair. U.S. law, for example, does not uphold so-called "contracts of adhesion," that is, inequitable contracts in which one party had no real choice. To justify rights by actual agreement, one must show that the conditions under which the agreement was reached were fair, and, in particular, that those who benefit most by the agreement did not coerce those who benefit least. This might be possible in an artificial community (e.g., an Israeli Kibbutz), but in any natural community this is surely not true. The last difficulty is that actual contract theories cannot be used to evaluate or amend legal systems. On an actual contract theory of rights, one could not have argued in 1867, before ratification of the 14th Amendment was complete, that the 14th Amendment should be passed because it protects rights, since the only rights people have are those already agreed to, as signified by law. Hence the "rights" the 14th Amendment protects do not exist until the 14th Amendment is passed.

Hypothetical contract theories avoid these problems, but are subject to three others. John Rawls's hypothetical contract view holds that political systems (including systems of rights) are just and fair when people would agree to them in what he calls "the original position." The original position is an imaginary, hypothetical situation in which people are fully rational, are mutually disinterested, have general knowledge about the world, but do not know whom they will be once they enter the social world—in particular, they do not know their own abilities, their own moral and personal preferences, their personal relationships, their race, gender, age, religion, or ethnicity, etc. So rights emerge from what people would agree to under a set of totally hypothetical circumstances. Tim Scanlon argues that moral claims (including rights claims) are true when they follow from any system of rules that no reasonable person would reject. More precisely, Scanlon says: "An act is wrong if its performance under the circumstances would be disallowed by any system of rules for the general regulation of behavior which no one could reasonably reject as a basis for informed, unforced general agreement."[33] Scanlon, thus, is adverting to what people would agree to if they were rational and acting in good faith. While various problems concerning the details of Rawls' and Scanlon's theory can be found in the extensive literature about them, three general problems with any hypothetical contract theory deserve mention. First, it is clear that I am morally bound by agreements into which I actually and freely enter, because by doing so I bind myself. That is what it means to enter freely into an agreement. But it is not at all clear that I am bound by what I would agree to under circumstances that do not arise. In short, the argument runs, actual agreements bind people, but hypothetical agreements do not. Some hypothetical contract views, such as Rawls', avoid this problem, at the cost of some justificatory power: Rawls claims only that the original position models the conditions of our shared conception justice, and, hence, what people would agree to in that situation is isomorphic to what fits our shared conception of justice (see below). The second problem is that people would agree to different things in different circumstances. Hypothetical contract theories claim that only one set of circumstances is privileged—what counts is not what you would agree to if you were a Buddhist, or what you would agree to if you were wealthy, or what you would agree to if you were extraordinarily talented, but what you would agree to under one specific set of hypothetical circumstances, x. (For Rawls, for example, x is the original position.) But why is that one circumstance the determining one? Thus hypothetical contract theories must justify why one hypothetical circumstance is morally privileged over all others. The most profound problem stems from the fact that, while what people actually agree to is, at least in part, a matter of empirical fact, what people would agree to is not an empirically verifiable fact. One cannot visit the hypothetical situation and see what happened. The problem, then, is determining the truth value of counterfactual claims about what people would agree to in a hypothetical situation. The more specific one is about the hypothetical situation, the easier it is to answer that question, but the less plausible becomes the claim that the hypothetical situation is privileged. Hypothetical contract views, thus, must balance sufficient generality to be plausible and sufficient specificity to obtain a result. If someone claims "those rights exist that people would agree to were they just like me," then it may be clear which rights result, but few people would accept that this criterion has any moral weight. Conversely, if one says "those rights exist that people would agree to if they knew all the objective moral truths," it becomes impossible without circularity to determine what people would agree to in those circumstances.

Scanlon's view, for example, adverts to what reasonable people would conclude. What does it mean to be "reasonable"? Few would deny that holding logically incompatible beliefs is unreasonable, but many conflicting and bizarre moral theories are not logically contradictory in any straightforward way. A much stronger notion of "reasonable" might yield results, but stronger notions are increasingly controversial and difficult to justify. This point emerges very strongly from a look at John Rawls' *A Theory of Justice* (TJ).

Rawls project in TJ is frequently misunderstood. As a result, many criticisms of Rawls are misguided. The persistence of these misapprehensions, despite their refutations in print, justifies belaboring a few points that have been made elsewhere. TJ attempts to capture, not justify, what Rawls takes to be our shared conception of justice in the United States and other liberal democracies. TJ, thus, is not attempting to provide an argument that might convince the Ayatollah Khomenei or Joseph Stalin. TJ begins with some assumptions about the general elements of a democratic notion of justice that Rawls takes to be widely shared in the United States, such as the claim that justice is impartial. To a Roskolnikov, who rejects the idea of impartial morality (that is, who holds that justice and morality do not apply equally to the superman and the ordinary person), TJ has little to say. The only kind of justification for the impartiality of justice TJ offers are a few somewhat cursory remarks (e.g., greater social harmony results when there are neutral grounds for the system to be acceptable to those with competing visions of the good—when a system is based on a vision of the good, it is hard for those with disagree with that vision to feel commitment to the system) and the idea of reflective equilibrium, and Rawls acknowledges that the results of reflective equilibrium may not be universal. Rather, Rawls' system is intended to model our conception of justice, much as economists' models are intended to model economic situations. Rawls is constructing a simulation machine, and, for a simulation machine to give an accurate simulation, only the relevant properties of the simulation need correspond to reality. (A computer can simulate a hurricane's behavior even though there are no winds inside the computer.) If justice, for example, is impartial between competing conceptions of the good, one way to model this is to consider a fictional world of persons independent of their visions of the good. It doesn't matter whether persons are actually independent of their visions of the good or not. The point is just that this representation of persons, whether veridical or not, captures the neutrality of justice. Rawls' argument, in other words, is roughly along these lines:

1) The original position models the relevant features of our shared conception of justice.

2) Therefore the results yielded by the original position are consequences of our conception of justice.

3) We (that is, most citizens of the US, for example) continue to adhere to our conception of justice. (That is, learning the results of the original position does not cause us to modify our conception of justice.)

4) Therefore we should adhere to the results yielded by the original position.

Thus criticisms of TJ based on the claim that the original position is not possible or has no innate special moral importance are irrelevant, as are criticisms that Rawls invokes a mistaken metaphysical conception of persons as Humean rational agents who are mutually disinterested beings independent of their values, desires, preferences, and social networks. That argument would constitute a legitimate criticism if Rawls were attempting to give an external justification of liberalism based on a claim about the nature of persons. But Rawls takes great pain, particularly in later writings, to point out that, in TJ, the construal of persons as mutually disinterested rational agents is not a metaphysical claim about persons, but a fictional construction designed to model relevant elements of our shared conception of justice.

On the other hand, communitarians like Michael Sandel[34] do mount a legitimate challenge to Rawls. Sandel's view is that justice should not be neutral between competing conceptions of the good, because adherence to one's community's (thick) moral stance is itself a central (perhaps the central) element of good human lives: it is, in large measure, what human life is about. The correct way to put this objection is not as a criticism that Rawls' project fails, but rather as a claim that it is the wrong project. Sandel wants to construct an alternative to what Rawls calls our shared conception of justice and to argue that the communitarian alternative is the better, more correct, conception. In other words, Sandel should acknowledge that Rawls' system does model a conception of justice (or, if it fails to do so, it fails on other grounds), but it is not the best conception of justice. Sandel's argument for the superiority of his conception does rest upon a metaphysical conception of the self. Rawls objects to theories based on a metaphysical theory of the self because such theories are meaningless, unknowable, essentially contested, lead inevitably to unbridgeable dissent, etc. Communitarians can answer this objection either by a) providing a viable epistemology for claims about the metaphysics of the self (hence showing that such claims are neither meaningless nor unknowable) or b) arguing that there is no special vice in the state's taking a stand on such matters (for example, by arguing that the state cannot help take a stand on this or that the relevant claims are no more unknowable or essentially contested than other things upon which the state cannot help but take a stand).

A more general and compelling argument is that formalist projects like Rawls' fail in one of two ways. Specifically, either the assumptions of the system are so general that no definite results emerge, or the assumptions are too robust to serve (they assume too much). One example may help illustrate the general point, which applies to many other elements of TJ as well.

TJ's conclusions depend upon what a rational person would choose in the original position. Hence the notion of what is rational is crucial to Rawls' system. As noted above, adopting a very "thin" definition of rationality, that is, a definition or account that makes only very weak assumptions and hence is acceptable to almost everyone, yields no substantial results. Too many incompatible choices emerge as rational ones. For example, there is nothing self-contradictory about someone in the original position's agreeing to a system in which there are ten masters and a hundred slaves, risking the possible hardship of being a slave for the possible benefits of being a master. Such a stance might be unwise in various ways, but it is not self-contradictory. So, if being rational merely means eschewing contradiction, persons in the original position could opt for a system of masters and slaves. What a rational person would choose in the original position depends crucially upon (among other things) what attitude toward gambling she takes. If the definition of rationality is thin enough that the attitude toward gambling it entails is unproblematic, too many disparate choices turn out to be rational ones.

Rawls himself employs a very thick definition of rationality—he claims, for instance, that rationality requires employing the maximin principle about the most fundamental elements of one's life: the most rational response to uncertainty about things of fundamental importance, asserts Rawls, is always to choose the alternative with the least bad worst-case scenario. This attitude of extreme aversion to risk is thick enough to generate results when imported into the original position, but also thick enough to be highly problematic and controversial. It is neither a widely accepted view of rationally nor an element of our shared conception of justice. After all, the maximin principle is not generally required by rationality. For example, it is hardly irrational to prefer a 99.999% chance of being a millionaire and a 0.001% of having $10,000 to a 100% chance of having $10005. Why then should choosing the maximin principle be a precondition of rationality about basic freedoms? Rawls' brief comments on this point fail to persuade most readers.

These few brief remarks cannot, of course "refute" either Rawls or Scanlon. They serve, rather, to illustrate a general tension in all hypothetical contract and ideal observer accounts of rights, a tension that, in my view, no one has satisfactorily resolved.[35]

Another approach to rights is to claim that they are morally basic and cannot be justified by other moral notions. Adherents of this view typically conflate two different claims. Claim 1) is an ontological claim, while claim 2) is an epistemological claim. The ontological claim is that rights exist as a brute ontological fact and that their existence does not derive from other moral notions. Claim 2) is a claim about our knowledge of rights—one cannot infer the existence of rights by arguing from other moral notions. Neither claim entails the other. That is, rights could be ontologically basic, but we could get knowledge of rights by reflecting on derivative notions. Conversely, rights could be ontologically derivative but the epistemological starting point in thinking about ethics. This is because reasoning can work in both directions. Suppose Adams scored 97% on a test and therefore deserves an A. Getting the 97 determines deserving the A—Adams deserves an A precisely because she scored a 97, and not the other way around. Thus, in the relevant sense, getting the 97 is ontologically basic. If I know Adams scored a 97 and know the grading scale, I know Adams deserved an A. But, conversely, if I know just that Adams deserves an A and know the grading scale, I can infer that Adams must have scored a 90 or above. So claims about epistemological priority and claims about ontological priority are independent claims. Claim 1), that rights are ontologically prior, leaves unaddressed the question of how rights claims can be justified. Those who hold claim 1) must still select among the other theories of rights under discussion when attempting to justify rights. Claim 2), that rights are epistemologically prior, is a competing theory. It asserts that rights are not justifiable in terms of any other moral notions. But then either a) rights exist but we have no way of knowing what they are or b) rights claims must be self-evident. Possibility a) is obviously unsatisfactory—it is a position one adopts only if no other position is available. Possibility b) is, simply, empirically false. Given the wide variety of divergent opinions about rights, they are clearly not self-evident. So the only feasible alternative for an adherent of Claim 2) is adopting a hypothetical self-evidence theory—rights claims would be self-evident under appropriate conditions. This view, a form of ideal observer view, is subject to the objections raised against hypothetical contract views.

The Need Theory argues that A has a right to x if A's having x is required to satisfy a pressing need. As Joseph Fletcher puts it, "rights are nothing but a formal recognition of society of certain human needs...."[36] For example, it might be asserted that, since we all need liberty, there is a right to liberty.

Once again, rights as warrants permit need to be used to justify some rights claims without requiring that all rights be justified solely in terms of need. A brief look at some difficulties with justifying rights entirely in terms of needs helps illustrate the attractiveness of viewing rights as warrants.

Two problems with the need theory, raised by Loren Lomasky, deserve mention.[37] The first centers on defining needs. In general, "need" is a relational concept: something is needed, under a given set of circumstances, in order to achieve a particular result. One can't call something a need without specifying what it is needed for (the result) and when (under what circumstances). Almost anything can be a "need" in this sense, since almost anything one might mention is needed, some time, by some one, in order to achieve some result. After all, if I wish to knit you a sweater, then I need yarn. In some sense, then, yarn is a need of mine, but, presumably, that does not give me a right to yarn. Thus need theories must distinguish between results sufficiently important to justify rights and results, like knitting you a sweater, that are insufficiently important, and that requires a mechanism for evaluating the importance of the result for which something is needed. Since objective importance has proven notoriously elusive and controversial, need theorists frequently advert instead to subjective importance, that is, the importance a given individual attaches to a given result. However, subjective importance varies considerably between persons. If I am truly obsessed, knitting you a sweater could be the most important thing in life to me. Is it impossible for a fanatical book collector to commit murder and risk hanging in order to obtain a rare book? Might a religious fanatic gladly give his life to wipe out masturbation? If so, then an end to masturbation is more subjectively important to him than his own survival, and, it would seem, his right to others' not masturbating is stronger than his right to life. Perhaps this problem can be met by defining the relevant result as survival: A needs x, on this view, if and only if A will not survive without x. However, I can survive with only one kidney. Is keeping my kidneys not a need? If not, do I have no right to keep my kidney? Some attempt to meet the objection by defining a special class of "basic needs" that are prerequisites for all other needs. It is argued, for example, that whatever else we might need for our projects, having it is of no avail without liberty. It does one no good to have ample yarn to knit if one lacks the liberty to knit. Thus liberty is a "basic" need. Basic rights, on this view, pertain to basic needs. However, since the liberty to knit is equally unhelpful if one has no yarn, further argument is needed to explain why such "basic" needs are privileged over more subjectively urgent needs. (Undoubedly, for example, at least one person exists who would readily trade the liberty to knit for a night with Jennifer Lopez.) The second problem is that the mere fact that A needs something does not, by itself, give B a rational reason to recognize A as a right holder. In response, some have argued that B must value her own needs and must recognize that the same reasons that make B's needs valuable to B also make A's needs valuable to A. Thus, it is held, B cannot rationally fail to value A's needs.[38]

The best known adherent of this sort of view is Alan Gewirth, who can be classified both as a need theorist and an autonomy theorist, as he argues that autonomy is a necessary condition (and hence a need) for all projects. The general idea is that each person values her own ability to pursue projects and must recognize that all other people value their own ability to pursue projects for exactly the same reason that she values hers. Hence, Gewirth argues, by the principle of universality (like cases should be treated alike), everyone must value other people's ability to pursue projects.[39] Gewirth was a teacher of mine at the University of Chicago for whom I bear considerable respect, so I must confess to a nagging sense that I am misunderstanding some part of his detailed argument, which appears to be as follows:

1) I am a valuer.
2) Therefore I must value being a valuer.
3) Therefore I must value my rationality and well-being as necessary conditions for being a valuer.
4) You have exactly the same reasons for valuing your rationality and well-being as I do.
5) Therefore I must value rationality and well-being *per se*, as the necessary conditions for being a valuer, and value them as ends.
6) Therefore I must value your rationality and well-being.
7) Therefore I must respect your rights.

The argument does not appear to follow. From the fact that I am a valuer it does not follow that I *value* being a valuer. Valuing x is a first order judgment. One can also form a second-order judgment about that first-order judgment. One can want x and also want not to want x. For example, Don Jose in the opera *Carmen* intensely desires Carmen and also, at times, wishes devoutly that he did not feel that desire. Similarly, one can consistently value x and hold that it is not valuable to value x. One can imagine a tormented theologian who believes that reason should be entirely subordinated to faith and yet finds that he cannot help but value reason. He values reason, but does not value valuing reason. Thus it is not inconsistent to wish that I were not a valuer, that is, that I had no preferences. For example, I could wish that whatever happened made me equally happy, that I considered all outcomes equally good, or that I were able to eliminate all desires and values. Each of these viewpoints has been suggested as an ideal by schools of thought with significant numbers of adherents. Of course, in wishing not to be an evaluator, I am being an evaluator, but it does not follow that I value being able to make that second-order judgment—that is a third-order judgment. That is, I can desire to have no first-order desires. That is a second-order desire. I can also desire to have no second-order desires. That is a third-order desire. At no level do my desires contradict one another. So 2), that I value being a valuer, does not follow from 1), the fact that I am a valuer. Consider also an alternate formulation Gewirth offers on page 52. Gewirth avers that agents act for a purpose they deem good, and, because without freedom they could not act, they must deem freedom good as a necessary means. This does not follow. I may value getting the result of an action without valuing my acting to get it. Freedom is necessary only for the action, not for obtaining the result. Thus I may, without contradiction, fail to value freedom. For example, I can value the sensation occasioned by tickling without placing any value on my acting to get that sensation, and I do not need to be free in order to feel the sensation of tickling. Even if I am totally paralyzed though sensate, and have no means of moving, speaking, or otherwise indicating my preference, someone might just come along and tickle me without my doing anything whatsoever to prompt it. So while Gewirth might perhaps argue that freedom is necessary for action, as he defines action, he gives no reason to think we must value action in that sense, even as a necessary means, since action in his sense is not always necessary to obtaining the good for the sake of which actions are undertaken. In other words, there is nothing contradictory in this situation: Jones values x, Jones can sometimes obtain x without acting (in Gewirth's sense), and Jones does not value acting as an end or as a necessary means of obtaining x. Therefore, the fact that freedom is a necessary condition for acting does not show that Jones' valuing x entails that Jones values freedom as a necessary means.

Put another way, I must value purpose satisfaction (that the facts of my life accord with my purposes), but I need value purpose fulfillment (that my purposing brings about that accord) only to the extent that it achieves purpose satisfaction. Because purpose fulfillment is not the only route to purpose satisfaction, I do not need to value purpose fulfillment as a necessary means. I can be indifferent as to whether purpose satisfaction is achieved by purpose fulfillment or by some other route: purpose fullfillment may be valuable only as a non-necessary means of obtaining purpose satisfaction.

Gewirth could reply by building into the very notion of a purposive agent that a purposive agent values his purposiveness. In that case, however, not everyone is a purposive agent, and hence Gewirth has not shown that there is any special moral significance to the fact that purposive moral agents, in his sense, value freedom.

Of course, most people do, in fact, value their autonomy. But is autonomy the most fundamental value? Gewirth's argument, as best I can determine, runs something like this:

1) Particular ends (desired states) are conditional.
2) The conditions for having any ends at all are not conditional, since they are the same no matter what our ends are.
3) Therefore the conditions for having ends are valuable as an end.

As suggested earlier, autonomy is not a necessary condition for having ends. Even if it were a necessary condition, universally necessary means remain means, not ends. Let "universal means" designate the means that are universally necessary for any of a given range of ends. The fact that some means are universal means does not make them any the less instrumental (valuable as means to something else, not as ends in themselves). A means is still a means, however universal it may be. For example, human beings cannot be said to value access to oxygen as an end in itself simply because access to oxygen is necessary to pursuing any human ends other than death.

Finally, if I value my agency, must I value yours as well? The following broad principle is clearly false: if I value my having x, and I recognize that you have the same relationship to your having x as I do to my having x, then I must value your having x. As Lomasky points out, what I must recognize is that other people's ability to pursue projects is valuable to them. It doesn't follow from universality that they should valuable to me. To use Lomasky's example, I recognize that all the other runners in the race value their own winning for exactly the same reasons that I value my winning. Does it follow that I am rationally obligated to value other runner's winning (and hence my losing)?

The discussion so far concerns disagreements within rights theory, that is, disagreements about some aspect of what rights are, what justifies rights, or which rights we have. Some writers have rejected the idea of rights altogether, either denying that rights exist or arguing that the idea of rights possessed by individuals is morally invidious. Since these attacks on the very idea of rights have come from a wide variety of quarters expressing disparate views, space permits but a brief mention of a small sample of these attacks.

Attacks of rights as such fall into two broad categories. One category of attack is founded on moral skepticism, amoralism, or deep-seated relativism. If there is no way of determining moral truth, or no moral truth at all, then no rights claims may reasonably be judged to be true. If all moral claims are relative, then rights claims are relative, and hence true only for an individual or a society. These attacks are met in two directions: positively, by providing an adequate moral epistemology, and negatively, by showing the unacceptable consequences of relativism, amoralism, and such thorough-going skepticism. Both require more space than can be allotted here. For a sketch of a moral epistemology, see "Environmental Ethics: An Aristotelian Approach" (*op. cit.*). For a response to amoralism, see *Moral Responsibility and Persons* (*op. cit.*). Responses to relativism abound in the philosophical literature.

The second category of attack on rights stems from a substantive moral objection. Such attacks must be addressed individually. This chapter concludes with a brief comment about three of the many objections in this category.

One view, sometimes (somewhat unfairly) attributed to Carol Gilligan but more properly found in the works of others influenced by Gilligan, asserts that rights are primarily concerned with justice and with interactions between disinterested parties. This "male" conception of ethical discourse is impoverished, mistaken, perverse, or in some other way inadequate. It should be replaced or supplemented by an ethic of care, concerned with people's mutual interestedness, their social and person bonds, their concern for and responsibility for each other. A second critique avers that rights talk is based on individual choice and ignores social institutions. Thus talk of rights fosters inequality, because it protects choice within institutions that are repressive. It is claimed, for example, that because rights draw lines limiting state action, rights prevent the state from modifying social institutions that oppress women. Hence, it is argued, individual rights oppress women by protecting non-state patterns of actions and social structures that adversely affect women. Both objections begin with a valid point: ethics is not exhausted by rules for the interaction of disinterested parties and state action to address oppression by non-governmental institutions and individuals (which may receive various forms of state support) is sometimes needed. These two licit points may tell against traditional views of rights. However, if rights are warrants and natural rights are requirements to make adequate provision, neither point shows that rights are invidious. Rather, they serve to influence the discussion concerning which warrants exist and what constitutes adequate provision: a licit network of warrants respects connections of care, both by leaving room for relations of care and by containing appropriate care-related warrants. It seems hard to deny that care and intimate relations are a necessary part of human flourishing, and hence societies, to be licit, must make adequate provision for the establishment and flourishing of such relations. Thus, it appears, if the view of natural rights advanced in this volume is correct, a legal system in which pursuing and enjoying such relationships is not feasible is illegitimate: it violates natural rights. Thus rights neither ignore nor undermine an "ethics of care," but support and respect relationships of care and their moral implications. Similarly, making adequate provision for human flourishing could well require state modification of harshly oppressive non-governmental institutions and practices. Nothing in the nature of rights, as articulated in this volume, rules out the claim that individuals may be warranted in demanding that the state interfere with non-governmental institutions. Rather, the issue becomes a substantive one of determining which warrants exist, and so which claims for such interference are justified. The issue concerns, using Jenkins' terminology (*op. cit.*), the contents of rights rather than the ground of rights. So, while some feminists may disagree with some of the arguments in this volume, those disagreements are substantive ones about the content of warrants, not broad theoretical ones about the nature or legitimacy of rights. One of the virtues of the holistic approach to rights is that it provides a framework for such disagreements within rights theory itself.

A third attack on rights begins with the assertion that communities are the meaningful units of human life, not individuals. What ultimately deserves and requires protection is the survival of and flourishing of communities as ways of life, with their particular value orientations and their particular institutions and practices. One form of communitarian critique argues that individual human beings are important but derive their identity only by participation in such communities. A more radical form asserts that individuals exist only to serve the community. In any case, the argument is that individual rights are evil because they serve to disrupt the shared life of the community and distance individuals from their community. This a substantial claim that deserves closer scrutiny than space permits: a brief hand-wave in the direction of a response must suffice. Human beings, it seems to me, are social individuals, and any adequate framework for human life must take cognizance of both the social and individual aspect of human life. While some liberal thinkers have downplayed the importance of community, the holistic view of rights leaves room for warrants and natural rights based on and supporting the importance of community. Several of the arguments in this volume attempt to do just that. Others may wish to go further in arguing for warrants based on the value and importance of community, but, once again, that is a substantial disagreement about the content of warrants rather than a theoretical disagreement about the nature of rights. On the other hand, the claim that rights are possessed by individuals does attribute some importance to individuals as individuals. Only the extreme view that human individuality is of no moral importance tells against the general view of rights proposed in this volume. Without denying in any way the importance of belonging to a community and of viewing one's life as part of an ongoing joint project with others, this volume will assume that the undeniable facts that individuals differ, have separate consciousnesses, and number among their important aims various personal ends are of significant moral importance.

Notes to Chapter One

1 Jenkins, Iredell, *Social Order and the Limits of Law*, Princeton: Princeton University Press, 1980, p. 252.

2 MacIntrye, Alasdair, *After Virtue*, Notre Dame: Notre Dame University Press, 1981, p. 69.

3 Ramsey, Paul, *Fabricated Man: The Ethics of Genetic Control*, New haven: Yale University Press, 1970. Cited in Fletcher, Joseph, "Ethical Aspects of Genetic Controls: Designed Genetic Changes in Man," *New England Journal of Medicine* 285, 1971, pp. 776-783.

4 *Griswold v. Connecticut*, 381 U.S. 479, 1965.

5 *Roe v. Wade*, 410 U.S. 113, 1973.

6 *Adkins v. Children's Hospital*, 261 U.S. 525, 1923; *Stettler v. O'Hara*, 243 U.S. 629, 1917; *Morehead v. New York ex rel. Tipaldo*, 298 U.S. 587, 1936.

7 Hohfeld, Wesley Newcomb, *Fundamental Legal Conceptions, As Applied in Judicial Reasoning*, ed. W.W. Cooke, New Haven: Yale University Press, 1919.

8 *New York Times Company v. Sullivan*, 376 U.S. 254, 1964.

9 See, for instance, Mackie, J.L., "Can there Be a Rights-Based Moral Theory?" *Midwest Studies in Philosophy* 3, 1978, pp. 350-359.

10 Benditt, *op. cit.*

11 Ross, who promulgated the idea of *prima facie* rights and duties, thought they did retain some force when overridden, but it is not clear from his account of *prima facie* rights and duties how they could retain some force. See Ross, Sir William David, *The Right and the Good*, Oxford: Clarendon Press, 1930.

12 Wellman, Carl, *Real Rights*, New York: Oxford University Press, 1995.

13 Legal positivists hold that legal rights are exhausted by the rights a given legal system recognizes, officially and/or *de facto*. Natural law theorists hold that some rights are inherent in all legal systems, whether acknowledged and enforced or not, by virtue of the very nature of law. I prefer to call such rights "presumptive rights," thus sidestepping the issue. A third category of legal rights, implicit rights, is introduced below.

14 Thomson, Judith Jarvis, "A Defense of Abortion," *Philosophy and Public Affairs* 1 (1) Fall 1971.

15 Fishkin, James, *The Limits of Obligation*, New Haven: Yale University Press, 1983.

16 *Regina v. Prince* Court for Crown Cases Reserved, 1875. L.R 2 C.C. R. 154.

17 As Chapter 3 reveals, some holders of one theory of rights, the will theory, deny that, in our present legal system, I have a right not to be killed, since the law does not permit me to waive my right (you will be punished if you kill me even though I consented to your killing me). The point made here, however, applies equally well to a legal system in which consensual killing is not a crime.

18 *Op. cit*

19 Judith Jarvis Thomson, in *The Realm of Rights*, Cambridge, MA and London: Harvard University Press, 1990, argues that a liberty is more than a privilege. I agree, but what I mean by "liberty" differs from what Thomson means.

20 For additional criticisms of the distinction between negative and positive rights, see Lippke, Richard, "The Elusive Distinction Between Negative and Positive Rights," *Southern Journal of Philosophy* 33 (3), Fall 1995, pp. 335-346.

21 See also Joel Feinberg's discussion of my argument in Feinberg, Joel, *Harmless Wrongdoing* [Volume IV of *The Moral Limits of the Criminal Law*], New York, Oxford: Oxford University Press, 1990, esp. pp. 62-64.

22 Raz, Joseph, *The Morality of Freedom*, Oxford: Clarendon Press, 1986.

23 Dworkin, Ronald, *A Matter of Principle*, Cambridge: Harvard University Press, 1985, p. 191.

24 Langlois, Anthony, *The Politics of Justice and Human Rights*, Cambridge and New York: Cambridge University Press, 2001, p. 90.

25 Devlin, Lord Patrick, *The Enforcement of Morals*, London: Oxford University Press, 1965.

26 Rowan, John, *Conflicts of Rights: Moral Theory and Social Policy Implications*, Boulder, Colorado: Westview Press, 1999, p. 140

27 Raz, Joseph, *op. cit.*, p. 166.

28 See Rowan, John, *op. cit.*, for a detailed discussion of the impact of the will and interest theories on major social issues such as abortion and pornography.

29 Rawls, John, *A Theory of Justice*, Cambridge, MA: Harvard University Press, 1971; Nozick, Robert, *Anarchy, State and Utopia*, New York: Basic Books, 1974.

30 Hill, Thomas Jr., *Autonomy and Self-Respect*, Cambridge, New York: Cambridge University Press, 1991, p. 36.

31 Schlossberger, Eugene, *Moral Responsibility and Persons*, Philadelphia: Temple University Press, 1992, pp. 70-71.

32 Schlossberger, Eugene, *The Ethical Engineer*, Philadelphia: Temple University Press, 1993.

33 Scanlon, Tim, "Contractualism and Beyond" in *Utilitarianism and Beyond*, ed. Amartya Sen and Bernard Williams, Cambridge: Cambridge University press, 1982, p. 117

34 Sandel, Michael, *Liberalism and the Limits of Justice*, Cambridge: Cambridge University Press, 1982.

35 See, however, Schlossberger, Eugene, "Environmental Ethics: An Aristotelian Approach," *Philosophy in the Contemporary World* 8:2, Fall-Winter 2001, pp. 15-26, for a sketch of a type of ideal observer theory about human goodness that, in my view, deals with this problem.

36 Fletcher, Joseph, "Ethical Aspects of Genetic Controls: Designed Genetic Changes in Man," *New England Journal of Medicine* 285, 1971, pp. 776-783, reprinted in John Arras and Robert Hunt, eds., *Ethical Issues in Modern Medicine* 2nd ed., Paolo Alto: Mayfield Publishing Company, 1983, pp. 401-407; p. 406.

37 Lomasky, Loren E., *Persons, Rights, and the Moral Community*, New York, Oxford: Oxford University Press, 1987.

38 For instance, Lomasky (*op. cit.*) argues that the commitment to pursue projects is a constituent of personal identity. Therefore persons are project pursuers. It follows, argues Lomasky, that if A is a person, there is some end that is directive of A's life-plan, E, so A values that which is necessary for the promotion of E by A. A's having the ability to be a project pursuer is necessary for that, so A values A's ability to pursue projects.

39 Gewirth, Alan, *Reason and Morality*, Chicago, University of Chicago Press, 1978.

Chapter 2:
The Many Flavors of Rights:
Entitlements, Liberties, Permissions,
and the Right to Die

Rights talk is complex and diverse. Like ice cream, rights come in different flavors that are as importantly different from each other as chocolate and vanilla. As Chapter 1 indicates, legal rights, moral rights, and social rights constitute three domains of rights: rights may be recognized in law, moral deliberation, and/or social dealings (e.g., the right to a response to an RSVP from someone who intends to attend). There are five broad sources of rights: natural rights, presumptive rights, moral rights, regulative ideals, and positive (legal, moral, and social) rights.[1] Natural rights are rights every person holds against every society to make adequate provision for certain things within its domain. Presumptive rights are rights that, generally, legal systems ought to recognize. A legal system that does not recognize a presumptive right may be, in that respect, flawed and should be changed. But it does not, on that basis alone, lose legitimacy. Natural and presumptive rights are addressed in Chapter 3. Moral rights are warrants provided by the correct moral theory. Ordinarily, I have a moral right not to be lied to. One important source of moral rights, discussed in Chapter 7, is the duty of "team loyalty" one owes to others engaged in the moral enterprise, the task of instantiating a morally good world. Regulative ideals are broad, defining ideals of a society, chosen from the set of defensible but not necessarily compatible ideals. For instance, equality is a regulative ideal of American society: a commitment to equality is one of the defining ideals of America as a nation and as a society. It is not a necessary ideal for any morally acceptable society—other good societies may not include equality in their regulative ideals. Regulative ideals are defining commitments that can be used to criticize or justify positive legal, moral, and social rights, which stem from the particular laws, moral beliefs, and social understandings of a given society. All of these rights may include several species of warrants, three of which are the subject of this chapter: entitlements, liberties, and permissions.

Some rights are entitlements, some are liberties, and some are permissions.[2] An entitlement right is a warrant to demand, insist upon, something as one's due. Liberties are spheres of socially approved aspects of life or activities such that a) they are sheltered from obligations to refrain and b) there is some force to (some consideration is owed to) fostering the conditions for engaging in that activity or realizing that aspect of life. Of course, when a form of support is enacted into law, it generally creates positive legal entitlements. The relevant liberty remains the ground or rationale for those positive legal entitlements and may be appealed to in legal reasoning concerning which specific entitlements law should recognize (as when a court finds that the liberty of movement demands handicapped accessibility) or disputes concerning the nature and scope of the positive legal entitlement. Permissions, which Hohfeld called "privileges," [3] are merely absences of duties to refrain. A permission to do x is much weaker than an entitlement to non-interference in doing x. If the law does not forbid spitting on the sidewalk I have a permission right to do so, but others may licitly interfere with my spitting in ways they may not licitly interfere with, for instance, my voting on election day.

The distinction between these three flavors of rights is often overlooked by rights theorists who concentrate on the difference between positive rights, that is, entitlements to be given something, and negative rights, or rights of non-interference. For example, the legal right possessed by children of Indiana to be provided a free education is a positive right. The right of free speech, it is generally held, is a negative right: the right to speech, common wisdom avers, entitles one not to free newspaper space to pronounce one's views, but merely to the government's not forcibly preventing citizens from broadcasting their views, not arresting those who do, and so forth. In fact, however, both positive rights and negative rights may include all three flavors of rights. For example, the right to vote may include absences of duties to refrain (permissions), such as the absence of a statute forbidding people to vote, social commitments to support the activity (liberties), such as transportation to the polls when needed, and entitlements, such as the entitlement that the state mount elections and the entitlement not to be forcibly prevented by others from entering the polling place. The "negative right" to freedom of movement might include an entitlement that others not lock one up against one's will, the permission to walk in one's garden (that is, the absence of a duty to refrain from walking in one's garden), and perhaps a liberty that calls for support of one's ability to move freely in the form of the creation of roads, police protection for roadways, handicap accessibility of public buildings, etc. A "positive right" to a free public education might include an entitlement to attend classes free of charge, a permission to study, and a liberty calling for such forms of support as the maintenance of public roads leading to the school. In short, a clearer picture of the scope and structure of rights emerges when one pays attention to the different entitlements, permissions, and liberties that a broad right *in rem* may include.

A. Three Species of Rights

Entitlements can be quite general, e.g., an entitlement not to be treated differentially on the basis of race, or quite specific, e.g., an entitlement to your standing on your head for three seconds after dinner, as you promised. To have these entitlements is to be warranted in demanding as one's due that you stand on your head for three seconds, to be warranted in demanding of others as one's due that they not treat one differentially on the basis of race and/or in demanding of the government that its policies do not promote differential treatment on the basis of race, and so forth.

A permission is merely the absence of a duty to refrain. In Hohfeld's infamous salad example, if you give me a permission to eat your salad, I have no duty to refrain from eating it, but you have no obligation to assist or even make it possible for me to do so—you may, for example, licitly gobble up the salad before I have a chance to taste a single leaf or deny me the use of your fork. In giving me that permission, you have merely removed the ordinary obligation I am under not to eat your salad. Thus, my having a fork with which to eat the salad is due no special consideration. Of course, there is rarely a point to a permission when the conditions for engaging in the relevant activity are lacking. I have a permission to jump to the moon unaided, in the sense that I am under no duty to refrain from doing so, though that permission is of scant value. But, although permissions may be of value only when engaging in the permitted activity is feasible, they exist whenever no duty bars the way.

Some theorists may be loathe to use the term "right" for a mere permission—only entitlements, they might be tempted to say, count as "rights." But if we insist on such a stipulative restriction of the use of the term "right," we must offer separate explanations of the force of the requirement that others not block my path to the polls (an entitlement) and the warrant I have for touching my desk (that no duty forbids it). If, instead, we regard rights as warrants, that is, as socially recognized sanctions (groundings, justifications) for someone to do, say, demand, believe, feel, or think something as his due, then we can offer a unified explanation of all of these claims. We can then distinguish between things we are warranted in doing because there is no duty to refrain, namely permissions, things we are warranted in claiming as entitlements, such as others refraining from forcibly preventing us from voting, and things we are warranted in asking society to endorse and support (liberties). But whether or not one chooses to employ the term "rights" for liberties and permissions, certain things follow from the fact that there is no duty to refrain from x-ing, that is, that there is a permission to x, while others follow from the fact that a society, either in law or public morality, has a commitment to fostering and supporting x-ing, that is, that there is a liberty to x. These facts, and their consequences, may be overlooked if one attends only to Hohfeldian claim rights.

Can mere permissions (privileges) create obligations? Judith Jarvis Thomson suggests that "no privilege entails any claim."[4] However, as Thomson herself points out on page 52, "if a person X has a privilege as regards Y then Y cannot complain that X wrongs Y if X exercises that privilege." This fact creates some obligations on Y's part. For example, D's permission to eat C's salad means that C is under a duty not to bring suit against D for eating it--C has no ground for that suit and has a duty not to bring frivolous suit. One might urge that it is not the lack of a right alone that puts C under a duty to refrain from bringing suit, but C's privilege coupled with a duty not to bring frivolous suit. In that sense, no claim ever entails another that is not definitionally equivalent to it. Nonetheless, the fact that C's permission gives him no grounds for a suit means that C ought not to bring suit. [5] Similarly, C is under a moral duty not to blame or excoriate D for consuming the salad. Again, this duty depends, in some sense, on a duty not to unjustly blame or excoriate others. But, clearly, if C cannot justly complain, then she should not. Thus C has a duty not to complain. Of course, C may licitly excoriate D for eating the salad if, for example, a starving person has just asked for a forkful, but the excoriation is for D's hardheartedness in ignoring the plight of the starving person, not for exercising the permission as such. C may sue D if, in eating the salad, D stains C's blouse, but the suit is for ruining the blouse, not for eating the salad as such. Thus, given obvious legal and moral background assumptions, permissions can entail claims. However, they do not entail the sort of robust and far-reaching claims that liberties frequently do.

A liberty, as I shall use the term, is much stronger. Liberties are penumbral. If doing x is my due, the conditions necessary for and surrounding my doing x deserve consideration. For example, other things being equal, it is preferable that nothing cast a chilling effect on my doing x. Again, since freedom of speech is of little meaning to those who lack a pen or other means of communicating, if speaking freely is my due, my having a pen (or other means of communicating) is of importance. It does not follow that I have an entitlement right to a pen, of course, but the value of my having a pen must be considered, along with other factors, in legislation, lawsuits, social arrangements, and the deliberations of other agents. No specific method of addressing that concern need be mandated: the government might subsidize the purchase of pens, or citizens might form a foundation for the distribution of pens, or individuals may freely loan others the use of their pens.

A liberty, then, is a permission that demands support in the exercise of the permission. With few exceptions, support requires some degree of sacrifice from others. A liberty, then, makes some claim to sacrifices on the part of others in order to support the exercise of a permission. Such support may take various forms. One form consists in providing means of engaging in the activity: laws requiring handicap accessibility, for example, provide some of the means by which those in wheelchairs can exercise their permission to enter a public building. Handicap accessibility may increase construction costs, diminish a building's aesthetic virtues, require greater devotion of land resources, etc. The liberty of movement warrants the sacrifices those costs require. Equal time provisions, which guarantee access to public forums, are another form of public support for the exercise of speech permission rights. In addition to support in obtaining the means to exercise a permission, liberties may support permissions via public relations campaigns designed either to disseminate relevant information or change attitudes, through other rhetorical devices such as legislative proclamations, or by publicly managed or funded data banks or other forms of record keeping. The State of Indiana, for instance, began permitting voters to register while renewing their vehicle registrations in order to make it easier for citizens to vote. By paying for this program, Indiana recognized that voting is a liberty, not just a permission or even a negative entitlement. Another form of support consists in debarring things that have a chilling effect on the exercise of the permission: the Supreme Court has ruled, in *Sullivan*,[6] that holding newspapers liable for false but non-malicious statements about public figures would have a chilling effect on newspapers exercising their permission to report on public figures, and is hence unconstitutional. The cost of this immunity includes widespread circulation of false statements about public figures, a cost borne both by readers and public figures. Thus the legal entitlement of the handicapped to ramps and the legal immunity of newspapers from certain libel suits derive from (are grounded in) the liberty of movement and the liberty of speech. One significant consequence of this derivation is that legitimate debate about such immunities and entitlements ought to center upon whether these are appropriate ways of supporting movement and speech, that is, a) whether the liberty in question is strong enough to justify the sacrifices required by the immunity or entitlement and b) whether that immunity or entitlement is the best method of supporting that liberty. Broader effects of the proposed legal policy must also be weighed: it is at least arguable that, in an age in which news reporting is increasingly driven by economics and increasingly viewed as entertainment, the *Sullivan* decision, by eliminating one of the greatest dangers of reckless reporting, significantly undermined responsible journalism. If so, this result must be counted among the costs of supporting the liberty of speech in the manner the court adopted. Thus the concept of a liberty helps clarify the debate about the still controversial *Sullivan* decision.

Liberties are of different weights. Some call for greater support (and greater sacrifices to create that support) than do others. However, if substantial numbers of citizens lack the means to communicate, societies are obligated to give consideration in some form to that problem. By way of contrast, my lack of a fork when you have given me permission to eat your salad carries no weight (makes no claim upon the consideration of others): I am not justified in demanding that others make sacrifices to support my permission to eat your salad. There may, of course, be circumstances in which such a demand is justified, such as, perhaps, when I am in danger of dying of starvation without a fork, but what justifies the demand is the goal of preventing my death, not the permission right to eat the salad, which serves, at most, to indicate that eating the salad is a licit means of preventing my death by starvation.

Liberties derive from a positive commitment toward something in public morality or law. Positive commitments require, in some form, support and encouragement, while negative commitments require, in some form, discouragement. In U.S. law, citizens have the liberty to marry, since it is public policy to promote marriage. For example, wills forbidding the beneficiary from marrying a particular person will be revised by the court. Permissions generally derive from relative neutrality on the part of public morality or law. Normally, I have a permission but not a liberty to trace lightly the number two with my finger on the bark of a healthy tree in a public park, since law and public morality are neutral on this point--they are committed neither to fostering nor discouraging my doing so.[7]

The distinction drawn here between liberties and permissions is a matter of stipulation. There is a licit distinction to be drawn, and I employ the terms "liberty" and "permission" to mark that distinction. Doing so accords well with many instances of common usage, but does not constitute a claim about common usage of the terms. Judith Jarvis Thomson, for instance, defines a liberty as a permission against everyone plus claims of noninterference against everyone in "a certain range of ways" (p. 53). The claims made here do not contradict Thomson's claim: it could be useful to demarcate both what I am calling a "liberty" and what Thomson dubs a "liberty." However, the claims that a "liberty," as I use the term, may entail are sometimes broader than non-interference—they may extend, in some cases, to positive duties to provide certain necessary means or conditions for exercising the liberty. Moreover, liberties, in my sense, need not entail claims of noninterference against everyone. While liberties provide some reason for noninterference, they need not be pre-emptive.[8] Consider the fact that I have the liberty to talk to my wife about our marital problems, even though she has a permission simply to walk away and refuse to listen. Spousal discussion of marital problems could be socially sanctioned to the point that there is a legal obligation on the part of the government to provide marital counseling to those who cannot afford it. But my spouse has the permission to walk away, thus interfering in a relevant way with my liberty to discuss our problems. Thus my construal of "liberty" is helpful in unpacking rights claims. In any case, those who demur at this use of the terms "liberty" and "permission" may substitute others. The primary point here is that it is useful to designate a term to refer to what I am calling "liberties."

These three species of rights may be linked. If I am giving a speech in support of an unpopular political party, I have the liberty to speak my views, I have an entitlement to reasonable police protection against violent disruption, and I have a permission to speak from notecards. In this example, presumably, the liberty of speech is the source of, the motivating factor behind the entitlement to police protection against disruption—it exists in order to safeguard the necessary conditions for engaging in the liberty of speech, a socially sanctioned activity. The law, public policy, and morality are neutral with respect to the use of notecards in public speaking, and hence I have a mere permission to employ them. In other cases an entitlement may be the legally or morally central item from which a liberty or permission is derived. Similarly, when a liberty and an entitlement conflict, although, perhaps, entitlements often carry special weight, there is no general rule about which must yield. A lesser entitlement might be overridden if respecting that entitlement renders impossible an essential condition for a liberty of central importance, as the court held in *Sullivan*.

B. The Presumption in Favor of Permissibility

One way in which permissions differ from entitlements and liberties is that a presumption exists in favor of permissibility. Obligations to refrain should not be imposed, in law or in morals, without a good reason. By contrast, the presumption is against entitlements or liberties: I need to show reason why I am entitled to x or that my doing x demands consideration from others, that is, stakes some claim on their making sacrifices to support my doing x. The burdens of proof, in other words, are on those who claim an entitlement or liberty and those who deny a permission.

It is worthwhile to distinguish my claim from some similar sounding claims others have made. Joel Feinberg argues for a presumption in favor of liberty.[9] While Feinberg does not define "liberty" as I do, it is clear that he means more than a mere permission. Such arguments are difficult to make because, while the absence of a good reason to prevent you from writing your name in your sneakers may indicate that it should not be illegal for you to write your name in your sneakers, that fact alone does not entail that any social consideration whatsoever is due to fostering your writing your name in your sneakers. Others argue for a presumption in favor of negative rights. Negative rights, however, go far beyond permissions—they are penumbral and include various duties of non-interference. Moreover, as noted in Chapter 1, the distinction between negative and positive rights is problematic.

Shorn of the terminology of negative and positive rights, this fairly weak claim is readily argued. Since the arguments are not unfamiliar, I will but sketch out the lines of argument. First, freedom of action is generally a good. Neither the law nor morality should deprive someone of a good without a good reason— it is contrary to the purpose of both law and morality pointlessly to suppress goods. Second, when actions are proscribed without good reason, the majesty of the law is diminished, costs and inefficiency increased, and unjustified punishments are meted out. We should not put people in jail or clog an already over-crowded court system without good reason. Thus a good reason is required in order for law or morality to proscribe something. Hence there is a presumption in favor of permissibility.

Jordy Rocheleau[10] has suggested that this argument in support of permissions *eo ipso* turns them into liberties: if freedom of action is a good, as I suggest, then all permissions are worthy of social support in order to promote the good of freedom of action. Hence all permissions are liberties. However, while freedom of action is a good, it is not such an overwhelming good that society should be committed to fostering everyone in doing anything he or she wishes to do. After all, social commitment to fostering does call for sacrifices of some sort. I should not be called upon to work extra hours in order to build a ramp to a tree just because Mike wishes to touch that particular tree. So the distinction between liberties and permissions remains an important distinction.

Notice that the presumption in favor of permissibility is readily explained if rights are warrants, as the next chapter argues: the absence of a good reason to impose a duty to refrain from doing x, given the arguments above, warrants me in doing x as my due. Indeed, if rights are warrants, the three flavors of rights and the link between them can be explained with a single set of concepts. The importance of free speech warrants me in speaking my mind as my due. That in turn warrants me in demanding, as my due, that the city provide police protection against improper disruption of my speaking my mind. Prescriptively, the absence of a good reason for imposing a legal obligation to refrain from reading from notecards while speaking warrants me in demanding, as my due, that the state not impose a legal duty on me to refrain from doing so. Moreover, to the extent that it is difficult to give speeches on complex issues without notecards, the liberty of speech warrants a permission to read from notecards and perhaps also an entitlement to protection against others tearing up my notes, other things being equal. Descriptively, the absence of a legal duty to refrain from employing notecards warrants me in doing so as my legal due, warrants my claim of immunity from punishment for reading from notecards, etc. In short, the notion of grounds that warrant something as one's due provides a useful framework for expressing and analyzing the network of complex legal and moral facts pertaining to my giving a political speech.

C. A Brief Illustration: The Right To Die

The usefulness of these distinctions emerges when one considers a purported right such as the right to die. Paying attention to the three flavors of rights and the presumption in favor of permissibility does not, of course, settle the issue of whether there is a right to die and what that right includes. But it does clarify the nature of the arguments that must be made.

Showing that no compelling reasons exist to outlaw voluntary passive euthanasia, for instance, is sufficient to show that the law should respect a permission right to do so—it ought not to be illegal. Indeed, since the presumption is in favor of permissibility, it is sufficient that proponents of outlawing passive euthanasia have not shown a compelling reason to do so. By way of contrast, arguing that social mechanisms be established to support patients in exercising this right (that is, the existence of a liberty), for example, a state sponsored data bank of living wills, requires much more, namely, showing that there is strong reason for public morality and/or law to take a positive stance toward people exercising this permission, reason strong enough to justify asking for sacrifices from others. Neither, alone, suffices to establish entitlements to passive euthanasia, e.g., a requirement that hospitals refrain from continuing treatment in violation of the patient's request. Such an entitlement would require a different form of argumentative support, e.g., that it constitutes an improper violation of patient autonomy. Conversely, a requirement that hospitals not violate living wills does not entail a liberty to engage in passive euthanasia, since one may have an entitlement to something that the state actively discourages, rather than supports (e.g., certain forms of non-interference with dropping out of high school at age 16). Similarly, a mere permission to receive physician-assisted suicide, that is, the absence of a law forbidding it, differs from an entitlement that physician-assisted suicide be provided to those who request it, from an entitlement that others not interfere, and from a liberty. The onus rests on those who would make it illegal to receive or offer physician-assisted suicide to show that there is some compelling reason to deny such a permission. The burden of proof rests on those who claim physician-assisted suicide is a liberty, which would require that consideration be given to governmental subsidy of or insurance coverage of the cost of the procedure for those who cannot afford it: proponents of this view must show that some deeply held value (perhaps autonomy over fundamental life choices or the alleviation of suffering) compels public morality to support the exercise of the permission. Finally, those who hold that physician-assisted suicide is a positive or negative entitlement must show that major violation of legal or moral principles occurs if others interfere (if it is a negative right) or if physician-assisted suicide is not provided for those who request it (if it is a positive right). Thus, those who argue for a right to die must indicate which specific permissions, liberties, and entitlements it includes. A presumption exists in favor of the purported permissions—the burden of proof rests on their opponents to give a good reason for denying the permission. The burden of proof shifts, however, for liberties and entitlements. Those who claim a liberty must give a good reason for thinking society should make sacrifices to support exercise of permissions, that is, that the value of exercising the permission is of sufficient strength to warrant the relevant sacrifices on the part of others and that the proposed means of doing so are reasonable methods of supporting the exercise of the permission. Those who claim an entitlement must give a good reason for thinking that claim is warranted, a reason of the sort appropriate to justifying entitlements.[11]

Thus, attending to the differences between permissions, liberties, and entitlements both clarifies the range of possible positions and indicates the nature of the arguments needed to support them.

Notes to Chapter Two

1 While Chapter 7 suggests there are objective as well as positive moral rights and Chapter 5 argues that positive law is required to conform to the demands of natural rights, no stance is taken here concerning whether there are objective, universal legal rights in addition to positive legal rights.

2 More strictly speaking, a right may include various entitlements, liberties, and permissions. These terms are used stipulatively—the term "entitlement," for instance, has been licitly used by others in quite different ways. No claim is being made that entitlements, liberties, and permissions exhaust the species of rights. Hohfeldian powers, immunities, etc., are not mentioned here because, as Hohfeld acknowledges, they can be defined in terms of entitlements and permissions. Whether permissions can be defined in terms of entitlements depends upon whether every entitlement, as I have used the term, corresponds to a duty. If so, then A's having a permission to do x is equivalent to no one's having an entitlement entailing that A not do x. Chapter 4, however, argues that this correlation thesis should be discarded.

3 Hohfeld, Wesley Newcomb, *Fundamental Legal Conceptions, As Applied in Judicial Reasoning*, ed. W.W. Cooke, New Haven: Yale University Press, 1919.

4 Thomson, Judith Jarvis, *The Realm of Rights*, Cambridge, MA and London: Harvard University Press, 1990, p. 47.

5 A similar point applies to whether an "is" can entail an "ought." Logical connections between predicates in ordinary predicate logic must be spelled out by a premise or axiom. Thus, in every case, one cannot move from one set of terms to another, whether "is" terms to "ought" terms or any other two sets of terms, without a statement that specifies the connection. The fact that one ought, other things being equal, to discharge one's obligations means that a) "A made a promise to do x and thereby obligated himself to do x" entails b) "A ought to do x, other things being equal". The argument going from one to the other is not valid without either a syntactic link or a specific statement linking the two (expressing the fact that one ought to keep one's promises), but this is true of any two sets of terms. So whether a) entails b) depends on whether we take for granted the fact that one ought, other things being equal, to discharge one's obligations or insist that this is a substantially new idea. The same point applies here. A suit by C against D is frivolous precisely because D's act is permissible. The fact that one ought not to bring frivolous suits means that C has a duty not to sue D.

6 US Supreme Court. *New York Times Co. v. Sullivan*, 376 US 254, 1964.

7 Some theorists wish to distinguish between basic and other forms of liberty, suggesting that only basic liberties deserve the name of "right." The concept of "basic liberties" does not seem helpful in this context, since there are various reasons why a society might commit itself to fostering the exercise of a permission. In the 1950's the United States adopted a commitment to fostering science education not because it is a "basic" liberty, more basic than, say, arts education, but because scientific discovery was perceived to be an important social good (partly for reasons pertaining to U.S.–Soviet conflicts) to which the United States, as a society, was committed. Concerns about energy conservation and dependence on foreign oil motivated tax rules that support the permission to insulate one's home. An argument would be needed to demonstrate that these are improper reasons for adopting a social commitment to fostering an activity.

8 Non-interference with a liberty may conflict with another liberty, an entitlement, or a permission.

9 Feinberg, Joel, *Harm to Others*, Oxford: Oxford University Press, 1987.

10 Rocheleau, Jordy, "Reply to Schlossberger," Central Division American Philosophical Association Meeting, Minneapolis, May 2001.

11 There exists, of course, widespread disagreement about the sorts of reasons that justify entitlements.

Chapter 3: Rights as Warrants

What is a right? Two views have dominated rights theory. According to the will theory, to have a right is for one's will to have sovereignty over something. So if Jones has a right to speak his views, Jones alone may decide whether or not to speak his views: Jones is, as it were, the king ruling over the realm of Jones' speech. The interest or beneficiary theory holds that to have a right is to be the beneficiary of a duty. Jones' right to vote is the benefit he derives from the duties other people bear not to prevent him from voting, to establish voting booths, and so forth: Jones' interest in voting is protected by relevant obligations upon other people. Well known problems exist with both theories (discussed in detail in Section C.), yet the beneficiary and will theories remain dominant because, Hillel Steiner avers, while both theories have serious drawbacks, no one has yet proposed a viable third option.[1]

It is time to remedy that deficiency: rights as warrants, it will be argued, constitutes that viable third option. Rights are networks of warrants: X's having a right to y consists in the fact that x has a network of warrants (usually of different sorts) concerning y under various sets of shifting circumstances. That is, "A has a right to x" means that some set of warrants exists, pertaining to A and x, each of the form *A is warranted in q under circumstances p.*[2] As noted in Chapters 1 and 2, the full meaning of any particular right claim must always be understood in terms of other, related, penumbral rights and the existence of a right may have a wide variety of direct, indirect, immediate, and tangential implications for legal and moral thinking. A major virtue of construing rights as warrants is that it captures the richness and complexity of rights talk.

A warrant, on this view, is a publicly recognized sanction (grounding, justification) for someone to do, say, demand, believe, feel, receive, or think something, x, as her due, reflecting her publicly recognized special status and her relationship to x. (The term "warrant," thus, serves to denote a special sort of justification.) Publicly recognized sanctions are elements of the public framework (legal, moral, or social) of discourse. When a right claim is *descriptive*, the claim is that the relevant sanction is *in fact* part of the public framework of discourse. When describing a given legal system's positive rights, the claim is that the relevant sanction is a part of the law in that system. When describing the moral rights recognized by the positive morality of a particular society, the claim is that the relevant sanction is in fact part of the public morality accepted by that society. A *prescriptive* rights claim avers that the relevant sanction *should be* part of the public framework of discourse. Moreover, one has a *vector warrant* when the warrant claimed has some legitimate weight in moral, legal, and/or social deliberations, for example, when there is some legitimate justification for one's demanding something as one's due, to be weighed against other relevant factors. One has a *resultant warrant* for that demand when one is overall (all things considered) justified in making that demand as one's due. Thus the importance of freedom of movement gives me a vector warrant to walk to work, but not a resultant warrant when, for example, public health requires that I be quarantined.

Chapter 3 begins by clarifying exactly what sort of claim the warrant theory makes (Section A). Section B. describes more fully the theory that rights are warrants. Section C. analyses in detail problems association with the will and interest theories and notes how the warrant theory resolves those difficulties. The chapter concludes with some remarks on the broader conception of law that the warrant theory reflects (Section D.).

Rights theorists will note that many of the claims and remarks below violate or appear to violate the correlation thesis, namely, that every right is correlated with a duty or obligation. I will assume in this chapter that the correlation thesis is not a constraint on talk of rights. Chapter 4 argues at length for the correctness of this assumption.

A. Theories of Rights and Definitional Stops

It is important to understand here that the claim that rights are networks of warrants is not a claim about the word "right" or the word "warrant." It is a substantial claim. In a wide variety of cases in which we generally employ the language of rights, something (usually a person, partial person, or constructive person), x, has a particular kind of special status and x's relation to something, y, has a particular kind of special status. In those cases, x possesses a network of publicly recognized warrants, societal imprimaturs, as x's due, in the circumstances, enabling x to do, to some extent, some or all of the following: fend off certain criticisms or challenges regarding y, justify certain kinds of actions regarding y, demand certain actions of others regarding y, fend off certain challenges to making that demand, take certain actions to insure those demands are met, influence others' deliberations, and so forth. This claim is perspicuously made by saying that rights are networks of warrants.

It is, of course, possible to make the same claim, less perspicuously, perhaps, by stipulating, for example, that the term "right" will refer only to

Hohfeldian claim rights and that what might otherwise be dubbed epistemological rights be called something else, e.g., "groundings." On that view, although there are no epistemological "rights," both "rights" and "groundings" are networks of warrants. Such a theory, which would simply be the theory that rights are warrants, masquerading under other terms, would not be incorrect. One is always free to use whatever stipulative definitions one likes, as long as one is consistent in their use and does not employ the fallacy of ambiguity by, explicitly or implicitly, shifting to a non-stipulative use of the term. Hence one may stipulate, as Matthew Kramer does, that one will use the word "right" only to describe correlates of duties and proceed to give a theory that explains rights, so defined. However, since the distinctive moral status of believers and the distinctive relationship that believers have to warranted beliefs must still be explained, an additional theory of what might ordinarily be called "epistemological rights" is required. A single theory that explains both is more parsimonious and perhaps more enlightening than two separate theories. Thus, if warrant theory succeeds in adequately capturing and explaining, wherever they occur, these significant features (something's being one's due and one's relevant special status and relationship to it, justification under a publicly recognized sanction, and so forth), then warrant theory is preferable to theories that do not do so.

A parallel point pertains to problems with the will and interest theories discussed below. It may be possible to rescue the will theory from the problem of unwaivable rights by insisting that what people are describing when they say "in U.S. law, citizens have rights not to be deliberately killed that cannot be waived" are not really rights but something else. But, when pointing to what is generally called "a right not to be deliberately killed," one is pointing to a feature of U.S. law that is importantly similar to other features the will theory does call "rights." In U.S. law, not being killed by others, absent certain special circumstances, is one's due, whether or not one consents to the killing, because U.S. law publicly recognizes the status of residents as warranting restraint from killing. That may be bad law. Our legal system may be mistaken in its construal of the status of residents, and one may argue that the law should be changed. But it is not an unintelligible claim. It is not clear what point is served by obscuring this common feature of what we normally call "the right not be killed" and the right to vote, in which the legal system recognizes enfranchisement as one's due because it publicly recognizes the status of citizen as warranting enfranchisement. A will theorist is not "wrong" if she insists on calling the latter a right because it involves the sovereignty of will but not the former because it does not—that is her choice of language. But it is a virtue of the warrant theory that it clarifies the nature of both and gives them a unified explanation. Similarly, it may be possible to rescue the will theory by finding, despite the difficulties raised below about doing so, some sovereign will that governs Smith's legal right not to be killed, such as the collective will of the people or the will of the public official charged with enforcing the law. But it is not clear what point is served by such mental gymnastics. Rather than saying, for instance, that in killing Smith with his consent I have violated the sovereign will of the district attorney, it seems clearer and more explanatory to say that I have failed to give Smith his legal due because the law recognizes not being killed as warranted by Smith's status as a resident. After all, if pressed to justify the law's refusal to recognize consent as exculpative of killing, one would hardly insist that the law was necessary to safeguard the autonomy of the district attorney. Rather, one would construct an explanation along the lines the warrant theory suggests.

In short, my claim is not that the arguments employed in this paper refute other theories of rights. Rather, the arguments serve to make two related points. First, to be fully adequate, other theories of rights must be expanded, modified, or construed in a fashion that, ultimately, is equivalent to warrant theory. Second, it is more perspicuous and enlightening to describe the entire panoply of legal, moral, and epistemological phenomena discussed below in terms of networks of warrants.

B. Rights as Warrants

Two key features of rights

The theory that rights are networks of warrants attempts to capture two characteristic features of rights that emerge clearly from Joel Feinberg's "The Nature and Value of Rights."[3] Any adequate theory of rights must capture these two features in two ways. First, Feinberg's remarks affect the range of things that are rights. If x possesses those two features then x is a right, and so an adequate account of rights must apply to x. Second, if, according to an account of rights, something could be a right without these two features, then that account is not fully adequate as an account of rights. These two features concern 1) the special status of right-holders that having a right implies and 2) the special status of A's relationship to x that A's having a right to or regarding x implies.[4] What Feinberg's piece makes clear is the importance of being able to assert something as one's due. As Jenkins puts it, "rights express demands for things and conditions that men insist are due them."[5] Feinberg makes clear the moral importance of having the status of being a right-holder and the moral importance of the specific relationship one has to that to which one has a right. The Grand Canyon, on this view, cannot not have rights, even though, arguably, duties to preserve the Grand Canyon could outweigh duties that correlate to someone's rights. What characterizes rights claims is not the strength of the duties involved. To have a right is to attain a certain moral status. As I have pointed out elsewhere,[6] if my neighbor forbids me, upon pain of torture, to eat stale bread when I have a brand new loaf, the infringement of my right has little to do with the value of eating stale bread, or even the practical value of liberty or choice in this situation, as I am extremely unlikely to have any desire whatsoever to do what is proscribed. Indeed, if for some reason stale bread is physically unavailable, I will not even notice, much less feel distress, over the fact that I cannot choose to eat stale bread. Rather, the importance of my enjoying the liberty to eat stale bread when fresh bread is readily available stems from the fact that forbidding me to do so demotes me from a certain status, and it is the lack of recognition of my attaining that status that occasions my anger, resentment, and so forth at my neighbor's behavior.

Having that status is not necessarily a matter of being morally more important. In certain cases, a given right-holder may be less morally important than a non-right-holder. It may be more important to preserve the Grand Canyon than to preserve the life of a visitor to the canyon. (For instance, if the only way to save the life of a reckless visitor would be to destroy the canyon, it is arguably wrong to do so.) Similarly, when one has a right to x, then x is one's due in a certain important sense. Being preserved is not the Grand Canyon's due, even though preserving the Grand Canyon may outweigh giving someone his due. Rights do not necessarily trump other moral considerations (if they do, as Dworkin[7] insists, this is a substantive claim about rights, not a matter of definition). But claims of being a rights-holder and claims of having a right are distinctive kinds of moral claims, and Feinberg's paper goes some way toward articulating the distinctive flavor of those assertions.

I suggest that something's being one's due has five related aspects. When X is my due,

1) my claimed relation to X is justified, but also
2) my claimed relation to X is, in some way, merited or earned, in the particular sense that
3) it is called for, mete, because of something about me, and so
4) to do or say otherwise is to deny some important truth about my status, because
5) X's being my due is a form of (publicly proclaimed and/or accessible) recognition of my status.

For example, autonomy-related rights, such as the right to choose my own mate, are called for and merited by my status as a moral agent, and so to deny them is to deny that I am a moral agent, to deny my moral agency. Autonomy rights are a recognition of my autonomy, and to recognize and respect those rights is to participate in the public recognition of me as a free agent. To say that a professor has a right to be treated respectfully by students is to claim that the professor is warranted in demanding such respect as her due because it is called for, merited, by her status as professor, that failing to show such respect is denying an important truth about the professor's status and failing to give required public recognition to the professor's status. Claiming that one has a moral right to the sexual fidelity of one's spouse amounts to claiming that one's spouse's sexual fidelity is one's due, insofar as public morality recognizes (or should recognize, if the claim is a prescriptive one) that such fidelity is warranted by one's status as a spouse. Underlying this public recognition is a moral paradigm (or complex network of paradigms) of marriage.

The nature of warrants

What is a "warrant"? McCloskey's view that rights are entitlements[8] is sometimes criticized on the grounds that the concept of an entitlement is no clearer than the concept of a right. Some readers might raise the same concern about the claim that rights are (networks of) warrants. Indeed, contrasted with the fairly substantial claims about rights made by the interest and will theories, the view that rights are warrants may appear disappointingly vapid. It is useful, thus, to expand somewhat on the nature of a warrant.

A warrant is a publicly recognized form of special protection or sanction that recognizes what is, in some important sense, the warrant-holder's due. More precisely, a warrant is a 1) *publicly sanctioned* 2) *justification, grounding, or entitlement to do, say, demand, believe, feel, receive, or think something* 3) *as one's due, 4) reflecting one's publicly sanctioned status and 5) one's publicly sanctioned special relationship to what is warranted.* A things' being "publicly sanctioned," in this sense, entails that express recognition of the importance and legitimacy of things of that sort is an element of the relevant public framework of discourse, e.g., the public morality in the case of a moral right or the law of the land in the case of a legal right. Something's being one's due, in this sense, means more than that one's having it is morally desirable. It is morally desirable that everyone have enough to eat. Asserting that having enough to eat is A's due, however, goes further, insisting that denying A enough to eat is denying A his publicly sanctioned status by virtue of which his having enough to eat is mete and proper, and, as a result, denying A's special relationship to having enough to eat. For example, one might argue that A holds the publicly recognized status of being a member of the kingdom of ends, that to be a member of the kingdom of ends is to be due special concern for one's ability to pursue rational ends, that having enough to eat is a publicly acknowledged precondition for this ability, and hence that members of the kingdom of ends' publicly sanctioned special relationship to adequate food justifies A in demanding enough to eat. If so, A is warranted in demanding enough to eat, and, if this is a resultant claim right, others are required to make requisite sacrifices, even should they prove onerous, to insure A has enough to eat. This goes much further than saying that it is desirable that A should have enough to eat.

Thus the concept of a warrant has considerable substantial content. Not every justification or *desideratum* counts as a warrant. The view that rights are warrants, then, is not empty or vapid.

Legal recognition (in the body of statutes and other enactments, constitutional provisions, regulations, precedents, and judicial reasoning) is the paradigmatic form of public recognition with regard to legal warrants. As the examples below indicate, other forms of public recognition are often pertinent to other sorts of warrants and the class of things that may be warranted include actions, claims, beliefs, verbal assertions, and feelings.

Warrants serve a variety of functions. They may positively justify certain kinds of things, render things immune from certain kinds of criticisms and challenges, confer a kind of stamp of approval, and give one grounds to stand up for something as one's due. A given right can consist of many different sorts of warrants. A right can warrant claims that others owe me something—either a particular other person owes me a particular duty or that I have a general entitlement to something. A right can fend off challenges to my doing, thinking, saying, believing, or feeling something, warrant actions taken to get something, or warrant Hohfeldian powers. A search warrant gives legal recognition to an officer's conducting a particular kind of search of a particular place because, in the circumstances, conducting such a search is the officer's due. The document called a "search warrant" actually confers several different kinds of warrants. It justifies the action of conducting the search, renders the officer immune from suit from (properly) conducting the search, justifies the officer in demanding that other parties forbear from interfering with the search in certain ways, renders the officer immune from suit or criminal charges against taking certain kinds of actions to insure that other parties do not interfere with the search, and so forth. In each of these cases, legal sanction is given to the officer as her due. Each of these warrants accords a special status to the officer and to the relationship between the officer and her action. The document also warrants, among other things, a prosecuting attorney's introducing in evidence, during a trial, evidence obtained as a result of the search—the prosecutor's warrant to introduce the evidence is partly dependent upon the searching officer's warrant to conduct the search.

Rights can warrant one in doing x in the sense that one is beyond reproach in doing x, in the sense that one's doing x is no one else's business, or in the sense that doing x is simply within one's realm of discretion. For example, I have a right to be rude in the sense that whether or not I am rude is socially recognized to be within my realm of discretion, and, in that sense, protected, but it is not protected in the sense of being justifiable, beyond reproach, or no one else's business. A judge might, despite parents' Constitutionally sanctioned warrant to refrain from providing religious instruction for their children, consider one parent's failure to provide religious instruction an adverse factor relevant to a custody ruling. Arguably, the law should proscribe such consideration: judicially enforcing such a bias against atheism is as unjustifiable as a judge's awarding custody to the Lutheran rather than the Catholic parent on the grounds that Lutheranism is superior to Catholicism, a ruling that amounts to judicial impropriety and would surely be overturned on appeal. Nonetheless, given that custody rulings should serve the best interests of the child, custodial decisions must often evaluate some parental actions that, in virtually every other legal context, fall entirely within parents' discretion. Thus warranted actions, in the sense of legally recognized as falling within the discretion of parents, may nonetheless become "the court's business" during custody litigation.

Warrants exist whether exercised or not. Wiggams may be warranted in filing whether or not Wiggams chooses to file. Maya Angelou is warranted in calling herself a poet whether or not she ever invokes this warrant to fend off criticism. The exercise of warrants may be non-discretionary in two important ways. First, a warrant can be licitly utilized by others in certain ways even against the warrant-holder's objection. For example, in United States law, Smith's warrant that Jones refrain from stabbing him grounds the District Attorney's warrant to prosecute Jones, whether or not Smith chose not to make (or even actively opposed) the legally warranted demand that Jones refrain and whether or not Smith chose not to make (or even actively opposed) the legally warranted demand that Jones be tried. Similarly, I can justify my calling you a poet by appealing to your warrant to call yourself a poet, even if you never choose to so describe yourself. Indeed, I may, licitly, appeal to your right to call yourself a poet when justifying my calling you a poet, even if you vociferously object to being called a poet. In that sense, I may use your warrant against you to defeat your criticism of my calling you a poet. Warrants (and/or the grounds of a warrant) can create or ground other warrants, and your warrant to call yourself a poet (or the ground of that warrant) warrants me in calling you a poet. Second, in some cases one may be obligated or duty-bound to employ a warrant—choosing not to employ a particular warrant on a particular occasion may not be a morally or legally permitted option. In some cases, an officer's failure to employ a warrant for someone's arrest could be grounds for disciplinary action against the officer. Note that the existence of the warrant alone does not require the officer to exercise it: there are times when an officer may choose not to employ a warrant without dereliction of duty. A search warrant is not itself a requirement to search, though in many cases the duties of a police officer may require employing it. On the other hand, these duties are not entirely external to and independent of the warrant: it was precisely by virtue of those duties that the warrant was obtained. Without the warrant, no duty to search exists—officers are not duty bound to conduct illegal searches. Thus the existence of the warrant is a necessary condition for the duty to search, and the very conditions that create the warrant can also, in some cases, morally or legally require that the warrant be exercised. In other words, the existence of the officer's search warrant in turn, given the circumstances, warrants superiors in demanding that the search warrant be exercised. We can call warrants that arise from the existence of another warrant "secondary warrants," although the distinction between primary and secondary warrants is not a rigorous one: it is simply a convenient way of noting the fact that, in a particular instance, one warrant can be viewed as providing the grounds for another warrant. The existence and range of secondary warrants is determined not solely by the logic of promising or the logic of rights, but also, in part, by any relevant considerations from the whole of the legal or moral system. A legal system may decide, for example, that it is socially beneficial, as a form of "social insurance," to permit anyone harmed by reasonable reliance upon a contract to sue for actual damages if the terms of the contract are not fulfilled. Again, if you fail to fulfill a contract to provide for my grandmother, the law might decide to permit anyone to file a suit in her behalf. These decisions would have unworkable consequences in a large, litigious society—the proliferation of lawsuits alone could render such a legal system helplessly backlogged. Either, however, might be workable and defensible in a legal system governing a small village. This alone shows that determining who has standing to bring suit and in whose name a suit may be brought requires not only examining the logic of rights but also taking into consideration a wide range of factors relevant to the workings of a legal system.

Thus warrants are not passive in the way that being the beneficiary of a duty is passive nor fully discretionary like the exercise of sovereign will. In many cases, warrant-holders may choose not to exercise a warrant.[9] However, the existence of secondary warrants means that warrants are not always realms of free choice for the warrant-holder: a warrant-holder may be obligated to employ a warrant, and other parties may sometimes licitly employ Jones' warrant in certain ways that may not please Jones or to which Jones may actively object. All three features pertain to what we often call "rights," and neither the will nor the interest theory can readily explain all three.[10]

Scope of right-holders

The warrant theory, as such, is compatible with different approaches to determining the scope of right-holders. A proper treatment of the scope of right-holders would require a lengthy discussion. Since it is an important element of a theory of rights, I will simply sketch out briefly the approach I advocate. It should be realized that one may accept the rest of the warrant theory while rejecting what I say about the scope of right-holders.

I suggest that right-holders are persons: rights may be held by full persons, partial persons, or constructive persons. One can accept this tri-partite division of right holders without accepting my account of what it is to be a full person, in the relevant sense, namely, as I have argued elsewhere,[11] to be a sufficiently developed worldview in operation, to be an entity whose behavior, physical, emotional, and conceptual, reflects a sufficiently developed network of concepts, goals, values, standards, attitudes, etc., in terms of which the world becomes meaningful. "Sufficiently developed" alludes to the sophistication and coherence of concepts, values, dispositions, and affective responses, degree of appropriate responsiveness to evidence, and so forth. Partial persons are those things that satisfy the criteria for personhood to some significant degree but fall short in some way. Otters and small children have rudimentary worldviews, and so count as partial persons. Partial personhood, obviously, is a matter of degree, since chimpanzees (apparently) have significantly more developed worldviews than do mice. Constructive persons are those things that we treat, for some good reason, as if they had a genuine worldview. In contract law, for instance, we can treat corporations as if they had goals, corporate outlooks, values and priorities, attitudes, etc., and so, in contract law, corporations are constructive persons. Constructions, of course, can be natural and intuitive or strained. They can be purely pragmatic fictions (akin to the fiction that all and only those over 18 years old have the maturity to vote). An environmentalist may wish to treat a forest as a constructive person, urging the usefulness of attributing to the forest, either genuinely or as a pragmatic fiction, goals such as survival and a diverse ecosystem. Thus the range of possible constructive persons is quite open-ended, particularly, as one would expect, in law, given legal systems' propensity to balance diverse considerations and the practical necessity of employing various legal fictions. (See Chapter 8 for a fuller discussion of constructive or virtual persons.)

It might be objected that including such a wide range of constructive persons dilutes the concept of right. However, while real full persons and real partial persons have real full and partial rights, constructive persons have constructive rights. After all, many legal systems, including our own, seem to be teeming with constructions that function much like rights. Calling them "constructive rights" simply recognizes the reality of how legal systems function. Whatever point is served by denying them the title of "rights" is equally served by denying them the title of "genuine rights," while the fact that the word "rights" appears in both the terms "genuine rights" and "constructive rights" emphasizes the genuine similarity in how they function in law. Thus distinguishing between genuine and constructive rights appears to be a perspicuous way of representing the situation. It also facilities a unified account of genuine and constructive rights. Otters have the prescriptive moral right not to be wantonly tortured because, as sentient creatures with sufficient worldviews to care powerfully about what befalls them and so experience significant distress, not being wantonly tortured is their due: public morality should include a recognition of their status as sentient creatures with worldviews warranting a demand to refrain from torture. A corporation has the legal right to sue for copyright infringement because seeking such remedy is its due: the law publicly recognizes corporations as constructive persons with sufficient relevant similarities to genuine persons (e.g., corporations have constructive goals that can be thwarted, and whose achievement compensation can assist, and corporations function as a participant in the community's commerce) that compensation for improperly suffered harm is warranted and courts are appropriate venues for effecting compensation.

Illustrating examples

The power and nature of the warrant theory emerges when considering a broad range of examples. Consider the following cases:

Case 1): The legislature of Connecticut passes a statute stating "Everyone has the right to like himself as he is."

Case 1) involves a proclamative right. It is a legal statute that carries no specific powers, liberties, or claims. In that sense, it is akin to the legislature proclaiming July 6 "National Dry Cleaners' Day." Proclamative rights do not fit readily into Hohfeld's schema. The statute proclaims that each person is warranted in liking himself. Having this warrant does not readily entail being warranted in making a claim of duty on anyone else, and so is not readily analyzable as being a benefit of another's duty. (My proclamative right to like oneself does not, for example, require others to forbear from saying derogatory things about me that would trample my self-esteem.) It is also not immediately clear in what sense the statute enables my sovereign will to govern my liking myself (except in the sense that I am warranted in so doing). The way in which liking oneself is within one's discretionary sphere is quite different from the way in which leaving money to my children in my will is within my discretionary sphere. While it may be tempting to say that proclamative rights are not legal rights at all, they are part of the law of the land and may enter into legal reasoning in a wide variety of ways. The proclamative right might be invoked by a Connecticut court in deciding what constitutes grounds for divorce, for example. (See Chapter 4 for several other examples.) But the primary force of the statute is to provide a publicly recognized sanction to liking oneself. The statute proclaims that we, as a society, believe individuals to be warranted, justified as their due, in liking themselves as they are: it confers a kind of public imprimatur on liking oneself. In a society such as ours, it does not go so far as to posit a duty on others not to criticize one for liking oneself—the right to criticize, entailed by free speech, clearly overrides any warrant granted by this proclamative statute. However, this proclamative right serves as a sort of defense against such criticism: one can reply that the law gives one that right, a response that does not automatically defeat criticism but is, at least, a relevant factor.[12]

Case 2:) A passage in a custody agreement reads as follows: Either parent shall have the right to keep the children when they would otherwise be in daycare.
Case 2), the right to remove a child from daycare, is not merely a Hohfeldian permission right, the mere absence of a duty to refrain, since one party violates the agreement if she attempts to stop the other party from exercising this right. It is not a power. Is it a claim right? It does impose some duties, of course, but the real force of this provision is not to impose a duty but to defeat a criticism or challenge to one parent's removing the child from daycare. It warrants the parent in removing the child and so renders the parent immune from criticism or challenge. After all, it is unlikely that one parent will be standing at the daycare door saying "you shall not pass," but plausible, in the absence of this provision, that one parent will mount a legal or other challenge as a result of the other parents' removing the child from daycare. In practical terms, the rationale for including this provision in the custody agreement is to obviate a challenge or criticism rather than to impose a duty. This is an important kind of warrant, as Case 3) demonstrates.

Case 3): Joan has published 15 volumes of poetry with major publishers, won two Pulitzer prizes for poetry, has been anthologized in virtually every collection of contemporary poetry since 1980, and has given over 400 readings in the past 15 years. Her poetry is the subject of 76 articles in academic journals. Mike's entire poetical output consists of one unpublished rhymed couplet: "Ice/is nice." Joan has earned the right to call herself a poet, while Mike has not.

Joan's right to call herself a poet, which is justified by her poetic accomplishments, must be distinguished from general speech rights, which include, among many other things, calling oneself a poet. Mike has a speech right to call himself a poet. The state, for instance, acts wrongly if it criminalizes calling oneself a poet. In this sense, Mike and Joan both possess the right to call themselves poets. But there is a different sense, illustrated by Case 3), in which Joan but not Mike has a right to call herself a poet: Mike is not warranted in calling himself a poet, even though he is, for example, immune to prosecution for his unwarranted assertion.

Feinberg's discussion of two key features of rights speaks only of claim-rights, but does not the dimension of social life Feinberg describes apply equally to being able to describe oneself as a poet? Feinberg[13] says that a right is something that can be insisted upon without embarrassment or shame. Saying, in this sense, "I have the right to call myself a poet" not only describes the factual situation that one has written significant poetry, but asserts that the term "poet" is one's due, that one has earned the sobriquet, that calling oneself a poet is protected in certain important ways, and that one may, without reproach or apology, no matter what anyone else says, appropriate to oneself that term, that one is immune to criticism in so doing (has a protection against, a defense against, anyone who questions one's doing so). Joan, unlike Mike, is entitled to insist upon calling herself a poet without embarrassment or shame, as her due. After all, calling herself a poet is not only justified, but merited by her status as a writer in the sense that her poetic output properly grounds public recognition of the special relationship she has to the title of "poet" and to say otherwise is to deny the relevant truth about her, while recognizing her right to call herself a poet is accepting a publicly accessible recognition of her status as a writer. Thus calling oneself is poet is something Joan, unlike Mike, is entitled to do as a matter of right. Jenkins avers that "when we assert our right to something…..we feel and mean that our demand is justified and that others are obligated to acknowledge and accord it."[14] Part of the force of saying that Joan has a right to call herself a poet is to enable her to meet a challenge or criticism. Joan's right to call herself a poet means that she is warranted in so doing, and this means that she can defuse, meet, or refute any challenge to her so describing herself. All of this may be expressed, using Feinberg's language, by saying one has a claim to be called a poet, but it is not a particular claim against anyone in particular: it is a *claim to*, not a *claim on*.[15] Again, Jenkins states that "to assert something as a right is to insist on its legitimacy and binding power" (*ibid.*), and it is precisely the legitimacy and binding power of my call to being a poet that is asserted by claiming the right to be called a poet. Thus there is good reason to include the right to call oneself a poet in the set of rights that theories of rights are meant to capture, since what is important about rights and what is significantly characteristic of rights claims applies to the right to call oneself a poet.

It is worth noting that in some cases a similar sort of "right to call" is protected by legal sanctions. In France, for instance, the right to call one's wine "Bordeaux" is legally defined and penalties attach to unwarrantedly calling one's wine "Bordeaux." Both cases involve a publicly recognized sanction to call oneself or one's product something, as one's due. (See also Case 6) below.)

Case 4): Given the sum of my relevant knowledge, six arguments give strong support to x while only one argument very weakly supports not-x. I have not been negligent in pursuing relevant knowledge. I say "I have a right to believe x."

Case 5): My wife is on trial for murder. I say "I have a right to believe in her innocence."

Cases 4) and 5) illustrate different senses of the phrase "the right to believe." Case 5) is an example of an either an autonomy right or a loyalty right. The husband may be invoking the right of freedom of belief. In this sense, I have a right to believe that 2+2=6, that is, I am immune to various penalties for the content of my beliefs, others may not forcibly attempt to change my belief, and so forth. It may be wrong and benighted to hold such a belief, but it is within my purview as an independent being to be wrong and benighted in this way. So I am justly prone to criticism for my belief but not justly prone to forcible attempts to change it. Alternatively, the husband may be claiming that spousal loyalty justifies him, as his due (acknowledging his status as a spouse), in believing in the innocence of his wife.

Case 4), by way of contrast, centers on an epistemological warrant, another region of warrants that does not fit readily into Hohfeld's categories. I am entitled to believe that 2+2=4 in an additional, stronger sense than my freedom of belief right to believe that 2+2=6. I am epistemologically warranted in believing that 2+2=4, while I am not warranted in believing that 2+2=6. To claim a right to believe x, in this stronger sense, is both to assert one's special status as a believer, as a rational enquirer, and to claim a special kind of protection for one's belief in x, that is, that one's belief in x is merited according to publicly recognized canons of evidence. A computer that prints out "x is true" lacks these features. I can claim to believe that 2+2=4 (though not that 2+2=6) "by right," in a way that computers cannot.

To be epistemologically warranted in believing something is not to be the beneficiary of someone else's duty. One might be able to articulate some tangential or cumbersome duty involved, but clearly the point of an epistemological warrant does not center on others' duties. True, my right to believe x warrants me in demanding, from others similarly epistemologically situated, an acknowledgment of the plausibility of x, but it does not impose a duty upon them to do so. I am, as it were, within my rights in demanding it (I am warranted in, have justification for, demanding such an acknowledgment), while it is within their sphere of discretion to refuse to do so, though they may be licitly criticized for exercising their discretion in this way. Thus my being warranted in demanding something is not necessarily the same as your having a duty to comply with my demand. Nor does an epistemological warrant mark a region over which the will has sovereignty. Arguably, one cannot "choose" to believe x in the sense that one can choose whether or not to waive a promise. More tellingly, if the evidence in support of x is strong enough, I might lack the epistemological right not to believe x—my epistemological right to believe x might be, in this sense, inalienable.

   Case 6): The rights of a daycare licensed by the State of Indiana.
Case 6) is in some ways akin to the right to call oneself a poet, but a licensed daycare has a special legal entitlement to call itself licensed. Having a license in Indiana is not a requirement to operate: operating an unlicensed daycare operation is not in any way illegal. In some states, perhaps, only licensed daycare centers are permitted to participate in certain state-funded programs, but, as this need not be the case, for purposes of discussion it will be assumed that in Indiana a license confers only the legal right to call oneself a licensed daycare, while unlicensed centers are not legally permitted to call themselves licensed daycare centers. If the right to call oneself a licensed daycare is a Hohfeldian claim right, to which obligations does this right correlate? It does not correlate to the duty of the state not to prevent one from calling oneself a licensed daycare. For example, the state may pass a law saying that one may not, in advertising, state whether one is licensed or not. (If that is unconstitutional, it is on free speech grounds, not because of the right conferred by the license as such.) The point is more that, if challenged, one has a warrant to call oneself a licensed daycare, a warrant sufficient to fend off legal criticism based on the claim that one has not met the requirements. Is the right to call oneself a licensed daycare merely a privilege that unlicensed daycares lack? It may indeed be a kind of privilege, but it is a very special kind of privilege. It is an earned privilege. The kind of warrants involved are importantly different from the warrant Hohfeld's salad-eater has to eat the salad. The right to call oneself a daycare cannot be removed arbitrarily. It supports certain kinds of procedural and perhaps substantial claims of due process. It is a privilege that can underpin libel or slander (while it is hard to imagine a court finding that Hohfeld's salad eater was slandered solely because the defendant said he did not have the privilege of eating the salad).

Criticisms of the theory
   Some may object that the warrant theory violates the correlation thesis and so must be false, that is, that some warrants appear not to correlate with duties. Chapter 4 argues that the correlation thesis should not be a constraint on theories of rights.

It might be argued that rights cannot *be* warrants because rights *generate* warrants. That is, it could be argued, one is warranted in demanding of a debtor that the ten dollars lent him be repaid precisely because one has a right to those ten dollars. Moreover, it is by exploring a right that one comes to learn which warrants the right confers: the way to decide whether one is warranted in using a four letter word in a public speech is by examining in detail the right to free speech. Judges do not determine what the right to free speech is by examining people's warrants. Rather, they engage in extensive legal reasoning about the nature of the right to free speech in order to determine which particular warrants citizens have. Thus rights cannot be warrants.

This objection is based on two errors: it confuses what a right is with what grounds a right and it confuses the ontological question of whether two descriptions refer to the same thing with the epistemological question of which of the concepts employed by two descriptions gives access to the others. The ground of a moral or legal right consists of the arguments, statutes, precedents, regulations, conventions, legal maxims and principles, etc. that justify the complex network of moral and legal warrants we can express simply and conveniently by saying that someone has a right to something. Strictly speaking, the right to be repaid the money one has lent a debtor does not generate the warrant to demand it. If Smith asks why Jones feels warranting in demanding that Smith leave Jones' house and Jones replies "because it is my right," Jones does not give a direct, literal, non-circular answer to Smith's question. Natural languages are quite flexible, so there are several things Jones might be licitly doing with his reply. Jones might mean by saying "because it is my right" that the law warrants him in so doing, in which case Jones' reply serves not to provide the (independent) ground of his warrant but to remind Smith of the law. Jones may be trying to remind Smith that his warrant to demand that Smith leave is one of the warrants deriving from his ownership of the house. Jones may be cutting short Smith's questioning by reminding him that they both know the answer. But one thing he is not doing is directly and literally providing independent moral grounds for his being warranted in his demand.

It is often convenient to speak of a right generating or justifying a warrant in order to express the more complex truth that the grounds of the right to be repaid the money create or justify the warrant for demanding its repayment. More precisely, the ethics of promising (or the laws regarding loans) ground, justify, and/or create the moral (legal) warrant to demand repayment that is partly constitutive of what we mean by "the right to be repaid the money." Moreover, the arguments, statutes, etc. may clearly indicate that some important set of warrants pertain to repayment of the debt, though spelling out precisely which warrants are involved may require considerable further careful scrutiny and argument. For example, an argument may establish that it is wrong wantonly to kill another person. That conclusion, as stated, leaves untouched such crucial questions as what constitutes wanton killing and what constitutes a valid justification for killing another person, questions whose resolution requires considerable further argument. One convenient way to express our limited knowledge, at this point, is to assert that we have a right not to be wantonly killed. After all, most citizens of the United States would agree strongly with the claim that persons have a moral right not to be wantonly killed without being able either to give a clear, non-circular moral argument supporting that conviction or spelling out in detail exactly what that assertion entails. Claiming that such a right *in rem* exists amounts to asserting the existence of some network of specific warrants, as yet unspecified, that pertain to wanton killing in the way that warrants typically pertain to *in rem* rights claims of this sort. Thus the linguistic practice of offering the existence of a right as the reason for believing that one has a particular warrant is a useful and reasonable one, provided one does not take the assertion too literally.

The points made above help explain the second confusion in the objection. In general, the fact that one can gain information about concept A by exploring or reasoning about concept B does not necessarily mean either that A and B refer to different things or that B is not reducible to A. If I observe George W. Bush walking on the beach, I may be able to learn things about the President of the United States by reflecting on properties I observed on the beach, even though "the man I saw on the beach" and "the President of the United States" refer, in 2007, to the numerically same object. Moreover, Lake Michigan is a collection of water molecules. The properties of the lake may be reducible to the properties of collections of water molecules, even though I can learn something about the properties of collections of water molecules by measuring and reflecting on the macroscopic properties of the lake. In short, there may be information epistemologically linked by me to one term whose link to another term is not at present evident to me, even if the two terms are synonymous or the former is reducible to the latter, and so I can gain information about one by reflecting or reasoning about the other. Hence the fact that judges sometimes engage in legal reasoning about rights to determine which warrants exist does not entail the falsity of the claim that rights are networks of warrants. A judge might believe the law recognizes a right not to be wantonly killed (i.e., that there exists some or other set of specific legal warrants appropriately related to not being wantonly killed), search for a rationale for the belief in the existence of such a right (network of warrants), and then reason from that rationale to the fact that a particular warrant exists (that is, that the particular warrant whose existence is asserted is a member of the network of warrants established by the rationale). In principle, of course, the logical relationship between the grounds and the warrant can be expressed without employing the term "right," but, in this case, the belief in the existence of a general right not to be wantonly killed played a crucial epistemological role. Similar accounts can be given of legal arguments that warrant X is a precondition for the enjoyment of right A or that the intention of the legislature in according right A must have included or entailed acknowledging warrant X: in the latter case, for example, one could argue directly from the premise that the point of a statute must be Y to the conclusion that the statute should be interpreted as establishing warrant X. Thus while legal reasoning will sometimes infer the existence of a warrant from the existence of a right, it does not follow that rights are not just networks of warrants.

It might also be objected that viewing rights as warrants dilutes the concept of a right: any kind of reason, however weak, for anything, however trivial, becomes a right, though perhaps a weak and/or trivial one. To a certain extent, this objection is justified. One can view rights as primarily resultant rights, yielding a system of relatively few rights with relatively few conflicts between them, or one can view rights as primarily a system of vector rights, with many conflicts. The former leaves unaddressed the force of claims that do not make it to the set of resultant rights. Suppose an editor receives a story exposing important shortcomings in nuclear security. Publishing that information compromises national security. The editor might, depending on the circumstances, have no resultant right to publish the story. But the force of freedom of the press, the right to publish and the right of the public to be informed, is certainly a powerful and important element in her deliberations. If rights are solely resultant rights, there is no adequate way to capture the force of that element. On the other hand, it is often important to refer to resultant rights, as when a court determines that the editor had no right to publish the story. In short, we need to be able to refer to both sorts of rights. The warrant theory begins by defining rights as vector rights and then singles out, from among those rights, a more restricted set of resultant rights. This produces no problems so long as it is clear, when asking whether X had a right to Y, whether one means a vector right or a resultant right. Nonetheless, the usefulness of referring to vector rights is vitiated if vast numbers of extremely weak and trivial justifications count as vector rights. It is worth remembering, then, that warrants are public proclamations: in order to ground a vector right, the justification for a warrant must be strong and important enough to be a publicly proclaimed sanction. Very weak or very trivial justifications are of insufficient magnitude to pass this test. To claim that one has a prescriptive moral right, for instance, is to claim that one's conduct, belief, etc. is covered by a sanction that should be ensconced in the public morality of one's community. To claim that one has a legal right is to claim that one's conduct, etc. is covered by a generalizable legal sanction. Neither the law nor the public morality concerns itself with trifles. Thus the proliferation of weak or trivial rights is not as much of a problem as the objection might make it appear. In any case, as John Rowan has remarked in conversation, the weaker or more trivial the vector right, the less likely it is that anyone will invoke that vector right. Thus the proliferation of weak and trivial vector rights might not be a problem in actual moral or legal discourse.

But conceiving of rights as warrants does make rights very responsive to circumstances. I suggest this is a virtue of the view, but Theodore M. Benditt thinks otherwise. Benditt suggests that if whether one has a right (as opposed to when a right is overridden) is too responsive to circumstances then right claims do no real work—such an approach "risks running the idea of rights into the ground." Hence, argues Benditt, "these considerations...rule out questions of cost in determining whether there are general, justificatory rights."[16] In fact, however, many legal rights are entitlements to conformity on the part of others to a reasonable person standard of some sort, e.g., a right to reasonable care or a right to reasonable accommodation. Such rights essentially invoke considerable sensitivity to circumstances, including cost. Of course, Benditt might suggest that whether I have a right to your putting up a neon sign warning of a danger, for instance, which is very sensitive to cost, is not a question about a general justificatory right. The general justificatory right is a right to reasonable care, and my having that right is not determined by cost. But it is not clear what is served or clarified by making a right more general and then putting responsiveness to cost inside the content of the right. It seems to be merely a verbal difference whether, following Fried,[17] one says that whether one has a right to a fair share of society's resources depends on cost (the example Benditt is discussing) or that having the right to a fair share of society's resources is independent of cost, but what constitutes a "fair share" is dependent on cost. In either case, adjudicating right claims requires weighing circumstances. If the need to make these weighing judgments runs rights into the ground, then rights are necessarily run into the ground. If making those judgments in determining the content of broad *in rem* rights does not undermine the role of rights, then why should making those same judgments to determine whether someone has an *in rem* right do so?

C. Problems with the Will and Interest Theories

The will theory has been criticized on several grounds. It limits the scope of right-holders: infants and animals, for example, appear to be precluded from having rights, as they are unable to exercise will, in the traditional sense, about many of the sorts of things to which rights typically pertain. Hart in 1955 suggested that children do not have rights, just compelling interests the state protects.[18] But a child can sue the trustee of a trust fund: a twelve year old child has a legal right to have the bank that manages her trust fund do so in a fiscally sound manner. The bank owes her this as a duty. She has an enforceable claim on the bank to do so. Duties and claims of this sort are explicitly recognized and articulated in statues and/or specifically employed in judicial decisions as the basis for findings. What more is needed to assert that the child has a legal right? Steiner responds that, in such cases, the relevant will is exercised by a proxy, such as a guardian. Benditt (*op. cit.*) replies to this that while we can exercise rights to our detriment, a guardian may not—guardians are bound to act in the interests of their charges. Hence rights exercised by proxies are not discretionary in the way the will theory requires. Moreover, children appear to have a variety of unwaivable rights. For example, it has been argued that children between six and sixteen have an unwaivable right to an education. Hart's 1982 reply (rejecting his 1955 position) is that the legal rights of children are, theoretically, hypothetical rights, in the sense that they pertain to what the child would have willed were she of legal age (*sui juris*).[19] It is, of course, difficult or impossible to determine what an infant would have willed were she 18. Hence, proxies act on the assumption that what a child would have willed is whatever is in that child's best interest.

However, even when it is fairly clear what a child would want, proxies are generally barred from acting against the specific interest of the child's that the proxy is appointed to protect. Supposed a distant relative has left 6 million dollars to Susan, a twelve year old child. The testator did not know Susan or her parents personally and left the money in a trust administered by a paid custodian. The terms of the trust stipulate that interest from the trust is payable yearly at the custodian's discretion. The trust will terminate on Susan's 18th birthday. In order to survive, Susan's father, her sole surviving parent, needs a costly operation. Susan's father will die unless she can raise a million dollars over and above available insurance, savings, etc. This year's interest from the trust amounts to $150,000. It is in Susan's best interest, presumably, for the trust to pay for the operation from its principal—most children are better off with 5 million and a living parent rather than 6 million and no parent. Since most 18 year olds would spend one of six million dollars to save the life of a parent, the probability is high that Susan would so choose were she *sui juris*. Nonetheless, should the custodian pay for the operation from the fund's principal, Susan could, upon attaining the age of majority, sue the custodian. Susan has a non-waivable right to the custodian's conserving the trust. True, upon reaching age 18, Susan can choose not to bring suit for compensation for the violation of that right. However, whether or not Susan brings suit at age 18, her right was violated—she has compelling grounds for a suit. And nothing Susan can do between the ages of 12 and 18 protects the custodian. Thus neither the custodian nor Susan can waive Susan's right that the custodian preserve the trust's capital.

Does the right belong, not to Susan, but to the deceased testator? Rights of the dead create problems for the will theory, since the dead cannot exercise sovereign will. However, deceased individuals were able to exercise sovereign will before they died. Perhaps the will exercised by the testator before he died is the one that governs the trust rights. But if the money is needed for an operation to save Susan's life, rather than her father's, would a court insist on the custodian's allowing Susan to die? Perhaps it could be argued that the custodian acts as a proxy for what the testator would have willed had he been alive. Normally the presumption is that the testator would have willed what he in fact willed in creating the trust. However, since it is pointless to preserve the capital for Susan if doing so has the result that Susan does not live to receive it, the court concurs that the testator would have waived his right to the custodian's preservation of the capital had he been alive. Of course, if the custodian does pay for the father's operation from the trust's capital, it is Susan who is entitled to bring suit in her own name, not the testator, and it is Susan who, at age 18, decides whether to

bring suit. Moreover, she does so for herself, not as proxy for the testator—
Susan is under no moral or legal obligation to consider whether the testator
would have wished her to bring suit, nor does that hypothetical play any role in
the court's deliberation should Susan bring suit. Hence, should the right belong
to the testator, a third party would have exclusive right to determine, based
purely on her own wishes, whether to seek compensation when the testator's
right is violated. This is surely a troublesome result for the will theory. If rights
protect the exercise of will, rather than benefits or interests, it is difficult to explain why a third party should be compensated when someone's will is improperly infringed. The testator is a stranger. Susan has no more connection to
whether the testator's autonomy is infringed, as such, than anyone else. Her special connection lies in the content of the testator's sovereign act of will, that is, in
the interest she has in the money, not in the testator's will as such. On the interest
theory, Susan's right to compensation is readily explained—her interest in the
million dollars was set back. Of course, a will theorist could insist that having a
right and being compensated for its violation are two independent issues: while
having a right pertains to sovereignty of will, compensation for the violation of
that right is based on interests. Indeed, a will theorist is almost forced to this
conclusion. If you violate my right to due care regarding the hole you dug, compensation I receive is based on the harm I sustained (the extent to which my interests are set-back), not the extent to which you infringed my autonomy.
Granted, punitive damages may be assessed as well in certain cases, but if I sustain no harm (I didn't fall in, etc.) despite your negligence, I cannot recover,
however much your negligence may have infringed upon my legitimate will to
walk on a safe path. The will theorist, however, can argue that violating my sovereign will makes the violator vulnerable to having to compensate for the harm
caused me by that violation—it is my will and my harm. In the case of Susan,
however, the will theorist would have to argue that violation of one person's
sovereign will makes one vulnerable to compensating for the harm that violation
causes to *anyone*, since, *ex hypothesi*, it as the testator's will that was violated,
not Susan's. This creates for the will theorist exactly the problem of third party
beneficiaries with which the will theorist berates the interest theorist (see below).
Hence arguing that the custodian acts as proxy for the testator's sovereign will is
highly problematic for the will theorist.

Perhaps, then, the right to have the trust conserved by the trustee belongs to
the court. But courts are not at liberty to waive this right at will. If Susan brings
suit at age 18 and a court "waives" that right by arbitrarily dismissing Susan's
suit, does the court not violate Susan's right? Susan can correctly observe that
the court improperly applied the law. But if properly applying the law requires
the court not to waive the right to have the trust conserved, then, if the will theory is correct, that right cannot belong to the court. In short, one can maintain
that the ultimate court of appeal has a will theory right here only if one insists
that the ultimate court of appeal is not bound by anything but its own will, that
there is no legal right the court has a duty to respect in its ruling. The process of

legal reasoning in which courts of ultimate appeal engage would indicate that such courts do not themselves subscribe to this view. One might hold, of course, that such exercises of legal reasoning are fictions that merely disguise the ultimately arbitrary or political exercise of the court's will, as some critical legal theorists hold. But on that view, only the court of final appeal, ultimately, has any rights at all. For example, you would have no right to the repayment of a contracted debt, since the court may, at its whim, simply ignore the *bona fide* contract in its ruling. This is hardly a result will theorists are likely to accept. In sum, then, children appear to have some rights not governed by their sovereign wills.

Warrant theory can readily accommodate the rights of children and animals. Infants and animals may have rights to the extent that they possess a relevant status publicly recognized in law or morals that some actions would inappropriately deny. If, for instance, as suggested above, infants and animals are partial persons, and if wantonly torturing infants or animals denies their status as partial persons, then infants and animals may have a right not to be tortured.

Fiduciary duties generally pose problems for the will theorist, since many fiduciary duties are, to a large extent, defined by law, leaving the fiduciary and beneficiary relatively little room to alter the relationship. Contrast a client's demanding that her financial advisor buy a bad investment with a patient's demanding that his physician prescribe a contra-indicated medication. The financial advisor's legal duties are normally fulfilled by advising against the investment. The physician, however, may be liable under U.S. law for malpractice if she advises against taking the medication but nonetheless writes the prescription. Such fiduciary duties are not the result of particular contractual arrangements between client and fiduciary, but general requirements of law applicable to physicians and financial advisors. To the extent that any such fiduciary duties correspond to a beneficiary right, fiduciary arrangements create non-waivable rights. While, generally, the beneficiary may end a fiduciary relationship, during the period in which the relationship is in effect the fiduciary has duties toward the beneficiary that the beneficiary cannot waive. The will theorist might reply that the beneficiary can waive his or her right by deciding not to bring suit. However, nothing the beneficiary says or does during the relevant period will protect the fiduciary from liability should the beneficiary later bring suit. In some extreme cases, a fiduciary may be duty bound to prevent the beneficiary from terminating the relationship: hospitals, in some jurisdictions, have had a legally imposed fiduciary duty to prevent a patient from leaving the hospital when so doing would endanger her life.

One consequence of many common fiduciary duties is that either the will theory or the correlation thesis (that all duties correlate to a right and/or vice versa) is false. For example, White, arguing against the correlation thesis, suggests that a physician's duty to refrain from indulging a patient's desire for drugs correlates to no right of the patient.[20] Kramer replies that the patient has a corresponding right to care in accordance with professional standards. Such a right, however, since it is designed specifically to include refusing to accommodate inappropriate patient demands, is not waivable. The same logic applies to any putative right to which the physician's duty might correspond. Thus either the physician's duty not to indulge the patient's desire for drugs corresponds to no right or it corresponds to a non-waivable right. Hence either the correlation thesis is false or the will theory is false. This result will trouble many will theorists, who cleave to the correlation thesis. More importantly, even if, as Chapter 4 argues, the correlation thesis should be discarded, the will theory requires that not even one of these unwaivable fiduciary duties corresponds to a right. As noted in Section A., there is no contradiction in stipulatively defining the term "right" in such a way that, while patients are legally entitled as their due to proper medical care, patients do not have a legal right to proper medical care, that, while students are entitled, as their due, to proper instruction, students do not have a right to proper instruction, and so forth. However, encumbering discussions of right claims with such stipulations seems less than helpful.

It is not hard to discover other examples of unwaivable rights, in the sense that the law does not recognize acts of waiving as valid, even though pursuing redress for violation of the right remains within the discretion of the right-holder. For example, courts will not uphold contracts with common carriers that excuse the carrier from liability for negligence. The ABC train company, in addition to the usual service, offers to ship goods at a reduced rate (or faster) if the consigner agrees to exempt ABC from liability for its negligence. Jones accepts this offer and sends 100 cartons via ABC. As a result of ABC's negligence, the 100 cartons are destroyed. The courts will still permit Jones to recover for damages, despite his voluntarily waiving his right to be compensated for negligence—he retains his legal right to compensation despite his waivure. Jones may, of course, decide not to sue, but he retains the right to recover. Thus Jones' right to recover for damages caused by negligence is unwaivable. The law recognizes an unwaivable entitlement to recover in order not only in order to promote due care by common carriers but also, among other things, to protect Jones against exploitive offers and contracts of adhesion. What clarity is gained by refusing to call such an unwaivable entitlement a "right"?

A particularly troubling category of unwaivable rights centers on rights under criminal law. Someone who stabs me, in many jurisdictions, is liable to prosecution even if he stabbed me with my consent and even if I insist that he not be prosecuted. Thus, in those jurisdictions, the right not to be stabbed turns out not to be a right under the will theory, since I cannot waive that right. It may, of course, be difficult in practice to convict the stabber if I refuse to testify against him, but he may nonetheless be charged and I can be required to testify on pain of contempt of court if I refuse or subject to perjury charges if I lie. Thus I cannot waive the right to be stabbed and redress for the violation of that right is not within my control. In fact, it is often charged that, on the will theory, we have rights to things until they become very important, at which point they cease to be rights. For example, I have rights over my body about such things as where I walk, but, as the importance of the interest involved increases, my right de-creases, so that with regard to being killed or maimed I have no right over my body. As Kramer points out, it is distinctly odd to say that I have a right to my nail clipper but not a right to life. (Once again, since I clearly have a duty not to stab you, the will theory seems to deny the correlation thesis: enforceable duties under the criminal law seem not to correlate to any rights.)

Steiner ingeniously replies that such rights are held by the prosecutor or other official in charge of implementing the criminal law. "Civil law confers will theory rights on private citizens, criminal law (now) vests them in state offi-cials." (p. 250). Thus, for example, my duty not to stab you correlates to the right of the appropriate official. But state officials have a duty to prosecute under ap-propriate circumstances: they are not permitted simply to waive their right. Steiner replies that immunity, plea-bargaining, etc. show that public officials can waive their rights. This appears to be an inadequate response, since public offi-cials may not waive the right to prosecute merely as a matter of will: they are required to show that these waivings are taken in the public interest. A prosecu-tor who refuses to prosecute a friend abuses his office. In short, prosecutors ex-ercising the right of prosecution are bound by, obligated to adhere to, the stan-dards of justice and public welfare. No doubt, Steiner would reply that the right is held by whoever evaluates those waivings. That is, to whom is a prosecutor answerable if she grants criminal immunity? A judge? The voters at election time? Whatever the answer, that is the person who holds the right. However, a judge asked to evaluate the propriety of a prosecutor's grant of immunity is also obligated to do so in light of the standards of justice and public welfare—a judge who rules on such matters on the basis of her personal will abuses her office. Voters cannot revoke or overturn grants of immunity or plea bargains—at most they can punish the official who granted them via removal from office. (Even then, voters are given only an overall choice between two or more candidates and so must consider many factors other than a particular exercise of immunity.) Thus voters cannot directly waive or exercise the right to prosecute. In any case, voters, too, it could be argued, are duty bound to evaluate the prosecutor's exer-cise of immunity in terms of the standard of justice and public welfare. Suppose, for example, that a prosecutor decides not to prosecute a rapist who is patently guilty simply because the rapist is popular. Poles show that 60% of the popula-tion approves of this decision, and the prosecutor is re-elected. Would anyone truly say that no one failed to fulfill an obligation? Would we not say that the rights of the person raped were violated?

Again, Steiner's view has the odd consequence that if I stab Jones I do not violate Jones' rights at all, though I do violate (e.g.) the Governor of Indiana's rights. This is not only counterintuitive—it fails the test of capturing the two distinctive features of rights articulated by Feinberg. On Steiner's view, Jones may not demand redress as his due—Jones has no ground to demand justice, though he may voice displeasure that justice was not done, and Jones does not have the special status of a right-holder (only the Governor does).

Hart's approach is to bite the bullet and deny that there is a right not to be murdered. A more plausible variant on this approach is to claim that the right not to be murdered is a tort right, which may be waived by refraining from bringing suit. The same action that violates the tort right of the victim also renders the perpetrator liable to criminal punishment, but they are two different things. The two trials of O.J. Simpson famously illustrated the difference between the tort right of the victim and the criminal penalty to which the perpetrator is liable. It does seem odd, however, to insist that the victim has no right to the prosecution of his killer. Suppose the Los Angeles prosecutors were convinced of Mr. Simpson's guilt and believed there was sufficient evidence to convict, but simply refused to prosecute Mr. Simpson because he was a personal friend. The Goldman family then filed a civil suit and won damages, thus redressing Ron Goldman's (or his family's) tort right. Would we insist that no unredressed violation of Ron Goldman's rights (or those of his family) occurred? Do not victims of serious crimes have a right to (at least procedural) justice? If a citizen reports to a police officer that she has been raped and the police officer responds "I don't like you—I just don't care," and refuses to investigate the crime, have not her rights been violated? Is this not because she has a right to the law's taking the appropriate steps, whether ultimately successful or not, toward bringing her victimizer to justice? It could, perhaps, be argued that the police officer violates only her right to equality before the law. But this response seems to presuppose that the law recognizes some right of the victim to a fair investigation that the police officer denies her. After all, if the only right violated by the rapist belongs to the public, then, in refusing to investigate, the police officer is ignoring equally the rights of every member of the public.

Kramer suggests that rights of this sort are public, collective rights. The case of the popular rapist, however, shows that the public collectively may not be free to waive this right. There may be no form of legal redress in this case, but that is not because no legal right was violated, but rather because public officials, with the approval of a majority of the public, refused to enforce the law. A hard core *de facto* positivist might disagree, but anyone else would recognize that it is possible for there to be a legal right, that is, a right clearly articulated in positive law, that courts and/or public officials fail or refuse to uphold.

By way of contrast, unwaivable rights present no difficulty for the warrant theory. There is nothing incoherent in saying that killing me, even with my permission, does take away something (my life) that is merited by my status as a person, that killing me, even with my permission, does deny an important truth about my status (the value of persons) and fails to give required public recognition to my status as a person. Many (including myself) will (prescriptively) disagree with these claims, but it is a legitimate disagreement about what is due persons: those claims may be substantially incorrect, but they are not mere confusions about the nature of a right. Hence, the warrant view can accommodate such non-waivable rights as the right not to be killed. In general, the existence of a warrant can ground others having warrants against the warrant-holder. You have a right not to be killed: you are warranted in seeking police protection from a demonstrably urgent threat to your life, taking certain actions in self-defense, etc. It could coherently be held (perhaps wrongly) that the arguments and conditions that ground those legal warrants (e.g., arguments from the value of human life) also legally warrant the state in preventing you from killing yourself. Similarly, it could coherently be held that the grounds for your warrant to demand that others refrain from stabbing you also warrant state officials in prosecuting someone who stabs you, even against your objection. In any case, the Goldman family is warranted in demanding the prosecution of Mr. Simpson (assuming he is in fact guilty). Similarly, you might be legally bound to exercise your legal right to an education, because the grounds of the relevant warrants involved also ground a legal duty to exercise those warrants. Put another way, it could be claimed that getting an education is merited by one's status as a rational being, and that in denying yourself an education you are denying your own status as a rational being, and hence violating your own rights. Again, I am not here asserting that these claims are true, but merely that they are not incoherent: disagreement about such claims is substantial disagreement about which rights exist, not a conceptual confusion about the nature of rights by adherents of those purported rights.

The interest theory also faces a variety of problems. Performances of duties may create a host of tangential benefits. Not all such benefits count as rights. If Hidalgo has a mild preference for seeing blue over yellow as she passes Jones' house while driving to work, Hildalgo benefits slightly when Conners performs her contractual duty to Jones to paint his house blue, but Hidalgo (unlike Jones) does not have a right to Conners' painting the house blue. To be plausibly accounted the basis of a right, the benefit conferred by the performance of a duty must be the appropriate sort of benefit. Interest theorists have attempted to spell out in various ways what constitutes an appropriate sort of benefit.

Promissory duties provide clear instances of the problem of third party beneficiaries, such as Hidalgo in the preceding paragraph. Promissory duties are generally regarded as owed to the person to whom the promise was made yet routinely affect third parties in ways large and small. If I promise you I will care for your grandmother Martha, then you are the right-holder, despite the fact that Martha is the primary beneficiary of my duty. If all beneficiaries of a duty are right-holders under that duty, then Martha also has a right under the promise. Moreover, many people might be indirectly affected by a promise. Thus Smith, who harbors a mild liking for Martha, is a right-holder under my promise, since he would be mildly pleased (obtain a small benefit) if I do my duty. Should I fail to honor my promise, I have violated Smith's rights, and so, if my duty to care for Martha is a legal duty, it would appear that Smith (as well as anyone else who likes Martha) would have grounds for suit. Similarly, if to have a legal right is to benefit from the performance of a legal duty, in jurisdictions that recognize breach of promise as grounds for suit, not only were the disappointed fiancé's legal rights violated but so were the legal rights of his friends, as well as the rights of the tailor shop, photographer, and catering establishment that would have benefited commercially from the carrying out of the promise. Similarly, when A fails to repay B, who planned to buy a couch from C with the money, C is harmed by A's failure to fulfill his legal duty. Did A violate C's legal rights? As the consequences for both law and ethics of such widespread third-party rights are unacceptable, holding a right cannot be identical to being the beneficiary of a duty.

Obviously, then, interest theorists must restrict the class of benefits that generate rights. One method is to impose a directness test: does a breach of that duty constitute a sufficient condition for that person's interests being set back? However, the sufficient condition test fails to exclude some cases in which a breach of duty does not violate someone's rights. If you promise Tremona that you will attend her tea, and the very thought of your not appearing makes me ill, your breaking your promise to Tremona is a sufficient condition to set back my interest. Yet I have no right to your attendance. A possible reply is that your nonappearance is not sufficient in itself to set back my interest, since your nonappearance sets back my interest only in conjunction with my intense desire that you attend. However, a parallel point could be made about Tremona, to whom the promise was made: your nonappearance sets back Tremona's interests only in conjunction with her actual interest in your attending. After all, if Tremona has bet $40,000 that you will break your promise, then your non-appearance advances rather than sets back her interests. One might reply that although your non-appearance advances some of Tremonas' interests (e.g., her interest in winning the bet), it sets back others, and it is the setback of those other interests that generates the right-violation. However, it is not tautologically true that your non-appearance sets back an interest of Tremona's--Tremona need not have any actual interest at all in your keeping your promise. Thus your nonattendance is sufficient to set back Tremona's interests only given her actual interests. In short, if "sufficient" is construed as "sufficient given the person's interests," then your nonattendance is sufficient to set back my interests. If "sufficient" is construed as "sufficient independent of the person's interests," then breaking your promise to Tremona is not sufficient to set back her interests. Thus, depending upon how "sufficiency" is construed, the non-performance of a duty is either frequently a sufficient condition to set back the interests of non-right-holders or rarely a sufficient condition to set back the interests of genuine right-holders.

Similarly, if an arsonist, without my advance knowledge or consent, burns down an insured, dilapidated building of mine, he may, in fact, advance my interests rather than set them back. Indeed, if the building is a hazard and I am subject to costs greater than the value of the building that cannot be avoided by abandoning or donating the building, the arsonist may set back no interest at all of mine. Does such an arsonist fail to violate my rights, since performing his duty to refrain from arson would not benefit me? Similarly, Steiner points out that a clerk's giving a potential robber the combination to a bank's vault is not sufficient to set back the depositor's interests, since their interests are not set back unless and until the robber uses the combination. Nonetheless, depositors clearly have a right to the clerk's not doing so. Of course, one could argue that the arsonist did withhold from me the benefit of retaining the ownership of the building, however much ownership of the building might be a liability. In this sense, however, almost anything confers some benefit on everyone. Kramer could argue that the bank clerk improperly withheld from the depositors the benefit of having their bank vault's combination known only to authorized persons. But if such a prospective benefit counts, then why shouldn't the benefit to the shopkeeper, C, of having a cash-flush prospective buyer, a benefit withheld by A when he failed to repay B? In other words, if merely potentially useful or harmful conditions (such as having the combination to one's vault remain secret) count as benefits or harms in some cases, why do they not count as benefits or harms in others? Just as bank customers would prefer the combination to the vault to remain secret, so shopkeepers prefer that those considering a purchase have the means to do so.

Of course, I benefit from the general duty not to commit arson, even if a specific observance of that duty would not benefit me, just as, arguably, Tremona benefits from the general duty of promise-keeping. Perhaps the interest theorist might propose that I have a right to A's doing x only if 1) x is an act of kind z and 2) my circumstances are of a kind y, where 3) people in circumstances of kind y characteristically benefit from the performance of someone's duty to do something of kind z, and 4) A has a duty to do x. However, there are an indefinite number of levels of generality, and so there will always exist some description of x and my circumstances, perhaps at a very high level of generality, that will satisfy the condition. In the case of your promising Tremona to attend her party, for instance, you have a duty to attend, your attending is an instance of the kind *keeping your promise*, and my circumstances are of the kind *having desires that are fulfilled by someone keeping a promise to another*. (The constructive benefit approach, discussed below, goes some way to meeting this problem.)

Bentham proposed a more sophisticated version of the sufficiency test, a version whose most perspicuous articulation is given by Kramer. Does finding that A has withheld, without justification, some benefit from B suffice to demonstrate that A breached a duty? Kramer argues, for example, that when A fails to repay B, who planned to buy a couch from C with the money, C's harm, that B did not buy the couch, does not sufficiently demonstrate A's breach of duty, since there might be all sorts of reasons why B did not buy the couch. Thus C has no right to A's repayment of the money. Presumably Kramer would employ a parallel argument to suggest that Bentham's version rules out harms such as the chagrin I feel at your nonappearance at Tremona's party.

Notice that there are three aspects of the demonstration invoked by the Bentham test. The test requires a demonstration 1) that a benefit was withheld from B, 2) that it was withheld by A, and 3) that A's withholding of the benefit was unexcused. Demonstrating that you withheld from me the benefit of your company by not appearing at Tremona's party does not suffice to show that you breached a duty. However, showing that your withholding of that benefit was <u>unexcused</u> requires showing that you breached a promise, since, absent that promise, you would have every right not to attend. That is, your nonappearance was unexcused precisely because you made a promise to Tremona to attend. Hence, it appears, your unexcusedly withholding from me the benefit of your company does suffice to show that you breached a duty. Thus Bentham's test does rule out my right to your appearance at Tremona's party. Moreover, since Benthan's test requires that a benefit be withheld, if the arsonist's act withheld no benefit from me, Bentham's test does not seem to certify the arsonist's act as a violation of my rights. In short, Bentham's test avoids some counterexamples only if the notions of benefit and demonstration remain amorphous and flexible enough to be used in an *ad hoc* manner.

Joseph Raz suggests that to have a right is to possess an interest that is a sufficient reason to impose a duty.[21] The shopkeeper's interest in A's repaying B, it might be argued, is insufficient to impose a duty on A to repay B. Hence the shopkeeper does not have a right to A's repaying B. However, an interest can be sufficient to impose a duty without constituting a right. My interest in seeing that Joe, a stranger, is not unjustifiably tortured is sufficient reason to impose a duty on you not to torture Joe, since, in order to set back my interest, you would have to torture Joe unjustifiably. Thus my interest is sufficient reason to impose a duty, even though it is not for the sake of my interest that you must refrain from torturing Joe. Hence, if Raz is correct, I have a right that you refrain from unjustifiably torturing Joe. But you violate Joe's rights, not mine, when you torture Joe. Of course, my interest in Joe's not being tortured is a sufficient reason to impose a duty on you to refrain only because it somehow incorporates Joe's interest in not being tortured. Perhaps, then, the difficulty can be solved by placing appropriate restrictions on the term "sufficient reason." If we ask why it is not my rights you violate by torturing Joe, however, the answer is that I am warranted in demanding that you refrain from torturing Joe as Joe's due, not as my due. Thus placing appropriate restrictions on sufficiency of reason that genuinely capture the underlying moral rationale explicitly or implicitly converts Raz's view to a version of the warrant view.[22]

Lyons' qualified beneficiary theory is more promising.[23] Lyons suggests that to have a right is to be the direct, intended beneficiary of a duty. Lyons points out 3rd parties can have rights when a promise is made. In Steiner's example, the depositors are direct, intended beneficiaries of the clerk's duty not to provide the combination to the vault. I am not the direct, intended beneficiary of your promise to Tremona to attend her tea, however chagrined I might be by your nonappearance. And I am the intended beneficiary of the arsonist's duty not to burn down my building, even if his forbearance does not, in fact, benefit me. Thus Lyon's theory is immune to the three counterexamples mentioned above. Kramer objects that appeals to intention are problematic. We can gauge an intention only by looking at other words, which in turn need interpretation, thus, suggests,

Kramer, generating an infinite regress. However, we gauge intentions, both actual and constructive, all the time in life and in law. Indeed, Lyon's view might be more precisely formulated as "to have a right is to be the direct, constructive beneficiary of a duty." The constructive beneficiary is determined by the moral or legal logic of the duty, and while this is certainly a matter of interpretation, it is not a form of interpretation that judges or moral analysts can readily avoid. Ordinance M forbids spitting in the street. Jones, a resident of K Street, is charged with spitting on the sidewalk. No resident of K Street has previously been charged under ordinance M. Jones argues that M does not apply to residents of K Street. Since M makes no mention of K Street and there is no precedent, the court must advert to justificatory features and the constructive intent of the law. What reason is there to think that K Street residents are not covered by M? Answering that question requires looking at the point or purpose or rationale of the ordinance. The legislative discussion preceding an enactment is instructive but not determinative--legislators voting to approve a statute do not thereby vote to approve comments made in discussion of the statute. Morever, a statute itself could be constitutional even if what each legislator in fact wanted the statute to accomplish would be unconstitutional. In short, judges work with a partly implicit and partly explicit analysis of the logic of such ordinances, which generates a framework of covered instances (does spitting blood count?) and exceptions (spitting out poison). Determining the constructive beneficiary of a legal or moral duty is no more (and no less) problematic. Similarly, Kramer points out that intentions conflict, particularly between levels (general and specific), as when the legislature passes a general amendment to the tax code specifically designed to help a particular company. If rights can conflict, however, this does not pose a problem. (In any case, the particular company is not the constructive beneficiary of the amendment, regardless of each legislator's actual motive for passing the amendment.) If rights may not conflict, then the word "overall" must be inserted before "duty," and plays the same role that "unjustified" plays in Kramer's construal of Bentham's test. Ultimately, Kramer accepts intentional analysis as one among several method of determining that an unexcused withholding of benefits has taken place. Perhaps, thus, he would be satisfied with the constructive interpretation of "intended," since looking at the intentions of lawmakers is only one method of determining the constructive beneficiary of a duty.

Notice that the constructive interpretation avoids the problems generated by the generality version discussed above. The problem with the generality version is that there always exists some general description that will meet the conditions. The constructive approach limits which sorts of general descriptions may be employed. Only those descriptions appropriate to spelling out the nature of the law in legal reasoning (or the nature of moral obligations in moral reasoning) are pertinent. A disadvantage of this approach, however, is that, since rights are defined by the result of legal reasoning, they cannot be used in legal reasoning without circularity. More generally, Steiner points out that the problem of third party beneficiaries has the consequence that, on the interest theory, who has a right to something and who may waive that right are unrelated facts, and so the concept of waiving a right becomes hard to explain satisfactorily.

Of course, in some instances third parties may have rights. F promises G to take H on a trip to Europe, at F's expense. G, with F's knowledge and consent, informs H of the promise. H, acting in reliance, cancels engagements, including an alternative travel opportunity, purchases various items for the trip, and so forth. The night before departure, G waives the promise and F decides not to take H. Does H have no moral right at all to demand that F follow the original plan or that G not waive the promise? In some legal systems, but not in others, H might have a right to compensation. A descriptive theory of rights must be able to explain both results. Prescriptively, it seems obvious that the relevant question is what, if anything, H is warranted in doing or demanding and that in answering that question one should weigh and consider the whole panoply of relevant considerations, whatever they might be. Morever, action in reliance is but one category of circumstances in which third parties might gain rights. The range of cases in which third parties might acquire some form of right is both broad and open-ended. The problem is particularly acute with respect to describing positive legal rights, since a given legal system could recognize rights very foreign to traditional Anglo-American law. Interest theorists are limited, by definition, to identifying setbacks of interest and so must construe all considerations in all third party cases, for all legal systems everywhere and at all times, however awkwardly, in terms of setbacks of interest caused by duty violation. Moreover, to the extent that tests such as sufficiency, directness, or constructive intent are rigorous, they may rule out the possibility of a legal right that a given legal system in fact recognizes (there is no guarantee that, in all jurisdictions and at all times, positive law will invoke the same test). Both points are illustrated by a legal system, S, that grants every citizen the right to demand redress in court of any unwaived or unwaivable legal wrong. In a litigious society, a system such as S might be impractical, but there is no contradiction inherent in S and, in some circumstances (e.g., a small village whose inhabitants share a general disposition against filing suit), S might function satisfactorily. In S, K has a positive legal right to demand redress on L's behalf when M violates her contractual obligation to L, yet it is unclear what interest of K's is set back by M's breach of duty, much less that M's breach of duty is a sufficient condition for setting back K's interest or that some benefit withheld from K is sufficient to establish a breach of duty. Ingenuity might produce such an interest (K's interest in seeing justice done), but, such a strained analysis may miss the point if, in S, the right to bring such suits is viewed as recognizing citizens' status as agents of justice with a fiduciary duty to justice as such. True, an interest theorist could insist that K's relevant interest is her interest in doing her duty as an agent of justice, but saying that K's right exists to protect that interest seems misguided. The case of S serves not to refute the interest theory, but to indicate how artificial the analysis of S becomes when constrained by an interest theory account of rights. Warrant theory, by contrast, more naturally holds that, descriptively, third party rights are the warrants recognized by a given legal system for whatever grounds legal reasoning within that system provides: within S, K's right is warranted by the importance of justice and the relationship citizens bear to justice, namely, K's status as an agent of justice. S holds, in other words, that barring K from bringing suit to rectify the wrong done L fails to acknowledge K's publicly recognized status as an agent of justice. Prescriptively, of course, third-party rights are the warrants (legal or moral) that are objectively justified, on whatever grounds objectively succeed in justifying them. If S's conception of citizens as agents of justice is objectively unjustified or if K's bringing suit improperly denies L's status as an autonomous legal agent, those facts provide grounds for urging that S's positive law be changed.

The warrant theory appears to solve the problem of third party beneficiaries. If A promises B to go to Indiana for a week and C, B's next door neighbor, benefits because when B is away B's lights are out, facilitating C's stargazing, C may be a beneficiary of B's fulfilling her promise, but B's fulfilling her promise is not C's due. If B fails to fulfill that promise, C cannot reasonably say that B's failing to go to Indiana denies an important truth about (and so fails to give appropriate public legal or moral recognition to) his status. Thus C has no right to B's keeping her promise. Similarly, the merchant is not warranted in demanding as his due that B repay A, however much he might benefit from the repayment, since B's failure to repay A does not deny the merchant's relevant status publicly recognized in law or morals. When F promises G to take H on a trip to Europe, G is warranted in demanding that F fulfill his promise. When H acts in reliance with F's knowledge and consent, H may also, on different grounds, be warranted in demanding as her due that F fulfill his promise. If F fails to fulfill his promise, he fails to respect properly G's status as a promise-holder as well, arguably, as H's status as one due consideration and fair dealing. If those claims are objectively true, then H has a prescriptive right under the promise. If a given legal system accepts those claims, then H has a relevant positive right in that legal system. Thus warrant theory can explain either the presence or absence in a legal system of H's rights under the promise. Moreover, I am warranted in demanding as my due that the arsonist not burn my building, even if his doing so would benefit me, since his doing so would deny my status as a property owner, a status recognized by law and public morality. Similarly, the bank depositors are warranted in demanding as their due that the clerk not reveal the safe's combination.

A second problem area for will and interest theories is conceptual rather than technical. In an important sense, the view that rights are warrants subsumes both the will and the interest theory. Some warrants may ultimately derive from the importance of an interest while others may ultimately derive from a delineated sphere of sovereign will. (Warrants may also be claimed to derive from additional sources, such as God's will or the ideal of the university—rights as warrants incorporates but is not limited to interest and sovereign will analyses.) For example, I may have a warrant for demanding that you refrain from stabbing me because of the compelling interest I have in my bodily integrity and I may be warranted in demanding that you not trespass on my land because control over who enters my land is a legitimate exercise of my sovereign will. This is an important theoretical advantage, because both regions of sovereign will and interests that deserve promotion and protection are legitimate bases of rights. The will and interest theories are forced to deny one in favor of the other. Interest theorists can attempt to explain the importance of a region of sovereign will as an interest in automony. Will theorists can attempt to explain the importance of an interest as a precondition for autonomy or as a result of autonomous choice. Neither is convincing.

Schwartz is a Jew who dislikes the taste of pork. Green is a fundamentalist Jew who is sickened to the point of nausea by the very thought of a Jew eating pork. Schwartz's interest in eating pork is trivial, while Green's interest in Schwartz's not eating pork is very important to him. There is no contradiction in saying either that the law deems Schwartz's trivial interest in eating pork if he chooses more worthy of protection than Green's deeply felt interest or that Green has a duty to refrain from compelling Schwartz to refrain from eating pork, a duty of which Schwartz is the intended beneficiary, however minor the benefit. But the interest theory appears to have it backward. Schwartz's interest in eating pork if he chooses should be protected precisely because he has a right to do so, a right centered fundamentally on his autonomy as such. Green has a duty to refrain from compelling Schwartz to refrain from eating pork precisely because Schwartz has a right to do so, because Green has no warrant to order Schwartz to comply, regardless of the strengths of the interests involved. The point here is not that the interest theory is wrong, but that it seems to distort the moral logic of rights. In other cases, it seems clear that the strength and importance of an interest is the driving force behind a right, rather than the exercise of sovereign will. In short, it is evidently true both that 1) some interests are so compelling that legal systems legitimately create duties to foster and protect those interests and that 2) constructing areas for the exercise of sovereign will as such is a legitimate goal of legal systems. Will and interest theorists are forced either to deny one of these statements or to attempt to show that one is reducible to the other. Rights as warrants accepts that some rights center on protecting interests and receiving the benefit of a duty, some rights center upon opportunities to exercise sovereign will, and others may stem from and center upon neither.

A third problem area for the interest theory emerges from the fact that, whereas the will theory appears too restrictive in its apparent exclusion of children and animals from the category of right holders, the interest theory appears to be too inclusive. Arguably, human beings have duties to the Grand Canyon. Citizens may have a legal duty not to deface the canyon walls. Officials of a particular governmental agency may have a legal duty to protect the Canyon's water sources. Of course, one might argue that these are duties *regarding*, rather than *to*, the Grand Canyon. In either case, they are duties and the Grand Canyon is the beneficiary of these duties—the point of the duties is to insure that the Grand Canyon is not damaged. Thus the Grand Canyon appears to be the constructive beneficiary of my legal duty not to sandblast its walls. So, on the interest theory, the Grand Canyon would have rights.[24]

Some interest theorists attempt to exclude counterintuitive right-holders by fiat, but, if having a right is being the beneficiary of duty, it is not clear what intelligible grounds justify this exclusion. The concept of rights, as explained by the interest theory, would seem to apply to inanimate beneficiaries, so it is only by an *ad hoc* stipulation that the interest theory is rescued. Similar remarks apply to Joseph Raz's suggestion, mentioned earlier, that a necessary condition for x's having a right to y is that x is the sort of being that can have rights. This condition could be used to rule out, by fiat, the Grand Canyon's having any rights. But, "being capable of having rights" either means "being capable of benefiting from a duty" or it means something else. If the former, it does not resolve the problem, as, arguably, the Grand Canyon can benefit from duties. If the latter, then Raz's qualification obliquely slips something else into the interest theory of rights—having a right can no longer mean being the beneficiary of a duty, or else "being capable of having rights" would, by definition, mean being capable of being the beneficiary of a duty. Thus the notion of a right must be expanded to include whatever feature of right-holders makes them right-holders, and the conceptual connection between that feature and duty-supported interests must be explained.

Granted, it is at least arguable that my duties regarding the Grand Canyon stem from duties to other people, e.g., future generations. (This, of course, is one of the major battlegrounds in environmental ethics, discussed in Chapter 8.) But even if my duties to the Grand Canyon are subsidiary duties, they are duties nonetheless, of which the Grand Canyon is the directly intended beneficiary (the duties are intended to protect the Grand Canyon). Even if the ultimate benefit accrues to, for example, future generations, I benefit those future generations by benefiting the Canyon. Hence the Canyon is a beneficiary (even if not the ultimate beneficiary) of a duty. Interest theorists cannot solve this problem by specifying that rights are held only by ultimate beneficiaries of a duty. For example, Netscape's right to freedom from unfair practices on the part of Microsoft ultimately benefits the consumer via product diversity, competitive pricing, and a healthy commercial environment. This, after all, is the primary motivation behind anti-trust laws. If only ultimate beneficiaries hold rights, then by engaging in unfair practices regarding Netscape, Microsoft would not have violated Netscape's rights. Sandblasting the Grand Canyon directly damages the Grand Canyon. Showing that I have improperly withheld certain benefits from the Grand Canyon is sufficient to demonstrate a breach of duty. For example, showing that, absent special justification, I have sandblasted the Canyon walls is sufficient to demonstrate a breach of legal duty. Thus on the sufficiency test, the constructive test, Lyons' test, and Kramers' version of Bentham's test, the Grand Canyon has rights.

It might be argued that it is impossible to benefit or harm the Grand Canyon--plugging up the canyon with cement does the Grand Canyon no harm, since the Grand Canyon is indifferent to its own existence. Adopting this view, however, makes it difficult to explain what is meant by "protecting" the Grand Canyon or even "defacing" it, since nothing one does to the Grand Canyon, *ex hypothesi*, harms it. One could adopt an extreme anthropocentric view and claim that "defacing" the Grand Canyon means altering it in a manner of which most people would disapprove. However, the reason most people would disapprove is that most people would regard it as defacing the Canyon. And what if most people came to think that painting the canyon walls in permanent day-glo colors was an improvement? One could not urge against them that this would deface the Canyon, since, *ex hypothesi*, the mere fact that they do not disapprove renders this claim false.

The most promising path appears to be distinguishing between "damage" and "harm," so that painting the Grand Canyon's walls would damage but not harm the canyon. Perhaps "harm" can be defined in terms of set-back of interests while damage is defined in terms of distance from proper perfection, or some other teleological notion. Since, it would then be argued, the Grand Canyon lacks interests but possesses a proper perfection, it can be damaged but not harmed. "Benefit" would then be defined in terms of advancing interests rather than progressing toward proper perfection, so that a law or regulation could be said to protect the Canyon from damage without benefiting the Canyon. A further argument would be needed to show that rights pertain to advancing interests rather than progressing toward proper perfection. Unfortunately, the notion of proper perfection, or any other teleological notion strong enough to do what the interest theorist requires, is highly controversial. To take this tack, then, an interest theorist must solve a problem that goes back at least as far as Aristotle, namely, defining and defending a notion of proper perfection that avoids the difficulties raised in the vast literature devoted to this subject. In short, the task of articulating a generally applicable concept of benefit such that inanimate objects are incapable of receiving a benefit is, at best, difficult and problematic.

Of course, an interest theorist could bite the bullet on this and insist that the Grand Canyon does have rights—a few environmental ethicists have claimed rights for natural objects. However, for most philosophers and jurists, if the interest theory entails that the Grand Canyon has rights, the interest theory is wrong.

On the warrant theory, the Grand Canyon, presumably, does not have rights, since the Grand Canyon has no warrant to make demands, fend off claims, and so forth. Various other individuals, of course, have rights concerning the Grand Canyon—I am warranted, for example, in demanding that you not sandblast the Canyon Walls. Importantly, that warrant may be a secondary warrant grounded in environmental duties that do not derive from either utility to or the autonomy of human beings. It could be argued, for instance, that we have a general duty to preserve ecosystems for their own sake and that my status as an inhabitant of planet earth warrants me in demanding that you not violate that duty. Hence, even if only persons have rights, warrant theory is not inherently committed to an anthropocentric environmental ethic.

A fourth perceived disadvantage of the interest theory is that it must embrace a theory of the good, while the will and warrant theories need not, on their face, embrace a theory of the good (since the question of what grounds rights is left open).

I should note, though, that in my view this is not an enormous advantage of the will and warrant theories over the interest theory. At one level of abstract description, all three theories can leave open the question of what is good. The interest theory, after all, in saying Jones has a right, need only claim that some or other benefit accrues to Jones from the performance of someone else's duty. It need not identify the benefit. At this level, the three theories are on a par. At a another level, as Chapter 5 suggests, any full-blown theory of rights must embrace a theory of the good, that is, that claims about the existence of a particular warrant, realm of free action, or benefit must ultimately be justified in terms of a background theory that takes a stand on the nature of the good. At this level, the three theories are on a par. The will and warrant theories, however, provide for an intermediate level of description lacking in the benefit theory. The will theory can, without providing a theory of the good, describe (but not justify) the particular realms of personal sovereignty for which the actual workings of a legal system provide. The warrant theory can, without providing a theory of the good, describe (but not justify) which particular warrants the actual workings of a legal system recognize. However, because law is always an ongoing process of interpretation, description cannot avoid some elements of prescription (*vide* the discussion above of spitting on K Street). In short, the additional level the warrant and will theories permit is sometimes convenient, but it is not a theoretical advantage. All three views, ultimately, are committed, when fully fleshed out, to a theory of the good.

A fifth problem applies both to will and interest theories. Unlike the warrant theory, the will and interest theories cannot readily account for epistemological rights, the right to be called a poet, and various other rights discussed in Chapter 4 and elsewhere in this volume. If the arguments given that such rights exist are convincing, the will and interest theories appear inadequate.

Group rights create a sixth problem area for both will and interest theories. Chapter 10 examines group rights in detail. For present purposes, three sorts of purported group rights may be distinguished:

A. Rights of organizations, countries, cities, corporations, or other entities including some executive function or governance procedure.

B. Rights belonging to each member of a category, as individuals, over which they have individual control or receive individual benefits.

C. Rights pertaining in some essential sense to a group as a group.

As Chapter 10 points out, despite widespread error on this point, organizations are not groups and organizations' rights differ importantly from group rights. Type A. rights are not group rights but rights of a virtual individual. Type

C. rights may be analyzed in two ways—they may be understood as rights of a group, that is, rights possessed by a group as a distinct entity, or, as Chapter 10 urges, as group-oriented rights of each group member. Either way, they differ from type B. rights. Type B. rights are individually-oriented rights whose possession is defined by group membership. The right of U.S. citizens over 18 to register to vote, for example, pertains to an interest that I have about myself—the primary relevant interest concerns my own voting, and while I might have a general interest in representative democracy, voting rights reflect no special interests I have in those over 18 as a distinctive group. I exercise my own sovereign will in this area about myself as an individual (I choose for myself alone whether to register or not), and I benefit, as an individual, from the opportunity to register. Type C. rights, by contrast, pertain to interests in the group as a group, interests that individual group members may or may not share. The asserted right of the Jews in 1946 to a Jewish state is not just about the interest each Jew may nor may not have in his or her own living in a Jewish state. It is also about, for example, the survival of the Jewish people as a people, the survival of some or other people as Jews, living out and evolving Jewish customs, traditions, world-views and attitudes, philosophies, theologies, and practices, who view their doing so as part of the continuing history of Jews that each claims as his or her own story.

Types A. and B. are relatively unproblematic for the will and interest theories. Type A. rights are rights of structured organizations which, as virtual individuals, exercise their sovereign will through, e.g., a vote or official organizational document. In addition, an organization may benefit from a duty even if not all the individuals who constitute the organization's base benefit from that duty. Thus rights of type A. rights present no special problems for the will and interest theories. Theoretical problems may attend clarifying the ontology of organizations, as well as identifying the base of and interests of organizations, but these are general questions about the nature of organizations rather than difficulties about their rights, as such. Type B. rights are ordinary rights whose possessors are identified via belonging to a particular category. Possession of the right to vote in Presidential elections is restricted to U.S. citizens over the age of 18, but each person in that category exercises sovereign will over whether to vote and benefits from the duty of election officials to count whatever vote, if any, he or she casts. Thus rights of type B. present no special problems for the will and interest theories.

Type C. rights, however, produce difficulties for the will and interest theories. Consider the right of Spanish-speaking Americans to have municipal warning signs printed in Spanish as well as English. Whether or not one thinks these rights exist, it does not appear unintelligible to assert that they do.[25] Yet Hernando H. cannot exercise his sovereign will over the provision of warning signs in Spanish. Indeed, he may prefer quite strongly that all municipal warning signs be printed solely in English. There is no official organization of Spanish speakers in which Hernando H. may cast a vote or which could in some other way exercise the sovereign will of Spanish speakers. If this right belongs to Hernando H., it is an unalienable right. Similarly, Hernando H. individually may not benefit in the least from the city's duty to provide warning signs in Spanish and it is not tenable to insist that Hernando H. in particular is a constructive beneficiary of the duty to post warning signs in Spanish. Thus the right is problematic for the interest theory if it belongs to Hernando H. Moreover, as Chapter 10 argues, there is no collective entity of Spanish speakers that can benefit from the duty to post warning signs in Spanish. In contrast, Type C. rights are unproblematic for the view that rights are warrants. To claim that Spanish speakers have a right to municipal warning signs in Spanish is to claim that Hernando H. is warranted in, e.g., demanding that the city post warning signs in Spanish, whether or not Hernando wishes to make that demand or benefits from the city's duty to post them or even opposes the posting of such signs, and that Jose C., Pedro M., and numerous others posses similar warrants. As noted above, warrants can sometimes be used against the wishes of the warrant-holder. Similarly, to claim that Jews have a right to a Jewish homeland is to claim that each individual Jew is warranted in demanding a Jewish homeland, whether or not a particular Jew wishes to make such a demand, benefits from its being met, or even opposes the establishment of a Jewish homeland.

Will and interest theorists might respond that their views perform the important task of showing that type C. group rights are unintelligible. However, it would appear that the real question when assessing such purported rights is whether Hernando H. and Yehudah Ben Israel are in fact warranted, justified, in claiming, respectively, that it is their due that signs be printed in Spanish and that a Jewish homeland be established, not whether such claims can be coherently stated. Arguments in support of such claims must be evaluated on their merits, not dismissed by definition. As noted earlier, a will theorist could insist that while in 1946 Yehudah Ben Israel's demand that the world support and permit the establishment of Israel is a valid demand and that it is his due to make such a demand, his entitlement to make that demand should not be called a "right." Such a claim, however, would only serve to highlight the unperspicuousness of the will theory, as it would then need to provide distinct accounts of the validity of Ben Israel's demand concerning Israel and his demand that Schmuel Smith repay him the ten dollars Smith borrowed from him.

Obviously, the question of group rights is complex and requires a more detailed examination. Perhaps some complex equivalent of Type C. right claims may be constructed by will and interest theorists. However, the ease with which rights as warrants analyzes Type C. rights claims and the difficulties, whether ultimately resolvable or not, such claims present to will and interest theories indicates an obvious advantage of rights as warrants over its two major competitors.

D. Rights and the Broader Conception of Law

Simmonds points out that the classical will and interest theories are linked to general conceptions of law. The classical will theory, Simmonds suggests, views the law from the standpoint of a Kantian kingdom of ends: the authority of the will is abstracted from the particular contents of what is willed, and the business of the law is to make autonomy compossible for individuals within a society, that is, to protect spheres of individual liberty from each other's interference. The classical interest theory, Simmonds contends, springs from a positivistic conception of law as regulating the battlefield of conflicting individual interests. Some modern versions of the will and interest theories, by contrast, have become merely analyses of the formal features of rights. Theories of major import, Simmonds avers, "have been converted into a regimentation of linguistic usage; such regimentation seems to be of doubtful value if disconnected from wider goals" (p. 198).

Simmonds' point is of great importance. Will theorists need not be Kantians and interest theorists need not be positivists. But theories of rights should link to important concepts of law and morals. The long-standing debate is not a purely technical one depending only on fine points of definition. Any fully developed theory of rights, to be worth the attention spent upon it, should express, cast light on, and/or importantly enlarge how major issues in law and ethics are conceived and understood.

What conception of the law does warrant theory express? Is the theory merely a regimentation of language, or does it connect to wider goals?

Warrant theory reflects a conception of the law as moral discourse in action. The law, on this view, is an intelligible system proclaiming the public morality as it is realized in a lived community of individuals whose status deserves public recognition. Legal systems and public moralities are complex networks of complexly related principles, values, ideals, commitments, and moral analyses. Moral discourse, on this view, is not simply a matter of deducing more specific from more general claims, though such deductions often do occur in moral discourse. It is, rather, an open-ended process of giving reasons for balancing, in a particular way for a particular case, the diverse pulls of a variety of sources, moral and pragmatic. This conception of moral thinking as giving case-specific reasons for adopting a particular balance between potentially conflicting moral considerations, as *The Ethical Engineer*[26] illustrates, is more satisfactory than attempting to find a single principle that resolves all moral questions. Similarly, law reflects diverse values and ideals. Equality before the law is one important ideal. Abstract justice, that a person's life situation should correspond to her moral situation, is another (e.g., evil should not be rewarded). Promoting good consequences is an important principle. Privacy is an important value. Each of these components of our public morality reflected in law generates a variety of particular (vector) warrants in particular circumstances. Often, the vector warrants conflict. The law must intelligibly (that is, in a way justifiable by reason-

giving) decide, in a given case, which resultant warrants emerge from the inter-
play of these vector warrants. What warrant theory reflects, thus, is a particular
model of ethical decision making (reason-guided casuistry) and a conception of
law as an intelligible system of public morality realized in the lives people make,
severally and collectively, in a community.

This conception of law accords nicely with the way legal reasoning in fact
proceeds. Judges engage in just such an open-ended process of drawing upon
constitutions, statutes, regulatory law, precedents, legal maxims, considerations
of practical and social welfare, principles of and conceptions of justice, and legal
customs. For example, an important legal maxim is that a felon should not profit
from his crime. A man who murders his father because anything is better than his
father's constant nagging does profit from his crime if sent to prison—he has
succeeded in escaping the nagging. When locked in his cell, the prisoner raises
his arms to heavens and proclaims "thank goodness! Peace at last!" To prevent
the felon from profiting from his crime, a guard could be employed to nag the
prisoner. This, it could be argued, constitutes cruel and unusual punishment. The
maxim appears to conflict with U. S. Constitutional requirements. Of course,
Constitutional strictures are usually interpreted in accordance with legal maxims—there is no algorithm for deciding what is "cruel and unusual" or which
instances fall outside the scope of the Constitutional provision. One could argue
that punishments required in order to prevent a felon from profiting from his
crime are not cruel and unusual. So legal reasoning is required. Which conceptions underlie the maxim and the Constitutional stricture? One source of the
Constitutional stricture is equality—punishments should be general, not *ad hoc*.
Employing a guard to nag this particular prisoner violates the ideal of equality.
Moreover, for the state to inquire into and respond accordingly to the particular
motivations of each felon in violating the law violates ideals of privacy, is inor-
dinately costly, fallible, and subject to abuse. Similar points apply to decisions
about whether an instant case is differentiable from precedent, since, as the discussion of spitting on K street indicates, every case will have some unique feature, however trivial, and, in deciding whether that feature differentiates the case
from previously decided cases, legal *desiderata* from any source may be relevantly invoked. In short, legal reasoning, even in such obvious and clear cases,
inevitably involves giving reasons for weighing and balancing an open-ended
spectrum of *desiderata* drawn from a variety of sources.[27]

Rights as warrants, thus, not only offers a solution to some of the technical
problems about rights that have troubled the will and interest theories, but offers
a conception that accords well with the actual practice of legal reasoning, rescues
law from being an arbitrary collection of rules and decisions, frees moral thinking from the problematic requirement of conforming to a single principle, and
restores law to an intelligible system of morality in practice that proclaims the
moral ideals of a community.

Notes to Chapter Three

1 All references to Steiner, Kramer, or Simmonds, unless otherwise specified, are to Kramer, Matthew H., Simmonds, N.E., and Steiner, Hillel, *A Debate Over Rights*, Oxford, New York: Oxford University Press, 1998.

2 As will appear below, A's being warranted in p may ground or entail someone else's being warranted in some other thing, q. When A's warrant to p grounds B's warrant to q, one can describe B's warrant as part of A's right to p or as a right of B's that is dependent upon A's right. While the latter option is usually more convenient, the important underlying facts remain the same: A is warranted in p, and A's warrant grounds or entails B's being warranted in q.

3 Feinberg, Joel, "The Nature and Value of Rights," *The Journal of Value Inquiry* 4, 1970, pp. 243-57.

4 Consider Carl Wellman's definition in *Real Rights*, New York: Oxford University Press, 1995, p. 8:

> A legal right is a system of Hohfeldian positions that, if respected, confers dominion on one party in favor of some second party in a potential confrontation over a specific domain and that are implied by the legal norm or norms that constitute this system.

A right, says Wellman, provides whatever associated advantages are necessary to give the right-holder a legal advantage under a variety of circumstances. (Wellman gives a parallel definition of moral rights on page 38.) While rights are frequently invoked in confrontational settings, they need not be. Sometimes the point of a warrant is not to confer an advantage in a dispute but to confer a certain status. This is the key point made in Feinberg's paper. Even if no one ever challenges my giving a political speech in the park, my right to free speech changes my attitude and others' attitudes toward my doing so—the fact that I do so as a matter of right makes a difference in how I regard both myself and my making the speech. Rights are proclamative as well as practical. The theory that rights are warrants captures this feature of rights. I am warranted in giving my speech, my giving that speech has a publicly recognized sanction, a fact of importance whether or not anyone challenges me or attempts to stop me from speaking. In short, Wellman's account doesn't fully capture the two distinctive features of rights articulated by Feinberg's article.

5 Jenkins, Iredell, *Social Order and the Limits of Law*, Princeton: Princeton University Press, 1980, p. 243.

6 Schlossberger, Eugene, Review of Boucher and Kelly, eds., *Social Justice from Hume to Walzer* in *Ethics* 111 No 4, July 2001, pp 804-805.

7 Dworkin, Ronald, *Taking Rights Seriously*, Cambridge: Harvard University Press, 1977.

8 McCloskey, H.J., "Rights," *Philosophical Quarterly* 15, 1965, pp. 115-127.

9 The term "choose" is used loosely here. In some cases, such as epistemological warrants, one doesn't generally "choose" to employ or exercise a warrant. I might not believe x even though I am warranted in believing it, and so not exercise my warrant, but this is not, strictly speaking, a "choice."

10 Richard Brandt, in *Morality, Utilitarianism, and Rights*, Cambridge: Cambridge University Press, 1992, pp.189-190, suggests that "X has a moral right to Y" be defined as follows:

"It is justified for people in X's society to be strongly motivated, overridingly so normally and always when in conflict with concern for merely marginal benefits in a given case, and to disapprove of others who are not so motivated, to enable X—always by refraining from interference, but when necessary also by cooperating substantially to bring about the opportunity, when appropriate by legal means—to do, have or enjoy Y primarily because of the importance to people in X's situation of being able to do, have, or enjoy things like Y; and it is justified for X to feel resentment if he is hurt or deprived because of the failure of others to have this motivation, and for him to feel unashamed to protest, and for him to take reasonable steps of protest, calculated to encourage others to have the motivation to enable anyone in a similar situation to do, have, or enjoy things like Y." Brandt's view already shares two key features with the view here espoused: the emphasis on justification and the invocation of publicity, of the importance of a social or public outlook. Pressure on Brandt's view will make it more closely approximate my own. Brandt is speaking specifically of moral rights, but accommodating epistemological rights, proclamative rights, and so forth would force Brandt to widen the scope of rights to include things other than obligations on others to enable a rightholder to enjoy something. Further, as argued earlier, Brandt must acknowledge that the "importance" of enjoying things like Y may stem purely from the importance of recognizing X's status as a rightholder. Understanding this aspect of "importance" again brings Brandt's view closer to my own. Finally, recognition of the importance of vector rights weakens the motivation necessary for a right to exist.

11 Schlossberger, Eugene, *Moral Responsibility and Persons*, Philadelphia: Temple University Press, 1992.

12 For example, the statute provides very weak evidence that liking oneself is morally justified: the fact that a belief is not only widely held but part of the legally proclaimed public morality of one's society certainly does not demonstrate the truth of the belief, but it does provide weak support. After all, while the cognitive processes and epistemological positions of most people in our society are imperfect, they are, in general, better than random. Thus, if a perfectly rational evaluator knew nothing else about a belief but that it was widely held and publicly proclaimed in our society, she would assert that the belief is slightly more likely to be true than false. More importantly, it is harder to fault someone for a belief that is part of the publicly recognized morality of his society than it is for an idiosyncratic belief.

13 Feinberg, Joel, *Social Philosophy*, Englewood Cliffs, New Jersey: Prentice-Hall, 1973.

14 Jenkins, *op. cit.*, p. 243.

15 A shortcoming of Feinberg's view that rights are claims is that some rights or constituent elements of rights appear not to be "claims" in any direct and natural sense. Rights as warrants captures this feature of rights, since one can be warranted in things other than claims.

16 Benditt, Theodore M., *Rights,* Totowa, New Jersey: Rowman & Littlefield, 1982, p. 70.

17 Fried, Charles, *Right and Wrong,* Cambridge, MA: Harvard University Press, 1978.

18 Hart, H.L.A., "Are There Any Natural Rights?", *Philosophical Review* 44 (2), April 1955, pp. 175-191.

19 Hart, H.L.A., "Legal Rights," in *Essays on Bentham,* Oxford: Oxford University Press, 1982.

20 White, Alan, *Rights,* Oxford: Clarendon Press, 1984.

21 Raz, Joseph, *The Morality of Freedom,* New York: Oxford University Press, 1986.

22 See also Rainbolt, George, "What Are Group Rights," in Christine Sistare, Larry May, and Leslie Francis, eds., *Groups and Group Rights,* Lawrence, Kansas: University of Kansas Press, 2001, who points out that rights are sometimes accorded for the sake of someone else's interests. The right of a judge to impose sentence, he suggests, is justified not by the judge's interests but by the interests of others in having guilty persons punished.

23 Lyons, David, "Rights, Claimants, and Beneficiaries," in *Rights, Welfare, and Mill's Moral Theory,* New York: Oxford University Press, 1994.

24 It is possible, of course, to claim that being the beneficiary of a duty is a necessary but not a sufficient condition for having a right, in which case it would not follow that the Grand Canyon has rights. However, such a claim does not amount to a theory of rights until one specifies which other conditions, when added to being to the beneficiary of a duty, constitute sufficient conditions for having a right. To the extent that those extra conditions are substantially unrelated to the possession of an interest, the resulting theory does not count as an example of the interest theory of rights.

25 Some such rights may be parsed as correlates of a duty, e.g., the right of Jews to a homeland may correlate with the duty of member organizations of the United Nations to vote in favor of the declaration establishing the State of Israel.

26 Schlossberger, Eugene, *The Ethical Engineer,* Philadelphia: Temple University Press, 1993.

27 Cf. Levi, Edward H., *An Introduction to Legal Reasoning,* Chicago: University of Chicago, 1949, for a more extensive discussion of legal reasoning.

Chapter 4:
Why the Correlation Thesis
Should Be Discarded

The correlation thesis, that every right corresponds to a duty and/or vice versa, is widely accepted among rights theorists in jurisprudence and philosophy. To many, the correlation thesis ranks among the truisms that can be safely assumed without argument. In some respects, this widespread acceptance is surprising.[1] A duty is an obligation imposed by a social, moral, or legal requirement, something that law, morals, or standards of socially accepted behavior requires one to do, a demand upon one made by law, morals, or social propriety. A right is, roughly, something one may insist upon as one' due with some degree of justification, either *in propria persona* or through a proxy. It is not obvious why it is always someone's due that I meet the demands of law, morals, and/or social propriety or why someone is always required to provide what is my due. Perhaps the driving motivation behind the correlation thesis is the sense, particularly with regard to law, that no point can be served by saying that something is my due except to impose requirements on others. What other import, some might wonder, could such a claim have? As the ensuing discussion will show, the perception that a right imposing no corresponding obligation would be vacuous overlooks the richness and complexity of the multifarious ways rights enter legal and moral reasoning.

Moreover, the widespread acceptance of the correlation thesis is partly illusory, since not all of those who accept the correlation thesis are actually accepting the same thesis. Previous discussions of the correlation thesis fail to make one or more of seven critical distinctions, thereby creating ambiguities in the arguments and rendering unclear exactly what thesis is being attacked or defended. Making the relevant distinctions yields 192 different possible versions of the correlation thesis. None, it will be urged, imposes a substantive constraint

on theories of rights: it should not count against a theory of rights that some duties correlate to no right the theory sanctions, and it should not count against a
theory of rights that it posits rights that correlate to no duty.

A. 192 Versions of the Correlation Thesis

Seven distinctions regarding the correlation thesis must be observed.

1) Correlation theorists must choose between the Denial and the Limitation theses. Hohfeld distinguished between liberties, powers, immunities, and claims. While claims might appear to be correlated to duties,
   liberties, powers, and immunities seem not to correlate to duties. Thus,
   holders of the correlation thesis must either a) deny that liberties, powers, and immunities are rights (the *Denial thesis*) or b) limit the correlation thesis to claim rights (the *Limitation thesis*).

2) Three possible versions of the thesis pertain to the scope of the thesis.
   The Half-Correlation thesis asserts that every right correlates to a duty.
   The Converse Correlation thesis asserts that every duty correlates to a
   right. *The Full Correlation thesis* asserts that every right correlates to a
   duty and every duty correlates to a right.

3) Two possible versions pertain to the content of the correlation. I will
   express them in terms of the half-correlation thesis, but analogous versions exist for the converse and full correlation theses. *The No Remainder thesis* avers that the correlated set of duties exhausts the content of
   a right. *The Material Correlation thesis* merely states that whenever x
   has a right to P, it is the case that someone, somewhere, has some duty
   by virtue of x's right to P.

4) The correlation thesis may be substantial or stipulative. According to
   the *Substantial Correlation thesis*, the entire panoply of what we ordinarily call "rights," and their legitimate role in legal and/or moral thinking, can be captured or analyzed exclusively in terms of rights that correlate to duties. The *Stipulative Correlation thesis* treats the correlation
   of rights and duties as simply a stipulation about how the term "right"
   is being employed. It concedes that there may be other things, ordinarily called "rights," that are both indispensible to legal and moral thinking and not included in or analyzable in terms of what the correlation
   thesis dubs "rights."

5) The correlation thesis can be essential or accidental. *The essential version* of the correlation thesis regards the correlation thesis as a claim
   about the nature of rights. *The accidental version* regards the correlation thesis as a statement that happens to be true but might well have
   not been—it is a contingent, accidental feature of the world. In other
   words, on the accidental version, although there could well be rights
   that do not correspond to duties, as it happens, no such rights exist.

6) The correlation thesis can be trivial or robust. The *Trivial correlation
   thesis* permits duties to which rights are correlated (or vice versa) to

have no substantial meaning apart from the right or duty to which they are correlated. For example, if A has a right to x, then others have a *prima facie* duty to refrain from doing any member of the set of things that would violate A's right. Even if this is the empty set, it is still, at least formally, a duty. For example, the right to call oneself a poet imposes on others the duty to respect that right, that is, to refrain from doing anything that would violate that right, other things being equal (even if, in the particular case, nothing would violate it). The *Robust correlation thesis* insists that correlated rights and duties are, in some important sense, conceptually independent of each other. The correlated duty must be comprehensible in some way that does not simply amount to, directly or indirectly, the bare existence of the right. The robust correlation thesis may appear to be inconsistent with the no remainder thesis, but it is not—one can claim both that the full content of a right is exhausted by its correlated duties and that the two are conceptually independent. The robust correlation thesis and the no remainder thesis, taken together, entail that a genuine reduction has taken place. The hardness of a table's surface is exhausted by the nature of its molecular structure—nothing additional is needed to explain the table's hardness. But the idea of hardness and the idea of a certain molecular structure are conceptually independent in the relevant sense. Obviously, a rigorous account of the requisite sense of conceptual independence is beyond the scope of this chapter—it is a topic that has generated lengthy debate in philosophy of science.

7) Finally, the *legal version* limits the claim to law: within the law, at least, rights and duties are correlated. The *general version* applies to all rights and duties, whether they are legal rights and duties or non-legal (e.g,. moral) rights and duties.

Not all 192 versions are of equal import. The correlation thesis has been employed to rule out various claims about rights. For example, it has been used to deny the existence of broad positive rights, such as a general right to an education, on the grounds that such a right would correspond to no specific duty borne by any particular duty bearer. It has been raised against my claims that rights are networks of public warrants for doing, thinking, saying, receiving, or believing something as one's due (Chapter 3) and that liberty rights are permissions due some level of penumbral public support (Chapter 2), because, the objection runs, liberties as well as some other warrants do not exhaustively correspond to a set of duties. Unless the correlation thesis can do theoretical work of this sort, it is not clear what advantage is gained by holding it. Thus, only versions of the correlation thesis that place genuine constraints on claims about rights require examination.

The legal version of the correlation thesis should be discarded because of the role that rights and duties, legal or non-legal, play in legal reasoning. It may seem tempting to say that if a right does not impose specific duties it has no legal meaning. However, something may be termed "legally meaningful" if it is a significant factor recognized by a court as the full or partial basis of a judicial decision. A right or duty may be said to be recognized within law when it is legally meaningful in this manner. Non-legal rights and duties may be recognized within law, in this sense, as Dworkin, Greenawalt, Levi, and Eisenberg, among others, point out.[2] Mistake in the criminal law provides two classic examples of non-legal obligations significantly affecting *mens rea* requirements. In *Regina v. Prince* Court for Crown Cases Reserved, 1875. L.R 2 C.C. R. 154, the defendant was charged with violating 24 & 25, Vict. c. 100 # 55, which made it unlawful to cause any unmarried girl under the age of 16 to leave her guardians' house without their consent. The defendant incorrectly but reasonably believed the woman in question was over 16, in which case his act would not have been a criminal offense. The court found the defendant guilty because what the defendant believed himself to be doing, while not illegal, was, in the court's opinion, wrong in any case. Thus the court held that while there was no legal duty to refrain from causing a woman over 16 to leave her guardian's house without consent, the (purported) moral duty to refrain from so doing is central to determining the *mens rea* requirement concerning age. Hence a purely moral duty became legally significant. Conversely, in *State v. O'Neil*, 147 Iowa 513, 126 N.W. 454 (1910) defendant was convicted of violating a statute after it was invalidated by the Iowa Supreme Court but before that judgment was reversed by the U.S. Supreme Court. Under those circumstances, found the Iowa Supreme Court, it would be unjust to convict someone for an act that is *malum prohibitum* (wrong because contrary to law) but not *malum in se* (wrong in itself). The court, thus, cited the absence of a purely moral obligation as a crucial factor in its decision.

In addition, legal reasoning concerning damages for breach of promise has historically adverted to courts' understandings of a fiancé(e)'s moral rights and duties. Moral rights and duties may play a role in determining the nature of a criminal charge (e.g., whether murder or voluntary manslaughter) and may function as mitigating or exacerbating factors in sentences and judgments. The fact that a defendant confesses may reduce the sentence because, in pleading guilty, a defendant "shows an appreciation of his obligations as a member of society and his consideration for the public."[3]

Similarly the role of moral duties in legal reasoning invoking "public policy" is complex. Wills that prohibit social relations with other members of a family are against public policy (*N.J.-Girard Trust Co. v. Schmitz*, 20 A.2nd 21, 129, N.J.Esq. 444), but *N.J.-Latorraca v. Lattorraca*, 26 A.2d 522, 132 N.J.Esq. 40 upheld a will prohibiting an overnight stay at the domicile of a family member. Total restrictions on marriage violate public policy and provisions encouraging divorce violate public policy (*Fineman v. Central National Bank*, 33) but partial restrictions frequently do not, e.g., requiring beneficiary to marry within a particular faith (*Shapira v. Union National Bank*, Ohio 1974; 27). The decision of the court, of course, does create specific duties, rights, powers, and permissions. In reaching these decisions, the court adverts to and gives consideration to purely moral obligations and rights not otherwise recognized in law, as one factor among others.

Similarly, non-duty conferring legal rights, such as proclamative rights, may become legally meaningful via their role in judicial reasoning. If the legislature of Connecticut passes a statute containing the phrase "everyone has a right to self-esteem," this right could be recognized within law in several ways. Courts continually determine what counts as "reasonable," and the (hypothetical) fact that Connecticut law affords a right to self-esteem may well affect, for instance, the court's determination of what constitutes "reasonable accommodation" in disability related cases. Determining what is "reasonable" requires weighing a broad spectrum of considerations, including not only precedents, statues, regulations, and legal maxims but economic factors and moral expectations. Proclamative rights may be cited when courts determine legislative intent, when courts weigh conflicting *desiderata* in determining the scope of a broad statute or regulation or setting boundaries between two statutes that might be viewed as conflicting, and in determining which factors are differentiable when evaluating precedent. A Connecticut court, for instance, when determining that public schools must install one ramp per six hundred students, might cite the right to self-esteem in its opinion. Since the proclamative right is only one factor influencing judicial decisions imposing obligations, the right cannot be said to correlate to the resulting obligation.[4] The hypothesized right to self-esteem in Connecticut does not correlate, for instance, to an obligation on the part of public schools to install one ramp for each six hundred students. (If any right correlates to that duty, it is a right created by disability legislation, not the self-esteem proclamation.) The right to self-esteem functioned as one factor, among many others, informing the judicial decision to set the number at six hundred. Absent the self-esteem legislation, the court might possibly have selected a different number of students per ramp, although it is virtually impossible to say what number of students per ramp the court would have selected. There is no determinate answer to what specific effect the proclamatory right *per se* had on the court's decision, although the court recognized it as a relevant factor affecting its decision. Thus the hypothetical right to self-esteem in Connecticut has legal significance without correlating to any particular duties. Similarly, the self-esteem statute might be cited by a Connecticut court of review in overturning a lower court's sentencing or custody decision that gave undue weight to the defendant's or one parent's high opinion of herself. While the protection the statute affords to self-esteem is a relevant factor in the review court's decision, it would be an overstatement to say that the statute imposed a strict duty on judges not to consider defendant's high opinion of herself a relevant adverse factor in sentencing.

In general, it is impossible to specify in advance the exact role a right or duty, legal or non-legal, will play in the entirety of legal reasoning: any right or duty can, under the right circumstances, play a role in judicial reasoning, even if only a subsidiary one. While many of the specific examples discussed below are non-legal, each may have legal significance under the right circumstances. Thus, if there are moral rights that correlate to no duties or moral duties that correlate to no rights, those rights and duties can receive judicial cognizance and so become legally meaningful. Thus, if all rights and duties recognized within the law must be correlated, then, in effect, all rights and duties, legal and non-legal, must be correlated. Hence, the legal version implicitly entails the general version.

The trivial form of the correlation thesis is tautologically true, but has no significant impact on theories of rights. Only versions of the correlation thesis that assume some form of independence condition on correlated rights and duties place genuine constraints on what can count as a right. The trivial form, in short, is true, but of no interest: it is surely not what those who held the correlation thesis have meant to assert. Similarly, the material version, even if true, has little impact on theories of rights: its requirements are weak enough that virtually any theory of rights meets them. The limitation version appears to reduce to the stipulative version, since Hohfeldian claims are generally defined as rights that correlate to duties.[5]

The stipulative version, while unassailable, lacks theoretical import. It merely forces those who wish to posit non-duty-correlated rights to use different words. Often, this stipulation is less than helpful. Consider, for example, Thomson's term "positivism," which she employs to describe the view that a duty exists when a penalty is attached to non-performance.[6] The stipulative versions of the converse and full correlation thesis must deny this version of positivism unless it substitutes some other term for "duty," since it is conceivable that there are actions whose non-performance carries a legal or moral penalty but are not correlated with any right. (Some candidates for such duties are mentioned below.) Such actions would be "duties" according to positivism as Thomson defines it but are not "duties" according to the stipulative thesis. The stipulative version does not deny that such actions exist. It simply insists that such actions not be called "duties." Note that the further thesis that there are no such actions, which would render the correlation thesis compatible with Thomson's positivism, amounts to the substantial correlation thesis. While any stipulation might prove useful in a particular context for a particular purpose, additional reasons will appear below for not adopting the stipulative version of the correlation thesis as a general linguistic convention for the discussion of rights.[7] Thus only the substantial version will be considered in the ensuing discussion.

It is unlikely that anyone holds the accidental version. In any case, the present concern is whether the correlation thesis can be employed to argue against a theory of rights, that is, to reject a proposed theory of rights on the grounds that it incorporates rights that do not correspond to duties (and/or vice versa). The accidental version cannot be so used, because, since correlating to a duty is purported to be an accidental feature of rights, the way to determine whether the accidental version is true is by looking at the rights that in fact exist. That no duck is pink is an accidental feature of ducks. That no duck is a rose follows from what it is to be a duck. If Carreras claims to have found a pink duck, one cannot argue, without examining the duck in question, that Carreras must be mistaken on the grounds that, while there could be pink ducks, there happen not to be any. One has to look at the duck in question and see if it is pink.[8] On the other hand, if someone claims to have discovered a duck that is really a type of rose, one has to wonder what she means, and whether her claim is even coherent. Thus it is the essential version, and not the accidental version, that could be employed to argue against a proposed theory of rights, and, hence, it is the essential version, which holds that the correlation thesis is a claim about the nature of rights rather than just an accidental feature of the rights that people actually happen to bear, that is at issue. Note that the essential version implies that talk of a right uncorrelated to a duty is not just false but in some sense incoherent, a conceptual error.

In short, we may define the *strong version* of the correlation thesis as the combination of the essential, no remainder, substantial, denial, robust, and general theses. In the ensuing discussion, I will argue against half, converse, and full versions of the strong version by presenting duties that do not correlate with rights and rights that do not correlate with duties.

B. Duties that Do Not Correlate with Rights

Are there duties that do not correspond to rights? Russell Grice suggests that supererogatory duties violate the correlation thesis: Schweitzer felt it was his duty to do what he did, but no one had a right to claim it of him.[9] Joseph Raz suggests that the owner of a Van Gogh painting has a duty not to destroy it.[10] This does not correlate with a right of others. Rather, says Grice, it comes from respect for those things that give life meaning.

Along similar lines, consider a specific instance of the duty to leave the world no worse than one found it,[11] namely, the duty of campers not to trash the forest (that is, to pack out their trash). To whose right do these duties correspond? Is it a right belonging to the forest? To all members of present and future generations? It certainly seems a bit strained for me to claim that a stranger who leaves behind a soda can in a remote Siberian forest has violated my rights. Perhaps with sufficient ingenuity one might locate a rightholder, however strained and unintuitive the claim might be. Perhaps, for instance, anyone who might have visited the forest is a conditional right holder. But when you leave a soda can in a Siberian forest, the harm to me, the infringement of my autonomy, and the denial of my status as a rightholder are at best faint and amorphous. Even were I in fact to visit the forest and see the lone soda bottle you left behind, it seems odd for me to insist that my rights were violated. Is it my due to see no empty soda bottles? Do you deny my publicly sanctioned status by leaving a soda bottle behind? In contrast, the duty not to trash the forest is quite clear and simple: if you litter the forest, you have committed a clear and direct violation of your duty. If we discard the correlation thesis, we can simply say one has a duty not to trash the forest, without having to find some corresponding rightholder. For what purpose should we be committed to such mental gymnastics? What is lost when we say simply that a duty is an obligation (as opposed to a mere *desideratum*), a requirement of law or morality, a legal or moral demand upon our conduct that may or may not be owed to someone, and a right is a warrant that may or may not create various robust obligations for others?

Duties to ideals seem not always to correspond to rights. As a professor I have a variety of duties. Some are owed to my university and defined by its rules, procedures, practices, and customs. Some are owed to my students. But my duty to uphold certain standards (regarding, for example, grades and course content) is not owed to any specifiable set of persons: it is a duty to an ideal, which may conflict both with the wills and the interests of my students and my particular university. Similarly, consider duties under a social code, such as the Mafia code of revenge, the machismo code of manhood, or the traditional Spanish code of honor. The injunction to a Mafioso or an adherent of machismo to "do your duty" does not mean "observe someone's rights." Duties under such codes are not necessarily duties to someone, though someone or something may function as an underlying basis—God, the honor of Spain, a certain conception of manhood, or, more abstractly, the moral order. If the correlation thesis is interpreted so loosely that a Mafioso who fails to take revenge has (putatively) violated the rights of each person of Sicilian ancestry or every member of the Mafia, then it is a pointless exercise. Moreover, for the correlation thesis to do any work, it must insist, as the essential version requires, that such conceptions of duty are not only untrue but incoherent, that is, confusions about the nature of duty. Are such claims of obligation incoherent—do they constitute a confusion about the nature of obligation? The code of machismo says that there is a regulative ideal of manhood that demands certain things of, places certain normative constraints upon the behavior of, each man. I would suggest that this claim is false. But in what sense, on what grounds, might one legitimately call it incoherent, a confusion about the nature of duty (other than the fact that it violates the correlation thesis)? Put another way, while codes of machismo and revenge are not defensible, they are not unintelligible claims of obligation: the wrongness of such codes stems from their moral content, not because having duties to an ideal is a conceptual confusion about the nature of duties. One could always deny, as a stipulation, that requirements on conduct imposed by an ideal are duties simply because their being duties violates the correlation thesis, and insist they be given some other name, such as "schmuties." But what is the point of such a definitional game?

Duties of self-development also present problems for the correlation thesis. If I have a duty to develop my talents, who has a right to my developing those talents? When Gauguin left his family to paint, he did so, rightly or wrongly, out of a sense of duty. It is not uncommon for those who believe they have something important to say to feel an obligation to contribute their idea to the common discourse (posterity), for those who feel a sense of mission about a project to feel it is their duty to pursue it, and so forth. Who has the corresponding right in such cases? Perhaps, for those who feel their mission is God-given, one could argue that God possesses the right. But this sort of sense of duty is frequently not theologically based at all. Is it posterity as an abstract entity that possesses the right? Do all art lovers have a right to Gauguin's leaving his family and devoting himself to art? Such claims sound unduly strained. If an art lover had demanded of Gauguin, that, as that art lover's due (or as the due of all art lovers collectively), Gauguin leave his family and devote himself to art, virtually everyone would agree that the art lover had exceeded his moral authority, just as Smith does when she demands, as her due, that Jones fall in love with her. An art lover, however, who criticizes a talented artist for not devoting himself to art does not exceed her moral authority in that sense—the art lover would be intelligibly asserting that the artist failed to do what he ought to do. In short, it is not incoherent to suggest that a duty exists, though performance of that duty is no one's due. Proponents of the correlation thesis can deny that these purported obligations should count as "duties," but to do so is to abdicate the substantial thesis in favor of the stipulative thesis, since these purported demands upon conduct function like "duties" in the sense that some moral penalty is attached to their non-performance, that they can be used to justify conduct or serve as the basis for reproach, form the basis of exhortations to act in accord with them, etc.. [12]

C. Rights that Do Not Correlate with Duties

Are there rights that do not correspond exhaustively to a set of duties? [13] If any rights fail to correlate with duties, such rights are not traditional claim rights, since, traditionally, claim rights are precisely those rights definable in terms of duties. But if rights definable in terms of duties are claim rights, then strong full or half version correlation theorists must insist that all rights are traditional claim rights. This insistence seems wrong or misguided. [14]

For example, general entitlement rights have been thought to pose problems for the correlation thesis. These Matthew Kramer calls "inchoate entitlements": to say that a child has a right to an education, says Kramer (following Hart), is just to say that this interest deserves moral or legal protection. [15] However, if a child is warranted, justified, in demanding an education as his due, it is not clear what point is served by denying the title of "right" to this demand.

In general, the denial version seems misguided. Something is lost if one denies the title of "rights" to certain sorts of permissions that correlate with no robust duties. Just as non-legal rights and duties may enter, in diverse ways, into legal reasoning, moral rights that impose no specific duties may enter into moral reasoning. A child's "inchoate" right to an education may help persuade voters and legislators to provide publicly funded busing for remote areas or persuade a parent with limited means to pay tuition for one child at the expense of a benefit, such as braces, for another. While a child's right to an education does not impose on parents a specific duty to purchase internet access to assist with homework, it does legitimately affect parental deliberations about how to allocate family resources. It is not merely that the child's interest in an education is a worthy interest: the fact, if it is a fact, that the child is warranted in demanding consideration for her education exerts a different and perhaps stronger claim on our deliberations than other equally worthy interests do.

Consider a custody agreement governing a three year old child that states "Either parent shall have the right to remove the child from daycare until the customary pickup time." This right, which serves to ward off criticism or adverse action, is more than a mere absence of a duty to refrain from removing the child. It is an entitlement, and differs markedly from an ordinary permission such as the absence of a duty to refrain from picking one's nose in private. For example, absent a duty to take Jones shopping, Smith may licitly refuse to take Jones shopping unless Jones ceases to pick his nose in private, even if Smith's only reason for so doing is to prevent Jones from exercising that permission. By way of contrast, while Parent A has no duty to offer parent B extra time with the child, parent A does act improperly if she threatens not to offer parent B extra time if A removes the child from daycare. While parent A, in doing so, does not explicitly violate a specific obligation, the court would frown upon such an action and may (or may not) intervene. To act explicitly to prevent the other parent from exercising this right, with no justification other than the desire to prevent the exercising of the right, is to act in bad faith. The difference is that the parent has a warrant to take the child from daycare, a warrant that deserves penumbral support of some sort. This penumbral support is not readily cast as a specifiable duty. While the court would be justified in intervening, should the court choose not to intervene, the court is not guilty of refusing to enforce parent A's legal duty. These and numerous other complex situations are readily explained by calling the appropriate warrants "rights." The court, for instance, in intervening when parent A threatens to deny parent B extra time if parent B removes the child from daycare, acts to protect parent B's right to remove the child from daycare: B's warrant to remove the child from daycare warrants the court in intervening in A's attempt to prevent B from exercising that warrant.

Consider also a form of ethical egoism that asserts that everyone has the right to pursue his or her own welfare. If this means no more than "no duty exists to refrain from pursuing one's own welfare," it appears to be indistinguishable from the amoralist's claim that no duty exists to refrain from pursuing one's own welfare, simply because no duties of any kind exist. Clearly, the ethical egoist is saying something more, namely, that people are warranted in pursuing their own welfare. That is, for the amoralist, nothing is anyone's due, while for the ethical egoist, pursuing one's own welfare is one's due. The ethical egoist of the stripe I am considering avers that each person can make a public claim, may justly proclaim as her due, may licitly insist upon public recognition of the warrantedness of, her pursuit of her own welfare. The moral force of this claim is most naturally captured by calling it a "right." The ethical egoist's claim, while it may be incorrect, is not obviously incoherent. Having a good of one's own, says the ethical egoist, perhaps in conjunction with having the ability to recognize that good and care about its realization, confers upon one a certain status, a status that, morally, demands public recognition. Whether or not this claim is true, it seems to be intelligible. So the strong half correlation thesis appears to be wrong.

The correlation theorist can abandon the substantive correlation thesis for the stipulative thesis, insisting that what the ethical egoism claims is not a right but a "shright." Alternatively, the correlation theorist can insist that the right to pursue one's own good, claimed by ethical egoism, correlates with the duty of others to recognize that right. But, since others are perfectly at liberty to interfere with the egoist's pursuit of her welfare, this is a trivial duty, in the sense described above. That is, the duty invoked has no content apart from the right. To make this move, then, is to abandon the robust for the trivial correlation thesis. The correlation theorist can insist that the ethical egoist's claim is wrong but not incoherent, thus abandoning the essential for the accidental version of the correlation thesis. But the example does seem to show that the substantive, robust, and essential versions of the half correlation thesis are mistaken.

Other rights claims create standards of appropriateness that fall short of duty, but which nonetheless may serve as grounds for resentment or criticism. When people say "I have a right to my emotions," they are often making at least three related claims: a) that feeling whatever they feel is their due, b) that they are immune from criticism for feeling whatever they feel, and c) that they should not be asked rationally to evaluate their feeling. Their claim goes further than a Hohfeldian privilege not to rationally evaluate their feelings. You have no duty to hop up and down, but there is no impediment to my requesting that you do so. By contrast, those who claim such a right may feel self-righteously angry when asked rationally to evaluate their emotions. On the other hand, their claim does not go so far as to insist that others have a duty, an obligation, to refrain from asking them to do so. Rather, the right adverts to a standard of appropriateness that constitutes part of the framework of appropriate expectations governing social interaction. While others do not quite have a duty to adhere to this standard, failure to do so is grounds for resentment and criticism and, in some sense, amount to giving someone else less than his or her due. Such standards, a common part of social life, are neither obligations nor mere permissions. Suppose that Williams says "hello" to a passing stranger, who averts his eyes without responding. Williams may well feel ill treated, take umbrage, and assert that the strangers' behavior is inappropriate. Williams may feel the stranger rendered him less than his due. But Williams is unlikely to assert that the stranger has violated a duty. Most people don't think we have a duty to return "hello's." Failing to do so is quite different from breaking a promise. Rather, politeness of this sort is not an obligation, a demand of morality that one is required to satisfy, but a standard of aptness deviation from which may justifiably incur criticism and resentment. One is more apt to say the stranger "wasn't nice" than that he was immoral or unethical. On the other hand, criticism of the stranger is a moral one—it is not just that his behavior violates a social convention, but that such rudeness is a less morally lustrous way of treating people than is returning the greeting, since it fails appropriately to respect others. (A variety of parental actions in custody litigation fall into a similar category: they are subject to judicial disapprobation and are relevant factors in making custodial decisions without violating any legal obligation.) Thus the purported "right to one's emotions" correlates, in part, to something between a duty and a permission.[16] Once again, refusing to treat these claims as rights claims obscures the fact that they enter into moral and legal deliberations in much the say way as other rights claims do.

Proclamative rights, the right to call oneself a poet, and epistemological rights also seem to violate the correlation thesis. Recall the hypothetical Connecticut statute proclaiming "Everyone has a right to self-esteem." This is a proclamative right. While it imposes no specific duties, it does warrant one in having a certain feeling, as one's due, and it serves to fend off certain forms of criticism. The existence of this proclamative right, the fact that, in Connecticut law, self-esteem is not just a desirable thing but everyone's due, is not without consequence: as noted earlier, it informs and influences legislative, regulative, and judicial thinking in matters as diverse as educational labeling, reasonable accommodations for disabilities, and any other aspect of publicly scrutinized life that may affect a resident's self-esteem. Yet it does not seem to correlate to any robust duty or set of duties.

Epistemological rights are also problematic for the correspondence thesis. As noted earlier, when one claims the right to believe x, one can mean two quite different things. If Jones wants to believe in the tooth fairy that is his "right" in the sense that no one is entitled to punish him or force him to stop—Jones has a right to freedom of belief. This right may plausibly be said to correlate with various duties. But "I have a right to believe x" can also mean that the evidence non-negligently available to one warrants the belief: one is claiming that one is entitled, as one's due, to believe x, and invoking public recognition of that fact. In this sense Jones does not have a right to believe in the tooth fairy. Jones then, has a warrant not to be interfered with for believing in the tooth fairy (freedom of belief) but not a warrant for believing in the tooth fairy (an epistemological warrant). The right to believe x, in this latter sense, is not empty. Epistemological rights may serve to ward off criticism, mitigate blame, and help determine the range or extent of others' legitimate emotions (e.g., "you should not be angry with me for believing x since I had a right to believe it"). Epistemological rights may also be relevant to setting standards (legal or moral) for negligence: the fact that Williams had a right to believe x surely tells against Williams' being negligent in believing it. Yet epistemological rights do not seem to correspond in any straightforward way to any specific set of duties. For example, as noted in Chapter 3, I may be warranted in demanding that others similarly epistemologically situated recognize my belief as justified without their having a duty to do so.

Finally, consider the statement, also discussed in Chapter 3, "I have earned the right to call myself a poet." (This right to call oneself a poet, which must be merited, differs from the speech right not to be prevented from or punished for calling oneself a poet, whether the sobriquet is merited or not.) That right is not, in any plausible way, correlative with a set of duties: it too, asserts that one is warranted in so calling oneself, as one's due, and serves to fend off certain kinds of criticisms. To what duty might the right to be a poet plausibly correspond? The strong version requires this duty to be non-trivial, so, for instance, the duty to respect my right to be called a poet will not serve. My right to call myself a poet does not entail, for example, a duty on your part not to scoff at me for do-ing so, although my right does give me a rebuttal to the challenge your scoffing poses. You have no legal duty not to scoff, and it is far from clear that you have any moral duty not to scoff. (Is it really morally wrong?) In any case, since you have fiduciary duties concerning your son's emotional development, you may also have a duty not to scoff at your twelve-year-old son's claim to be a poet even though his poetic output does not give him a right to call himself a poet in this sense. If so, your son has the right not to be scoffed at by you for calling himself a poet but not the right to call himself a poet, and it is the former, not the latter, that correlates with your duty not to scoff at his calling himself a poet. In any case, the right to call oneself a poet includes much more than immunity from being scoffed at, and so cannot, given the no-remainder thesis, be the cor-related duty. My right to call myself a poet does not correlate to the duty others have to forbear from interfering with my calling myself a poet—that aspect of the right to free speech is shared alike by Nobel Laureates and those whose life-time poetic output is one rhymed couplet.

In short, while the right to call oneself a poet may impose some duties on someone, somewhere, it is hard to imagine what duty would capture all of the substantive content of this right non-trivially.

This conclusion is significant because the right to call oneself a poet is more than a mere Hohfeldian privilege. Calling herself a poet is Maya Angelou's due (that is, she has earned the right to do so), in a way that having a shot at eating the salad, in Hohfeld's example, is not: Maya Angelou's relation to calling her-self a poet goes far beyond the absence of a duty to refrain from calling herself a poet. She also has positive grounds to do so, and is entitled to do so in a special way, without embarrassment or shame and with social sanction. (Similarly, Maya Angelou's right to call herself a poet is not simply a liberty in Thomson's sense, namely, a Hohfeldian privilege plus certain claims on other's forbear-ance.)

In sum, there appear to be a wide range of right claims that do not correlate, non-trivially and without remainder, with claims of specific duties. Many read-ers might be inclined to say, about one or more of the above examples, that, al-though what is claimed may be commonly referred to as a "right," it is not really a right that is being claimed, but something else. However, all of these are claims for publicly sanctioned warrants to do, think, believe, feel, receive, or say something as one's due. The right to vote and the right to call oneself a poet, for instance, both invoke a publicly recognized sanction that warrants one in doing something as one's due. All are linked in sophisticated ways to other warrants. All affect the conditions for proper interpersonal converse, in the sense that, were the purported right not held, the conditions for proper interpersonal con-verse would be different. All function in importantly similar ways in legal and moral reasoning. As the above examples show, what we commonly call "rights" may serve to impose duties, stave off criticism or liability, impose standards of appropriateness that fall short of duty, and point to a pro-attitude that demands penumbral support, or influence in a rich varieties of ways judgments about what is reasonable or about resolving conflicts between apparently conflicting legal or moral considerations. A right imposing a duty may also impose a standard of appropriateness or be linked with a right that does. Calling them all "rights" makes clear the richness of rights talk. Nothing prevents one from insisting that common parlance is mistaken in calling them all "rights" and, instead, giving each a different name. It is not clear what is gained by this maneuver, since everything no longer called a "right" would simply have to be readmitted into the moral arena under a different name and given its own explanation. The result, in other words, would be a panoply of moral and legal warrants, each with its own account. Since they all function in similar ways, we would soon find ourselves employing a collective term for all these warrants, a term such as "shrights." (Convenience alone dictates such a term, since we often want to claim something as our due, with the appropriate ramifications for moral and legal discourse, without having to stop and determine whether it correlates exhaustively with a duty.) Correlation theorists could then spend their days correcting those who claim a right to believe or a right to call themselves a poet, informing them that what they mean to claim is a shright, not a right. It is clearer, less cumbersome, and more intuitive simply to call them all "rights": greater explanatory power is gained by following common usage in dubbing them both "rights" and capturing what they have in common.

D. Conclusion

While I have not "disproved" the correlation thesis, the above considerations strongly suggest that the correlation thesis is either weak enough to have no substantial import, false (or at best accidentally true), or an unhelpful stipulation. It is not incoherent to posit legal or moral requirements usefully called "duties" that correspond in no strong and straightforward way to rights, and it is not incoherent to posit warrants usefully called "rights" that correspond in no strong and straightforward way to duties.

Notes to Chapter Four

1 Historically, the appeal of the correlation thesis sprung from several sources. Some moral positivists were inclined to say that duties must owed to someone, and, hence, that all duties correspond to rights. Some have held that all rights are contractual, and so the existence of a right implies a contract holder and hence a contractual duty. Yet others have seen the role of rights as trumping pursuit of the good, and hence the only possible content of a right would be the imposition of an obligation restricting pursuit of the good. While this chapter will not include an explicit argument against such conceptions of rights, it does point out some functions of rights claims that show such conceptions, however correct they may be about some kinds of rights, are too limited to capture the full realm of rights.

2 Levi, Edward, *An Introduction to Legal Reasoning*, Chicago: University of Chicago, 1949, Dworkin, Ronald, *Law's Empire*, Cambridge: Harvard University Press, 1986, Eisenberg, Melvin Aron, *The Nature of the Common Law*, Cambridge, MA: Harvard UniversityPress, 1988 and Greenawalt, Kent, *Law and Objectivity*, New York and Oxford: Oxford University Press, 1992.

3 Comment, "The Influence of the Defendent's Plea on Judicial Determination of Sentence," *Yale Law Journal* 204, 210, n. 28, 1956.

4 It might be argued that the right correlates with the duty of the court to take the right into consideration whenever and in whatever fashion it is relevant. But in this sense, even the fact that two plus three equals five correlates with a parallel duty on the part of the court to take that fact into consideration in whatever ways are relevant. In short, the duty has no significant content apart from the right itself. Such a correlation is relevant only to the trivial version of the correlation thesis.

5 More precisely, the claim-right element of a right corresponds to one or more duties. A right, as Chapter 3 suggests, is a network of warrants. Thus claim rights do not exist in isolation. Carl Wellman, in *Real Rights*, New York: Oxford University Press, 1995, points out, for instance, that Smith's right to be paid ten dollars by Jones includes (is associated with) a power to waive the claim. While Smith's claim to be paid correlates with Jones' duty to pay, the power to waive does not precisely correlate with a specific duty.

6 Thomson, Judith Jarvis, *The Realm of Rights*, Cambrige, MA: Harvard University Press, 1990.

7 Kramer, for example, repeatedly emphasizes that the correlation thesis is merely an analytical stipulation, but acknowledges that it could be rejected as an analytical system if found to be impractical or less useful than some other system. See Kramer, Matthew, "Rights Without Trimmings," in Kramer, Simmonds, and Steiner, *A Debate Over Rights* Oxford: Oxford University Press, 1998, pp. 7-111.

8 Of course, it is logically possible that some other feature of reality might necessitate the correlation thesis. For example, someone might claim that all rights are created by divine dispensation, and while non-correlating rights are logically possible, God's nature is for some unknown reason incompatible with creating a right that correlates to no duty. However, since it is difficult to imagine a plausible example, I will ignore this abstract possibility until someone actually proposes a plausible version of it.

9 Grice, Russell, *The Grounds of Moral Judgment*, Cambridge: Cambridge University Press, 1967.

10 Raz, Joseph, "Right-Based Moralities" in Frey, ed. *Utility and Rights*, Minneapolis, University of Minnesota Press, 1984, pp. 42-60.

11 For a discussion of this duty and an argument for its existence, see Schlossberger, Eugene, *The Ethical Engineer*, Philadelphia: Temple University Press, 1993.

12 Two additional, oft-discussed arguments should be mentioned: public duties and imperfect duties appear to present problems for the correlation thesis.

Public duties do not obviously correlate to rights. To whose right does the duty to pay taxes correspond? Kramer, an interest theorist, suggests that the duty to pay taxes corresponds to a public collective right: we collectively, as a society, have a right that you pay your taxes, and someone who does not pay taxes improperly withholds a benefit from the "regnant political-legal system or public as a whole," p. 83. Since this suffices to show that the tax dodger has violated a duty, for Kramer, tax dodging violates the rights of "the public or its political-legal regime", p. 84. Steiner, a will theorist, argues that the corresponding right belongs to the public official who can waive that duty (e.g. the head of the Internal Revenue Service or the judge with ultimate jurisdiction). (Steiner, Hillel, "Working Rights," in Kramer, Simmonds, and Steiner, 1998.) But, as Chapter 3 points out, neither the head of the IRS nor a judge is at liberty to waive the "right" according to personal preference: they are obligated to represent justice, not exercise their sovereign wills. Furthermore, as noted in Chapter 3, this response has the unhappy consequence of divorcing the holder of the right from the point, justification, or purpose of the right, since the point of the right held by the judge with ultimate jurisdiction that Jones pay her taxes is surely not to protect the judge's interests, autonomy, and so forth. Public duties, then, seem more problematic for correlation theorists who hold the will theory than for those who cleave to the interest theory.

Imperfect duties, it is sometimes argued, correspond to no rights. Smith, for example, has a duty to contribute to charity, but no one has a right to Smith's making charitable contributions. Whatever having a right entails, it must entail some color of justification to claiming, *in propria persona* or through a proxy, something as one's due. It seems distinctly odd to insist that anyone may justly claim or demand Smith's giving to charity as his or her due. Thus, it is argued, there are duties that correlate to no rights. (Cf Feinberg, Joel, "The Nature and Value of Rights," *Journal of Value Inquiry* 4, Winter 1970, pp. 243-257.) This argument, of course, does not apply to the converse correlation thesis.

Kramer suggests that Smith's duty correlates either to God's right, the human species' right, or the right of Smith's community. On what grounds could Smith's community demand as its due that Smith give to charity? Perhaps some ground could be found, e.g., that giving to charity is part of the social contract. Kramer's response requires that such a ground be discovered for every imperfect duty, without exception, a daunting task.

In any case, imperfect duties have two features that ill fit the concept of rights espoused by most will and interest theorists. Imperfect duties are imperfect in two distinct ways:

1)   Imperfect duties are non-specific, in the sense that no particular actions are required by them, although they do require that the totality of one's actions display certain features.

2) Imperfect duties are less stringent than perfect duties. For example, imperfect duties are to be satisfied with the resources that remain after perfect duties are satisfied and a person who fails to fulfill an imperfect duty is judged less harshly than someone who fails to fulfill a perfect duty. Not giving to charity is less damning a fault than neglecting one's children or reneging on a debt.

If a right corresponds to Smith's imperfect duty, it must be a nonspecific and less stringent right. Since Smith's duty is merely to make some or other reasonable set of charitable contributions over the course of his lifetime, the corresponding right possessed by Smith's community would be simply that Smith's life exhibit the feature of having contributed reasonably to charity. Indeed, it is at least arguable that Smith satisfies his duty, even if he never gives to charity, if he participates in a reasonable way in a community that makes reasonable provision for those in need in one way or another. In any case, most ethicists would agree that such an imperfect duty, which we may call the duty of reasonable participation, exists, whether or not a duty to give to charity also exists. In addition, if Smith's duty corresponds to a right possessed by Smith's community, that right is less stringent than Jones' right that Smith repay her the money Smith borrowed from her. In short, the correlation thesis can be saved only by creating two categories of rights.

Are there imperfect rights, that is, do nonspecific, less stringent duties correlate to nonspecific, less stringent rights? This suggestion has at least some plausibility, and it would rescue the correlation thesis from these sorts of counterexamples. Imperfect rights appear more congenial to interest than to will theories. An interest theorist might correlate Smith's duty of reasonable participation with the following rights: those in need have a right to the community's exhibiting the global feature of exhibiting reasonable provision for those in need, if and when the community's perfect duties are satisfied, and the community has the right to Smith's life exhibiting the global feature of reasonable participation in the community's fulfilling its duties, if and when Smith's perfect duties are satisfied. Since interests can be specific or broad and interest theorists focus on conflicts of interest, this analysis involving broad interests and conditional (prioritized) obligations should not be unduly troubling to an interest theorist. Will theorists, however, must construe the correlative rights in this manner: if and when the community's perfect duties are satisfied, those in need exercise their sovereign will over whether the community exhibits the global feature of making reasonable provision for those in need, while, if and when Smith's perfect duties are satisfied, the community exercises its sovereign will over whether Smith's life exhibits the global feature of reasonable participation in the community. This analysis so distorts the basic notion of the exercise of sovereign will that a will theorist who embraces it may justly be accused of expanding the notion of exercising sovereign will beyond recognition. Thus imperfect rights are more congenial to interest than to will theories. They are, of course, quite congenial to rights as warrants, since warrants can be specific or broad and strong or weak.

13 One oft discussed example can be found in MacCormick, D.N., "Rights in Legislation" in P.M.S. Hacker and J. Raz eds., *Law, Morality, and Society*, Oxford: Clarendon Press, 1977. In Scottish law, the children of an intestate has a right that the executor of the estate give them ownership of the intestate's property. But since the right exists before an executor is appointed, the children have a right to which no one has a correlating duty. The obvious response is that the legatee's right corresponds to a conditional duty. If A makes a will in accordance with the provision of S.9 of the Wills Act, 1837, then the executor of the will has duties x, y, and z. So, for example, failing to have enough wit-

nesses is not a "breach" of a duty but rather ensures that the antecedent of the conditional is not true, and hence the duty does not arise. It is quite possible for a duty-imposing law not to apply to any particular individual at a given time, especially when the duty is conditional. Suppose that in 1998 a statute is passed requiring any individual whose net worth exceeds one trillion dollars to fill out a particular form, k. That law creates a conditional duty to fill out form k (that is, for all x, if x possesses a net worth over one trillion dollars then x has a duty to fill out form k), although, in 1998, the duty did not apply to any actual person. Similarly, in MacCormick's example, the inheritee's rights can correlate to the duty of "the executor, whoever he or she shall be," that is, the will creates a conditional duty (for all x, if x is the executor of y's will then x has a duty to do z). The duty that correlates to the legatee's right belongs to anyone who comes to satisfy the antecedent of that conditional. H.L. A. Hart suggests that power-conferring and duty-imposing laws have radically different functions. Powers, Hart argues in *The Concept of Law*, Oxford University Press, 1961, p. 28, cannot be reduced to conditional duties because an invalid will is not a breach of duty. But, as Wellman notes, the fact that power-conferring and duty-conferring laws have different functions does not mean that one cannot be reduced to the other: power-conferring laws may be a particular form of duty-conferring laws that perform a different function from other power-conferring laws (i.e., duty-conferring laws may serve two quite different functions). "Social insurance" torts serve quite a different function from negligence torts, but they are both torts.

14 An interesting argument against the correlation thesis comes from Thomson's definition of "cluster rights." Thomson defines cluster rights as "rights that contain other rights" (*op. cit.*, p. 55). A cluster right, notes Thomson on page 56, "is not correlative with a duty" since cluster rights can contain liberties, powers, and permissions. The correlation thesis, Thomson holds, pertains only to rights "in the strictest sense." But the arguments given earlier show that virtually every right is a cluster right. My entitlement that you stand on your head for 3 minutes after dinner as you promised contains the permission to complain if you fail to keep your promise (both, of course, are equally overridden by compelling circumstances, etc.), the power to release you from your promise (though not all entitlements to promise-keeping include this power), the immunity from criticism if I demand that you keep your promise, etc. That is, the entitlement may be expressed as purely an entitlement, but it carries with it a variety of rights in the broadest sense that are not entitlements (and may not correlate with duties).

15 Kramer, *op. cit.*, "Rights Without Trimmings," pp. 7-11.

16 Again, I would deny that we actually have such a right, but it is a perfectly intelligible rights claim whose falseness is unrelated to the correlation thesis. It is false, I would suggest, because emotions of this sort involve judgments that may be correct or incorrect, appropriate or inappropriate, and even fair or unfair. For example, to resent someone, I have argued in *Moral Responsibility and Persons*, Philadephia: Temple University Press, 1992, is (in part) to judge that the person resented has wronged one in a way that betrays trust. If the person resented has not done so, then the resentment is unjustified and may constitute doing an injustice to the person resented. Hence there are criteria for judging emotions to be inappropriate or even unjust. It is this fact about emotions, not the correlation thesis, that defeats the claim that we have a right that others not judge or ask for justification for our emotions.

Chapter 5:
A New Theory of Natural Rights

Natural rights are very strong claims. To say natural rights exist is to insist that, regardless of the laws any regime enacts, persons have some claims on each government or society so strong that failure to meet those claims impugns the legitimacy of that government or society.[1] That such powerful and universal claims exist is not, despite the Declaration of Independence, self-evident. Bentham famously pronounced such talk of natural rights to be "nonsense on stilts." In any case, such a strong claim requires firmer justification, in the view of many, than has yet been provided.[2] Moreover, adherents of natural rights disagree about which natural rights exist. Despite its adoption by the General Assembly of the U.N., Article 24 of the *Universal Declaration of Natural Rights*, which proclaims a universal right to "periodic holidays with pay"[3] finds few scholarly supporters. A somewhat larger number hold, to the derision of others, that a government's proscribing the use of a particular obscene word on television violates natural rights. The theory of rights advanced in this chapter, called "T" for convenience, attempts to remove natural right claims from Bentham's stilts and ground them firmly. Natural rights, on this account, stem from the very thing that makes questionable the use of force against persons, and so, it will be argued, either there are natural rights or there are no moral constraints on killing or maiming our fellow persons. T's second major task is to correct the prevalent conception of natural rights. T views the natural right to free speech not as a shield against governmental regulation of speech, but as a claim each person has upon his or her government or social system to *adequate provision* for speech and advocacy within its domain. What counts as adequate provision depends on the circumstances of a society and the totality of its laws. Thus, in determining whether a society or government violates natural rights, one must examine not just a particular law or custom but the laws and practices of the society as a whole. After all, it is at least arguable that some degree of time apart from labor is a necessary condition for human flourishing, and so it is not blatantly absurd to suggest that there is a natural right for some degree of leisure, broadly understood. But societies may employ numerous methods of providing for leisure. Rather than demand a specific form of leisure, such as paid holidays, as the *Universal Declaration of Human Rights* does, or a line in the sand that no government may cross in restricting leisure, as some traditional theories of natural rights must do, or a minimal baseline of leisure to which everyone throughout history is entitled, T more plausibly suggests that a natural right to leisure is simply a requirement on governing systems to insure, within their domain, opportunities for leisure that are, under the circumstances, adequate. Third, T provides a general framework for determining which natural rights exist. Surprisingly, if T is correct, some harsh critics of natural rights turn out to be committed to natural rights, disagreeing with traditional natural rights theorists about the content, rather than the existence, of natural rights. T is a convenient framework for formulating, focusing, and perhaps resolving major disputes about natural rights.[4]

In short, T attempts to provide an alternative conception of natural rights that follows naturally from the claim that there are moral constraints on the use of force against persons.

A. Two Preliminary Points

The idea behind T can be outlined briefly. Any enduring human society needs some method of enforcing its rules, laws, or mechanisms for settling disputes within its borders, whether formal or *de facto*, that relies ultimately upon force or the threat of force. What makes morally permissible a society's use of force against its inhabitants? The answer lies in the difference between persons and dandelions. It is perfectly acceptable to destroy a dandelion marring the beauty of one's lawn and quite unacceptable to kill a tall person in a movie theater blocking one's view of the screen. What is it about persons that gives them a moral status different from dandelions? Let us dub "P" the feature of persons that makes morally questionable the use of force against them. Governments, it will be argued, are justified in using force against persons exactly when that force is necessary to preserve P. Thus, any government that does not make adequate provision for P is not legitimate (its use of force is not justifiable). Hence every inhabitant of any region has a claim against his or her government to adequate provision to P. Thus there is a natural right to adequate provision for P.

Obviously, this line of argument requires considerable filling out, but even this cursory summary of the theory suggests two salient points.

First, T is a three-tiered framework. Level I is very broad: T argues that each person has a claim against his or her government to provide adequate provision (understood in light of that society's means and circumstances) for P (and certain things without which the reasonable pursuit of P is not feasible), where P is the feature of persons requiring that persons be accorded moral respect. It is in this sense that people have a natural right to P (and appropriate conditions for achieving P). Level II, defining P (and determining what is necessary to make feasible the reasonable pursuit of P), makes the theory more specific: T plus a definition of P yields a broad conception of which natural rights exist. Level III, adding a definition of "adequate provision," produces a fairly detailed theory of natural rights.

Second, natural rights, on this view, are rights that legal systems and societies must respect on pain of illegitimacy (loss of political authority in the prescriptive sense of the term). T takes what William J. Talbott calls (and attributes to Rawls) a "minimal legitimacy interpretation" of natural rights.[5] Natural rights are supplemented by presumptive rights, rights that, generally, legal systems ought to recognize. Much of what is sometimes claimed as a natural right, with some degree of implausibility, is better understood as a presumptive right. A legal system that does not recognize a presumptive right may be, in that respect, flawed. It should be changed. But it does not, on that basis alone, lose legitimacy. Thus the set of natural rights does not exhaust the set of rights in virtue of which a legal system may be evaluated or to which an appeal may be made in deciding what the law should be. The sources of presumptive rights are varied. Presumptive rights may arise from particular moral arguments. For instance, if a compelling moral argument exists for the principle of "finder's keepers," then there is a presumptive right to own what one finds: legal systems ought to respect that right, but an otherwise salutary legal system that does not respect such a right to keep coins found lying on the street, although flawed, does not lose legitimacy. Presumptive rights claims may be justified on pragmatic grounds. For example, legal systems ought to fulfill their duties in the best way they can, all things considered. Hence, if X is by far the best manner of respecting a natural right, then there is a presumptive right to X. But a legal system is not illegitimate if it respects natural rights in a way that is good, but less good than some other arrangement would be: persons do not have a natural right to the very best form of government possible. Hence there is a presumptive right to X but not a natural right to X.

The distinction is important: there are good reasons for distinguishing between natural and presumptive rights. First, the distinction captures the general understanding that natural rights require more stringent respect than most other rights and that violating natural rights is a deeper and more serious wrong than violating most other rights. Moreover, flawed but legitimate states deserve certain sorts of respect that illegitimate states do not. The exact nature of that respect is controversial. Talbott makes the very strong claim that viewing natural rights as requirements for legitimacy is equivalent to identifying natural rights as those whose violation justifies military, economic, or other serious interventions compromising the sovereignty of the offending state. Talbott's claim would require arguments that no such forms of intervention toward a legitimate state are ever justified and that some set of such interventions toward an illegitimate state are always justified. Nonetheless, few would deny the weaker claim that the legitimacy of a state always counts (as one factor among others) against coercive intervention and a state's illegitimacy always mitigates, to some extent, some morally significant reasons for not intervening. Thus the distinction marked here by the terms "natural rights" and "merely presumptive rights" is of some moral importance and the use of those terms both captures and justifies an important aspect of our common discourse: one reason violations of natural rights are especially serious is that states that violate natural rights impugn their legitimacy, with the result that such states are no longer entitled to (the same degree of) some important forms of respect.

B. Level I: The New Theory of Rights

The argument that there are natural rights may be summarized as follows:

1. If the use of force against persons does not require justification then there are no genuine moral constraints on conduct concerning persons.
2. If the use of force against persons requires justification then it is by virtue of some feature P of persons.
3. Thus, either there is some feature of persons, P, that requires the use of force against persons to be justified or there are no genuine moral constraints on conduct concerning persons.
4. There are genuine moral constraints on conduct concerning persons.
5. Thus, there is some feature of persons, P, that requires the use of force against persons to be justified.
6. Every government must, ultimately, rely upon the use of force against persons. More specifically, without (continuing) government use of force, the reasonable pursuit of P is ineluctably unfeasible.
7. No use of force is wrong when the reasonable pursuit of P is ineluctably unfeasible.
8. Therefore governmental use of force is not wrong when the reasonable pursuit of P is ineluctably unfeasible.
9. Thus, continuing governmental use of force necessary to make feasible the reasonable pursuit of P is not wrong.[6]
10. Governmental use of force is not justified if it is not necessary to preserve P (make feasible the reasonable pursuit of P within its borders).
11. Thus, governmental use of force against persons is justified exactly when that force is necessary to preserve P and reasonably successful, overall, given the prevailing circumstances, in making the reasonable pursuit of P feasible.
12. Thus, governmental use of force against persons is not justified unless that government makes adequate provision for P within its boundaries.
13. Thus, no government is legitimate unless it makes adequate provision for P within its boundaries.
14. Thus, for any person, A, and every government or society, B, where B is willing to use force against A to enforce its dispute settlement mechanisms, A has a moral claim against B to make adequate provision for P within the domain affected by B's mechanisms.

15. Thus, there is a natural right to adequate provision for P.

This argument requires elucidation and support.

Statement 1. suggests that, *in fact*, force against persons requires justification or there are, *in fact*, no significant moral constraints on conducts regarding persons. While a moral theory denying 1. can be imagined, the claim made by 1. is that no such theory is true. [7] Would anyone seriously propose that, when asked an embarrassing question, it is wrong to lie but perfectly acceptable to kill the questioner to prevent him from hearing the truthful answer? The reasons against proposing such a theory are obvious. First, moral constraints on conduct regarding persons become otiose, since one can achieve the proscribed result through acts or threats of violence that, it may be noted, are usually seen as more repugnant than the proscribed acts. Second, it is hard to provide such a theory with a plausible moral rationale. Why might someone think it wrong to lie? Because it violates the hearer's autonomy? So do acts of random killing. Because it violates the principle of universalizability? So do acts of random killing. Because a life of unswerving dedication to truth is noble or valuable? If so, then random killing, which puts an end to such a life, and hence destroys something noble or valuable, must need at least some justification.

Statement 2. would seem to be true unless morality is essentially arbitrary. If, for example, someone tells me I am morally obligated to endure a life of poverty rather than kill a distant relative, Jake, who stands between me and the inheritance of a fortune, I might legitimately ask "What is it about cousin Jake that is so valuable and important as to require me to endure much suffering and sacrifice the fulfillment of many of my desires and aspirations?" The answer to that question is P. There are thus two alternatives to admitting the existence of P. One can reject the relevant moral restrictions on killing or one can insist that while persons possess no feature of special moral value or significance, everyone must suffer great hardship rather than kill one. It is hard to see the latter as a convincing response. Of course, constraints on conduct might stem from some abstract general principle rather than from a feature of persons. But an abstract principle must apply in some crucial way to persons, and the way in which the principle applies generates P. If it is the sanctity of life that proscribes the killing of Jake, then persons are of special moral importance because they are alive. If what requires us to refrain from killing Jake is obedience to God, who has forbidden killing, then P becomes "being protected by God's will." Most theologies offer some rationale for that protection, e.g., human beings are fashioned "in God's image." In that case, P becomes being fashioned in God's image. It is, of course, possible to construct a theology that renders P trivial. A theology might hold that persons are of no intrinsic value whatsoever--God has arbitrarily forbidden killing persons merely in order to test our obedience. Further reflection suggests, however, that if my being (or striving to be) obedient to God's commands is of moral importance, other persons' being or striving to be obedient to God's commands is also of moral importance. So the ability to obey (or strive to obey) God's commands is a morally significant feature of persons that requires respect. In general, then, if the use of force against persons requires justification, there must be some feature P of persons, however trivial, by virtue of which force against persons requires justification. Furthermore, it appears that any plausible moral theory makes P non-trivial.

In this volume, the truth of statement 4. will be presumed: there are genuine significant moral constraints on conduct regarding persons. It will also be presumed that people have reasonable epistemological access to those constraints: however fallible or provisional our knowledge of those constraints might be, it suffices to make reasonable the judgment that a political system is illegitimate. Amoralists are fully answered by appending to the present discussion an argument supporting 4.[8] Similarly, criticisms of natural rights theory based on radical moral skepticism are fully answered by producing an adequate moral epistemology.[9]

Statement 6. seems clearly true in any currently plausible human social world. In every known human society to date, disputes between persons are inevitable and threaten to render unfeasible the attainment or reasonable exercise of P, given any plausible account of P.[10] Moreover, any effective P-preserving mechanism for settling disputes employs force (or the threat of force). For example, suppose rational pursuit of one's projects is an essential condition for or an element of P. It is not feasible rationally to pursue my projects unless agreements are reasonably enforceable and others generally and foreseeably refrain from killing me or wantonly destroying the fruits of my labor. Similarly, opportunities for the exercise of autonomous choice are severely limited if others are free to kidnap, kill, or maim those whose choices provoke displeasure. Establishing these conditions has required, in every known human society to date, at least the *de facto* use or threat of force of some kind. Some societies have relied on threats that do not directly employ physical force, such as banishment, but banishment must, ultimately, be backed by the threat of force. While the threat of social ostracism might effectively deter most individuals, societies cannot passively endure individuals who refuse to depart and openly rape, kill, and steal at will with complete physical impunity. Thus, if P is or includes either the rational pursuit of one's projects or the ability to make autonomous choices, then effective P-preserving mechanisms for settling disputes use force or the threat of force. Since parallel arguments exist for any plausible account of P, it seems safe to conclude that effective P-preserving mechanisms for settling disputes employ the use or threat of force.

7. seems unavoidable if one remembers that P is defined precisely as that feature which makes morally questionable the use of force against persons. Since it is precisely P that gives rise to the proscription against the use of force, in circumstances in which it is not feasible reasonably to pursue P, proscribing the use of force seems as pointless as watering a dead flower: the rationale for proscribing force has disappeared.[11]

10. can be established by demonstrating that other purported justifications of state use of force either fail or entail that governmental force is necessary to pre-

serve P. For example, plausible utilitarian justifications of state power generally hold or imply, implicitly or explicitly, some version of the claims that P is happiness and that state use of force is necessary to preserve happiness. Since a detailed treatment of rival views is clearly beyond the scope of this paper, the argument here must rely upon the extensive literature on the subject.[12] Note, however, that whatever P proves to be, it must be of enormous moral importance. (It hardly seems plausible to tell me that I must endure lifelong poverty, rather than kill cousin Jake, simply because he has an opposable thumb.) P must encapsulate, directly or indirectly, the heart of moral life. Since it seems hard to countenance the use of governmental force if people generally can live rich moral lives without the use of state power, it seems plausible that any successful justification of state force would at least entail that such force is necessary to preserve P.

If indeed governmental force is justified exactly when that force is needed to preserve P, it follows that there is a natural right to adequate provision for P (and the conditions necessary for P), since any government that does not make adequate provision for P is illegitimate (and so its use of state force is not morally permissible). Thus, either there are no constraints against the use of force, or everyone has a moral claim on his or her government to make adequate provision for P within its boundaries.

The above argument for natural rights may not seem to go far enough: it guarantees neither that natural rights be equal rights nor that natural rights protect everyone. This appears to be an odd result. Human rights, says Alan Gewirth, "are moral rights which all persons equally have simply because they are human,"[13] and many have shared Gewirth's sense that natural and human rights must be held equally by all persons.

How might one justify the claim that natural rights must be equal rights? One might argue that any system of dispute settlement that does not recognize equality before the law either fails to preserve P or fails to meet minimal requirements of justice (or both). But equality before the law does not entail that all citizens have equal rights. Equality before the law (EL) requires that the law, whatever its content, be applied equally to everyone, not that laws themselves make no distinctions between categories of citizens. The principle of equal rights (ER), which claims that the laws themselves must grant equal rights to all, is a much stronger claim.[14] While EL requires that each category of persons has clearly articulated rights, different categories of citizens could have different natural rights. Several arguments that might establish EL do not establish ER. For example, since human flourishing is questionable if one's ability to carry on projects depends upon the caprice of judges, a reasonable level of anticipatibility is required. Thus it may be argued that the law must be equally applied to all: any legal system that fails to meet this requirement also fails to provide the level of anticipatibility required for human flourishing. However, citizens can reasonably anticipate courts' rulings as long as their legal system clearly articulates the relevant categories of citizens and spells out the rights and responsibilities of each category, the categories and duties are reasonably specific, explicit and clear, the courts consistently adhere to those criteria, and the rights and responsibilities themselves provide for reasonable stability and anticipatibility. In such a system, EL but not ER is satisfied. Thus the argument from anticipatibility justifies EL but not ER. Again, it might be argued that a system that violates EL is not a bona fide legal system at all, because it is the essence of law to settle particular questions by reference to a general framework of rules and principles that treats like cases alike. But this argument does not establish ER--by definition, cases involving different categories of right holders are not "like cases," that is, they are differentiable according to the rules and principles ensconced in (positive) law. Such an argument might establish a weaker version of ER, ER1: the law may distinguish between categories of right holders only when those categories are justifiable. ER1, however, begs the present question. The issue is precisely whether it justifiable to distinguish between slaves and citizens when such a system maximizes P. Perhaps ER could be independently justified.[15] If so, that independent justification can simply be added to T. In any case, natural rights provide only one of several constraints on the law. Suppose a society prohibits political speech on Tuesdays, except for Brahmins, who are entitled to argue among themselves. While such a law would normally, it will be argued, not violate non-Brahmin's right to free speech, there are other, powerful reasons to protest such inequality. Even if natural rights need not, inherently, be equal, there might be a presumptive right to equality of rights. In short, either ER is not true of natural rights or it has an independent justification that can be appended to T.

Yet more troubling is the fact that, while the argument given shows that every citizen has a claim against her government to make adequate provision for P, it does not show that the government must make adequate provision *for her*. For example, if P is the life of the mind, and if a society like ancient Athens produces the most P, then is the state's use of state force licit, even though the slave population has virtually no opportunity to live the life of the mind? The problem here is not just that the slave and the citizen have unequal rights. If slaves are given adequate provision for P and citizens more than adequate provision, slaves and citizens have unequal rights. More problematic is the situation in which the slave's rights, if any, do not meet the minimum level of procuring adequate provision for P for the slave. Does a state's making adequate provision for P within its boundaries require making adequate provision for P for each individual? A Benthamite might claim that P is pleasure and that adequate provision for P consists in maximizing P. Thus, the Benthamite could say, all that the argument given above demonstrates is that everyone has a natural right to his or her government's generally maximizing the aggregate balance of pleasure over pain.

This objection poses a problem for all theories of rights that do not simply assume that individuals may not be used for the benefit of others.[16] If no argument against doing so exists, then no theory of rights can answer the objection. If such an argument is available, it can be deployed within T. In other words, T does not rule out Benthamism—nor should it. T is a framework for posing and resolving rights disputes. T helps clarify the nature of arguments against Benthamism—they are arguments about the nature of P (Level II) and/or the nature of adequate provision (Level III).

However, T does shift the onus of proof from the anti-Benthamite to the Benthamite. After all, it is clear that if governmental force is necessary to make the rational pursuit of P feasible *for Jones*, then the government is clearly justified in using legal force *against Jones*. Thus T clearly justifies the use of force of a government or society that makes adequate provision for P for every person within its boundaries. T itself is silent, however, about whether force against Jones is justifiable in order to make the rational pursuit of P feasible for Smith. Thus, if a government wishes to claim that it is justified in using force against Jones to make P feasible for Smith, it must show why such a trade-off is permissible. The latter, unlike the former, requires additional justification. In other words, T justifies a society in which natural rights apply substantially to all. It neither justifies nor rules out a society in which the rational pursuit of P is feasible only for some. Thus the onus is on the Benthamite to provide the additional justification needed. For example, one argument might be that it is simply not possible to make P feasible for every citizen—P for some is presumably better than P for none. But it is at least hard to see how a government might justify its use of force against Jones that does not make P feasible for Jones when it *is* possible to make P feasible for everyone, including Jones.[17]

In sum, a system of natural rights for all is justifiable in terms of the arguments here presented. A system of natural rights for only some would require further argument to justify its use of legal force, to be legitimate. Thus the claim that natural rights apply substantially (though perhaps not equally) to everyone is a rebuttable presumption.

A second objection is that what the argument justifies does not count as "natural rights" in the traditional sense. For example, the argument in this chapter does not yield "natural rights" in Mabbott's sense of rights that are self-evident and absolute.[18] More generally, entitlements to adequate provision do not provide the kind of clear line in the sand, beyond which the state may not cross, that some rights enthusiasts seek.

In response, let us call the kind of rights argued for within this paper "rights*." Since rights* impose considerable restraints on government, it is of considerable significance that people have rights*. Rights* are "natural" in the sense that they do not spring from any particular circumstances or actions (such as contracting) and serve as constraints upon the legitimacy of social and political institutions. Rights* display many of the features numerous writers have attributed to natural rights.[19] In particular, they serve as antecedent constraints upon every legal system or society. Thus, it is morally and politically significant that persons have rights*, whatever other rights they might have. Certainly, rights* do not exhaust the constraints on government: some things a government might wish to do violate considerations of justice, prudence, or efficiency, even if they do not violate a right*. It could be held that, in addition to rights*, people have more traditional natural rights, such as a natural right, held equally by all, that government not cross some clearly specified line in regulating speech. While no definitive argument is presented here that more traditional natural rights do not exist, I will point out some advantages of rights* over more traditional conceptions.

Others might object that T views natural rights as held against societies and their legal systems, while other conceptions of natural rights view natural rights as held against all other individuals.[20] This difference, however, has little effect in practice. For example, Jones has a claim on his government to establish mechanisms disallowing Smith's wanton killing of him, and, given a viable theory of political authority, Smith has a *prima facie* obligation not to violate those mechanisms. Thus, if Jones' government is legitimate, Smith has a *prima facie* obligation not to kill Jones wantonly. Moreover, by wantonly killing Jones, Smith indirectly violates Jones' natural rights by interfering with the government's fulfillment of its natural rights obligations toward Jones, much as Williams indirectly violates Washington's right to be repaid $10 by Garcia by forcibly preventing Garcia from repaying Washington. Indeed, if, as Chapter 3 argued, rights are warrants, then Jones' natural right to life, held against the state, warrants Jones in claiming that Smith is obligated to refrain from wantonly killing Jones, and hence generates a claim right Jones holds against Smith that Smith refrain from wantonly killing Jones. Jones' right to life against Smith is a consequence of his natural right to life held against the state. A difference does arise when Smith and Jones inhabit a region whose governing social mechanisms are not legitimate. In the worst case, that is, a Hobbesian war of all against all, T suggests that Hobbes may be correct that the only right is the permission right of doing what is necessary to survive. However, there are powerful moral and prudential reasons for persons in such a situation to act to change that situation: after all, in such a situation, the opportunity reasonably to exhibit or pursue P is minimal. In any case, there may be other moral reasons, in addition to natural rights, for not engaging in wanton killing.[21] A second difference arises if Jones lives by himself or in a world in which no P-disrupting disputes arise. In that case, Jones might have Lockean natural rights, if Locke is correct, but would not have rights*. However, in such a situation, there would be no need or motivation to invoke natural rights of any sort: they would play no significant role.

C. Level II: Defining P

The argument so far, if successful, shows only that people have some natural rights. Determining which particular natural rights exist requires articulating the nature of P. The more precisely one defines P, the more specific is the resulting set of natural rights. An act-utilitarian, for example, might define P as the ability to achieve happiness. If so, citizens have a moral claim on their governments to make adequate provision for the opportunity to attain happiness. Further defining "happiness" (and the pre-conditions for achieving it) yields more specific rights.

For example, if happiness cannot feasibly be reasonably pursued without a modicum of education, then there is a natural right to a modicum of education (either the education itself or the opportunity to gain it: see below). Similarly, if a minimal level of health is required to experience happiness, then there is a natural right to adequate provision for a minimal level of health. If, by contrast, P is, as some neo-Kantians seem to hold, the ability to make autonomous choices, then citizens have a claim upon their governments to make adequate provision for the exercise of autonomous choice. A more precise definition of "autonomous choice" yields more specific right claims. People cannot make rational, informed choices without adequate opportunity to become informed, hear arguments, and test their ideas in the laboratory of debate. So if "autonomous choice" means free, fully informed, and rational choice, then the opportunity for free debate and inquiry is required for the exercise of P, and hence there is a natural right to adequate provision for free debate and advocacy.

For reasons given in *Moral Responsibility and Persons* and elsewhere, I would urge that P, in the case of human beings, be understood as the ability to take feasible, rational steps toward formulating, pursuing, and instantiating (individually and collectively) a morally defensible conception of a good human life. (For non-human, partial, or constructive persons, the definition must be appropriately modified.) The argument for this claim is too lengthy for repetition here. While the few brief remarks below hardly constitute an argument, they may serve to assist readers in seeing the plausibility of my claim. This account of P suits well two theses, defended elsewhere: 1) persons are worldviews in operation, where a worldview is a network of attitudes, perceptions, values, standards, predilections, and so forth that give meaning and significance to the dance of subatomic strings (or whatever physics discovers to be the nature of physical reality) and 2) it is only via worldviews that morality and meaning have purchase. So much metal moving so many centimeters is, as such, neither good nor bad. Morality comes into play only when the movement of that metal is viewed not only as Brutus stabbing Caesar but also as a betrayal of friendship and as an act of sacrifice for the perceived greater good, notions that intrinsically invoke standards against which the world can be measured. It seems plausible, then, that P bears some intimate connection to persons' ability to experience and construe the world in terms of such concepts and standards and their commitment to worlds that are better, according to those standards, over worlds that are worse, according to those standards, a commitment expressed in the way people lead their lives. Moreover, assuming that some worldviews are more "correct" on these matters than others, it is at least plausible that directedness toward a more correct, or at least defensible, worldview is at the heart of what gives persons and not dandelions their special moral status. After all, few would be convinced, in a lifeboat situation, that one must surrender one's own life solely in order to protect complete wrongheadedness. The definition of P urged here captures these intuitions. Some implications of this account of P are mentioned in section E. below and throughout this volume.

That determining our natural rights depends upon defining P will appear troubling to many. However, every society with a moral code is committed, explicitly or implicitly, to holding that some such property as P exists, for the society's moral code has both a base and a boundary. The obligations of the code do not extend to everything: one does not need to ask the air's forgiveness when sneezing. P, explicitly or implicitly, is what distinguishes things to which one has such moral responsibilities from things to which one does not. This distinction is not wholly arbitrary. Every society's moral code has some theoretical base, implicit or explicit: it is not an arbitrary collection of strictures.[22]

Similarly, every fully developed political theory already contains, explicitly or implicitly, a stand on the nature of P. Every political system must set limits to the realm of right-holders, to the realm of those due moral consideration. Consider the following actions:

1) cutting open a seven-year-old girl to use her blood as a color swatch
2) cutting open a caterpillar to use its blood as a color swatch
3) cutting open a water melon to use it's pulp as a color swatch
4) cutting open an ordinary rock to use its interior as a color swatch

Somewhere between 1) and 4), presumably, legal systems and political theories prescribing legal systems draw a line. The line might be not sharply drawn. There might be several lines marking several categories (e.g., seven-year-olds may have a right to life but not a right to vote). But no viable legal system and virtually no prescriptive political theorist can avoid drawing at least one critical line.[23] No viable legal system can avoid proscribing some instances of pointless killings such as 1) while leaving at least some destructive uses of inanimate objects such as 4) legally permissible. To the extent that there is any moral basis for a legal system or political theory, this line must not be arbitrary—it must reflect the morally relevant features of seven-year-olds and rocks. In particular, the line drawn must reflect the reason that brutal force used against a seven-year-old girl requires justification, while brutal force used against an ordinary rock does not. Of course, there can be disagreement about the rationale for a given legal system's drawing the line where it does. However, some definitions of P draw the line at different places than others. For example, sentience draws the line after 2) while rational autonomy draws it after 1). Hence legal systems must at least rule out some definitions of P (and hence take at least a partial stand on P). Thus legal systems, and fully developed political theories that prescribe a legal system and provide its rationale, explicitly or implicitly, must take a stand, complete or partial, on what P is.

Cultural relativism, a second-order view about such moral codes and political theories, appears to assert that P legitimately varies from society to society. As a result, cultural relativism may seem to deny the existence of universal properties like P that ground moral respect: each society is morally free to choose its own boundary and base, and, concomitantly, to choose its own definition of P. Since, according to cultural relativism, whatever definition of P a society adopts is true for that society, natural rights vary from society to society (if T is correct).

While convincing arguments against cultural relativism are frequently encountered in print, many anthropologists and family therapists, among others, continue to cleave to some form of cultural relativism. It is thus worth noting that
unless cultural relativism asserts that members of society have an obligation of
some sort to adhere to their society's dominant moral codes and dominant political theory,[24] cultural relativism amounts to a form of amoralism (that is, it ultimately denies the existence of any moral constraints on action). Cultural relativists who do accept a universal obligation to conform to one's society's moral
code seem committed, by the argument given above, to asserting that residents
have a claim on their society to adequate provision for carrying out that society's
moral code.[25] Thus, even for cultural relativists, either there are natural rights or
there are no genuine moral constraints on actions concerning persons. Similar
arguments pertain to views such as subjectivism, emotivism, and the views that
any proposed definition of P is merely a mask for advancing a political interest
and that there are no neutral tools for evaluating proposed definitions of P. In
general:

1. Views that appear to deny the tenability of any definition of P ultimately fall into two categories. Category A consists of views that are,
   ultimately, amoralist, either ontologically or epistemologically: they are
   forced, ultimately, either to deny the existence of moral truths or to
   deny that we have reasonable access to them. Category B consists of
   views that, ultimately, embrace or are forced to embrace some definition of P.

2. Views in Category A, as noted earlier, are beyond the scope of this volume, which relies on arguments presented elsewhere that such views are
   mistaken.

3. Views in category B are compatible with T : T can accommodate these
   views.

4. Therefore views that appear to deny the tenability of any definition of P
   are either beyond the scope of this volume or compatible with T.

Defining P may also trouble a certain brand of liberal. Liberals can be
roughly classified as metaphysical or formal liberals. Metaphysical liberals base
their political philosophy on substantive moral theories that, implicitly or explicitly, define P. Kantian liberalism, for example, is rooted in the idea that what is
morally distinctive about persons is the ability to make free, rational choices: P
is, for Kant, autonomy in this rich sense. Mill can be interpreted as rooting liberalism in the distinctive ability of persons to form communities freely experiment-
ing in the pursuit of higher and lower pleasures. Thus metaphysical liberals already hold theses about P. Formal liberals, such as John Rawls,[26] attempt to
avoid such defining metaphysical theses. The state, a formal liberal is tempted to
hold, should be neutral with regard to competing definitions of P, perhaps because claims about things like the nature of P are essentially contested, or unknowable, or merely subjective, or even meaningless. Formal liberals attempt to
replace substantial moral views, such as claims about P, with some set of (pur-

portedly) purely formal distinctions (amplified, when necessary, by minimal assumptions about the good), such as the supposed distinctions between negative and positive rights, self-regarding and other-regarding interests, etc. To a formal liberal, then, theories that try to base rights on claims about P might seem misguided.

Strong reasons, some of which receive mention elsewhere in this volume, exist for thinking formal liberalism inadequate. At present it suffices to note that each brand of formal liberalism has a close analogue consistent with T. T can accommodate formal liberal views by adopting a "thin" definition of P, thus remaining neutral between certain important claims about the good. When P is thinly defined, T yields a thin set of natural rights. For example, P can be defined as the ability to function within a society governed by a particular shared conception of justice. *A Theory of Justice* can then be viewed as an attempt to spell out that conception of justice and what is required for P. Thus one can adopt T and still be, with suitable minor changes, a good Rawlsean. Alternatively, one could argue that because P is essentially contested and/or unknowable, political systems should strive to make adequate provision for those things widely regarded as necessary for any reasonable account of P. Systems that do so can then be regarded as observing natural rights, while systems that do not may be regarded as violating them. Again, if P is defined as the ability to pursue self-regarding interests, then natural rights will center on adequate provision for pursuing self-regarding interests. In general, T can generate a close analogue of any formal liberal theory by suitably defining P.

Moreover, as noted earlier, a stand on P is already present in any fully developed political theory that is not amoralist. If a definition of P must be used to determine who holds rights, there seems to be no relevant reason why it should not be used to determine which rights there are. If P is essentially contested, then the category of right-holders is essentially contested, and if the state is not neutral in this regard, why should it be neutral with regard to which rights those right-holders possess? If P is unknowable, the category of right-holders is unknowable, and if the state nonetheless takes a stand on who holds rights, why should it not do so with regard to which rights those right-holders possess? Similar points apply, *mutatis mutandis*, about the claims that statements about P are meaningless or merely subjective. In short, since any adequate political theory and every rationalized legal system must define P, the fact that discovering natural rights requires P to be defined adds no new requirements to legal or political theory.

Some alternatives to liberalism seem to reject the very notion of rights. However, if the alternative theory is not ultimately amoralist, the arguments advanced earlier show that the theory must ultimately embrace some definition of P, in which case the theory is consistent with T and generates some natural rights, though perhaps not traditional liberal rights. Marx, for example, appears to regard P as creative production, and so T would generate a natural right to creative production and the conditions necessary for creative production. While the language of rights may be foreign to Marxism, when P is defined as creative production and "adequate provision" is defined along Marxist lines, T yields a set of natural rights congenial to Marxism. Similarly, if P is the ability to live compassionately or sustain relationships of care, then there is a natural right to adequate provision for compassionate living and/or a natural right to adequate provision for sustained relationships of care. Hence some feminist critiques of liberal rights can readily be accommodated by T.

This result appears to be correct, and so demonstrates an advantage of T over traditional theories of natural rights. Presumably, feminists influenced by Carol Gilligan would not deny that persons have a compelling claim on governments to make adequate provision for sustained relationships of care, and so would be disinclined to dispute the claim that legal systems are illegitimate if they make inadequate provision for sustained relationships of care. Similarly, Marxists would presumably not deny that people have a compelling claim on their societies to made adequate provision for creative production—that claim, after all, is at the heart of Marx's critique of capitalism. Hence T locates the dispute between Rawlsean liberals, Marxists, and certain feminists where it belongs, namely over how P is defined and hence which natural rights we have, not over whether there are any natural rights.[27]

Finally, T can meet the criticism offered against traditional theories of natural rights by, for instance, Anthony J. Langlois.[28] Langlois suggests that the doctrine of human rights is committed to a universalist picture of human life that is supported neither by pure reason nor anthropology. T can readily acknowledge that very diverse sorts of human lives can count as good human lives: the universalist core required by T is somewhat limited. T permits a great deal of cultural variety in what counts as adequate provision and distinguishes between natural rights and regulative ideals. Much of the difference between societies can understood as differences in regulative ideals and what counts as adequate provision. For example, given the rendering of P suggested above, there is a natural right to participation, to playing some significant role in shaping one's own destiny, since, roughly put, playing such a role is part of and necessary for formulating and taking reasonable steps to instantiate in one's life a defensible conception of a good human life. Society A is governed by elected officials while society B is governed by a tribal council before which everyone is entitled to speak. Both societies respect a natural right to adequate provision for participation, though each society has a different regulative ideal about how participation should be realized. The legitimate difference between A and B poses no problem for T. On the other hand, a natural right to adequate provision for participation does seem to be violated by society C, an extreme theocratic society in which individuals are required to obey, without question, discussion, or appeal, the dictates of the high priest about any aspect of life upon which the high priest might choose to pronounce. Societies A and C appear committed to incompatible views of P, so T does seem to require that either society A or society C is incorrect. However, that much universalism is required by almost any theory that is not amoralist, since virtually any constraint on conduct may be denied at some time by some society. *Pace* Langlois, arguments do exist that render plausible the claim that society C is flawed.[29]

D. Level III: Adequate Provision

In order to generate specific natural rights from P, one must determine what counts as adequate provision for P, a task that requires an answer to two questions: a) which things are necessary (in the right way) for P and b) how much of each is adequate, given the circumstances of the society. A defensible account of adequate provision for P must be responsive to several different kinds of constraints, both practical and theoretical. While defining P is a general task, intended to apply to all human cultures, defining "adequate provision" is culture-specific. Even within a society, what counts as adequate may change rapidly as circumstances change. T is thus universal at Levels I and II but culture-specific at Level III.

Some constraints on defining "adequate provision" are primarily theoretical. If there is a natural right to property, what counts as an adequate system of legal property rights depends, in part, on independently argued claims about the justification of property ownership. For instance, if Locke's theory of property were both true and applicable (e.g., the Lockean *proviso* were, in fact, satisfied), then a legal system would make adequate provision for property only by being consistent with Lockean property rights. Thus other, independent, elements of moral theory can set side constraints on what counts as "adequate provision."

Defining "adequate provision" also determines whether there are "positive" natural rights or only "negative" ones.[30] Assume, for the moment, that P is the ability to make rational decisions. If most individuals in societies S and S1 are woefully uninformed about the crucial facts relevant to the decisions they must make and are unversed in the barest rudiments of logical thinking, they are, in an important sense, unable to make rational decisions about a wide variety of important topics. In S, every inhabitant can afford to learn the relevant logical skills and pertinent facts without enduring what most people in our society would consider to be drastic sacrifices. In S1, most citizens cannot afford to obtain the relevant skills and facts and also meet minimal health and safety needs. In S2, inhabitants are both logically sophisticated and well informed but choose not to make decisions rationally. No laws in S, S1, or S2 explicitly restrict either the gathering of pertinent information or the attainment of competence in logic. S, S1, and S2 make adequate provision for P in the sense that they contain no explicit legal impediments to evidencing P. S1 does not make adequate provision in the sense that necessary means for evidencing P are not widely available. S does make adequate provision in these two senses, but fails to make adequate provision for P in the sense of ensuring that individuals in fact possess the means for P, for example, by requiring universal education. S2 makes adequate provision in the above three senses, but not in the sense that it ensures that P occurs.

Which sense of "adequate provision" do natural rights demand? Does S, S1, or S2 violate natural rights?

Some progress may be made by considering society S3, whose laws explicitly proscribe a great many of the steps necessary to obtain the information needed to make rationally defensible decisions: in S3, the publishing of information is forbidden, debate concerning many major issues is illegal, etc. S3 clearly violates natural rights. People living in S3 are not generally able to make fully rationally defensible decisions, and so there is little merit to S3's claim that its use of force against persons is justified because that force is needed for the making of rationally defensible decisions. The lesson of S3 appears to be that adequate provision for P rules out a state's explicitly proscribing, to an unreasonable degree, the means directly employed in exercising P. Further progress results from considering society S4, which contains no laws or *de facto* mechanisms for safeguarding the lives of its inhabitants. Inhabitants of S4 are regularly and commonly subject to unpredictable homicide. Rational decision-making cannot be exercised from the grave. Moreover, the ever-present threat of homicide undoubtedly distorts the decisions that people do manage to make. Thus the extent to which rational decision-making is preserved in S4 is minimal, and so S4 cannot plausibly claim that its use of force is justified because it preserves rational decision-making. It appears, then, that "making adequate provision" must include reasonably safeguarding those conditions directly essential to and crucial for exercising P.

These principles require consideration clarification. The idea of what is "reasonable" plays a crucial role. No current society can indefinitely stave off death from illness, accident, or misadventure. "Adequate provision" cannot mean that the state guarantees P is never truncated in any fashion. S4 is not required to eliminate homicide or natural death, but rather to institute those safeguards against death that can be reasonably expected of S4, given S4's circumstances and resources. At the other extreme, a state's use of force does not seem justified merely because its use of force results in a minuscule increase in P, given that other feasible arrangements would result in P's widespread instantiation. If S5, a social arrangement that fosters and enables widespread rational decision making, is feasibly available as an option for inhabitants of the region governed by S3, S3 cannot justify its use of force because decisions made within its boundaries can be marginally more rational than they would be in a Hobbesian state of nature.

Unlike S3 and S4, S2 does seem to be able to justify its use of force. S2's use of force makes P a feasible choice for its inhabitants, whether or not they choose to instantiate P, while instantiating P would not be a feasible choice without that use of force. (Of course, if inhabitants of S2 choose not to be rational because they are required by law to take an "apathy" drug, then S2 would violate natural rights.)

In sum, assuming that both negative and positive rights to an education are consistent with all side constraints imposed by independent aspects of moral theory, if negative rights securing the pursuit of education are sufficient, in a given society, to render P feasible for persons within the state's boundaries, then the natural rights of members of that society do not include the right to be given an education. If, in a given society, it is not feasible for citizens to achieve P without a state supported educational system, and it is feasible for that state to support an educational system, then, in that society, natural rights include the right to a state supported educational system (that is, the state would violate its citizens' natural rights were it not to provide one). The ultimate criterion is whether the society would be justified in claiming that its use of force is justifiable, in the circumstances, by virtue of the extent to which it preserves P within its domain.

Other constraints on adequacy are practical ones, often specific to a society. Two things must be decided, given the actual circumstances of a society: what members of that society need in order feasibly to pursue P reasonably and what it is reasonable to expect that society to provide. Prohibiting candidates for town office from using photographs in their campaign brochures has little effect in a town with 42 voters and a 100% literacy rate. While such a law might be a bad law, it does not seem to violate the citizen's natural right to free speech—no one in that town can reasonably claim, on that basis, that it is not feasible for her reasonably to pursue P. In another society, photographs may be essential in order for a significant number of voters to identify the candidates, and hence the ban on photographs could have a significant impact on inhabitants' ability to participate in shaping their destiny, given that the society is governed by elections. Mass media are crucial to a society of 260 million, less essential to a society of 200 persons. Since needs vary from society to society, so does what constitutes "adequate provision." In addition, different societies have different resources. Members of a nomadic desert tribe and members of a prosperous industrial society may have similar nutritional needs, but the food and health resources of the latter are considerably greater than the food resources of the former. Thus what constitutes adequate provision for nutrition and adequate provision for health may well differ in the two societies. If there is, for example, an *in rem* natural right to minimal health care, it does not follow that Athens in 400 B.C.E. violated its citizens' natural rights because it did not provide them with antibiotics, even though the United States in 2002 might violate that right if it fails to provide those who suffer from life-threatening respiratory infections with the inexpensive antibiotics that would cure them. Again, how much education is adequate depends both on the circumstances of the society and its resources: more education is needed in a complex industrial society than in a traditional village, if only because the task of achieving *eudaimonia* is more complicated (and so more education is needed) and the greater resources of a modern society make it reasonable to expect more education. If the physical conditions of life in a society demand 16 hours a day in the fields to avoid starvation, it is unreasonable to expect that society to provide eight hours a day of instruction, just as it is unreasonable to expect pre-literate societies to teach children to read. Thus the extent of the education to which citizens have a right depends not only on how much education is needed, given that society's circumstances, but also on how much education it is reasonable to expect, given that society's resources.

The adequate provision standard, thus, does not draw a sharp line between states that violate natural rights and states that do not: while some states can clearly be said to violate a natural right and some states can clearly be said to respect a natural right, there is a gray area between them, an area in which a state may make some provision for an aspect of P that is neither clearly inadequate nor clearly adequate. In this respect, T is closer to moral reality than theories that insist on a sharp line: the legitimacy of states, in one respect or another, can be genuinely marginal, and the insistence that, in every such case, taking some tiny further step would convert a clearly illegitimate state into a clearly legitimate one seems unrealistic.

E. Illustrations and Advantages

In order to illustrate how T works and understand its advantages, assume the correctness of my claim that P is the ability to take feasible steps toward formulating, pursuing, and instantiating (individually and collectively) a defensible conception of a good human life. Since it seems reasonable to assume it is impossible for persons in a crowded world rationally to pursue a defensible vision of flourishing in the absence of a political system that enforces its mechanisms for settling disputes, it follows that the use of state force (formal or *de facto*) is necessary to preserve the very feature that makes morally questionable the use of force against persons. Hence it is permissible for a political system to use force to make feasible the rational pursuit of a defensible vision of *eudaimonia* within its boundaries. Conversely, a political system that does not make feasible the rational pursuit of a defensible vision of *eudaimonia* for its citizens fails to meet the criterion for the legitimate use of force. Thus all political systems are obligated to make feasible the rational pursuit of a defensible vision of *eudaimonia*. Conversely, all persons have a claim upon their governments to make feasible the rational pursuit of a defensible vision of *eudaimonia*: there is a natural right to (adequate provision for) the rational pursuit of a defensible vision of *eudaimonia*. In the ensuing discussion, certain assumptions will be made about defensible visions of *eudaimonia*, since the discussion is meant not to prove the existence of a particular set of rights but merely to illustrate how T might be deployed.

Debate and advocacy

Without copious opportunity for free and thoughtful debate and advocacy, it is not feasible rationally to pursue a defensible vision of *eudaimonia*: citizens could not subject their own pursuits to appropriate rational scrutiny or appropriately pursue those projects that require the co-operation of others, and, undoubtedly, any defensible vision of *eudaimonia* in a crowded world includes some projects requiring the co-operation of others. It might also be argued that thoughtful inquiry into the nature of reality, which requires free debate, is itself an important element of human flourishing. Thus, a generous dose of free and thoughtful debate is an element of and/or a precondition for rational pursuit of a defensible vision of *eudaimonia*. Hence, from the argument given above, it follows that any government or political system is illegitimate if it fails to provide its citizens with generous opportunity to debate freely. Thus there is a natural right to adequate provision for free debate and advocacy. (See Chapter 6 for a fuller exposition of these points.)

This argument does not establish that certain speech acts are inviolate. Rather, it establishes that governments are obligated to insure that persons within their domain have sufficient opportunity for free debate and advocacy to enable them rationally to pursue a defensible vision of *eudaimonia*. What constitutes "sufficient opportunity" depends upon the nature of *eudaimonia*, the circumstances of the society, and its laws as a whole. Consider a law that forbids political debate on Tuesdays. If the society is a large one, whose only mass media are newspapers, and if newspapers are published only on Tuesdays, this law severely interferes with citizens' ability rationally to pursue a defensible vision of *eudaimonia*. In a small village, in which debate may be freely conducted during the other six days of the week, it does not. Such a law, in other words, would violate natural rights in some societies but not others. Moreover, Mill's vision of the rational pursuit of *eudaimonia* requires more debate and advocacy than does Burke's.

In addition to imposing restraints on governmental regulation of speech, the right to free speech imposes positive requirements on governments to protect speech against certain actions of private citizens. Certainly, there are differences between what governments and private individuals may licitly do. For example, governments are generally not permitted to grant the use of public facilities (such as a park pavilion) only to groups whose views are congenial to the government while a private citizen is entitled to deny the use of her home for a fundraising event to a candidate whose views diverge from her own. Nonetheless, governments must provide reasonable safeguards against private citizens' systematically preventing others from speaking (for example, by systematically disrupting public rallies by screaming and shouting through megaphones so that the speaker cannot be heard). These facts are readily explained by T: the right to free speech is a right against the government to make adequate provision for free speech and debate, a task the government has not accomplished if the actions of other citizens render free speech and debate impossible or unfeasible. By way of contrast, in most societies, people cannot reasonably assert that they lack adequate provision for speech and debate because they do not have the use of Jones' home for a fundraising event. In short, it is hard to see how the complex and shifting network of restrictions and requirements imposed by the right to speech can be explained without adverting, implicitly or explicitly, to the notion of adequate provision.

Privacy

The right to privacy has proven difficult to define. The "penumbral" right to privacy in American law appears to defy clear definition: it has been held, for instance, to cover sex between a man and a woman but not between two men. A woman's decision whether to abort is private as is a college student's grade and whether a patient has cancer. Pictures, images, and body parts have also been held to be protected by privacy. Some instances of recording conversations or eavesdropping violate privacy. Some instances of this purported right cover protected actions or decisions, others pertain to protected information, some to what others may see or hear. No clear line in the sand seems obvious. Yet the traditional view of natural rights requires such a clear line that is roughly the same across the globe. The traditional account of natural rights seems forced to say that, if a given law violates the natural right to privacy in France or Spain, it would also violate the natural right to privacy in an African village, for if natural rights are truly natural (not the result of particular covenants or social customs), and if they are boundary lines a state may not cross, then the same boundary must exist in Somalia and Seville. Granted, the traditional view allows one method by which social circumstances may play some role in determining which rights *in personam* follow from an *in rem* right to privacy: social circumstances may help determine the value of a variable in the description of a right *in rem*. Suppose, for example, the right to privacy is defined as the right to control information most persons would find it embarrassing for others to know. Information falling under this rubric in Somalia might not do so in Spain. So the natural right to free speech may give rise to different rights *in personam* in Spain and Somalia. Many legal headaches result from this need to find an appropriate generalized description of natural rights *in rem* that can be universally applied to particular laws. For example, the definition of privacy cited above fails in several respects: there are non-informational aspects of privacy, some private information is not embarrassing, etc.[31]

What, then, is privacy? Human beings are social individuals. Conservative writers characteristically stress the social aspect of human good, while liberal writers characteristically celebrate individuality. Burke and Hume, for example, emphasized the key role of tradition. More recently, Lord Devlin insisted upon the importance of social cohesion. A shared moral tradition constitutes the moral tradition necessary as a basis for moral reflection. As William Sullivan suggests,

"a tradition of moral life is...continuity in the kind of character and vision of life that define the actual projects of people over time. A living tradition is a continuing, often dramatic and conflictual, dialogue concerning those things [that] matter most deeply to its participants. A moral tradition of virtue is thus a continuity among varied forms of activity that is recognizable, at least to those participating in its practices, as valuable by reason of the sense of self and world that it sustains."[32]

A shared moral culture is not only the starting point for individual moral reflection. It is the starting point for responding to a differing way of life. It is only when I regard another culture, with sensitivity and careful attention, with the whole of my social and personal commitments, that I am moved by the goodness or badness of that way of life

But a history of social ties is more than causally necessary for developed human thought. Much of what is significant in human experience is essentially social. Stanley Cavell[33] and Charles Taylor[34] have argued in detail that our conceptions of ourselves depend in crucial ways upon our having a place in a social order. Moreover, not only friendship, gratitude and anger, but also many moral attitudes, depend upon viewing oneself as part of a moral community. Michael Walzer's *Obligations*[35] and Alisdair McIntrye's *After Virtue*[36] articulate some of the ways in which our sense of duty and obligation is rooted in ties to a community. Anthropologists have well documented the ways in which persons in different societies derive their sense of self from the social roles they play.

By contrast, Kant stressed the value of individual moral choice and Mill emphasized the freedom to pursue new and different approaches to the business of living a life. The ability to formulate conceptions of the good under the *aegis* of rationality is a crucial component of P. To surrender one's judgment to a collective will and deny the claim of reason upon our judgments is to make oneself unworthy of enfranchisement, to cede the very characteristic that makes human life valuable. A person is an individual judge, however much one's judgments are rooted in social life, who must try to make her findings about the world conform, as best as she is able, to truth, to the demands of reason. To give up the task of attempting to develop coherent and rational standards to which one is committed is to give up something essential to human flourishing, one's moral personhood.

In any case, societies are enriched when their members display important differences in values, aims, judgments and perceptions. In *On Liberty*, Mill pointed out that exposure to a diversity of views and styles of life has a variety of benefits. An unpopular opinion may nonetheless be true, or supplement the truth embodied in received opinions. In any case, to understand the truth fully, one must "feel the whole force of the difficulty which the true view of the subject has to encounter and dispose of...." (II, 23.) Otherwise "the shell and husk only of the meaning is retained, the finer essence being lost." (II, 26.) So the search for truth thrives on difference of opinion. But suppose we had indubitable knowledge of moral truth. Suppose we all shared the correct moral views, and had no need of experiments or disagreements to test our beliefs. Still, society would benefit if different people realized the common morality in different ways. Intellectual achievement and compassion are both good. So it is good for a society to have a Socrates and a Mother Teresa, not only because of the actual good they accomplish, but because it is good to have exemplars, ideal examples, of the virtues of intellection and service. Moreover, it would not be good if everyone devoted her life entirely to service, or entirely to intellection. This is only partly because the crops need to be harvested and the dishes washed. It is also because many smaller goods would be missing from human life. The little things of life, such as enjoying a good wine, growing potatoes on one's fire escape, strolling along a quiet stream and making friendship quilts, also have an important place in human life. In dedicating one's life to art or service, one necessarily gives up a great deal in human life that is of value. The life of the kind and thoughtful shoemaker is also a good one, though perhaps not as shining as that of a saint or an artist. A society that includes saints, artists, philosophers, and kind, thoughtful shoemakers realizes human good more fully than a society of only saints, philosophers and artists. So a society is stronger and richer, a better realization of human potential, when its members flourish in different ways, and seek different (if not opposing) goods or conceptions of a satisfying life.

Human flourishing requires that both dimensions of human life be adequately realized. Human beings are not purely social beings like ants nor purely private beings: they are distinct individuals who belong to a community, and both aspects of human existence must be recognized and given a chance to flourish if a human being is to achieve *eudaimonia*. Both make strong claims on legitimate states. Indeed, the social and the individual aspects of the good life are inseparable. One can't be an individual on Tuesdays and a social being on Wednesdays, or an individual in one's moral beliefs and a social animal in one's work. Our individuality depends in deep ways on our shared social goals, concepts, understandings and interactions. Obviously, we can't develop rich worldviews without being taught and raised by others. But also much of what is significant in a human life depends upon conceiving of oneself as part of a community, as belonging to a social order. Conversely, belonging to a good human community means bringing to the social order one's individual values and perceptions. Human communities are not like ant farms; they depend essentially upon differences of aims, views, outlooks and so forth.

These remarks suggest it is essential to P that individuals have adequate scope for private (non-social) time, concerns and activities, and thus that there is a natural right to adequate provision for the private. But the specific division between the private and the public is, to a large extent, a matter of custom. A law requiring persons to disrobe publicly would be a drastic incursion on privacy in our society, in which it is, perhaps irrationally, widely and deeply felt that the features of one's genitalia are an essential element of the private, i.e., that which pertains to life as an individual and not to life as part of the community. For most Americans, control over who views their genitals is central to feeling that one's body is one's own. Given the cultural milieu of American society, a law requiring public nudity would seriously undermine most citizens' sense that the legitimacy of the non-social aspects of their lives is respected. Moreover, the balance and harmony between the social and individual aspects of people's lives is threatened if appropriate forms of privacy are not viewed as entitlements, as fundamental aspects of the good life that must be respected, and which one may enjoy without the sufferance of others. Americans feel that the integrity of the private is respected not only because there are, in fact, no laws requiring public nudity, but because they feel *entitled*, warranted as their due, to keep their genitalia unviewed. It is not, after all, the fact that the shape and size of their genitalia are not generally known that makes Americans feel that their bodies are their own. It is rather a sense that others recognize an *obligation* not to view their genitalia without permission. Unless this loss to the integrity of the private lives of citizens is compensated for in some other way, an American law requiring public nudity would violate the right to privacy. In a (more rational) society in which human body parts are considered as much a part of the natural landscape as tree parts, such a law would not violate the right to privacy.

More generally, the important question is not whether particular items are kept private, but whether, given the circumstances of the society, the law as a whole makes adequate provision for citizens to feel that they can maintain key elements of life as an individual, that citizens have sufficient privacy to flourish (according to a rationally defensible vision of flourishing). An individual law may so severely infringe on the realm of the private that it may be judged, by itself, to violate the right to privacy. But, in general, the proper object of evaluation is not a particular law or policy but the laws and policies of the society as a whole. T recognizes that both Somalians and Spaniards have a right to adequate provision for the private, but recognizes that what counts as adequate provision in Somalia may be quite different from what counts as adequate provision in Spain. Indeed, it is hard to imagine an adequate generalized description of privacy that does not, implicitly or explicitly, advert to the notion of adequate provision.

Property

Leading a good human life requires some sort of special usage rights over various things. Special usage need not be ownership in the traditional sense, though such ownership is certainly one form of special usage right. Another form is usage priority. For example, others may use this hammer when I am not using it, but when I wish to use it they must cede it to me. Yet another form is having decision-making power over something. For example, while anyone may use this hammer, I may lay down rules for its use. Special usage rights may be permanent, rotating, or re-assignable either by the right-holder or by others. Thus by "property rights" I will mean something much broader than what is generally meant in discussions of property. A property right is any right of special usage over material objects, ideas, trademarks, land, organizations, etc. There is necessarily some degree of fuzziness in defining the scope of property rights. If Sheila alone has the right to have sex with her husband James, then in some sense Sheila has a special usage right on her James, though we would not ordinarily wish to call this a property right and are uncomfortable with speaking of Sheila's "usage" of James in this way. However, an employer in the United States does have a kind of property right over an employee's time during work hours. One can choose not to call this right a "property" right, but it does seem to function like a property right: the employer has priority over the employee's time, the employer has the right to lay down certain kind of rules over the use of the employee's time during work hours, etc. As a result, I will use the term "property right" somewhat loosely. The arguments are intended to show that there is natural right to adequate provision for special usage. If those arguments also establish a natural right to some things we would not normally call property rights, no harm is done, provided we really do have a natural right to those things, whether or not we call them property rights.

The argument for natural rights to property, in the sense described above, can be outlined simply:

1. Feasibly pursuing projects in some sort of rational way is a prerequisite for *eudaimonia*.
2. The feasibility of rationally pursuing such projects requires adequate provision for special usage rights.
3. Therefore adequate provision for special usage rights is a prerequisite for *eudaimonia*.
4. Therefore there is a natural right to adequate provision for special usage rights.

If thinkers as diverse as Locke, Marx, and Aristotle are correct that human beings are essentially creative producers, then feasibly pursuing projects in some sort of rational way is a central element of human *eudaimonia* (premise 1.). More specifically, if the human enterprise essentially involves (individually and/or collectively) fashioning a life and refashioning the world, in some ways, in accordance with standards or values (in the widest sense), then, since doing so constitutes and/or incorporates pursuing projects, feasibly pursuing projects in some sort of rational way is a prerequisite for human *eudaimonia*. Moreover, most of our way of life is based on the premise that people's projects matter. Contract law, for instance, has as its primary motivating goal establishing sufficient anticipatibility that individuals can rationally pursue their projects. It is not feasible to mount an opera if the theatre owner can, with impunity, change his mind and simply deny the use of his theatre, on the day of the performance, to the performers and audience who gathered to hear and play it. The penalties and remedies of contract law assure those who toiled to create the performance and those who paid to hear it that they can be reasonably sure of access to the arranged theatre and reasonably sure of compensation in the unlikely event they are denied that access. Similar points can be made about much of human life as we know it, including the moral duty of honesty, the social duty to respond to an RSVP before attending, the practice of inheritance, laws against homicide, and the institution of marriage. If people's projects are not of great importance, then much of our way of life is a mistake.

In virtually every society, and certainly in any modern society, the feasibility of rationally pursuing such projects requires adequate provision for special usage rights (premise 2.). Agriculture, for instance, is not feasible if others are at liberty, just before harvest, to pave over fields that have been cultivated all summer, a point as true of collective farming as it is of individually farmed fields. The building of shelters is not feasible if others are at liberty to push out the inhabitants in the middle of a storm or dismantle the shelters and walk off with the materials employed. Again, this point is as true of a single shelter used by an entire tribe or a system of collectively built shelters used on a rotating or assigned basis as it is of individually owned suburban houses. If I want to write, I need to be reasonably sure that the paper I have written on will not be taken away by someone else, shredded, and used as cat litter. Without some reasonably extensive system of special usage rights, formal or *de facto*, life becomes, using Hobbes' famous phrase, perhaps not solitary but nasty, brutish, and short.

Thus there is a natural right to adequate provision for special usage rights, since a society that does not make such provision within its boundaries, whether formally or *de facto*, does not make P feasible within its boundaries, and hence its use of force is not legitimate.

What specifically follows from this general argument is that *some* form of property rights are necessary for well-being. It does not follow that a free market system of absolute individual ownership is a natural right. Can it really be argued that unless I may buy a Rembrandt and burn it I cannot take feasible steps toward a rationally defensible conception of the good life? Unless such an argument (or an independent argument establishing the moral inviolability of absolute ownership) is forthcoming, the natural right to property does *not* mean the right of absolute ownership. Rather, a system of absolute ownership is merely one of many ways a society could observe the natural right to property. Indeed, it is arguable that a system of ownership violates natural rights if it entitles one farmer to poison his neighbors by spraying on her field highly toxic pesticides or entitles a company to endanger the environment by destroying all the rain forests, since, for example, it is not feasible to take rational steps toward well-being if one is dying of poison.

Instead, the natural right to property requires that each society, formally or *de facto*, maintain some or other network of special usage rights that is, overall, adequate to make feasible within its domain the rational pursuit of a rationally defensible conception of *eudaimonia*. There are, of course, many different ways a government might do this. In a modern industrial society, in which one person's decision affects others in a wide variety of ways, the only feasible way is to es-tablish a variety of different special usage rights appropriate to different types of property. It is more important to my well-being to be able to throw away my diary than it is to a farmer's well-being to be spread long-lived, dispersible poi-sons on his farm. Conversely, destroying my diary does not impede others in taking rational steps toward well-being the way that a farmer's spraying danger-ous pesticides does. Thus it seems that, in a modern industrial society, a government must establish a variety of public/private ownership relationships (special usage rights) in order to preserve its citizens' natural rights.[37] Personal clothing and toothbrushes, for example, might be owned absolutely, but not land or scarce and crucial resources. The owner of a mom and pop store might have greater special usage rights to their store than the owners of a multinational corporation have to their corporation, since their need to control what happens in their store is greater and the consequences to others of their decisions less pervasive.

Once again, the holistic approach to natural rights yields more plausible results than traditional views. While it is plausible to maintain that some sort of natural right to property exists, it is implausible to insist that a government that does not allow me to cut down a tree in my backyard violates my natural rights. Rather than engage in the difficult (and so far unsuccessful) task of drawing defensible lines in the sand that apply to all societies at all times in human history, T simply requires that some or other system of special usage rights be in place that, overall, in that particular society at that time, is sufficient to make reasonably feasible, under the circumstances, the rational pursuit of *eudaimonia*. Vastly different systems in different cultures and different times can meet this requirement. Kibbuzim, small villages operating largely on free market principles, tribal cultures, and mixed systems of regulation and private ownership, such as the United States in the year 2007, can all observe the natural right to property, in their own very different ways.

Conclusion

This holistic approach to rights generates more plausible results than does the piecemeal approach of evaluating separately each piece of legislation to see whether it crosses some imaginary line in the sand. It seems distinctly odd to say that a government is illegitimate simply because it does not permit a person to say a particular four-letter word on a particular occasion, just as it seems an over-reaction to say that a government violates natural rights simply because it requires everyone's weight to be reported to health officials, when those governments provide copious opportunity for free debate and generous spheres of privacy. Contrary to the assumptions of some U.S. politicians, neither the right to vote nor the right to capitalistic ownership is a natural right. Rather, the relevant natural rights are the more general rights to significant participation and to adequate provision for special usage. A system of elections and capitalistic ownership is but one way, among others, of realizing these natural rights. Conversely, on traditional accounts of rights, natural rights are not violated when a government systematically undercuts individuals' ability to debate freely by instituting a series of restrictions, none of which goes quite so far as to cross the imaginary line. The holistic approach eliminates both these undesirable results. Individuals may be prohibited from using particular words on particular occasions without violating their natural right to free speech,[38] provided that, overall, adequate opportunity exists for inhabitants forcefully and freely to advocate their views. Legislation or policies that restrict speech, no matter how innocuous if taken singly, are impermissible if, collectively, given the rest of the law and the society's circumstances, they do not allow adequate opportunity for debate and discussion.

In sum, the new theory of rights provides a firm basis for the existence of natural rights (a basis as firm as the grounds for claiming that wanton killing of persons is wrong), provides a mechanism for determining which natural rights exist, eliminates some infelicities to which more traditional theories of rights are prone, and has significant practical consequences for law and political theory.

Notes to Chapter Five

1 For the sake of simplicity, the difference between "persons" and "human beings" will be ignored. That difference becomes crucial, however, when considering non-human persons or human beings who are not full persons. The rights, if any, of alien life forms, dolphins, and neonates raise issues beyond the scope of this chapter. T could be expanded to generate partial rights for partial persons, as I would urge, or applied directly to dolphins or neonates should they qualify as full moral "persons." After all, if dolphins are full moral persons then P pertains to dolphins and so, absent further arguments to the contrary, dolphins too would have a warrant to adequate provision for P.

2 Richard Wasserstrom, for example, in "Rights, Human Rights, and Racial Discrimination," *Journal of Philosophy* 61, October 29, 1964, pp. 628-641, reprinted in David Lyons, ed., *Rights*, Belmont, CA: Wadsworth Publishing Company, 1979, pp. 46-57, cites as one of the common objections to doctrines of natural rights "the lack of any ground or argument for any doctrine of natural rights", p. 47. Many insightful discussions of rights lack such a foundation. For example, Bruce Russell says of Judith Jarvis Thomson that, in her *The Realm of Rights*, Cambridge: Harvard University Press, 1990, "she has not yet thoroughly explored the bedrock which underlies that realm", p. 172. Russell, Bruce, "Exploring *The Realm of Rights*," *Philosophy and Phenomenological Research* 52:1, March 1993, pp. 169-172.

3 *Universal Declaration of Human Rights*, adopted by the General Assembly of the United Nations on December 10, 1948.

4 Loren Lomasky, for example, in *Persons, Rights, and the Moral Community*, New York, Oxford: Oxford University Press, 1987, p. 11, suggests that rights "spring from a commitment to the value of the individual" and "the notion that each person possesses a kind of sovereignty over his own life." Richard Posner, in *The Economics of Justice*, 2nd ed., Cambridge: Harvard University Press, 1983, has argued that rights have their roots in economic efficiency while Richard Bosanquet in *The Philosophical Theory of the State*, 4th ed., London: Macmillan Publishers, 1951, and L. Sumner in "Rights Denaturalized" in R.G. Frey, ed., *Utility and Rights*, Minneapolis: University of Minnesota Press, 1984, pp. 20-41, have argued that rights spring from maximizing utility. T is consistent with all of these claims, that is, each of these claims can find a congenial home in some version of T.

5 Talbott, William J., *Which Rights Should be Universal*, Oxford, New York: Oxford University Press, 2005, p. 9.

6 The alternative, that governments may use force just until the reasonable pursuit of P becomes feasible, then must stop until the reasonable pursuit of P becomes unfeasible, and may then immediately (briefly) resume the use of force, is clearly absurd, even if, as is doubtful, it is possible at all to make the reasonable pursuit of P feasible for individuals who know that it will shortly become unfeasible.

7 Certain forms of relativism or subjectivism might appear to deny 1). For example, if the only constraint on conduct concerning others is that I treat others consistently with my own moral code, whatever it may happen to be, and if my own moral code permits any use of force I wish to employ, then there is a moral constraint on my conduct concerning others but the use of force against persons requires no justification. It is not clear, however, that in such a case the constraint on my conduct concerning others counts as a genu-

ine constraint. Since my own moral code allows me to treat you any way I feel like treating you, it amounts to saying "I am morally required to treat you any way I feel like treating you." This appears to be, at best, a *pro forma* constraint.

8 For one such argument, see Schlossberger, Eugene, *Moral Responsibility and Persons*, Philadelphia: Temple University Press, 1992.

9 A sketch of such a moral epistemology may be found in Schlossberger, Eugene, "Environmental Ethics: An Aristotelian Approach" *Philosophy in the Contemporary World* 8:2, Fall-Winter 2001, pp. 15-26.

10 Cf., for example, Wellman, Christopher Heath, "Towards a Liberal Theory of Political Obligation," *Ethics* 111 #4, July 2001, pp. 735-759; p. 743: "coercive states are the only feasible method of ensuring territorially defined authorities, and this is why I presume that they offer the only viable solution to the perils of a state of nature."

11 Arguably, this insight provides plausibility to Hobbes' claim that, in the kind of world Hobbes calls a "state of nature," there is no proscription against the use of force.

12 See, for example, Simmons, A. John, *Moral Principles and Political Obligations*, Princeton: Princeton University Press, 1979.

13 Gewirth, Alan, *Human Rights: Essays on Justification and Applications*, Chicago: University of Chicago Press, 1982, p. 1.

14 Of course, virtually no legal system conforms strictly to ER: legal systems routinely and legitimately distinguish between categories of litigants, e.g., executive privilege accords special rights to the president, as president.

15 Gregory Vlastos, for example, in "Justice and Equality" in Richard B. Brandt, ed., *Social Justice*, Englewood Cliffs, New Jersey: Prentice Hall, 1962, pp. 31-72, argues that equality of rights derives from the purported fact that when any two individuals enjoy the same good, their enjoyment of that good is of equal intrinsic value. Such views require significant caveats. For example, if incarcerating criminals is justifiable, the enjoyment of liberty of a convicted felon does not have the same intrinsic value as the enjoyment of liberty of an innocent citizen. Even when properly hedged with caveats, however, Vlastos' principle is controversial.

16 Suppose, for example, that Alan Gewirth in *Reason and Morality*, Chicago: University of Chicago Press, 1978, is right that each person must admit that she values her autonomy and that others have as good a reason to value their own autonomy as she does to value her own. An additional argument is required to show that seeking to maximize aggregate autonomy is not an appropriate response to this fact.

17 Jeremy Waldron, in "Theoretical Foundations of Liberalism," *Philosophical Quarterly* 37, 1987, pp. 127-150, reprinted in Waldron, Jeremy, *Liberal Rights*, Cambridge: Cambridge University Press, 1993, pp. 35-62, says that the "justification of the social world....its legitimacy...must be made out to each individual....If there is some individual to whom a justification cannot be given, then so far as he is concerned the social order had better be replaced by other arrangements", p. 44. If Waldron is correct, the view that natural rights apply substantially to all has an obvious advantage.

18 Mabbott, J.B., *The State and the Citizen*, London: Arrow Books, 1958. Similarly, L. W. Sumner, in "Rights Denaturalized," *op. cit.*, p. 22, says "We will count as a natural-rights theory any moral theory that satisfies the following four conditions: 1) it contains

some rights, 2) it treats its rights as morally basic, 3) it ties possession of its rights to possession of some natural property, and 4) it accepts some form of realist moral episte-mology." T does not count as a natural right theory by Sumner's definition. For example, T does not necessarily treat its rights as morally basic in the sense that right principles are "grounded by no other moral principle in the theory",, p. 25. Right principles stem from an account of P, and the claim that it is necessary to justify force against things possess-ing P might be derived from more basic moral grounds. Richard Wasserstrom (in "Rights, Human Rights, and Racial Discrimination," *op. cit.*) suggests that human rights are possessed equally by all human beings, are not the result of any particular status or relationship, and are assertable against all other human beings. The arguments given for T do not require that natural rights be possessed equally (though additional arguments may require this). Moreover, on T, rights are assertable specifically against societies or governments rather than against all other human beings.

19 Bentham, in *Anarchical Fallacies*, T. J. Bowring (ed.), *Works*, v.2, William Tate, Edinburgh, 1843, appears to define natural rights as rights "anterior to the establishment of governments," which rights* are, logically if not chronologically: they are conditions upon the legitimacy of any government, rather than an artifact created by one. In a similar vein, Margaret Macdonald, in "Natural Rights," *Proceedings of the Aristotelian Society*, 1947-1948, reprinted in Melden, A.I., ed., *Human Rights*, Belmont, CA: Wadsworth, 1970, pp. 40-60, describes natural rights as rights people have "as human beings, inde-pendently of the laws and governments of any existing society", p. 42. Similarly, rights* are natural rights in what R.G. Frey calls "the broad sense," that is, they "are preinstitu-tional moral rights" that "antedate such institutions and serve as constraints on which institutions we should have." Frey, R.G., "Act-Utilitarianism, Consequentialism, and Moral Rights," in *Utility and Rights, op. cit.*, 61-85: p. 63. H.L.A. Hart identifies two central features of natural rights: they are possessed by all persons, regardless of which special relationships they might have, and are not created by any voluntary actions. (Hart, H.L.A., "Are There any Natural Rights?" *Philosophical Review* 64, April 1955, pp. 171-191.) Rights* exhibit both features. Rights* are also what Mackie defines as "basic ab-stract" rights, in that "any specific moral or political theory or system can be defended or criticized (or both) by considering to what extent its provisions and workings....can be seen as applying, implementing, and realizing those basic abstract rights." Mackie, J.L., "Rights, Utility, and Universalization," in Frey, ed., *op. cit.*, 86-105: pp. 87-88. Rights* also qualify as "natural rights" by Tibor Machan's definition. Machan defines rights as "social conditions that ought to be maintained, moral principles pertaining to aspects of social life", p. 2, and natural rights as rights we have "just by virtue of being human and living with other human beings", p. 3. Machan, Tibor, *Individuals and their Rights*, La Salle, IL: Open Court, 1989. A right, suggests Henry Shue in *Basic Rights*, Princeton: Princeton University Press, 1980, "provides (1) the rational basis for a justified demand (2) that the actual enjoyment of a substance be (3) socially guaranteed against standard threats", p. 13, and rights* meet these three criteria. They are rights in Feinberg's sense of "valid claim" (Feinberg, Joel, "The Nature and Value of Rights," *Journal of Value Inquiry* 4, Winter 1970, pp. 243-257) and "natural" in the sense that those claims do not arise from any special circumstance or action (such as contracting).

20 I am indebted to John Rowan for raising this point in conversation.

21 For example, Chapter 7 argues that there are moral rights, in the sense of justified moral expectations, based on duties of "team loyalty" members of the moral enterprise

owe to one another. Wanton killing would violate those duties and hence violate a moral right.

22 Even if the code is based entirely on following tradition, the importance of adhering to tradition becomes the moral basis of the code. In such a society, P would be understood as membership in the broad community encapsulating the traditions. (I say "broad community" because it might include land or trees, for example.) If that view is correct, then there is a natural right to adequate provision for realizing and preserving tradition.

23 One exception might be an extreme view that the only legitimate aim of the state is to impose order, where the nature of the order imposed is unimportant. Were that view correct, the only natural right would be to adequate provision for order. However, presumably order is an instrumental good: order, even on such a view, is most plausibly understood as important because it enables certain other things, e.g., sufficient anticipatibility to pursue projects. In that case, the ability to pursue projects becomes the underlying rationale for state force (and so P becomes the ability to pursue projects). If something else besides order, Q, is necessary to the pursuit of projects, it is unclear why a state is legitimate if the order it imposes forbids Q, since the order imposed by that state blocks the very thing that makes the imposition of order important. Similar points could be raised against other exceptions.

24 An interesting dilemma then arises if the dominant code of the society requires individuals to flaunt their societies' predominant views when their own consciences so dictate, e.g., a society whose most cherished dictum is "to thine own self be true."

25 What counts as adequate provision would vary radically from society to society, but T, as section D. points out, is quite consistent with that form of cultural relativity.

26 Rawls, John, *A Theory of Justice*, Cambridge, MA: Harvard University Press, 1971.

27 Another feature of T is that it helps clarify the conceptual link between theories of natural rights and concepts of personhood. Louis G Lombardi, for example, suggests on p. 112 of *Moral Analysis: Formulations, Guides, and Applications*, Albany: State University of New York Press, 1988, that there is much overlap in result between the views of Dworkin, Richards, Melden, Vlastos, and Wasserstrom because "underlying each view is a conception of personhood." Whether or not Lombardi is correct about these particular views, T makes evident which specific aspects of theories of personhood ground natural rights. What counts in determining natural rights is 1) which features of persons require the use of force against persons to be justified and 2) what is necessary to make the instantiation of those features feasible. Claims about those two categories are not unrelated to theories of personhood, but different accounts of personhood might nonetheless agree about those claims. Moreover, even theories of personhood that disagree about those two claims might yield similar sets of natural rights. Suppose, for example, that, it follows from theory A) that P is happiness and that free debate is essential for the feasible pursuit of happiness, while it follows from theory B) that P is the rational exercise of autonomy and that free debate is essential to the rational exercise of autonomy. Then both A) and B), despite their vast differences, yield a natural right to free debate, although what counts as adequate provision might differ between the theories. Conversely, two theories that both define personhood in terms of the rational exercise of autonomy could yield quite different sets of natural rights if they define autonomy (or what is necessary for autonomy) differently.

28 Langlois, Anthony J., *The Politics of Justice and Human Rights*, Cambridge: Cambridge University Press, 2001.

29 Some reason for holding C to be mistaken emerges from section E.'s discussion of privacy. While space does not allow the detailed development of such arguments, it is worth noting that there are good reasons, both theoretical and historical, to believe that if societies A and C are allowed to converse and observe each other freely, without imposing physical force, over a long period of time, A's view of P will become predominant in C. If it is correct that in "fair" conditions A's view will win out in the long term, that fact provides at least some reason to think A's view is correct. See Schlossberger, "Environmental Ethics: An Aristotelian Approach," *op. cit.*

30 As noted in Chapter 1, the distinction between "negative" and "positive" rights is at best a loose *facon de parler*.

31 See, for example, Fried, Charles, *An Anatomy of Values: Problems of Personal and Social Choice*, Cambridge, MA: Harvard University Press, 1970 and Benn, Stanley I., "Privacy, Freedom, and Respect for Persons," in J. Roland Pennock and John W. Chapman, eds., *Privacy* [*Nomos* v. 13], New York: Atherton Press, 1971, pp. 1-26.

32 Sullivan, William M., *Reconstructing Public Philosophy*, University of California Press: 1986, p. 111.

33 Cavell, Stanley, *The Claim of Reason*, Oxford: Oxford University Press, 1979.

34 Taylor, Charles, *Human Agency and Language*, Cambridge: Cambridge University Press, 1985.

35 Walzer, Michael, *Obligations*, Cambridge, MA: Harvard University Press, 1970.

36 MacIntyre, Alisdair, *After Virtue*, 2nd ed., University of Notre Dame Press: 1984.

37 It is worth noting how Locke's view of property rights, beloved of many free market advocates, fares when coupled with the notion of opportunity capital argued for in Schlossberger, Eugene, "A New Model of Business: Dual Investor Theory," *Business Ethics Quarterly* 4, Fall 1994, pp. 459-474. Locke's view, roughly put, is that a person gains property rights in a thing when she mixes her labor with it, providing she leaves as much and as good for others. Now, when a person makes a pot or plows a field, she is mixing not only her own labor with the clay or land, but also the labors of those who provided the opportunity capital employed (such as the inventors of the relevant agricultural and ceramic techniques). Thus, if Locke is right, those who provide the opportunity capital are partial owners of the field or pot.

38 It might nonetheless be argued that the right to use "obscene" words at will is a presumptive right or a right ensconced in our society's regulative ideals. See Chapter 6.

Chapter 6
The Right to Speech: Regulating Violence and Pornography in the Media

Does the right to speech protect pornography from government regulation? This question has tended to be the focal point for debates about speech rights, although many other questions, such as the right to broadcast falsehoods and the right to advocate violence, are not without importance. This chapter begins with some analysis of speech rights and the nature of pornography and concludes with a practical proposal for regulating violence and sex in the media, a proposal that illustrates the "holistic" approach to balancing rights and public goals that should inform our thinking not only about pornography but about such pressing issues as privacy versus security.

A. Five Levels of Speech Rights

It is a mistake to speak of *the* right to free speech. Rights are networks of warrants, and several different kinds of rights pertain to speech. Speech rights might include a permission to recite the names of the planets in my back yard, an entitlement to government protection from being forcibly prevented by my neighbor from reciting them, and various forms of public support for the ability to exercise the right of speech (a liberty). The natural right to free speech, as Chapter 5 suggested, is a warrant each of us has to demand, as our due, that governments make, within their domains, provision for free speech adequate, in the circumstances, for the feasibility of P (the feature of persons that requires force against persons to be justified), that is, to take reasonable measures to safeguard the taking of feasible rational steps toward formulating, pursuing, and instantiating (individually and collectively) a morally defensible conception of a good human life. In addition to the natural right to free speech, there may be moral and presumptive rights regarding speech, warrants that should be part of the law or public morality of a society, but whose absence does not render the govern-

ment illegitimate. For instance, the presumption in favor of permissibility
suggests that legal systems should not outlaw a speech act without a strong reason.

More specific than natural, presumptive, and moral rights are the positive
rights a given society adopts. The positive legal speech rights of a society are
those rights in fact recognized by that society's law. The right of a newspaper to
be non-maliciously reckless in reporting on a public figure became a positive
legal speech right in the United States after *New York Times Co. v. Sullivan*, 376
U.S. 254 (1964). Some systems of positive law violate natural rights in various
ways, but many, quite different systems of positive rights are consistent with
natural rights. Mediating between positive rights on one hand and natural and
presumptive rights on the other are regulative ideals of public law or morality.
As Chapter 1 indicated, a regulative ideal is a particular vision, a particular conception of how natural, presumptive, and moral rights are to be embedded in a
society, which is partly definitive of a society and may be used to criticize or
evaluate that society's positive law.

Thus speech rights may fall into five categories: natural, presumptive,
moral, regulative ideal, and positive. Each speech right, in any category, is a
network of warrants that may include liberties, permissions, entitlements, powers, or other forms of warrant.

B. Six Conceptions of Freedom of Expression

An adequate discussion of speech rights must incorporate a conception of
the role of speech. There are at least six quite different ways of understanding
speech that lead to quite different results, both substantially and in the ways in
which questions about what is protected by the right of speech are posed and
answered. Speech may be conceived:

1) As an instance of general autonomy:

Since freedom of expression is a major instance or example of the exercise
of autonomy, rights of expression are instances of rights protecting autonomy.

2) As a precondition of general autonomy:

Freedom of expression is necessary in order for people effectively to exercise their autonomy. Rights of expression are protected necessary means or
preconditions for autonomy, making them either derivative of autonomy
rights, if viewed as merely instrumentally useful, or more basic, in the sense
that the exercise of other rights depends upon their possession.

3) As free debate and discussion:

Free debate and discussion are essential ingredients for forming rational
and/or true beliefs. The process of thinking and discovering is valuable,
and/or having rational or true beliefs is valuable, either in itself or as a
means for some other end. Rights of expression protect free debate and discussion.

4) As a personal good:

> We have a direct personal interest in expressing ourselves, either because expressing oneself is itself a goal or because expressing oneself is a means of achieving pleasure or intimacy or some other personal good. Of particular interest is the view that expression is an essential aspect of self-realization. Rights of expression serve to protect that interest.

5) As an important social condition:

> Freedom of expression is important because societies flourish best when issues, ideas, etc. are freely discussed within them. Thus freedom of expression is important because of its salubrious effect on community life.

6) As a precondition for political equality and/or an implicit condition or value of democracy:

> Political equality requires that speech as an instrument for effecting one's will must be equally available to all. Some maintain that speech rights are, in some sense, implicit in the right of self-governance.

These six views of speech need not be mutually exclusive. Free speech might be important for several independent reasons, e.g., free speech may be an important good both for individuals (4) because it conduces to self-realization and for societies (5) because it acts as a peaceful vent for conflict and hence enhances the stability of a society of individuals with conflicting interests. Two or more of these conceptions of speech can be linked. For example, among the most venerable conceptions of the importance of free speech is the "marketplace of ideas": when all ideas are freely presented, John Stuart Mill suggests in Chapter 2 of *On Liberty*, the best ideas will win and truth will prevail, or, at least, truth is more likely to prevail in the long run. If the marketplace of ideas is an essential corrective in a democracy to errors of government and democratic societies are to be preferred, then speech rights protect free debate and discussion (3) as essential ingredients in reaching truth, a protection whose importance lies in the fact that free debate and discussion is an important social condition (5), namely, that it is required for the health of a democratic society (6). C. Edwin Baker's view, that free speech and democratic government are related aspects of the fundamental commitment to liberty as such, entails both 1) and 6).[1] Different conceptions may be given unequal weight or status: some of the six may be held as primary and others as secondary. Each of the six views of speech may consistently be held by someone who holds that one or more of the other five views are either incorrect or not directly relevant to the reason speech deserves protection. For instance, one could hold that speech is a major instance of individual autonomy (1) while also insisting that speech is no more of a precondition for the exercise of autonomy than wealth, health, or any other major good (2), that debate and discussion are no more important instances of autonomy than yelling randomly chosen phonemes (3), that autonomy, while the central right, is, *per se*, less of a good than many other things not given legal protection (4), that the social benefits of free speech are either nugatory or irrelevant (5), and that the best form of government is not electoral (6) but a committee of the wisest setting rules and practices that optimize autonomy within the society. Alternatively, one could hold that free speech is conceptually entailed by democracy (6) without claiming that it produces any particular social benefits (5). A third possible view asserts that the pre-eminent moral concern is that individuals live and/or believe correctly (rather than autonomously) and that free speech as debate and advocacy (3) is necessary for individuals to reach truth or make the best decisions, while denying both that general autonomy is important *per se* (1 and 2) and that democracy is a good form of government (6). These are only a few of the possibilities.

Selecting a conception of speech has significant consequences. For instance, each conception of free expression gives rise to different arguments concerning the protection of pornography. In addition, different conceptions give different content to the right of freedom of expression. Since viewing or producing pornography is an expression of autonomous choice, pornography would appear to fall within the realm of speech-rights protection on conception 1). On conception 3), however, political, scholarly, artistic, and moral debate are protected by rights of expression, as is the production of artworks that can be viewed as attempts at understanding or thinking through issues and experiences. Pornography would not be protected by the right of expression, on conception 3), unless it could be shown that pornography is a form of debate and discussion. John Rowan[2] finds it unclear how pornography can lead to the discovery of moral truth, and so concludes that pornography is not protected by the marketplace of ideas argument that "the public is best served when there is exposure to the ideas and beliefs of others, regardless of how bizarre or extreme they seem" (p. 137).[3] Rowan defines pornography as "explicit depiction of nonegalitarian sexual activity" (p. 136). Can some explicit depictions of nonegalitarian sexual activity be viewed as urging or promoting the idea that nonegalitarian sex is good? Rowan wrote, in correspondence (November 17, 2004), that "explicit depiction of nonegalitarian sexual activity does not, in itself, promote the public discovery of ethical truth. However, public discussion of the particular claim that 'nonegalitarian sex is good' might well further the discovery of moral truth." Depiction, however, is often a form of advocacy. The manner in which Upton Sinclair depicts working class life is not only advocacy, but a form of argument. Similarly, one can readily conceive of a film that explicitly depicts nonegalitarian sex in a manner that urges and highlights the (purported) merits of nonegalitarian sex, and hence effectively advocates the view, whether explicitly stated or not, that nonegalitarian sex is good. Pornography, as a rule, does not just depict nonegalitarian sex, but depicts it with approval. Such approving depiction may be both an irreplaceable method of capturing the purported merits of nonegalitarian sex and a defining characteristic of pornography. After all, we might hesitate to call "pornographic" a film that depicts nonegalitarian sex in a harshly negative way, however explicit the depiction might be. It is by advocating and promoting ideas, e.g., that women are merely objects of desire and that nonegalitarian sex is good, that pornographic films, in the eyes of many feminists, support the oppression of women. In short, the explicit depiction of nonegalitarian sex may well expose the public to the idea and belief that such nonegalitarian sex is good, in which case it would seem to fall within the scope of the marketplace of ideas argument, unless one assumes not just that "nonegalitarian sex is good" is a bizarre or extreme view but so benighted that thinking about the view that "nonegalitarian sex is good" cannot possibly contribute in any manner to discovering moral truth. In any case, pornography may not fall within the protected range of less extreme versions of conception 3), that is, versions that do not protect every idea, however benighted. Conception 4), by contrast, sees rights of expression as protecting self-expression, and thus rights of expression would include pornography to the extent that pornography is a form of self-expression. Since conception 5) views rights of expression in terms of their useful effects on social life, pornography would be included in rights of expression to the extent that permitting pornography enhances the life of the community and excluded to the extent that it does not. Conception 6) protects pornography only to the extent that pornography can be a form of contribution to the political process. Rowan claims that pornography "fails to meet the criterion of being intended and received as a contribution to political deliberation" (p. 138). While Rowan may be correct about the intentions of pornographers, as noted earlier, graphic depiction of nonegalitarian sex can function as advocacy of the view that nonegalitarian sex is good. Promoting the idea that nonegalitarian sex is good could constitute a contribution to deliberation concerning at least one law, regulation, judicial ruling, tax code, electoral decision, or other element of the political process, particularly in light of the fact that the sex lives of various politicians has in fact been made an issue in several elections. While pornographic films may not be regarded by their viewers as political speech, they can contribute effectively to the political process: some instances of pornography can be regarded as advocacy of views that pertain in significant ways to political issues. Reasons for protecting political speech, then, can apply as well to pornography: to take away the ability to distribute pornographic material is to take away one vehicle for contributing to political deliberation. Thus, whether or not pornography is intended as a contribution to political deliberation, it can arguably be a contribution to political deliberation and so arguably deserve protection on conception 6).

If pornography is within the scope of rights of expression, then there is at least a *prima facie* reason not to ban pornography. It does not follow that pornography should be permitted: most views include some form of liberty-limiting principle. On 4), for example, while expressing oneself through pornography might be a personal good for pornographers, permitting pornography could be detrimental to someone else's personal good, and so the good of pornographers' self-expression must be weighed against the concomitant setbacks to other peoples' interests. Similarly, even the most ardent advocates of autonomy typically propose some limits on autonomy rights. Someone who holds 1), for instance, might believe in the harm principle: it is a legitimate reason (perhaps the only legitimate reason) for proscribing x that x harms other people. 1) might thus be consistent with banning pornography if it can be shown that permitting pornography harms other people (people other than the voluntary viewer or the voluntary creator of the pornographic material).

The natural right to free speech, I suggest, centers on 3), 4), and 5), that is, on speech, discussion, expression, and advocacy as necessary conditions for and/or crucial elements of the feasible pursuit of (objectively) good human lives, individually and communally. In general, since it is dubious that people cannot feasibly pursue objectively good human lives without access to pornography, pornography, as such, is not protected by the natural right to free speech. However, people may be warranted on other grounds in claiming, as their due, immunity from restrictions on access to pornography: natural rights are not the only kinds of rights. Indeed, if freedom of expression is, other things being equal, a good, and if pleasure is, other things being equal, a good, and if some people derive pleasure from pornographic material, then the presumption in favor of permissibility suggests that access to pornography should be permitted unless a strong argument is mounted in favor of proscribing that access. In any case, people would have some (vector) rights to view pornography, though perhaps no resultant rights. Moreover, 6) is a regulative ideal of the United States, and hence there is some reason to think that, in the United States (as well as other countries that share this ideal), there exist speech rights rooted in regulative ideals. To the extent that pornographic material can constitute a contribution to the democratic process, then, there is a vector right within the United States to possess and promulgate pornography. The question then becomes how strong these vector rights are and how strong is the case for proscribing or limiting access to pornography.

A closer look is thus warranted at each of the six aspects, what each involves, what scope it offers for speech protection, and why it is or is not a crucial element of P.

Speech as self-realization

Speech is a major aspect of self-realization in at least three (related) major ways. First, speech as proclamation is an essential aspect of self-realization. As moral beings, we realize our worldviews, we express our personhood (the unique persons we are), partly through the rhetorical dimension of proclaiming, through our words and our actions, our values, principles, attitudes, perceptions, and stances. I have suggested elsewhere that the Kantian principle of universality should be understood as "live in a way that proclaims 'this is a good way of life for our society.'"[4] This basic moral precept applies to actions, of course, but it applies equally to words and even feelings. The moral life involves not just a behavioral fit between morality and how one lives, that is, that one's life conforms to the requirements of morality, but that one's life expresses and proclaims that morality. The moral life is a commitment, a public stance, not merely insuring that one's conduct conforms to certain rules. Some religious individuals speak of the imperative to "bear witness." Shorn of theology, it is a useful concept—the moral life involves bearing witness. If this conception of the moral life is correct, then some significant provision for free speech, at least with regard to values and life-stances, is an essential element of realizing ourselves as moral beings and so is an important aspect of or precondition for P.

Second, human beings are storytellers by nature. We experience our lives, both individually and as a community, as a story, where events have point in the narrative, where some things are narratively significant and others are not, because they have meaning in terms of the narrative framework of the story, the network of operating concepts, motifs, and so forth, that make it a story and not just a collection of events or details. Storytelling creates the personal reality of events—in a sense, from your point of view, if you don't tell your story, it didn't happen. I am not denying an objective reality in saying this. When Brutus stabs Caesar, so much steel moves so many inches, regardless of whether anyone says anything about it. But we don't live, psychologically, in a world of steel moving so many inches. We live in a world of betrayal, of revenge, of placing public weal above personal feelings, and so forth. Without storytelling, the world exists, but it is not a human world, for a human world is a world of meaning within a story. To realize ourselves as fully human, we must tell stories. Even memory, I would suggest, functions as a storyteller. We do not generally remember events or sensations as such. We store various cues, and when remembering something, we invent a story from the cues. Thus if I am recalling visiting Sharon's house in winter, I access my memory template for *house*, my memory template for *winter*, and perhaps a few other stored cues (e.g., *brick*), and from them construct a visual or verbal picture. I will perhaps see snow on the roof in my memory image because I mistakenly think the visit took place in winter, though, in fact, it occurred on a hot July day. Storytelling is at the heart of our experience as human beings, and storytelling is essentially a social interaction. We can and do tell stories to ourselves, but, when we do, we play two roles, much as when playing chess against oneself. The model of storytelling always involves an implicit speaker and an implicit hearer in a social relationship. In some sense, telling a story to oneself is parasitic upon telling stories to others. (There is a reason why solitary confinement is held to be a harsh punishment.) Thus being free to tell our stories is an essential aspect of self-realization. If this conception of human experience as narrative is correct, then some significant provision for free speech, at least with regard to our stories about ourselves and the world as we experience it, is an essential element of realizing ourselves as human beings and so is an important aspect of or precondition for P.

Finally, we are social beings. It is the social eye that fixes, at least to a significant degree, who we are. How we are seen and heard by others defines, in part, the self one is. What Tom Holland said of ancient Rome applies to many societies: "Only by seeing himself reflected in the gaze of his fellows could a Roman truly know himself as a man."[5] If this is correct, then some significant provision for the ability freely to tell our stories, proclaim our values and life-stances, explain ourselves, and influence how others understand us is an essential element of realizing ourselves as persons, and so is an important aspect of or precondition for P.

Speech as free debate and discussion

"Free debate" does not mean absolutely unrestricted debate about anything. What is at stake is the ability to explore ideas, follow lines of argument and evidence in the broadest sense (including, for example, how it feels to live a particular way), consider positions, develop theories and perspectives, etc. The natural right to free speech, construed as free debate and discussion, requires only that adequate provision is made for persons to engage in these activities within a society's boundaries. Forbidding the use of split infinitives, for instance, restricts debate in some sense, but, generally, does not preclude rational consideration of ideas. One can convey and make manifest the joys of devoting oneself to one's children without splitting infinitives. In contrast, severe punishments for asserting that the earth revolves around the sun do effectively preclude rational investigation of astronomy, as well as, for example, theories of gravity and certain views about the place of human beings within the cosmos.

Free debate and discussion may be considered critical for the living of good human lives for any of several reasons, including:

A.   Free debate and discussion are important for formulating, fully understanding, and applying correct views, reasonable conceptions of the good, life plans, projects, etc.

B.   Free debate and discussion are important for convincing others to share in and co-operate with projects, conceptions, social institutions, etc.

C.   Free debate and discussion are important for resolving disputes between individuals and/or groups.

D.   The exercise of the mind in free debate and discussion is developmentally necessary for and/or itself an important element of a good human life.

The most familiar rationale for free debate and discussion is Mill's marketplace of ideas argument. C. Edwin Baker, in perhaps the most detailed treatment of speech rights in print,[6] suggests that this argument in support of speech rights makes three assumptions:

1)   that objective truth exists,

2)   that people are basically rational, that is, the fixation of their beliefs depends primarily upon rational and objective evaluation of ideas and not social perspective or advertising and packaging, and

3)   that truth is the best basis for action.

Baker denies all three assumptions. His arguments for these crucial points are, he admits, cursory. However, he bases several major claims and arguments upon the purported falsity of these three assumptions and the arguments he does give do not support the conclusions he later draws. Baker argues that objective truth does not exist since scientists replace an old theory with a new one when the new one does more of what we value, and, hence, what scientists believe is based in part upon value judgments. This argument, of course, confuses the fixation of belief with objective truth. Even if deciding what to believe always involves value judgments, the beliefs chosen could still be objectively correct or incorrect. However, even if we are only talking about whether the content of people's beliefs are "chosen" or "discovered," Baker's statement that a new theory does more of what we value presupposes an objective truth about some things, e.g., that the airplane really does fly or that we really do have a sense experience of a needle pointing at the numeral "3" on the dial. That is, in saying that we adopt theory 1 instead of theory 2 because theory 1 is more useful to us when we build airplanes one implicitly asserts that it is a (discoverable) objective fact that we build airplanes. If, instead, one asserts that we adopt theory 1 because we believe it is more useful to us when we are doing what we believe is building airplanes, then one is implicitly asserting that there is a (discoverable) objective fact about what we believe. Not only does Baker's argument fail to show that there is no objective truth: it assumes that there is one. Perhaps some more careful formulation could avoid this problem. But, at least on the face of it, Baker's remarks seem to assume that there are at least some discoverable objective truths. And, indeed, in a footnote on page 13 he insists that he does not mean that "everything is 'up for grabs.'" But by page 48 he employs an argument that depends upon the strong claim that everything is up for grabs. "Given that truth is chosen or created, not discovered," says Baker, "advancement of knowledge and discovery of truth are merely aspects of participation in change." This is obviously not true if any aspect of reality objectively waits to be discovered: the use of the word "merely" requires not just some element of choice in the fixation of belief, as his Kuhnian argument about scientific theories suggests, but the much more radical claim that fixation of belief is mere choice. Baker thus slides from the relatively uncontroversial claim that belief involves some element or degree of choice or values or uncertainty to the strong claim that belief is entirely a matter of choice or values or uncertainty.

Similar points pertain to Baker's rejection of reason. From the obvious fact that most people do not fix their beliefs *entirely* on the basis of careful and competent rational evaluation, Baker concludes that reason plays *no* major role in the fixation of belief. Baker may not explicitly assert this strong claim, but his later arguments and assertions require it. It is perfectly obvious that people as well as some other animals frequently draw logical conclusions and come to believe at least some of the logical consequences of their beliefs. When Curacao sees six people die from eating a plant's red berries and as a result Curacao refrains from eating any of the plant's berries, Curacao is generalizing that eating those berries is or may be fatal and inferring that if he eats the red berries he may well die. Anyone who did not frequently form beliefs in this way would not long survive. So while social perspective and advertising and packaging may play some role in the formation of belief, it is obvious that reason also plays some role. The example of the poisonous red berries also shows that truth is at least sometimes the best basis for making decisions.

Once we recognize that some significant truths are discoverable and that reason often plays some important role and that truth is not infrequently the best basis for making decisions, Baker's arguments no longer invalidate a weaker version of the marketplace of ideas theory, namely, that free speech should be protected because not infrequently some important (and useful) truths will come to be accepted as the result of the free and open exchange of ideas. Baker is correct that this argument does not show why other determinants of belief should not be accorded special protection. Sometimes, as a matter of fact, they are. The argument merely shows that speech deserves protection, perhaps along with other things. However, if one adds that fixation of belief as a result of the rational evaluation of freely exchanged ideas and arguments is the *preferred* method of social and perhaps individual fixation of belief, then there are grounds for giving free speech *special* protection. There are numerous reasons why one might plausibly hold such a view. For instance, it is a peaceable method. It offers some check on beliefs that may be harmful to others. It is a method that promotes social cohesion of a particular sort. It is a method that gives some (though perhaps unequal) degree of access to the poor as well as the rich. In principle, reason is neutral between rich and poor. In practice, while the educational and other resources of the rich is often an asset in formulating and promulgating rational arguments, relative lack of money is not, as history has shown, an outright bar to doing so. Thus fixation of belief via the rational evaluation of freely exchanged ideas and arguments gives the disadvantaged at least some (if not equal) voice they might not otherwise have.

In short, Baker's arguments tell only against a very strong version of the marketplace of ideas theory, a version rarely strictly believed but often adverted to in legal and political rhetoric, according to which merely insuring that opposing voices are legally permitted to be heard guarantees that truth will always prevail. Baker's arguments remain useful as a warning against this strong version. The more plausible, weaker version, that the vigorous exchange of ideas and arguments can and should play an important role in reaching truth and making wise decisions, both escapes Baker's criticisms and more closely matches what most adherents of the marketplace theory actually believe.

In general, it seems hard to deny that reasonable opportunity to debate and discuss is necessary for assessing and formulating reasonable conceptions of the good as well as means, practices, and institutions for pursuing and instantiating those conceptions. It is necessary to test and develop one's ideas in conversation with others, to hear new ideas and evidence, and to advocate in order to secure others' co-operation. The (more or less) disinterested pursuit of truth,[7] conducted in large measure in this fashion, whether within one's own mind or with others, is itself, I would urge, a constituent of good human lives.

On this conception, the basic form of speech protected by speech rights is sincere rational discussion, in the broadest sense. It does not protect every form of advocacy. The core concern of speech rights protection, on this view, is neither the ability to convince others by any means, fair or fowl, nor the ability to enter the arena of conflicting wills through any and every verbal or pictorial means. The core concern is protection of reasonable deliberation. Thus a regulation does not violate this conception of speech rights merely because it limits a rhetorically effective form of making one's point. Irrationality and reckless disregard of the truth are not protected, since they are not part of reasonable deliberation. Obviously, however, reasonable deliberation in human affairs cannot be limited to what is provable in a court of law. Something is clearly amiss if pro-government speakers are permitted highly effective manipulative techniques of suasion and anti-government speakers forbidden their use. Obviously, since there is disagreement about rationality and judgments sometimes are biased, governments have to be extremely cautious about removing arguments from protection on the grounds that politicians or judges deem an argument to be irrational. Practical considerations bring this conception closer to current practice than first glance might suggest. Nonetheless, it would not warrant a claim that proscribing the use of a particular four-letter word violates speech rights because of the rhetorical punch that word has in certain contexts.

Speech as a social good

Aristotle said that a person alone is either more or less than human. Perhaps a god has no need of others, but ordinary mortals require life in a community to realize fully their humanity. The ways in which this is true are manifold and familiar, even if some claims for the central role of community are highly controversial. I will but mention briefly a few of the ways in which adequate scope for free speech as a social good is crucial to P.

Aristotle pointed out that we learn moral judgment by practice. In particular, we learn by initially imitating the ways of our community and participating in its practices and institutions, reflecting upon what we see and do, making adjustments that may require modifying those practices and institutions, then seeing and reflecting upon how those adjustments play out in one's own life and the lives of others. That process is undeniably at least an important part of acquiring moral competence. So acquiring moral competence requires both interaction and critical reflection. A healthy and vibrant social milieu is thus necessary for individual moral development. In addition, I would argue that there is more than one licit conception of *eudaimonia*, and that some of those conceptions cannot exist within the same community. A wise cosmopolitan, enlightened by the breadth of many cultures, and a thoughtful farmer, rooted in community traditions both lead good lives, but the diversity and clash of outlooks required for the former cannot coexist in the same social milieu as the common purpose and outlook required for the latter. Individuals must seek good lives appropriate for the community in which they dwell, and so a healthy community environment is necessary for individual flourishing. As mentioned above, social perception is a significant component of self-definition. Living in a benighted society distorts one's own view of and conception of oneself.

Finally, a crucial aspect of what is important about human life is commitment to something beyond oneself. Attachment of this sort is itself an element of moral good. Moreover, human life is brief. Individual instances of pleasure or exercise of autonomy are fleeting events in a tiny corner of the universe. It is through commitment to something that endures beyond the tiny span allotted to us that such events acquire meaning: the events in a human life are part of the history of a community, whether a small tribe or a community of thinkers across continents and generations (e.g., the enterprise of science). (See Chapter 8 for further discussion of these points.) In some important sense, salubrious communities are an essential aspect of or precondition for P.

Healthy and vibrant communities require the freedom to exchange perspectives and insights and challenges. This is as true in a traditionalist society as a cosmopolitan one. Jewish communities during the formation of the Talmud were certainly traditionalist in many ways, but that tradition flourished and endured by means of continual debate and argument and reflection within the Jewish tradition. Shared understandings and goals and outlooks that are not explored and pondered and wondered about gradually lose meaning. Practices and institutions bereft of critical discourse become rigid and stultified. I will not dwell on this argument, since its key points are widely known. The conclusion, however, is sometimes misstated. A healthy society is crucial for P, and healthy societies require vibrant discussion. This does not necessarily entail unfettered speech, as is sometimes assumed. It does require ample opportunity, provision, and support for: the exchange of ideas, insights, perplexities, problems, and personal experiences; social bonding through speech; criticisms of other people, social practices, and institutions; proposals for modification; and expression of wonder.

Speech as political equality

Speech as an aspect of political equality is powerfully present in the regulative ideals of American society. Since regulative ideals are not universal, I will describe rather than argue for speech as political equality.

Speech as political equality has two primary emphases, one relating to the public life of the *polis* and the other to the ability of speech to bring about desired results:

A. Everyone should have an equal shot at using speech to effect his ends, through persuasion and rhetoric.

B. Participation in a *polis* as an equal demands the ability to contribute one's ideas and language to public deliberation.

This conception of speech rights affords much broader protection. The idea behind A. is that the arena of conflicting wills is governed by a set of rules of combat, such as rules concerning libel. The rules of combat are intended to be relatively neutral (absolute neutrality being infeasible) between the vast preponderance of competing parties (not including, for instance, those who have taken vows of silence). Within those rules, equality is effected by permitting each individual to employ whatever tools of suasion he or she can muster. A. suggests, then, that any persuasive speech be afforded protection so long as it remains within the set of relatively neutral rules governing discourse. The focus here is not on speech as a means of reaching truth, social bonding, or conducting wise deliberations, but on speech as a political instrument, a means of effecting one's will. Of course, this conception of equality as free opportunity within neutral rules has detractors. It is oft observed (by, for example, feminists) that such a system preserves *de facto* inequalities. For instance, it preserves the advantage of those who are better educated over those who are less well educated, and so, through the easier access of education to those who are wealthier, the advantages of the more monied. Since I share some of these concerns, I will not defend this conception of speech rights. However, to the extent that it is an implicit element of the regulative ideals of American and several other societies, it can serve as a basis for urging broader protections within those society's laws than are extended by speech as the search for truth.

B. focuses as well upon the individual's ability to make a contribution rather than upon the value of the contribution made. It differs in this respect from speech rights based on the importance to a community of public discussion or the search for truth. Inflammatory and manipulative speech could lack protection if the goal is salubrious communal deliberation, a healthy public life, or the search for truth. But if the goal is giving citizens a chance to participate in public life and/or letting the voters decide, such speech can be a vital means of doing so. Again, I do not want to defend this particular democratic conception of governance or public life, but merely to point out that to the extent that it is integral to the regulative ideals of a society it can serve as a basis for urging broad protections of speech within that society's law. Note, however, that these arguments, since they stem from the regulative ideals adopted by, for instance, American society, are limited in application to American law and the laws of other societies that accept similar regulative ideals. Those who suggest that such broad protections are guaranteed by natural rights are mistaken, since neither democratic governance nor an unregulated speech arena for effecting one's will is necessary for P: what is of special moral significance about human beings can flourish in the absence of inflammatory rhetoric or voting. Morever, the weaker claim that other societies should (rather than must) adopt these broader protections on this basis would require showing that American regulative ideals are superior. This is no easy task, since the required comparison of U.S. regulative ideals is not with systems of governance that permit the arbitrary execution of political dissidents, but with, e.g., systems that permit free rational debate but regulate certain kinds of rhetorical devices. Freedom and democracy are not identical.

Speech as autonomy

While autonomy itself is a good, it is not, as such, a pre-eminent one. Rather, the most important aspects of autonomy are subsumed under other categories. For instance, wholehearted commitment to a good way of life is a crucial aspect of P, and the wholeheartedness of a commitment bears some relation to autonomy. The search for truth is important but impeded if beliefs are commanded rather than arrived at. In short, all of the above conceptions of speech (as free debate and discussion, social good, self-realization, and political equality) require some exercise of autonomy. For speech as autonomy to be a separate ground of the natural right to speech, autonomy would have to be important apart from all of those. Bare autonomy, autonomy for the sake of autonomy as such, would have to be a crucial element of P.

Bare autonomy, Chapter 1 suggests (following the more detailed argument in *Moral Responsibility and Persons*),[8] is not the basis of strong, robust rights. No major right of the Wanter (an organism that had no goals and desires, standards, moral commitments, etc., but spent its life pressing a red button or a white button as the whim took it) would be violated if someone safely borrowed the Wanter's buttons while it slept, without its permission. If we add to the story that the Wanter would feel distress about being deprived of its buttons during sleep, then preventing distress becomes a reason for not doing so, rather than respect for bare autonomy, and if the Wanter would feel distressed about the very idea of temporary losing its buttons even though it remained unaware of the loss, then it must have value-driven life goals, so it is no longer bare autonomy that is in question. In short, the presumption in favor of permissibility is an adequate response to autonomy as such. No further speech rights are necessary to respond appropriately to autonomy for its own sake.

These six conceptions provide the means of answering critics of speech rights. For instance, Lee Kwan Yew, former Prime Minister of Singapore, accused those who criticized his censorship of opposition to government policies of insensitivity to "Asian values,"[9] such as the priority of the community over the individual. However, even if the community is more important than the individual, speech as free debate and discussion remains important. Leaders, however wise, are not infallible, and thoughtful debate can raise issues and ramifications of or aspects of decisions that the government had not properly considered or appreciated. (Virtually every enduring society has in fact evidenced considerable debate, at least at the highest levels, even if the debate must be conducted in terms other than the straightforward and open ones to which Americans are accustomed.) In addition, members of the community who can voice their perplexities and disagreements can receive answers that enable them to enter more fully into community life, and the process of discussion itself can reinforce community bonds (speech as a communal good). Thus even if obedience and social order are preeminent values, some significant degree of free speech remains a precondition for P. Of course, as long as speech suppression is limited, by law or *de facto*, societies can function. For example, forbidden speech can occur in secret. In such cases P remains feasible only to the extent the government is not entirely successful in its attempts. Human ingenuity in circumventing a restriction does not render the restriction legitimate.

C. The Holistic Approach

Whichever conceptions of free expression are ultimately adopted, this volume urges a holistic approach to balancing speech and other rights against public interests and goals. This holistic approach focuses on rights as ensuring adequate provision for certain key aspects of individual and social life. It focuses on general, global aims, such as increasing the general level of security or affecting the overall tone of media attitudes toward sex and violence. And it seeks, as much as feasible, discretionary methods that have an overall impact on the problem while retaining considerable choice for people and institutions: ideally, the solution to such problems changes the playing field on which choices are made rather than mandating particular choices. The holistic approach suggests striving for a reasonable weighted balance between being sensitive to the important aspects of speech and a wide variety of public considerations, theoretical and practical, in a manner that is as unobtrusive as reasonably feasible.

Thus the holistic approach is "holistic" in several, related ways:

a.   It focuses on broad global aims, e.g., affecting the overall attitudes toward violence predominating in the media, rather than proscribing particular programs or images.

b.   It conceives of rights in terms of adequate provision rather than as lines in the sand that should not be crossed.

c.   It resolves conflicts through the reasoned balancing of a wide range of considerations for a particular situation, through an open-ended process of justification drawing upon an open-ended list of analyses, moral principles and values, some theoretical and some practical.

d.   It prefers solutions that have a broad effect on the bigger picture without mandating particular, individual choices.

The holistic approach has implications both for policy making and legal reasoning. The holistic approach requires a change in our legal thinking, with is historically rooted in decisions about the application of principles to individual cases. The holistic approach does not focus on whether a particular instance of speech falls under some principle, but upon policies designed to affect the general tenor of a society's discourse. Moreover, the holistic approach suggests that it is a mistake to look for rigorous principles to draw a line between protected and unprotected speech. It is always a matter of balancing, with the ultimate arbiter, in the case of natural rights, being whether the totality of speech rights, given the society's circumstances, makes adequate provision for P and the things necessary for P. This is not to say that analysis of speech rights depends purely on "intuitions." It is to say, rather, that, given the broadness of the notions of P and "adequate provision," instead of defining principles to be rigorously applied, legitimate analysis of speech rights articulates and gives reasons for weighing, in each case, a variety of factors, perhaps with different rationales and sources, some of which tend to generate stronger vector warrants than others.

Looking carefully at one particular kind of speech, threats, helps illustrate that speech protection is a matter of balancing diverse factors rather than a line drawn in the sand by some principle.

Consider the following threats:

A. Robbing someone at knifepoint: "Give me your money or I will kill you."

B. Blackmail: "Pay me or I will tell your husband about your affair."

C. "Pay me or I won't be your friend."

D. "Pay me or I won't say 'hello' to you."

E. "Pay me or I won't have sex with you."

F. One spouse saying to another: "if you make fun of me again, no sex to-night."

G. "I will not have sex with you unless you marry me."

H. Jones is about to lose his house because he cannot make his mortgage payment. He appeals to his neighbor Smith, a taxidermist, for a substan-tial loan. Smith has no special reason to lend Jones the money. Smith says "Say that you are a dummy or I will not loan you the money."

Obviously, some of these examples of speech acts are protected by speech rights and others are not. What more or less rigorous principle draws the line? A. and B. are both proscribed by law while C. is not: C. is protected speech while A. and B. are unprotected. In A., the speaker is threatening to do something she has no ordinary right to do, while, in B. and C., she is demanding money to re-frain from doing something that, absent the demand for money, she would have every legal right to do (not being the hearer's friend in case C. and, in case B., telling the hearer's husband about the affair, which, tellingly, would be a pro-tected speech act absent the demand for money). Thus the fact that the threat-ened behavior is *per se* permissible is a relevant but not decisive factor. Baker points out that the response the blackmailer wants is unrelated to what she might reveal, and (so) the blackmailer "has designed her speech as a means to under-mine the other's autonomy and get him to act in a manner she chooses" (p. 60). But this is equally true of the persons saying C. and D.: both speakers' desired response (the payment of money) is unrelated to saying hello or being a friend, and both speech acts are designed as a means to undermine the other's autonomy and get the hearer to act in the manner the speaker chooses, in quite the same way that blackmail is. Yet both C. and D. are instances of protected speech. In fact, in this respect, the blackmailer's activity is a trade like other trades—she trades her silence for money. In many trades the response one wants is unrelated to what one is trading, and in virtually all trades one's speech in offering the trade is designed as a means of getting the hearer to act in the way the speaker wants. Indeed many instances of manipulative speech, including political and commercial advertisements, are both specifically designed to undermine the hearer's autonomy and protected. Baker suggests on p. 61 that "people must be able to use speech as part of the activity of pursuing or implementing their substantive values" and that blackmail does not meet this criterion while whistleblowing does. But much protected speech does not meet this criterion, including permitted threats ("stand on your head or I won't eat my spinach"). Of course, one might suggest that the key difference is that A. and B. are "coercive" because of the harshness of the threatened result while C., D. are not, because of the relative mildness of the threatened results. While I would question the rigor of this distinction, note that for some individuals it might be easy to say "publish and be damned" and much harder to lose a friend on whom one dotes. The law often makes simplifying assumptions based on the average reasonable person, and that could be the case here. However, note that this response suggests that, while as a practical matter B. should be prohibited and C. protected, in some ideal sense B. should be protected and C. prohibited when the loss of the friendship would be acute and the revealing of the secret a minor embarrassment, just as in some ideal sense an extremely mature 14 year old should receive a driver's license and a wildly reckless 30 year old be denied one. Most of us agree with the latter claim, although we think it improper for the law to attempt to make such discriminations, but most of us are uncomfortable with the former—one should be able to deny one's (purely personal) friendship for any reason one chooses, however onerous the loss might be to someone else. A. and B. threaten positive actions while C. through H. threaten withholdings. The severity test does not seem to hold for withholdings. E. is generally proscribed in most states in the United States, while the law is neutral with respect to F. and perhaps mildly encouraging to G. In E. and F. the threatened consequence is the same, so the severity of the consequence is not a factor. In any case, the severity of the withholding in E. through G. is much less than in H., where the consequence of the withholding is severe—Jones will lose his house. Yet H. is permitted while E. is not. (Since, in general, the withholding of a substantial loan is more detrimental than the withholding of sex by a stranger, the response that the law makes a simplifying assumption will not serve.) The law permits the selling of sex for marriage but not for money, so perhaps the difference rests in what the law deems one has a right to offer, though again it is unclear what principled difference grounds this legal distinction, or why offering a loan in exchange for a self-denigrating comment is permitted. It appears to be a matter of enforcing positive public policy rather than some formal principle, and the limits upon the law's regulating speech to enforce public policy do not appear to conform to any nontrivial and rigorous formal principle.

Consider also the range of cases falling under singing and inchoate speech, including rude noises made at random while walking down the street and Bronx cheers designed to disrupt a meeting. What rigorous principle will draw a line between the permitted and the unpermitted? The fact that a given act of speech disrupts the speech of others is generally a factor mitigating protection. But not all disruptive speech is unprotected, while other disruptive speech is prohibited by law. In some cases, speech that disturbs the peace of others is regulated or forbidden and in others protected. At what point does singing or inchoate speech in a public place become disturbing the peace? If I am humming to myself softly on a park bench, is my speech protected? If I am singing opera at full voice? If six passersby gather to listen? If I put out a hat in which passersby might put money? Is the offensiveness of the lyrics a factor? If so, how do mildly offensive lyrics sung loudly compare to grossly obscene lyrics sung very softly? Are there principled cut-offs in such cases?

This brief discussion of a few examples merely raises questions. While it does not prove that no ingeniously drawn line in the sand exists, I suggest that similar worries can be raised regarding any reasonably rigorous formal principles meant to delimit protected and unprotected speech. It is not clear, in any case, why we should expect the range of speech rights to fall neatly within some rigorous line. Speech is important for several different reasons, each of which confers, upon different elements of speech (e.g., speech as a form of self-expression and speech as a means of reaching truth), some claim to consideration, the strength of which varies considerably in different contexts. A variety of reasons tell in favor of various sorts of speech restrictions (e.g., protecting individuals against the spread of malicious falsehoods and creating a salubrious social environment for human flourishing), each of which confers, upon different restrictions of different elements of speech, some claim to consideration, the strength of which varies considerably in different contexts. Many of these reasons apply less to particular utterances than to the overall milieu in which human lives unfold. Intuitively, this situation calls for an open-ended, sensitive process of balancing and weighing for particular cases with attention to the overall result of protections and restrictions. Intuitively, more than one resulting milieu is acceptable and several different combinations of restrictions and regulations may produce similar milieus. Hence more than one set of protections and restrictions is acceptable. If these intuitions are correct, the holistic approach matches moral reality.

D. The Nature of Pornography

Having cast some light on the nature and logic of speech rights, we now turn to consider the nature of pornography itself. Disagreement rages not only about whether pornography should be regulated but even about what pornography is. Four distinct criteria for identifying pornography are commonly encountered:

1. The content test: Material is pornographic that explicitly depicts human sexuality or sexual acts.
2. The affect test: Material is pornographic that appeals to prurient interests: to the extent that material is sexually arousing, the material counts as pornographic.

3. The offense test: Material is pornographic that offends the sensibilities, with regard to sexuality, of a majority of the relevant community.
4. The attitude test: Material is pornographic that conveys with implicit approval or at least neutrality certain kinds of attitudes about human sexuality, e.g.:
    a. people are mere objects of sexual desire, or
    b. the degradation of people is acceptable, or
    c. sex is a good to be consumed for the purpose of experiencing "highs."

As a stipulative definition, of course, each of these may be legitimately employed, but the point of each definition, the purpose of so defining pornography, derives from the following four claims:

1) Pornography, in asserting or depicting woman as mere objects of desire, both libels women and/or men, because women and/or men are not merely objects, and contributes to the oppression of women and/or to the prevalence of sexism by virtue of providing support for an oppressive system of patriarchy and or gender roles and stereotypes.
2) Pornography is a causal contributor to instances of rape and violence.
3) Pornography contributes to an individually or socially wrong/ insalubrious/harmful/evil view of sex and sexuality.
4) Pornography induces lustful feelings, which are intrinsically evil.

The content and affect test derive their point from claim 4), since if sexual arousal and activity are not bad there is no reason to suppress material that induces or contains it. The point of the offense test depends ultimately upon claims 2) or 4) as well. After all, few would pay much attention to one who asserted that while wearing yellow is not itself bad, other people's wearing yellow in the privacy of their homes should be criminalized because it offends him. There is no general, reasonably powerful reason for proscribing or limiting private access to material simply because it fits definition 3): the fact that x offends me does not, *per se*, give me a strong reason to prevent someone else from seeing it:[10] at the very least, my offense must be justified. At the heart of the offense test for regulation of private materials, then, is the sense that what makes the material offensive is its evilness, either because sexual arousal is evil, or because the effects on individuals who view the material are evil, or because the attitudes it conveys are evil. If so, then the offense test is merely an indirect way of measuring the extent to which material meets definitions 1), 2), or 4). Claim 2) could provide some point to definitions 1) and 2) if it is arousal *per se* or depiction of sex per se that causes rape and violence, but that claim is so dubious as not to warrant consideration here:[11] to the extent that claim 2) is true at all, its truth depends upon certain attitudes conveyed by the pornography that promote violence, not merely upon whether it reveals nipples or arouses desire, and so claim 2) gives point primarily to definition 4). Claims 1) and 3) give point to definition 4), in that both claims focus on a particular attitude conveyed by pornographic materials.

Claim 4) is simply false. Sexual arousal is not, *per se*, bad, harmful, or undesirable under the proper circumstances. The arguments for this view are too well known to be rehearsed here. Some *forms* of sexual arousal may be undesirable, e.g., arousal from degradation or sadism, but it is the pro attitude toward degradation or other's pain, rather than sexual arousal as such, that is objectionable. The argument for regulating sadistic pornography properly focuses on the question of regulating sadistic material, as such, of which sadistic pornography is merely one instance. Claim 2) lacks confirmation. The various studies frequently cited are inconclusive for a variety of reasons. Control groups can be used to look for very specific immediate effects of viewing pornography, but these are poor predictors either of long term, cumulative effects, of general behavior in a normal social setting, or of other specific immediate effects. Demographic studies of large populations over time correct these defects, but it is virtually impossible to control for the possibly relevant variables—the reasons people in our society may be drawn to pornography may be causally linked to the effects being measured, in which case restricting pornography would have little impact on those effects. In short, a reasonable person looking at the evidence and arguments presented by both sides of the debate would conclude that the broad effect on pornography in our society on rape and acts of violate is unknown. Finally, I would suggest that to the extent that claim 1) is significant and true, it is subsumed under claim 3).

Thus the present discussion will focus on claim 3) and the definition of pornography, definition 4), to which it gives point, namely, that something counts as pornography when it tends affectively to promote in a reasonable viewer acceptance of morally objectionable views of sexuality and pertinent human interaction. The word "affectively" is inserted because a closely argued dissertation advocating objectionable views of sexuality ought not to count as pornography, however poor the arguments or benighted the conclusions. There is a clear difference between such a tract and a photograph of a dog urinating on the face of a naked woman, although it is difficult to spell out that difference rigorously. The picture is not perspicuously an argument for or analysis of anything. However, as noted above, the distinction between argument and analysis on one hand and depiction on the other is hardly a rigorous one. A fictional depiction of a particular way of life may well be a powerful argument of recognition for the goodness of that way of life. So representation can function as argument, when the representation serves perspicuously to illuminate the aspect being argued for (e.g., the horrors of unbridled capitalism or the crushing brutality of life in Stalinist Russia, to take two cold-war examples). Trying to make and apply this distinction brings to mind the difficulties encountered by courts in applying the standard of "redeeming social value." How much social value is redeeming? Does placing a 30 second lecture on the Bill of Rights in the midst of an orgy film redeem it? Similarly, does a 30 second plea for world peace qualify a film as debate and advocacy? To some extent, the fact that speech rights are primarily rights to adequate provision mitigates these difficulties. If "redeeming social value" forms a line that divides the bannable from the non-bannable, the task of placing films and books and photographs on one side of that line seems hopelessly arbitrary. If, however, the requirement is to make adequate provision, then the question is whether, if a given item is regulated, there remain adequate opportunities to disseminate the views in question. In the U.S. today there are certainly adequate opportunities to plead for world peace even if the film mentioned above is restricted in some fashion. Hence restricting it does not violate the natural right to speech, the 30 second plea notwithstanding. Moreover, the holistic approach suggests the goal should not be to ban items purveying objectionable attitudes, but merely to influence the general tenor of the attitudes publicly disseminated. Thus the distinction between thoughtful urging of objectionable views and affectively fostering objectionable views is easier to make, since judgments are less absolute and mistakes in making them less critical: the question is not whether to ban or not to ban, but simply whether adequate venues for urging the relevant views remain if it is in some way more costly to broadcast or disseminate this item. Nonetheless, there remains an irreducible element of subjective discretion in making such judgments. However, that subjective element is inescapable in law generally: a degree of subjective discretion is an ineradicable element of any reasonable legal or political system, as the copious use of the term "reasonable" in law demonstrates.

Pornography and Speech Rights

Ready access to pornography, defined as materials that tend to promote in reasonable viewers acceptance of morally objectionable attitudes toward sexuality, is not a central social good in the sense articulated above. In fact, the goals implicit in the reasons given earlier for the importance of speech as a social good are served by ensuring that public discourse is not dominated by messages that violence is the way to solve problems[12] and that sex is a commodity. Thus wise holistic regulation of pornography supports rather than undermines the very reasons that speech is a social good. Of course, healthy societies must have venues for reasonable challenges to their mores, including sexual mores (speech as discussion and debate). But it is not clear that pornography is a necessary means of so doing. As long as governmental policies that render more costly or difficult the dissemination of a given piece of pornography leave ample opportunity for holders of the objectionable view to raise their challenge, speech as social good is adequately respected. Similarly, speech as self-realization may involve depiction of one's life experiences, views, attitudes, etc. in a way that might appear to promote objectionable attitudes. Again, the relevant question is whether making it more difficult or costly to disseminate these materials leaves ample opportunity for the disseminators to achieve reasonable self-realization through speech. As long as regulators are sensitive to this constraint, holistic regulation of pornography does not violate speech as self-realization. Speech as autonomy, it was suggested, was adequately addressed by the presumption in favor of permissibility. Having some impact on the general tenor of public life with respect to objectionable attitudes toward sexuality and violence is a legitimate and significant social goal. Holistic approaches are sensitive to this presumption in that they avoid directly prohibiting actions. Regulators should keep in mind, however, that regulation does impact autonomy and should be used with a light touch. Finally, while speech as political equality is not an aspect of the natural right to speech, it is part of the regulative ideal of American society. The democratic aspect of speech as political equality, the more central aspect, does not often come into significant play with respect to pornography and violence. The comments made earlier about depiction as argument, suitably modified, give adequate reason to think this factor will not pose insuperable problems. However, as a vehicle for effecting one's will, pornographic and/or pro-violent materials can be highly effective, as a glance at contemporary advertising reveals. Thus, arguably, pornographic and pro-violence materials can claim some protection under the American regulative ideal of political equality. However, we regularly accept that some moderate and reasonably neutral constraints may be placed on methods of effecting one's will. Our society as a whole adopts a moderated, not a strong libertarian view: there is widespread acceptance of government requiring seatbelts, requiring prescriptions for various medications, and so forth, based on a conception of government as balancing free choice against various social goods. Thus the strongly libertarian view cannot properly be said to be embedded in the regulative ideals of American society. The impact of moderate and reasonably neutral regulation of pornography on speech as an instrument of effecting one's will cannot plausibly be asserted to violate the regulative ideals of American society.

Given these conclusions, the proposal below adequately respects speech rights, so long as regulators remain sensitive in their judgments to the constraints mentioned above. Actual regulators may err by being insensitive to these constraints, but the nature of the proposal limits significantly the impact of regulators' benighted judgments. Hence I suggest that, so long as regulators' judgments are not wildly egregious, the proposal made below does not violate natural rights or regulative ideal rights in the United States. When regulators' judgments are so egregious as to violate natural rights or regulative ideals, the remedy to improper governmental action that currently exists, judicial review, remains available. I would urge as well that the proposal does not violate presumptive rights. Finally, I suggest briefly below why the proposal does not violate those positive speech rights in United States law granted by the U. S. Constitution.

E. A Proposal for Regulating Sex and Violence in the Media

No particular television show or image caused the shooting death of Balbir Singh Sodhi on September 15, 2001, who was shot and killed simply because, according to Maricopa County Attorney Rich Romley, he was dark skinned and sported a turban.[13] But when ordinary citizens committed acts of violence against Arab-Americans, Sikhs, and Muslims in the wake of the World Trade Center tragedy, their actions fit the insistent message of thousands of movies and television programs that violence is how problems get solved. How can we balance exercising some control over our social landscape with preserving essential freedoms such as speech? The issue goes deeper than *Friday the 13th* and *Debbie Does Dallas*. Balancing individual rights and social needs has come to the forefront of the public agenda. 74 percent of respondents to a poll conducted on Sept. 13 and 14, 2001 by The New York Times said it was necessary to "give up some personal freedoms in order to make the country safe from terrorist attacks," up from 49% who answered "yes" to a similar question posed by the LA Times after the 1995 Oklahoma City bombing. It is not a matter of simply choosing safety or freedom: as Robin Toner noted in the New York Times, "The buzzword on Capitol Hill is balance."[14] Representative Dick Armey, for example, has stressed the need to "equip our anti-espionage, counterterrorism agencies with the tools they want while we still preserve the most fundamental thing, which is the civil liberties of the American people."[15] More recently, James Feron, during a panel discussion sponsored by the Stanford Ethics Center on Nov. 1, 2006, spoke about the need to find a defensible balance between security and civil liberties.[16] How can balance best be achieved?

In the case of violence and pornography, most discussions have focused on the wrong questions. The real problem with media pornography and violence is not the particular images broadcast, such as nipples or severed heads. It is also not about drawing some imaginary line in the sand the state must not cross in using its power. Framing the issue this way forces both sides to sound implausible. Children do not suffer lifelong harm by seeing a naked body part or a bloody knife. A pair of nipples shown on TV does not provoke a rash of rapes. The proper object of speech regulation, with regard to violence and pornography, is the overall cultural setting, the framework of discourse, the texture of everyday life. Equally, Katie Couric's natural rights aren't violated because she may not say a particular four-letter word on network television. Instead, the debate should focus on finding a satisfying compromise between, on the one hand, having some control over the powerful global effects on society of repeated messages and attitudes presented by an omnipresent mass media and the need for free and open discussion reasonably independent of government.

It is hard to deny the pervasive acceptance of violence that permeates our media. Some films present graphic images of violence as something to be savored and enjoyed. Many more films and programs without graphic depictions of violence suggest that violence is the way to solve one's problems. In *The Great Panda Adventure*, an otherwise salutary Disney film about human connection both to nature and to other persons, the panda reserve is ultimately saved by fisticuffs. Unfortunately, *The Great Panda Adventure* is not alone. The list is huge of films and programs in which the "good guys" win, presumably with the viewer's

approval, by shooting, punching, physically threatening, or otherwise using violence against the "bad guys." The message implicit in such programs, that violence is the solution, is particularly effective because it is conveyed not as an
explicit statement or image, which the viewer might ponder, but as implicit in the
plot of a story in which the viewer is emotionally engaged. People respond to
images in varied ways—with disgust, excitement, apathy, curiosity, or disapproval. Messages implicit in a narrative tend to bypass critical judgment. Few
viewers ask themselves whether, in cheering on the "good guys," their thinking is
being subtly shifted toward violent solutions. And the message is widespread and
rarely challenged. In the past, when citizens' ideas came from books, newspapers, pamphlets, and their neighbors, the "marketplace of ideas" provided great
variety. In an age in which the average person spends 18 to 32 hours a week
glued to a small number of channels,[17] it does not. The vast cost of mass media,
and the resulting need to grab huge numbers of viewers in order to sustain them,
guarantees that the realities of the market produce a great deal of uniformity. TV
is watched at home and costs nothing to turn on, so viewers, especially those
who turned on their televisions in the middle of the show, will turn off a show
that does not constantly grab their attention. Sex and violence are attention grab-
bing, visual, require little context to understand, and can be comprehended by
everyone. So it comes as no surprise that violent solutions to problems are uni-
formly popular on TV and that sex is often portrayed as a commodity.[18] Network
executives and screenwriters are not sincerely advocating using violence or
viewing sex as a commodity. They are merely responding to the nature of the
technology and the conditions of the market.

   So the problem is not the purported harm done by individual salacious or
violent images. Rather, the problem is that the effects of millions of viewers
cheering the use of violence and sharing a story's assumption that others are objects of consumption, day in and day out, are deep and widespread.[19] The omnipresent barrage of such messages affects our relations with one another as individuals as well as our public outlook in law in policy, in ways large and small,
blatant and subtle. Road rage is no aberration in American life. It is symptomatic
of our public attitudes toward sex that when a stranger's child falls down on the
playground and begins to cry, a man risks arrest by giving that child a simple
hug. Since the thousands of moral messages by which we are bombarded daily
on television, movies, and advertisements have a profound effect on the values
and social realities of the community in which we must live and interact, societies have not only a right but an obligation to exert some control over that milieu.
Societies are responsible for the public morality expressed in their public discourse, in part because the nature of those public attitudes significantly affects
the kinds of lives people can practically live within a society's boundaries. If
virtually every major medium projects the image that manipulation is the appropriate way to deal with others, that practice has a major impact on my life, both
because most others in my life will be manipulative and because my own words
and actions will be perceived as manipulations. Thus I cannot be open and

straightforward with people in the way I would like. As Hume famously noted, one cannot be the only honest person in a den of thieves for very long. So harmful public discourse is not only inherently bad, but also sets back the flourishing of individuals within that society, who find it unfeasible to live the kinds of lives to which they are (properly) committed.

Thus traditional forms of regulation, that proscribe or regulate individual programs or images, do not directly address the problem, which is the preponderance or general tenor of media messages. They are also unduly obtrusive. Regulator's judgments are notoriously parochial. *Macbeth* is certainly bloody, but hardly unfit viewing. Moreover, a regulatory body's proscribing a program completely deprives both viewers and vendors of choice. A new, holistic approach to weighing rights against the ability of a society to control its public life is sorely needed, moderating the overall messages shouted by the media while tempering the effect of regulators' dubious judgments and maximizing viewers' and programmers' opportunities for choice.

In other words, a society must exert some influence over the overall tone of its public life without unduly restricting individuals' ability to advocate their views and without heavy-handed control of public forums like television. Put this way, it becomes a practical problem calling for a practical solution.

That solution is to establish a committee, reasonably free of political interference but ultimately answerable to the public (like the Federal Reserve or the EPA),[20] to rate each television program for the extent to which it appears to present with explicit or tacit approval either the use of violence, the suggestion that violence is something to be enjoyed, or the notion that sex is a commodity to be imbibed like root beer. Committee actions will remain subject to judicial review in the same way that other regulatory bodies' actions currently are. The committee's deliberations should focus on the attitudes conveyed by the program. Sex, violence, and manipulation are all facts of life, and television should not be precluded from representing those facts. It is not the presence of sex, violence, and manipulation in a program that should concern regulators but the attitude conveyed toward sex, violence, and manipulation. The character Ted on *The Mary Tyler Moore Show* was often shown being manipulative, but he was presented as a figure of ridicule rather than emulation. Showing even a single fist punch with approval has a greater effect on certifying violence as an acceptable method of settling disputes than showing a gory massacre with obvious disapproval and portraying realistically the human pain and cost of violence. A show containing images of fully clothed actors that treats sex as a commodity can be more "pornographic," in the sense that matters, than a show including frontal nudity. For example, a film about a woman executive so obsessed with her work that, even stepping out of the shower dripping wet, she is on the cell phone concluding a business deal is not pornographic, even if the shot of her talking on the phone doesn't hide her pubic hair. The committee would employ a "constructive attitude" standard: to what extent would a reasonable average viewer see the program as approving of these attitudes toward sex and violence? Decisions about such questions are necessarily somewhat subjective and discretionary, but the "constructive attitude" test is no more problematic than either of the tests for obscenity that courts have typically used, the affect test (does it arouse prurient interests) and the offense test (does it offend average members of the community). Just as important, the way that point ratings are used insures that the committee's rating of a particular program has a much less direct and dire impact on the program rated than, for example, the EPA's determination of a safe level of toxic emissions does on manufacturers. Presently, a court's decision that a book violates the community standard test may bar the book from sale, while, if this proposal is adopted, the committee's giving a program a high rating merely imposes a cost on a broadcaster who wishes to air it. Finally, unlike affect or offense tests, the constructive attitude test addresses the real problem. Our society can handle being pruriently aroused or offended. Similarly, while graphic images of violence may be disturbing, being disturbed is part of the price of a free society. More significant is the constant iteration of the message that violent behavior is acceptable. Unlike being offended or aroused, being beaten or shot is not a legitimate part of the price of a free society. The constructive attitude test directly addresses the legitimate reason for regulating violence and obscenity. The purpose of the committee's rating points is not to root out or regulate particular programs because they are prurient, offensive, or disturbing, but to have some influence on the general tenor of messages broadcast daily into millions of homes, in as unobtrusive a way as feasible.[21]

The kinds of messages that should receive attention from point raters are those that are likely to have a widespread negative effect on the lives of those who live in the society, rather than those that contravene parochial beliefs of either the raters or the general public. When the public media persistently and overwhelmingly present violence as an acceptable solution to one's problems, the effects are powerfully discernible in the lives of every citizen. A show that presents a positive view of abortion, however objectionable it may be to some people, does not have the same kind of widespread negative effect on the lives of citizens. Widespread and repeated approval of manipulation as a means of interpersonal dealing and a positive attitude toward the objectification of others has a global and powerful effect on the kinds of lives citizens can feasibly lead. A show approving of a couple thoughtfully choosing a non-traditional marriage, however objectionable some might find it, does not. Moreover, judgments should be made on the basis of the overall communication—a solitary statement that violence is bad does not undo the damage of a program in which the heroes, whom the audience is asked to admire, solve their problems with violence. Rating points, in other words, should reflect the totality of the messages of the communication as a reasonable person in our society would understand or perceive them.

The committee merely assigns points to programs. How the point system is used depends on which of four levels of regulation government employs. Government should employ the lowest effective level of regulation. I will discuss network television, but other methods can be employed with respect to major films, cable broadcasting, major internet media, and other mass media as they develop.

Level I merely requires broadcasters to post the committee's rating at the beginning of the broadcast. Level II uses a station's average monthly point total as one consideration, among others, in granting licenses. Level III creates tax and other incentives for broadcasters who maintain a low point total. Level IV requires broadcasters not to exceed a particular (fairly liberal) yearly point total.

Levels I, II, and III are not significant departures from current practices. Level I is not significantly different from warning labels on drugs, USDA meat ratings, etc. It simply informs consumers of the government's rating, leaving both viewers and broadcasters free to exercise informed choice. Level II is also not a radical change in practice, since the FCC currently considers, when awarding licenses, such factors as the amount of time devoted to religious programming. Tax incentives, such as those employed by Level III, as well as taxes on disapproved behavior, like smoking, are also familiar. If the government may use tax incentives to reward citizens for insulating their homes, it may also use tax incentives to reward broadcasters for moderating messages approving of violence. In both cases, the government does not mandate any behavior. It merely makes the environment for engaging in disapproved behavior more costly. Level IV is a significant departure, and should be avoided if at all possible.

All four levels give both viewers and broadcasters significant choice and discretion. Level I is purely informational. Levels II through IV affect only the overall offerings of a network or magazine, not individual programs or articles. Even Level IV does not prevent a broadcaster from airing any particular program it wishes: Level IV affects only the preponderance of what a broadcaster airs. Level IV permits a broadcaster to air highly violence-approving programs. It requires only that such programs not predominate. No level proscribes or precludes the offering of even a highly objectionable article or show. Thus all four levels preserve a great deal of freedom of choice for viewers and networks. They exert some influence upon the general tenor of television broadcasts without directly mandating or prohibiting any particular broadcasting choices, thus leaving considerable room for objectionable or controversial programming. Equally important, they mitigate the effect of particular decisions by program raters: even should a benighted committee assign a high rating to, for example, *Macbeth*, networks remain free to air *Macbeth*. They must merely either balance the program with lower rated programs or pay some form of higher cost, e.g., lose a tax incentive.

Does this proposal violate natural rights or constitutional safeguards on speech? The natural right to freedom of speech is a claim each person has on governments to made adequate provision within their boundaries for free discussion, debate, and advocacy, as well as adequate self-realization through speech. Nothing in the proposal prevents governments from doing that: no one can reasonably claim that even Level IV deprives him or her of adequate opportunity for free discussion, debate, or advocacy or prevents adequate self-realization through speech. If speech is viewed instead as a central form of or precondition for autonomy, the proposal nonetheless leaves copious room for autonomous choice, as well as the gathering and testing of information needed and freedom of advocacy that might be necessary for the exercise of autonomous choice. The proposal is not likely to have a major impact on electoral politics or the political exercise of democracy.

The Supreme Court's interpretation of the First Amendment has changed considerably over the years. The First Amendment states:

> Congress shall make no law respecting an establishment of religion, or prohibiting the free exercise thereof; or abridging the freedom of speech, or of the press; or the right of the people peaceably to assemble, and to petition the Government for a redress of grievances.

Would the proposed mechanism "abridge" freedom of speech or of the press? While courts have often shown sensitivity to any "chilling effect" speech regulation might have on expression, the courts have, throughout their history, recognized categories of speech that receive less than full protection, including libel or slander and certain forms of pornography, and upheld the right of government to employ certain forms of speech regulation to secure compelling government interests. The lines of unprotected or less protected speech, what constitutes a compelling government interest, and which forms of regulation are permissible have shifted over the years. However, a general framework remains that identifies three key factors in the government regulation of speech: 1) some categories of speech are less protected than others, 2) government has some compelling interests that justify regulating speech, and 3) some forms of regulation are acceptable and others are not. Within this general framework, it can be argued that advocacy of violence or sex as a commodity is less protected, and/or that the government has a compelling interest in exerting some influence upon the public discourse of the nation, and/or that the methods of regulation proposed are sufficiently non-obtrusive, like regulations concerning time and place of public meetings, to be acceptable. If these three claims can be adequately supported, a strong argument exists that the proposal is not unconstitutional.

Nonetheless, some will worry that a step on the road to censorship, however benign, is a dangerous step toward book burning and imprisoning critics of government. This fear seems unfounded. It seems unlikely that Supreme Court justices who come to see this proposal as Consitutional will suddenly countenance government book burnings and jailing of dissidents. After all, the Supreme Court has for many years permitted governments to stop the publication of certain items of pornography, a power far stronger than any this proposal would give government, yet no wholesale erosion of speech freedoms has resulted.[22]

Others might object to the very idea that a society exercise some control over the general tenor of its social milieu. But note first that media such as television or movies are not like soap boxes in public parks, which anyone may assume. For most of us, those decisions are already made by others. It is not clear why leaving them exclusively to network and studio executives is preferable to our, as a society, having some influence on the playing field on which executives make those decisions. It could be argued that we vote with our dollars, either directly or with our remotes, given the advertising value of viewership numbers. (While, arguably, each dollar counts the same, each viewer does not, given the importance advertisers place on demographics. The "remote vote" is non-egalitarian.) To an extent this is true, but that argument ignores certain features of the marketplace, e.g., that the market pushes toward "lowest common denominator" programming because of the cost of major films and television time, the nature of the technologies (television, for example, requires no viewer commitment, panoramic images are ineffective on the small screen, the convenience of viewing at home means programs must be comprehensible to viewers who came in during the middle, etc.), and the fact that television and movies now define our public culture, so that those who are unfamiliar with blockbluster movies and shows are effectively shut out. If ten people preferred *Hamlet* to *Rambo*, another ten preferred opera to *Rambo*, and another ten preferred nature documentaries to *Rambo*, but all 30 had some interest in *Rambo*, *Rambo* would win the "dollar vote," because, with limited exceptions, televison shows with very small audiences cannot survive. In any case, the "dollar vote" is not eliminated by my proposal, since it does not, like most other suggestions for regulation, give veto decisions on programs or images to government officials, but merely permits regulatory decisions to make some overall programming choices more economically attractive to programmers. Viewers make the ultimate decision with their remote controls.

At the very least, assigning rating points to programs deserves closer attention. But whether or not we as a society implement rating points, we should take seriously the three key ideas behind the holistic approach to trade-offs between rights and social needs, such as privacy vs. security. The holistic approach sees rights as entitlements to adequate provision. It focuses on general, global aims, such as increasing the general level of security. And it proposes discretionary methods that have an overall impact on the problem while retaining as much choice for people and institutions as feasible: ideally, the solution to such problems changes the playing field on which choices are made rather than mandating particular choices. These three ideas are essential to a thoughtful and workable modern society.

The holistic approach requires a change in our legal thinking, which is historically rooted in decisions about individual cases. But in a world that is increasingly global, a change is long overdue.

Notes to Chapter Six

1 Baker, C. Edwin, *Human Liberty and Freedom of Speech*, New York, Oxford: Oxford University Press, 1989.

2 Rowan, John, *Conflicts of Rights*, Boulder, CO: Westview Press, 1999.

3 Rowan also suggests that only public speech can contribute to public discovery of truth, and hence the private possession or production of pornography would not be protected by the marketplace of ideas argument. However, private speech can contribute to private discovery of truth. The marketplace of ideas argument is intended, by most of its adherents, to include the value of an individual's own efforts to discover moral truth for herself. In any case, ideas conveyed in private speech can be made public later: a private conversation with my neighbor may influence her subsequent public speech. Perhaps Rowan is correct when he states (in correspondence, Nov. 17, 2004) that "a reasonable distinction can be made between private discovery of truth and (at least the means of conveying one's ideas in the process of) public discovery of truth," but since private deliberation is an essential part of the process of public discussion, protecting the public discovery of truth would seem to require protecting the private production of relevant materials, just as it protects private discussion of public issues.

4 Schlossberger, Eugene, "With Virtue for All: Against the Democratic Theory of Virtue," *Southwest Philosophy Review* 5, January 1989, pp. 71–76 and "Is Morality Universalizable?", Colloquium Paper, Central Division American Philosophical Association Meeting, April 1989.

5 Holland, Tom, *Rubicon*, New York: Anchor Books, 2003, p. 5.

6 Baker's own view is that speech rights center on protecting the liberties of self-expression and participation in change. He attempts first to give a general theoretical grounding for this view and then to spell out is implications in detail. Whether right or wrong, Baker's book is a major contribution to speech rights theory.

7 While human beings are never entirely disinterested in any of their activities, and while it may not even be clear what absolutely disinterested pursuit might mean, the ideal of disinterested pursuit of truth, however imperfectly instantiated or even defined, remains important as a goal and corrective. Of course, if no coherent content at all can be given to the notion of being "disinterested" then the ideal is empty. However, that very strong claim seems false to me, and the usual arguments against the possibility of disinterested pursuit plausibly tell only against the claims that individuals can be absolutely disinterested or that disinterestedness can be rigorously defined. While those two claims may be necessary for some epistemological theories, they are not needed for the claim I am making here.

8 Schlossberger, Eugene, *Moral Responsibility and Persons*, Philadelphia: Temple University Press, 1992.

9 Cited in William J. Talbott, *Which Rights Should Be Universal*, New York and Oxford: Oxford University Press, 2005, p. 39.

10 See, for instance, Feinberg, Joel, *Offense to Others*, Volume 2 of *The Moral Limits of the Criminal Law*, New York and Oxford: Oxford University Press, 1985.

11 Cf. *Attorney General's Commission on Pornography: Final Report*, Washington, D.C.: U.S. Department of Justice, July 1986, p. 328, which admits that "the evidence lends some support to the conclusion that the consequences we have identified here [i.e., increased aggression and attitudinal change] do not vary with the extent of sexual explicitness so long as violence is presented in an undeniably sexual context." Thus the Commission concluded that sadistic pornography is harmful, while recognizing that it may be no more harmful than any other form of sadistic material.

12 It is worth noting that, according to TV-Free America, the average American has seen 200,000 acts of violence on television by age 18 (cited by Norman Herr, The Source for Teaching Science, http://www.csun.edu/science/health/docs/tv&health.html). While the actual number may be disputed on several grounds, if the figure is reliable within an order of magnitude (even if the figure is overstated by a factor of 10), the number is disturbing.

13 Lichtblau, Eric, "After the Attack: Anti-Muslim Violence Up, Officials Say," *Los Angeles Times*, September 18, 2001, A3.

14 Toner, Robin, "Bush Law-Enforcement Plan Troubles Both Right and Left" *New York Times* September 28, 2001.

15 "Everyone Should Worry about Civil Liberties," *Seattle Post-Intelligencer*, October 2, 2001.

16 Rhode, Deborah L., "War on Terror Undermines Moral Legitimacy, Human Rights," *Stanford Report*, November 7, 2006, http://news-service.stanford.edu/news/2006/november8/ civil-110806.html.

17 According to the U.S. Bureau of Labor Statistics, the average American in 2005 spent 2.6 hours a day, half of their leisure time, watching television (Bureau of Labor Statistics News: http://www.bls.gov/news.release/atus.nr0.htm). Nielsen Media Research placed the figure for 2005-2006 at 4 hours and 35 minutes a day, which is more than 32 hours a week (Nielsen Media Research: http://www.nielsenmedia.com/nc/portal/site/Public/menuitem.55dc65b4a7d5adff3f65936147a062a0/?vgnextoid=4156527aacccd010VgnVCM100000ac0a260aRCRD).

18 The problem is compounded by the fact that television is expensive and so generally requires large numbers of viewers, forcing programmers to seek the "lowest common denominator."

19 Some suggest that only abnormal or weak viewers' attitudes are changed by television. Perhaps only the weak or abnormal are so affected by a particular image that their behavior radically changes as a result, e.g., copycat killings. That is one reason why the argument for controlling particular images is so weak. By contrast, it seems implausible to insist that few ordinary viewers' attitudes will be even subtly shifted by hearing the same messages hundreds of times a day, each day of their lives, an effect reinforced by the fact that their friends and families are similarly influenced by omnipresent media messages.

20 Because the committee must sometimes make decisions that are unpopular and that run contrary to powerful interests (such as the networks), a considerable degree of independence is necessary. But, as the case of power industry regulators shows, for those very same reasons, significant accountability is also necessary. There are various ways of

achieving this balance. For example, point raters could be appointed to a fixed term by the President, with Congressional approval, subject to removal by a 2/3 vote of Congress. The committee structure might consist of a primary rating board and an appeals committee.

21 Among the attitudes toward sex I would urge the committee to support are the following: Sex is a small but important part of life. It is not dirty or obscene. The body is not shameful. Children are not harmed by seeing penises or nipples. On the other hand sexual attractiveness and success are not the main criteria of personal worth. Our society's obsession with sex is harmful, whether the obsession be on the part of Cosmo girls, leftist feminists, or religious fundamentalists. Finally, sex is not a commodity, but a personal exchange. Personal exchanges take many forms, and we should be aware of the diverse forms of legitimate ways in which sex and sexuality can be personal, from mutual enjoyment of sensuality to companionable touching. There is no one model for sex.

22 Formally, the slippery slope argument is a fallacy: almost everything is the first step toward something undesirable. Therefore this argument:

    1. x is the first step toward y
    2. y is bad
    3. therefore we shouldn't do x

is a fallacy. The cogent form of the argument reads, roughly:

    1. X is the first step toward y.
    2. Y is bad.
    3. If x is done, the chance of y happening is increased by z.
    4. The expected benefit of x minus the increased expected harm of y (roughly, z times the disvalue of y) is significantly less than zero.
    5. Therefore there is some reason, to be balanced against other reasons, for not doing x.

For the reasons given above, condition 4. is not true of this proposal.

Chapter 7:
Moral Rights and the Right to the Truth

Do we have a right to the truth? When people insist, as they often do, that they have a right to the truth, they can mean one of two things. One can have a *specific* right to the truth, that is, a right to know something specific, or, more precisely, a right that someone make a good faith effort to inform one, or at least answer forthcomingly one's questions about, some particular thing. For example, a wife might claim a right to the truth about her husband's fidelity, meaning that her husband violates her rights if he is not forthcoming about the status of his fidelity to her (as opposed to whether he rode a blue or a red bus to work). She could also be making the broader assertion that she has a claim on others not to withhold information about the state of her husband's fidelity (as opposed to the color of their underwear). An employer might claim a right to the truth about her employee's credentials (but not about his favorite sexual positions). A patient speaking to his physician may insist he has a right that she inform him truthfully of his medical condition, a right he normally lacks about her stock portfolio. This sort of specific right to the truth is, as a rule, based on particular circumstances and relationships. Juliette has a specific right to the truth about her husband Mark's marital fidelity, while her neighbor Martha does not, because Mark is Juliette's husband and not Martha's. In addition to such specific rights to the truth, people often claim a *general* right to the truth. A general right to the truth suggests that, while your neighbor does not have a right to know whether you were born in New Jersey, he, like everyone else, has a right, other things being equal, that you not lie to him about it. The general right to the truth is not a right to know, but a right not to be treated dishonestly, where dishonesty generally includes lying and may, in some cases, include deception. It is the general right to the truth, rather than specific rights to the truth, that is the subject of this chapter: in this chapter, the term "the right to the truth" will mean the general right to the truth unless otherwise indicated.

What kind of right is the general right to the truth? It is not a legal right: while there are various circumstances in which one has a legal right to the truth about something in particular, those rights are specific rights to specific truths. It may be actionable for the seller of a house to lie to the purchaser about the termite history of the house, but it is not normally actionable for the seller to lie to the buyer about the color of the underwear the seller is wearing. While courts, for instance, may have a right to the truth regarding statements made under oath in response to a valid question or representations of attorneys before the court, few if any legal systems grant private citizens a general right to the truth: lying to a private citizen, *per se*, is neither criminal nor actionable.[1] The general right to the truth is also not a natural right: one cannot claim that, in general, that someone's lying to one renders P infeasible. Rather, the general right to the truth is a moral right.

What is a moral right? The most central sort of moral right legitimates moral expectation: A has a moral right, in this sense, to some action on the part of B when, were A to expect B to consider herself morally obligated to perform the action because B owes it to A to do so as A's due, A's expectation would be morally justifiable. Here "because" means constitutes a sufficient reason. B might have additional reasons for performing the action. Moreover, A need not actually expect B to perform the action: what matters is that an expectation on A's part that B perform the action would be morally justified, whether or not A actually has such an expectation. Again, the expectation must be morally, not epistemologically, justified. A might have every reason to believe that B will, in fact, be extremely unlikely to perform the action or to regard herself as obligated to do so. Finally, a right, in this sense, can be overridden by more pressing moral concerns while remaining an enduring moral claim.[2] Smith has a moral right, in this sense, to Jones' keeping her promise to have lunch with Smith, even when she must break the promise to save a drowning child, and thus Jones owes Smith an explanation and a vigorous attempt to make it up to Smith in some way.[3] By way of contrast, if Jones breaks her lunch appointment with Smith because she learns Smith intends to shoot her at the restaurant, she does not owe Smith a vigorous attempt to make it up to him. The obligation to keep the promise is not overridden, but void.

A right, then, as the term will be used in this chapter, is a particular kind of warrant for a moral expectation. For example, students who inquire about how their grade was determined have a right to an honest explanation. Students have a moral warrant for expecting that the obligation to students of providing an honest explanation constitutes sufficient reason for faculty members to regard themselves as obligated to do so, as the students' due, even if, in special circumstances, another moral consideration might take priority over that obligation.

At issue in this chapter, then, is the general moral right to the truth, that is, the legitimate moral expectation that, in general, others tell us the truth. Do we have such a right? Three grounds for such a warrant are examined below. Two are familiar: respect for autonomy and the principle of universality. The third ground, duties of team loyalty to those who participate in the shared project of constructing a good world, is somewhat novel.

Can we lose the right to the truth? As will become evident, some people, in some instances, by virtue of their conduct or attitude, are no longer morally entitled to expect others to tell the truth. In at least this respect, the ethical demand to tell the truth does not require martyrdom. Morality and prudential common sense are not conflicting guides to conduct.

A. The Problem

Williams, the Chair of a Department of Philosophy at a public university, is a prominent member of a group calling for the criminalization of same-sex relationships and the removal of gays from schools, government, and the media. Her previous decisions about raises, tenure, and promotion give faculty members ample reason to believe that personal politics strongly affect her actions. Moreover, Williams is suspicious, prone to grilling subordinates, and quick to jump to conclusions. Finally, tenure at her university cannot be achieved without the vigorous support of the Chair. Williams, in idle conversation, asks an untenured junior philosophy faculty member, Perez, where he spent his break. Answering the question honestly would suggest that Perez is a closet gay. Perez has several options. He might say, tactfully: "That is none of your business." He might give a vague reply that does not really answer the question. He might try to think up a misleading but, strictly speaking, true reply. However, given Williams's predilections, being evasive or telling her, however politely, to mind her own business would effectively guarantee that Perez will not receive tenure. Instead, Perez might lie. The lie may be an excuse not to answer the question or a false answer to the Chair's question, such as saying that he went to Martha's Vineyard.

Little practical advantage accrues if Perez tells a deliberately misleading truth. After all, if the facts later emerge, Williams's chagrin at having being misled is not likely to be assuaged by the fact that what Perez said was, strictly speaking, true. Williams is not more likely to trust Perez in the future. Nor is much moral advantage gained by saying something specifically intended to mislead by violating the rules of conversational implicature. The principle of universality is violated by both responses, since lies and such "truths" alike are specifically crafted to deceive by violating rules of social converse without which we could not function. Both answers fly in the face of a personal commitment to truth and fair dealing, since in both cases one deliberately spreads error. James S. Ellin[4] suggests that, in the case of a misleading truth, the deceived is at least partially responsible for the deception. But Williams would have to cross-examine Perez for several days in order to rule out all possible misleading answers. It seems as odd to fault Williams for not subjecting Perez to this cross-examination as it is to say Williams would be partially at fault for being deceived by a direct lie because she did not hire private investigators to verify Perez's statement. In both cases, Williams can avoid being deceived only by acting in ways that are unreasonable and socially inapposite. A direct lie and a craftily misleading response both impinge on Williams' autonomy.

Does Williams have a general right to the truth, or is Perez entitled to lie? While some hold that persons have an inalienable right to the truth, it seems at least troubling that Perez is morally required to throw away his chance of tenure in response to Williams' idle question. (As noted above, telling a misleading truth, as some moral philosophers suggest,[5] does not resolve the problem.) Others might suggest that Williams has a right to the truth that is overridden by Perez's duty or right of self-preservation. But it is unclear that Perez owes Williams what someone would normally owe people when their right to the truth is overridden. For example, suppose you innocently ask where Michelle is. If I lie to you in order not to reveal Michelle's whereabouts to a stalker hidden behind the door, I owe you, at the very least, an explanation of why I failed to tell you the truth, as well as an expression of regret or apology. But most people would agree that I have no duty, overridden or not, to answer truthfully a burglar who asks where my jewels are hidden. There is no need to make it up to the burglar after lying about the jewels' whereabouts.

Some moral philosophers have held that there is no general right to the truth. If they are correct, then it follows immediately that Perez may lie without violating Williams's right to the truth, since Williams has no such right. Thus, for the sake of argument, let us assume that there is a general right to the truth. (Grounds for asserting there is such a right will emerge below.) In that case, the Chair, it will be argued, has lost the right to the truth in this instance. While there may be personal moral reasons for Perez not to lie, Williams is not entitled to an honest answer to her question. There may be internal moral considerations prompting Perez to tell the truth and let the consequences come as they may. Telling the truth may be a matter of personal integrity. Bowing to career pressures may diminish his sense of personal dignity or autonomy as a person. Perez may have a moral commitment to truth in all its forms, a commitment that would be violated by spreading a falsehood, however convenient. But no moral requirement to tell the truth derives from Williams's entitlements. Telling the lie would not violate Williams's legitimate moral expectations.

B. Autonomy

It has been noted by Sissela Bok and Thomas E. Hill Jr. that liars deprive listeners of some degree of autonomy.[6] Respect for autonomy, thus, provides one ground for the set of warrants that constitute the general moral right to the truth: generally, the truth is one's due as an autonomous agent and lying to others fails to respect their publicly recognized status as autonomous agents. It is less often noted that lying can restore autonomy to the liar in circumstances in which autonomy has been improperly impaired.

By asking her question, the Department Chair places the junior faculty member in a position that threatens his autonomy. In a perfect world, he could answer truthfully without fear. The answer, after all, is irrelevant to whether he should be tenured. But this is not a perfect world, and Perez knows that giving an honest answer will, improperly and unjustly, deprive him of his livelihood. Perez finds his autonomy unfairly and improperly threatened. By lying, Perez regains some measure of control over his destiny. Whether or not he gets tenure will depend upon the quality of his teaching, the quality of his research, and other legitimate factors over which he has some control, not on the prejudices of his colleagues over which he has virtually no control.

More generally, by asking an inappropriate question, the questioner improperly imposes a choice on the hearer. Autonomy considerations suggest that the hearer need not accept the terms of this choice. We are morally entitled to use commensurate methods of freeing ourselves from an improperly imposed choice situation, even if those methods would ordinarily be unacceptable. For example, in *Sophie's Choice* a Nazi officer, pointing a gun at Sophie's children, tells her she must choose one child to live or he will kill both of her children. Sophie is not obligated to accept the parameters of the choice. She may reject the choice and she may use otherwise morally unacceptable means to do so. For example, it is perfectly licit for her to wrest the gun away from the Nazi or even shoot him, if doing so would effectively eliminate the improper choice situation the Nazi has imposed on her. Similarly, a stranger at a bus stop who insistently asks Ozawa an emotionally troubling, prying question improperly gives Ozawa a choice between being rude and confrontational or revealing a private and troubling matter. The stranger has no entitlement to place Ozawa in that choice situation, and it is clear that his doing so violates standards of good faith and consideration. Autonomy considerations suggest that Ozawa may reject this choice situation. Obviously, asking a prying question is not comparable in seriousness or culpability to the Nazi's action in *Sophie's Choice*, but, equally, telling a small lie to avoid the choice is not as serious as shooting someone. In both cases, the method used to reject the choice situation is morally commensurable with both the moral flaw involved in imposing the choice and the harm the choice imposes. Thus Ozawa is entitled to lie to the stranger just as Sophie is entitled to shoot the Nazi.

More generally, people who take autonomy seriously accept some sort of reciprocity limitation on respecting autonomy. I am permitted to violate your autonomy, in certain ways, when your exercise of that autonomy improperly limits mine, in order to avoid having my autonomy improperly limited. If you, without justification, lock me in your room, I am permitted to break your window in order to escape, though, ordinarily, breaking your window without your consent would violate your autonomy. By asking the question, the stranger similarly employs his autonomy in a way that improperly limits Ozawa's, and Ozawa is entitled commensurately to perform actions that would ordinarily violate the stranger's autonomy in order to avoid having his autonomy improperly limited. Of course, imprisoning you in my room when I have the right to do so does not entitle you to break my window. Similarly, asking an embarrassing question does not, *per se*, entitle the hearer to lie. The argument from autonomy sanctions lying only in response to improper questions (that is, when the asker improperly restricts or violates the autonomy of the hearer by asking) the answer to which is not protected by a specific right to the truth.[7]

C. Universality

A second ground for a right to the truth stems from the principle of universality. The arguments that lying violates the principle of universality are too well known to require detailed exposition.[8] In any case, there are nearly as many versions of the principle of universality as there are philosophers. The general outline of the argument, however, can be formulated simply. Effective human interaction requires that people generally place a high value on telling the truth and that they generally do so. Thus everyone must insist that others commit themselves to general participation in the social institution of truth-telling. To exempt oneself from the general obligation to tell the truth is thus to assert that there are different moral standards for oneself and for everyone else, an assertion incompatible with the very notion of a moral standard. We should not freeload on others doing their duty. Thus, we should generally participate in the social institution of truth-telling. More specifically, others are morally warranted in expecting that we will regard ourselves as obligated, out of considerations of fairness and reciprocity, not to lie to them, and lying to others fails to respect their status as equals in the eyes of morality.[9] But a closer look at this argument suggests that, in some cases, telling a lie might not violate the principle of universality. The driving moral concepts behind most versions of the principle are reciprocity and fairness. The heart of the principle of universality is the notion that we should not freeload on others doing their duty. While reciprocity might be violated when someone lies to a dedicated truth-teller, lying to a liar observes reciprocity.

This consideration led Kant, as his discussion of capital punishment shows, to claim that the principle of universality must be applied only to individuals who abide by it. People who choose a maxim opposed to the categorical imperative, Kant suggests, should have their own maxim applied to them. If the enemy's armies are hungry, I need not send them food until they surrender: I have no general duty of beneficence toward people actively devoting themselves to destroying me without justification. Even Kant's famous claim that one must tell the truth even to a potential murderer about the intended victim's whereabouts is not a counterexample to this interpretation of Kant, since the potential murderer does not, according to Kant's story, violate the maxim of truth-telling. [10]

Thus, even for Kant, lying to a liar does not violate the principle of universality. As she is described earlier, Williams is not a liar. But Williams's question does abuse the institution of truth-telling. If it abuses the very principle that requires telling the truth, then lying to Williams does not violate the duty of reciprocity. Society has established a social obligation to tell the truth because that obligation is necessary for a number of legitimate purposes, including making fair and reasonable hiring decisions. Making use of the institution of truth telling for inappropriate purposes or in inappropriate ways is as much of an abuse of the institution as is telling a lie. Were everyone to abuse truth-telling in those ways, the institution could not survive. For example, society can maintain an institution of truth-telling only because most people generally refrain from asking questions that grossly violate others' privacy.[11] The principle of reciprocity requires that people do not make inappropriate use of social institutions as much as it requires people to perform the actions the institution demands. Someone who knowingly asks an obviously unfair and inappropriate question violates the rules of truth-telling as surely as does someone who tells a lie. Hence, the principle of universality does not require Perez to give Williams a truthful answer.

D. Duties of Team Loyalty

Different kinds of rights have different sources. Some rights derive from special roles that individuals assume: clients may legitimately expect a degree of confidentiality from their attorneys that it would be inappropriate to expect from their grocery clerks. One ground of the general right to the truth is active membership in the moral community: active members of the moral community are morally entitled to expect that others will not lie to them.

The term "moral community" is often used to refer to the collection of all beings who have moral standing. Here, however, "moral community" will refer collectively to persons who participate in the common moral enterprise of making a good world. Not all persons choose to assume this role, but many of us do take part in the task of making, together, a world worthy of moral respect. There are many ways of contributing to this project. The Buddhist monk who devotes his life to isolated contemplation dedicates himself, in his own way, to the moral enterprise, as does the honest and industrious grocer, the dedicated teacher, and the wise and loving parent. More specifically, active members of the moral community are persons who can reasonably be seen as assenting, in some broad sense, through their conduct and attitudes, to a morally defensible conception of the good life and who live their lives in adherence to that conception. Thus individuals can fail to be members of the moral community in three distinct ways. They can live without genuine commitment to a moral vision, their moral vision may not be properly reflected in their lives (in their conduct, feelings, perceptions, predilections, etc.), or their moral vision may be indefensible. A sincere and dedicated Nazi is committed to and reflects in his life a moral stance, but not a defensible one.

This formulation contains two somewhat controversial assumptions. It contains the assumption that some values are morally defensible and some are not. But unless some values are objectively indefensible, there is no reason for Perez to refrain from lying. If there is nothing objectively wrong with general disregard for the truth, then Perez is morally free to place no value on truth-telling. Unless some values are morally defensible and others not, there is no general right to the truth. Thus any account of the general right to the truth must presuppose that only some values are morally defensible.[12] The formulation also contains the assumption that, in some important sense, the moral enterprise is a co-operative project. People working toward a moral vision are invested in each other's success, and so have reason to support each other's efforts. Several reasons for thinking that the moral enterprise must be, at least in part, communal are found elsewhere in this volume.

Membership in the moral community is a matter of degree. Some people work harder than others. Some people's moral visions are more deeply flawed than the moral visions of others. Some people's lives more fully reflect their moral commitments than others'. For the sake of simplicity, however, let us temporarily consider membership in the moral community as if it were an all or nothing matter, and treat later the special problems that pertain to people who are partially or faultily members of the moral community.

Why does membership in the moral community give rise to a general right to the truth? Just as there are standards of concern and conduct members of an Olympic team may legitimately expect from each other as co-participants in an activity to which they are dedicated, so there are standards of concern and conduct that members of the moral community may legitimately expect from each other as co-participants in the moral enterprise. The very same arguments that belonging to Team U.S.A. creates duties of loyalty to other members of the team suggest that belonging to what might be called "Team Morality" creates duties of loyalty to fellow members of the moral community. For example, if someone is dedicated to an enterprise, that person has a stake in the success of people whose success advances the enterprise. In addition, it is puzzling to see how one could, absent special circumstances, hold that a goal is worthy but devoting oneself to the goal is not worthy, and so, if the worthiness of the goal commands one's allegiance, so, presumably, would the worthiness of committing oneself to the goal. So respect for the goals of the enterprise seems to imply respect for those who dedicate themselves to those goals. Moreover, trustworthiness and fellowship among teammates are necessary for an effective effort at achieving the goals of the enterprise.

Two arguments suggest that a general commitment to refrain from lying is, indeed, among the duties of loyalty that moral teammates may legitimately expect from each other. Just as football teammates should expect help and support from teammates in employing the playing skills directly used to achieve their common goal, so members of the moral community should expect help and support from teammates in employing the moral skills directly used to achieve their common goal. At the very least, players are entitled to assume that, other things being equal, teammates will not directly impede their ability to play well. Playing well, as it were, in the moral arena, means making wise decisions. Active members of the moral community have a mutual stake in each other's having the information to make wise decisions. At the very least, active members of the moral community are entitled to assume that, other things being equal, teammates will not directly impede their ability to decide wisely. Lying, however, directly promotes error and, if the lie is believed, guarantees that the hearer falls short of the ideal of the rational moral agent, since the hearer lacks full command of the facts. Lying to a person directly impedes his or her ability to make wise decisions, and so active members of the moral community are entitled to assume that, other things being equal, teammates will not lie to them. In general, honesty fundamentally supports efforts of others to achieve the common goal, while dishonesty generally undercuts ability of others to help the team. Thus the duties of team loyalty forbid lying to an active member of the moral community, other things being equal. Members of Team Morality are warranted in expecting, as their due, general honesty, and lying to a member of Team Morality fails to respect her status as a member of the moral community.

Note that the argument from wise decisions does not apply to people not actively engaged in the moral community. The decision not to participate in any significant way in the moral enterprise is, almost by definition, (morally) unwise. The decisions of those who ask improper questions are unwise in the relevant respect, namely, the respect by virtue of which their questions are improper, otherwise the question asked would not remove them from the set of persons actively engaged in making a good world. The burglar who asks where my jewels are is acting unwisely in robbing me, and it is the robbery that makes his question improper. Honestly informing the burglar the location of the jewels does not assist him in wisely choosing not to rob me. Williams acts unwisely in abusing her position, and it is that abuse that makes her question improper. By honestly informing Williams where he spent his break, Perez does not assist

Williams in wisely deciding not to abuse her position. In general, lying to non-members of the moral community no more undermines their ability to make wise decisions than putting corpses in air-tight coffins undermines the ability of the dead to breathe. Of course, non-members of the moral community can become members, while corpses cannot become breathers. This consideration suggests a principle of conservatism, articulated below.

The second argument that moral teammates owe each other a commitment to truthfulness takes it that general straightforwardness among persons is itself an element of a good world. In a morally ideal world, persons interact with honesty and honor: personal relationships are based on justified trust. To the extent that relationships among people are not honest and honorable, the world is morally flawed. While football players may expect opposing players to try prevent them from winning, football players are entitled to expect that their own teammates will try to help them win. Similarly, while active members of the moral community may expect lies from those not dedicated to morality, they are (generally) entitled to expect that their teammates in morality will not lie.

The argument from general straightforwardness also fails to provide people who are not members of the moral community a right to the truth. A relationship with someone who is not a member of the moral community is not governed by honesty and honor. If it were, then, presumably, the other person would be, to some significant extent, a member of the moral community. Thus, even if someone does not lie to such a person, the relationship will not be one of honesty and honor. Hence the importance of relationships of honesty and honor provides no special reason not to lie to non-members of the moral community.

In general, if the general right to the truth lies among the duties of loyalty to fellow members of the moral community, then, at least on these grounds, non-members of the moral community do not possess a general right to the truth, although they retain whatever rights they possess on other grounds, e.g., a specific right to the truth from medical providers about their medical condition, based on the moral implications of the patient-provider relationship. Unethical and amoral persons have chosen to opt out of the common moral enterprise, much as does a player who consistently harms the team's chance to win in order to make himself look good. Such players cannot legitimately expect the same loyalty from his teammates as can a loyal team player. Indeed, a player who throws the season is due no team loyalty at all, for the very considerations that engender loyalty no longer apply to him. For the same reasons that a football player who opts out of the team activity in certain respects loses the right, in certain respects, to the loyalty of his or her teammates, a person who opts out of the moral enterprise in certain respects loses the right, in certain respects, to the loyalty due fellow members of the moral community. That, I suggest, is why one has no duty to answer truthfully a burglar's question concerning the whereabouts of one's jewelry. Similarly, Williams abuses her position. Her question, however she herself perceives it, by insuring that in at least one case tenure is unfairly denied to those who are honest, constitutes a direct blow to the project of making a better world. Williams is no more entitled to an honest answer to her question than a ballplayer who throws the game is entitled to the loyalty of his teammates.

It may be objected that even if some moral stances are objectively indefensible, we have no infallible method of determining which ones they are. Williams believes that it is right to use the Chair's power to purge her university of gays, and Perez cannot, with apodictic certainty, prove her wrong. It is always possible, however unlikely, that Williams' stance is defensible and Perez's stance is indefensible. Moreover, it is impossible for Perez fully to know the heart of Williams. Thus, it may be argued, Perez is not entitled to treat Williams as having lost the general right to the truth, because he cannot be certain she is not a full member of the moral community.

While the fallibility of our moral beliefs provides good reason for conservatism in acting on those beliefs, it should not cause paralysis. We act on fallible moral beliefs all the time. Indeed, we cannot help but do so. Because Perez must decide whether to tell a lie or a self-destructive truth to Williams, Perez must decide if Williams is a member of the moral community. If he decides wrongly, then, in lying, he acts wrongly. In lying, Perez runs the risk that he tells a small lie when he should have told the truth. This does not seem to be an unconscionable risk. It is a much smaller risk than we frequently take when making moral decisions. While uncertainty might provide a presumption in favor of truth-telling, it is not always irrational to take the moral risk involved in telling a lie to someone whom we believe not to be a member of the moral community, particularly when the lie is a small one and the consequence of truth-telling severe.

The earlier arguments concerning the principle of universality might suggest that all persons, not just members of the moral community, have a general right to the truth. However, people who are not members of the moral community are not members by virtue of the fact that they are not doing their duty. Hence, in lying to someone who is not a member of the moral community, we are not freeloading on others doing their duty. Universality does not require truthfulness to people who are not members of the moral community. More specifically, effective social intercourse requires more than most people telling the truth most of the time. The nature of lies is as important as their frequency. Imagine, for example, the chaos that would ensue if a university registrar told random lies to students one sixth of the time. We can rely on others only if most people adopt truth-telling as a standard: we must be able to assume that most people will not lie without a fairly good reason. The institution of truth-telling requires more than refraining from knowingly uttering falsehoods. For example, social rules about what information must be volunteered in response to a question that does not expressly call for that information are equally necessary for effective human interaction. The standard of truth-telling most people must adopt in order for complex societies to thrive calls for striving to instantiate a certain ideal of human interaction, not a simple restriction on telling lies. Christopher McMahon, for example, articulates a principle of openness:

> When one acts with the intention of eliciting from another a reasoned response by providing an ostensible reason for it, one must make a good faith attempt to ensure that she is in possession of any apparent fact (this is, anything one believes to be the case) that one thinks she would regard as a reason for or against producing this response.[13]

Without general commitment to such ideals, complex societies cannot function. Universality, thus, requires us not so much to refrain from speaking falsehoods as to strive to instantiate fair and honorable human interactions.

The universality argument for truth-telling, thus, does not establish an abstract connection between moral agents and the truth. The connection between truth and individual moral agents is indirect, mediated by a particular ideal of human social interaction. What the argument suggests is not that agents are morally constrained by the truth as such, but that persons must be committed to a particular sort of human interaction characterized by reciprocity and honorable dealing. Speaking the truth is a consequence of striving for that ideal, of striving to instantiate a particular ideal of human interaction.

But people who are not members of the moral community, at least in the kinds of cases under discussion, have already made that ideal of human interaction unrealizable. For example, Williams has made impossible the kind of honorable relationship to which Perez is committed. It would be an exercise in futility for Perez to make his contribution to such an honorable relationship, since Williams has already guaranteed that it will not obtain. In general, our commitment to an ideal of human interaction no more requires us to try to interact with someone else in that way when his or her actions prevent that kind of interaction than our commitment to a flourishing garden requires us to water a dead plant.

The argument from moral community suggests that persons who are fully disengaged from any moral enterprise have no general right to the truth. At first glance, this may seem an overstrong result. But, if Adolf Eichmann inquires about the time, it does not seem implausible to say "I do not owe him, quite literally, the time of day." Of course, even if people who are not members of the moral community lack a general right to the truth, other considerations might entitle them to honest answers to particular questions. For example, the special responsibilities physicians have to their patients give even evil patients a right to an honest answer to questions about their medical conditions. Losing the general right to the truth does not, *per se*, entail losing whatever specific rights to the truth one might have. Moreover, there are reasons not to lie gratuitously, even to evil people. For example, lying about the time to someone is likely to cause him, or, yet worse, innocent others, some ill effect. If there is no compelling motivation for me to lie to him, then my lie gratuitously poses the risk of causing harm. We should not gratuitously harm others, even people who are not members of the moral community. Moreover, people change, and it is impossible fully to know the mind of another person. It is easy to be mistaken about the extent to which someone is not a member of the moral community. Finally, it is better to speak the truth to someone who has no right to the truth than to lie to someone who does have a right to the truth. Lying only when the motivation for lying springs from a clear moral defect in the hearer helps limit lies to hearers who are not members of the moral community in the relevant respect at the time the question is asked, and, by reducing the number and scope of lies told, lessens the probability of causing harm or violating other duties. For these reasons, it seems appropriate to treat others as losing the right to the truth only in contexts in which their improper behavior is immediately relevant to the motivation for lying. The moral fault must be clear, and the lie told should be as small as feasible. Since truth-telling and honesty are, in general, good things, a small lie is preferable to a big lie. In short, the principle of conservatism suggests that lies should be as small as feasible and be restricted to occasions in which the moral fault of the hearer is both clear and directly productive of the motivation to lie. The harm done by the lie must be commensurate with the harm done by asking the improper question. Moreover, the benefit of the doubt belongs to truth-telling: when in doubt about any of these conditions, tell the truth.

For people who are partially or faultily engaged in morality, losing the right to the truth is a more complex issue. Some loyalty is due anyone who participates, in any significant way, in a moral enterprise. But the honesty due moral teammates is not an all or nothing matter. The principle of conservatism provides some assistance here. Williams might be tireless in her fundraising to relieve world hunger and fastidiously honest and responsible in matters of personal finance. She might possess numerous other virtues, which entitle her to some degree of loyalty from Perez. The principle of conservatism, however, permits Perez to lie to her only in instances in which her moral faults create the motivation to lie. Thus Perez may respond with loyalty to Williams's admirable efforts on behalf of the starving, but withhold loyalty when her willingness to abuse her position threatens his career. This seems an appropriate way to express limited loyalty to a partial member of the moral community, as the arguments from universality and autonomy provide some independent justification for Perez to lie to Williams in that instance.

In other instances, the extent to which someone is fully a member of the moral community determines the degree of candor owed. Among persons of honor, the duty of honesty goes beyond mere truthfulness. The appropriate way to treat such teammates is not to stoop to deception or to make use of misperceptions. If a person of honor is considering buying my home, I will not attempt to give him or her the wrong impression or seek to hide drawbacks of the house and will actively correct misperceptions she produces on her own. I would certainly mention to a person of honor that the highway is audible from the backyard when the wind blows south, while, with someone else I might simply not bring up the subject of highway noise, though I would be straightforward about the topic if specifically asked.

E. Applications and Examples

People lose the right to the truth when they ask questions that undermine morality in some significant way, abuse the social institution of truth telling, or violate the hearer's autonomy by imposing an illicit choice. Not all inappropriate questions meet these criteria. Suppose a stranger in an internet chat room asks me to share one of my poems with her. I reply "I only share my poems with people who have sex six times a week or more. Do you?" While this is clearly an inappropriate question, the hearer has no moral claim on seeing my poetry, and can choose, without significant hardship, simply to ignore me. A chat room is not a captive audience situation: it is easy enough for a stranger in a chat room to ignore the situation and simply post no reply to me. My question imposes no significant illicit choice on the stranger. Similarly, because I am entitled to set whatever odd conditions I choose on showing my poetry, I do not abuse the social institution of truth telling. Refusing to show someone my poems, for whatever reason, does not significantly impede the effort to build a better moral world. I do not lose the right to the truth. By contrast, I would lose the right to the truth should I demand an answer to the same question as a prerequisite for throwing her a life preserver when she is drowning, since I am imposing on her the illicit choice of drowning or revealing private information to which I have no right and I significantly undermine morality. Even if, as some argue, I have no duty to save a life at no significant cost to myself, refusing to do so is morally reprehensible. Again, a woman who dishonestly agrees to go out with a man who respectfully asks her out, when in fact she has no intention of showing up for the date, usually does violate his general right to a truthful reply. In most contexts, respectfully asking her is not a wrong and whatever harm she suffers from the choice imposed on her, namely, saying "yes" or experiencing any discomfort she may feel at ignoring or gracefully declining his offer, is not commensurate with the harm he suffers as a result of her lie (preparing for the date, setting aside all plans for the evening, perhaps purchasing flowers, and so forth, in order to be hurt and humiliated.) However, the more that he consistently refuses to accept "no" as an answer, especially in a captive audience situation (e.g., she is at work and cannot leave), or the more that their particular circumstances make his asking her improper (e.g., he is married to her sister), the more that his asking does count as doing something wrong and/or imposing an improper choice upon her. For example, if he is unremittingly persistent, gracious refusal must give way to more stressful measures, such as making threats or even calling the police, and that choice, between saying "yes" or calling the police, he is not entitled to impose. Moreover, in such circumstances, the harm to her of his asking becomes increasingly commensurate with the harm done by the lie. In such cases he may lose the right to a truthful answer.

By these criteria, Williams has lost the right to a truthful answer to her question.[14] However, the principle of conservatism restricts the lie Perez may legitimately tell. Williams retains whatever specific rights to the truth she might have, including those she has as Chair. Perez should not mislead the Chair in a manner that affects the Chair's legitimate decisions, for such a lie would violate the special duties of trust members of a university have toward one another. It would be inappropriate for Perez to say that he attended a professional conference he did not attend. Similarly, Perez should restrict himself to a lie whose foreseeable consequences are of only minor importance, and the lie's divergence from the truth should be no greater than needed. Perez should not say that he went to France or Madagascar.

Job interviews present interesting cases. It is not appropriate to lie about licensure or degrees acquired, since this constitutes information directly relevant to the hirer's legitimate decision, and, in some cases, people have a special role responsibility not to misrepresent this information. Consider, however, these examples.

An employment questionnaire for a janitorial position in a public university[15] contains the question: "Did you ever know anyone who smoked marijuana?" The job applicant is aware that answering "yes" to this question will eliminate her from consideration. While it may be appropriate to inquire whether or not the applicant uses or has used illegal drugs, the fact that a neighbor or acquaintance of the applicant once smoked marijuana is neither the fault of the applicant nor relevant to determining that the applicant would perform well as a janitor. Indeed, few members of a certain generation could honesty answer "no." Similarly, while an employer may have a specific right to the truth concerning an employee's own use of illegal drugs, an employer has no specific right to the truth about the drug use of an employee's acquaintances. The employer has abused the power to hire and created a situation in which an irrelevant question brings it about that no one who gives an honest answer will be hired. The employer penalizes honesty and rewards dishonesty. An applicant who lies on this question does not treat the employer unfairly.[16] The employer acts wrongly, in the circumstances, in asking the question. The employer improperly imposes the choice of lying or rendering oneself ineligible for a public position for an irrelevant and improper reason. The harm done by the lie is nugatory. Finally, the lie does not interfere with the employer exercising any legitimate prerogative or making any appropriate decision.

Job interviewers may lose the right to a truthful answer even when their question bears some relevance to assessing suitability to the position. Consider an employer interviewing graduate students at a prestigious public university for a part-time, minimum wage, filing job in the library. The interviewer asks: "How do you feel about filing?" No graduate student at that institution could honesty answer "I love filing: it is my favorite activity on earth." Yet that is the answer for which she is looking. Previous applicants who gave other tactful but honest replies were turned down on those grounds. Here again, the employer has misused the power to hire and created a situation in which only those willing to lie may be hired. The question is not entirely irrelevant, but the standard imposed by the employer is inappropriate. Feigning intense enjoyment of filing does not treat the employer unfairly.[17]

A job interviewer at a public institution who has unrealistic expectations contrasts illuminatingly with a date who has unrealistic expectations. Suppose Jack makes it clear that he is only romantically interested in women who have never had the faintest interest in any other man. Jack asks Susan, a thirty-two year old woman, if she has ever had even a twinge of interest in any man other than himself, including wistful adolescent thoughts. Jack's question may seem similar to the employment questionnaire item concerning marijuana. Both make an impossible demand and so penalize honesty. But Jack is entitled to set any criteria he likes for his romantic inclinations. While the law and most moral philosophers hold that job applicants (especially for jobs at public institutions) have some entitlement to fair consideration, Susan has no moral claim of any sort on Jack's romantic interest. Thus the job applicant is wronged by an inappropriate job criterion in a way that Susan is not wronged if she is excluded from Jack's romantic consideration for an inappropriate reason. Jack's question, however absurd, does not abuse the institution of truth-telling. It does not violate Susan's autonomy by imposing an illicit choice or seriously undermine morality. Thus, although Jack is being unreasonable and foolish, he does not lose the right to the truth by asking his question.

Asking an inappropriate prying question may also lose someone the right to a truthful answer to that question. The stranger who insistently asks a couple with fertility problems "Why don't you have any kids?" is not entitled to an answer. It is none of his business. By asking, he violates the rules by which we are permitted to ask questions, and violates them in a fairly invasive and disturbing way. His abuse of the social institution of question-asking puts the couple needlessly in an uncomfortable position. He forces the couple either to be rude and confrontational or to reveal something private and painful, unless the couple lies. A small lie here does no instrumental harm. It does not deprive the listener of any information to which he is entitled or needs to know to make a rational decision about anything of import. Thus the couple is justified in telling a small lie to avoid the disturbing unpleasantness of either telling the questioner to mind his own business or revealing a private and painful fact.

In sum, people lose the right to the truth by asking inappropriate questions that undermine morality, abuse the institution of truth-telling, or impose an illicit choice. We are entitled to lie in response to such a question, although the lie should be as small as possible, providing that the moral fault of the hearer is directly productive of the motivation to lie and the lie does not significantly impede the asker in performing legitimate tasks, violate specific rights to the truth, or cause incommensurate harm. Thus the ethics of truth-telling does not require self-destructive behavior in response to unfair questions. Morality is less harsh a master than is sometimes believed.

Notes to Chapter Seven

1 While, as noted earlier, moral rights may be legally meaningful via their role in legal reasoning, lying as such is not actionable.

2 That is, a vector right may not be a resultant right: see Chapters 1 and 3.

3 Simmons, A. John, *Moral Principles and Political Obligations*, Princeton, N.J.: Princeton University Press, 1979.

4 Ellin, James, "Lying and Deception: The Solution to a Dilemma in Medical Ethics," *Westminister Institute Review*, May 1961: p. 1.

5 Bok, Sissela, *Lying: Moral Choice in Public and Private Life*, New York: Pantheon Books, 1978.

6 Bok, Sissela, *op. cit.* and Hill, Thomas E. Jr., "Autonomy and Benevolent Lies," *Journal of Value Inquiry*, 1984, 18:4, pp. 251-267.

7 For example, it is arguably improper to ask a spouse "do you love me or our children more?" In addition, arguably, a spouse has a specific right not to be misled about the extent of the other spouse's love for her. If so, the question is improper but a lying response would violate a specific right to the truth: the only morally appropriate responses would be answering truthfully or not answering the question (by refusing to answer, giving a vague or unresponsive reply, or finding an excuse for not answering).

8 For a more detailed discussion of the argument, see Korsgaard, Christine M., "The Right to Lie: Kant on Dealing with Evil," *Philosophy and Public Affairs*, Fall 1986, 15:4, pp. 325-349.

9 The requirement here is not that we recognize others as of equal moral worth, but that we recognize that moral requirements, whatever their content, applies equally to ourselves and to others. This distinction is parallel to that drawn in Chapter 5 between ER and EL.

10 Kant, "On a Supposed Right to Lie from Altruistic Motives", 1797, in *Immanuel Kant: Critique of Practical Reason and Other Writings in Moral Philosophy*, trans. L.W. Beck, Chicago: University of Chicago Press, 1949.

11 While there is no logical contradiction in imagining a society in which both egregiously prying questions and truthful, rude replies to those questions are widespread, pragmatically, such a society of human beings would not long endure in that state.

12 For an argument against amoralism, see Schlossberger, Eugene, *Moral Responsibility and Persons*, Philadelphia: Temple University Press, 1992.

13 Christopher McMahon, "Openness," *Canadian Journal of Philosophy* , March 1990, 20:1, pp. 31-32.

14 Cf. Robert N. Van Wyk, "When Is Lying Morally Permissible? Casuistical Reflections on the Game Analogy, Self-Defense, Social Contract Ethics, and Ideals," *Journal of Value Inquiry*, April 1990, 24:2, pp. 155-168.

15 Some would argue that for a "purely private" concern employers are entitled to impose whatever odd conditions on hiring they might wish, while others view jobs as semi-

public commodities (see Chapter 10). A public university, supported by tax dollars, is not a "purely private" concern.

16 For a discussion of inappropriate job interview questions, see Albert Carr, "Is Business Bluffing Ethical?" *Harvard Business Review*, January-February 1968, 46:1, pp. 143-153.

17 Arguably, an employer has a specific (vector) right to a truthful reply. If so, that right is overridden rather than lost, that is, the employer has a vector right but not a resultant right to a fully truthful reply.

Chapter 8:
Rights of and Obligations
to Future Generations

Many of our decisions are significantly shaped by what we owe to posterity. Sensible public policy appears to presuppose that we bear obligations to those yet to come. For instance, if we have no obligation to future generations, then, it would appear, we are entitled to consume all the earth's non-renewable resources and engage in practices that will leave the earth uninhabitable by human beings in a hundred years.[1] Common sense suggests that we have discounted obligations to future generations and that future generations have some (if lesser) rights.

Several objections to this common sense view have been raised. How, for instance, could we have obligations to future generations, since they do not yet exist? Future persons seem to be merely possible entities. How can mere possibilities have rights? Richard T. de George, for instance, suggests that since future generations do not now exist, they can't be "the present bearer or subject of anything, including rights"[2] and argues that, if future generations had rights equivalent to ours, given the limited supply of oil and the potentially vast number of persons who will be born after us, we would each be restricted to perhaps a mere thimbleful of oil. Before the commonsense view can be adopted and used as a basis for economic and environmental policy, these and other objections must be addressed. I will argue, specifically, for two related claims. First, we are obligated to strive reasonably to insure that there will be future generations and that our actions now, given that there is a future generation, do not ensure or render unreasonably probable the violation in the future of the rights that will be held by those who will then exist. Second, we now bear obligations that restrict our conduct because of our conduct's likely effect on future generations. These two claims are sufficient to ground most of the relevant claims of the commonsense position. In addition, some reason will be given for believing a third, stronger claim: the people who will actually exist in the future can have rights now.

A. The Commonsense View

The commonsense view holds that we owe discounted duties to those yet to come. Consider Jose, who has two twin infant children and plans to have a third. Jose has at present $100,000 available for education but, for various reasons, is unlikely ever to be able to add that amount. It would seem unfair, absent special circumstances, to give, irrevocably, $5000 to one twin and $95,000 to the other: absent special circumstances, their college funds should be roughly equal. Similarly, it would strike most as unfair to place $50,000 irrevocably in each twin's account, leaving nothing for the planned third child. Assuming that parents have some obligation to treat their children fairly, in the sense of not strongly disadvantaging one in favor of another without a good reason, the third child, if born, would have grounds for reproaching Jose for not retaining at least some of the money for future distribution. Yet few would reproach Jose were he to give each twin 40,000, reserving 20,000 for the planned future child. The third child does not yet exist, and its existence and future circumstances are somewhat uncertain. In short, commonsense deems that, other things being equal, Jose must make some, but not necessarily equal, provision for a planned third child: Jose has discounted duties to the future child.

The use of the term "discounted," borrowed from finance, is perhaps unfortunate. Investors discount future gains against present ones for two reasons: uncertainty and the loss of earning potential during the interim. If obligations to future generations are discounted in this way, then even a small gain in utility now might outweigh a vast amount of disutility in the distant future.[3] The analogy fails, however. Dollars invested possess three key features: they are fungible, durable, and there is no practical limit to their earning power. Dollars endure while happiness fades. While invested dollars continue to earn returns indefinitely, a unit of utility produced today will not necessary result in a hundred units of utility ten years from now. Most moral theories do not treat happiness and welfare as completely fungible. These factors impose limits on the amount we may discount future generations. Suppose my expected lifespan were 500 years. It is rational to prefer receiving five hundred dollars now to receiving a thousand dollars 400 years from now because, if I invest the five hundred dollars wisely now, I will have vastly more than a thousand dollars at the end of 400 years. But it would not be reasonable to eat a bite of pizza now knowing it would cause me a year of agony 400 years later, since the pleasure of the bite of pizza does not endure and does not continue to beget happiness. The fate of future generations is closer to the latter situation than the former. On the other hand, it is reasonable to give some degree of preference to a bite of pizza now over a bite of pizza 40 years from now, since I may not live 40 years longer, my feelings about pizza may change, and I inhabit the present: while I have very intimate ties to the self who will inhabit the future 40 years from now, a certain degree of self-preference (preference for the self I am now) is surely permissible. Thus limited, moderate discounting of future generations seems reasonable.

The commonsense view discounts the future via related, overlapping, broad moral *desiderata* rather than rigorous obligations. Three examples will serve to illustrate the character of these obligations.

1. We should do our best to insure that conditions are reasonably favorable for the continued flourishing of human life and of what is good, noble, and significant about human accomplishment as a common enterprise.

Arguably, we owe Obligation 1. to past generations, from whose devotion to the common enterprise of human accomplishment we have greatly benefited (see Section E.). Obligations 2. and 3. can be seen both as supplementing and further specifying Obligation 1.

2. We should generally strive to ensure, as feasible, that what we pass on to future generations is not grossly worse, all things considered, than what we received from previous generations.[4]

We inherited a reasonably copious supply of oil, and so we should try to ensure that the next generation inherits a reasonably generous supply of oil. Oil is but one resource, and our depletion of oil is to some degree offset by developing reasonable substitutes. While it is impossible to provide a reasonable supply of natural oil for a million generations, if each generation both strives to ensure that the oil received by the next generation is not grossly more limited than the oil it inherited and gives thought to developing alternatives to natural oil and improving overall life in ways not dependent on oil supply, future generations will generally not have licit grounds for accusing previous generations of serious injustice.

3. We should do our best to take reasonable steps to avoid acting in ways that will cause great hardship for large numbers of person in the future.

Unavoidably, large numbers of persons will endure hardships in the future. To determine what steps are "reasonable" one must balance the likelihood, severity, and extent of a risk against the costs of taking the step. Moderate discounting applies to each of these factors. If each generation does its best to take such reasonable steps, future generations will generally not have licit grounds for accusing previous generations of serious injustice.

Such commonsense dicta may seem hopelessly vague, but they do serve to rule out a variety of behaviors some have advocated, such as the widespread use of (present technology for employing) nuclear energy (with its attendant accumulation of nuclear waste),[5] unrestricted population growth in a world already endowed with over 6 billion people, and extravagant depletion of the world's oil, without requiring as much as others have urged, such as the elimination of the automobile (whatever other merits that proposal might have).

I will not discuss further, except tangentially, issues concerning discounting the future.[6] This chapter focuses on several arguments that future generations cannot possess rights or be the subject of obligations, not on the content of those rights or obligations.[7] Readers may find elsewhere discussion of additional arguments based on the difficulty of feeling connected to or knowing the needs and/or desires and/or moral concerns of future generations[8] as well as objections based on justice as reciprocity.[9]

B. Future Generations and Non-Existence

One simple and very general line of argument against obligations to future generations runs as follows:

1) Obligations can be owed only to things that actually exist.
2) Future generations do not actually exist.
3) Therefore there can be no obligations to future generations.

Is premise 1) correct, or can there be obligations to non-existent objects? Non-existent objects fall into two categories:

a) Things that do not presently exist but are actual at some time (departed and future objects), and
b) Things that are not actual at any time, such as merely possible objects, fictions such as "Mickey Mouse," and virtual objects such as those posited by certain interpretations of quantum mechanics.

For premise 1) in its present form to support the conclusion, "non-existent" must mean "not presently existing" and so include items in category a), since otherwise future generations, if indeed there will be any, are not "non-existent." Hence, if premise 1) of the above argument is true, then there can be no obligations to departed objects, since they do not actually exist (though they once did). Thus, for example, there is no obligation to the deceased establisher of a scholarship fund to use the funds as directed (rather than use them to buy oneself a swimming pool). It may be wrong to do so for other reasons: the trustee might, for example, have an obligation toward those who would have received the funds. But, on this view, once the person who established the fund dies, the fund's trustee has no obligation to her.

I will argue briefly, following and supplementing Joel Feinberg,[10] that there are obligations to departed objects, and so premise 1) of the above argument is incorrect. Let us suppose that Wilma works very hard, and through honest means that well serve society has accumulated a significant degree of wealth. Wilma believes very strongly in the value of education, and so established, with most of her wealth, a scholarship fund for worthy poor students. She lives another ten years in modest circumstances. During those ten years she was very active in pursuing the goals of the fund. Wilma had a strong interest in deserving students' receiving an education, and made considerable life sacrifices to further that interest. Her interest was not in feeling good about the fund or receiving praise or publicity: while those things might have given her some pleasure, her interest, that to which she dedicated herself and about which she most cared, was the furtherance of education itself. Education and its furtherance do not cease with her death. Thus the extent to which her interests are served, the extent to which her life goals are met, depends partly upon what happens after she dies. If the trustee of the fund absconds with the money after Wilma's death and uses it to buy a mansion, the trustee has set back Wilma's interests, that is, she has brought it about that the things Wilma cared about and to which she devoted her life did not occur. She has made Wilma's life less successful, diminished the extent to which Wilma has realized her life goals. Of course, if all that matters in life is the subjective sensation of happiness or pleasure, avoiding distress, the subjective feeling resulting from believing that one's preferences are satisfied, or any other subjective feeling, then Wilma's life's being diminished in this way is of little consequence, since it never occasioned any subjective experience of Wilma's. However, there are well known arguments, such as the pleasure machine argument,[11] against the view that subjective feelings are all that really matter. (See also Feinberg, Joel, *op. cit.*) Thus Wilma's interest in the use to which the fund is put survives her death and is set back if the fund's money is embezzled. The trustee accepted the trusteeship on the solemn assurance that she would uphold those goals and serve that interest and she was given the trusteeship only on the basis of that assurance. Thus the trustee has an obligation to Wilma not to set back her interest in the furtherance of education by abusing the trust Wilma placed in her.

That Wilma's interest in the fund's use remains an important moral factor after her death becomes clear if we suppose that, after her death, world government assumes all costs of education for all students. To continue to give scholarships to students whose every expense is already paid would not further Wilma's interest. What should the trustee do with the fund's money? It seems clear that she should neither continue to give scholarships (so her obligation is not merely to the explicit terms of the job or contractual position) nor buy herself a mansion (she does have continuing obligations): the reasonable course is to use the funds' money, if the law allows, to advance some other worthy project dear to Wilma's heart. If Wilma held a deep and lifelong personal interest in cancer research and little interest in multiple sclerosis research, and if cancer research and multiple sclerosis research are both equally in need of and deserving of support, it is more appropriate to use the money for cancer research than for multiple sclerosis research. Some obligation to serve Wilma's interest with her fund remains. It may not be the only or even the most important ethical concern, but it is an ethical factor.

This is not a proof, of course: perhaps the facts about Wilma's trust may be explained in some other way.[12] It is, rather, an attempt to make clear why it is plausible to say that there can be obligations to departed objects: people have interests in things that happen after their death, quite apart from any feelings or experiences they themselves might have. As Feinberg puts it, "we can think of the deceased's interests....as surviving their owner's death."[13] People have world-oriented interests, that is, interests not in their own experience but in the world's being a certain way. World-oriented interests can extend beyond one's death, since the object of the interest, what one has an interest in, does not cease with one's death. The extent to which one's life was a successful life is affected by how well those things to which one dedicated oneself fare after one's death: if

I dedicate my life to Harvard University, and Harvard closes down shortly after my death, then my life was, as a whole, less successful a life that it would have been had Harvard continued to flourish. Thus I can be harmed and my interests set back by what happens after I die. People often work hard and make considerable sacrifices to advance such interests. One's relationship to the work done by Jones while alive may create an obligation, based on those interests, even after Jones is dead. The trustee's relationship to Wilma's lifetime struggles illustrates one such relationship. These appear to be strong reasons for thinking that one may have some obligations toward departed objects.

It is instructive to examine George Pitcher[14] and Mark Bernstein[15] on this issue. Bernstein avers that Leopold Mozart after his death is nothing but bone and dust. Since bone and dust cannot be harmed, if Leopold Mozart is harmed by a posthumous event, the harm must have occurred during Leopold Mozart's lifetime. This conclusion can be challenged. While Leopold Mozart's body may be nothing but bone or dust, it is possible to disagree that Leopold Mozart is nothing but bone and dust without invoking reincarnation or disembodied spirits. A single example suffices to make the point. The causal view of persons regards a person as the sum of his causal contributions to any event or state of affairs (including his own mental states). This definition may sound circular, since it refers to "his" contributions, but that reference is merely a convenient method of indicating a particular set of causal contributions, which may be identified in any of several ways that do not refer to Leopold Mozart's identify (such as enumeration), just as saying "you are your body" is not really circular, but merely a more convenient way of saying that you are a particular body that may be identified in any of several ways that do not refer to your identity (e.g., the body that occupied space m at time t and space q at time y).[16] In this sense Leopold Mozart continues to "exist" after his death when, for example, someone makes a decision heavily influenced by his reading of Leopold Mozart's diary. Thus there are conceptions of what a person is, such as the causal view, according to which persons are not merely dust and bones after they die. In any case, one can say that, in some sense, Leopold Mozart exists timelessly; "Leopold Mozart is dead" does not fail of reference, so one must be predicating being dead of something, and, presumably, one is not predicating being dead of the scattered molecules that once composed his body. Whatever the ultimate analysis of the dead Leopold Mozart is, it must permit a variety of predicates to be applied to him, and so far no reason has been provided to suppose that being harmed by an occurrence after his death cannot be among them. As will emerge soon, there are reasons for holding that it is true in 1760 that Leopold Mozart's interest in his son Wolfgang's living a long life will not be satisfied (Mozart died in 1791). In that sense, at least, we can accept Pitcher's view that posthumous harm accrues during one's lifetime. Bernstein provides two arguments against the view that posthumous harm accrues during one's lifetime: the backward causation argument and the double jeopardy argument. The backward causation argument avers that if Leopold Mozart can be harmed by the posthumous death of his son, then the death of his son reaches backward in time to cause harm to Leopold Mozart while he lived. The double jeopardy argument avers that, if posthumous events can harm one, "not only is an individual harmed by the event that is responsible for one's desire being unfulfilled, but one is antecedently harmed as well by the fact that this event is going to take place. There is enough suffering in the world without recruiting novel efforts to increase it" (pp. 65-66). Where Pitcher suggests that if Leopold Mozart's friend knew what Leopold did not, that Wolfgang would die relatively soon after Leopold, that friend would feel sad for Leopold, Bernstein suggests the friend would more naturally be glad for Leopold that he will not live to experience his son's death.

In response, it should be said that most human beings have two kinds of interests, two kinds of things about which we care: we care about our own experiences, as experiences, and we care about the world. Put another way, as I argued in *Moral Responsibility and Persons*,[17] persons are worldviews in operation, bringing to the world as they find it attitudes and standards in terms of which some futures are understood as better than others as well as a commitment to the instantiation of better rather than worse futures. One future may be viewed as preferable to another because the world, so understood, is better, according to one's standards, and insofar as that is true, we have world-oriented interests. Most people, for instance, do care about whether or not their spouses are in fact unfaithful even if their infidelity is never discovered. In addition, one future may be viewed as preferable because my own experience of it is preferable: we have interests in our own experience regardless of the actual state of the world. I will call such interests "solipsistic interests," meaning merely that they remain interests even if nothing exists outside our own minds.[18] Thus, if I am like most people, when I discover that my wife is having an affair at least two of my interests are set back, namely my solipsistic interest in not feeling the pain of discovering her infidelity and my world-oriented interest in my wife's in fact being faithful. As noted, earlier, unless only subjective experiences matter in life, setbacks to both sorts of interests make one's life, in that respect, a worse life than it would otherwise be, and the pleasure machine argument gives strong reason for denying that nothing matters in life but our subjective experiences, e.g., the feeling of satisfaction or pleasure or contentment. Hence, one's life can be made worse both by the world's failing to conform to one's world-oriented interests and by knowing or experiencing that lack of conformity. Leopold Mozart's friend may reasonably feel both sad for Leopold that his son will die young and glad for Leopold that he will not experience the pain of seeing his son die, since two different interests are involved. The "double jeopardy" of which Bernstein complains, then, is an inevitable result of counting as important anything except what happens inside our own heads. It is unclear why the fact that we can be harmed in two ways by having two sorts of interests shows that we should give up or count as insignificant one of the two, particularly as we can, in parallel fashion, be benefited in two ways when the world does conform to our conception of a better future. One might as well say that life affords few enough benefits that we cannot afford to give up a whole category of benefits.

Bernstein's backward-causation argument also fails to prove tenable. First, the question of backward causation and time's arrow remains problematic in quantum mechanics—it may turn out that backward causation of the most straightforward sort is common in fundamental physics. Regardless, the sort of backward causation involved in posthumous harm is relatively unproblematic. Since, as Bernstein points out, the extent to which one's world-oriented interests are satisfied is a relational property, involving a relation of fit between the world and one's interests, posthumous harm would constitute backward causation of only a relational property. Such "backward causation" is both common and unproblematic: when R is a relational property between A's having P1 at time t1 and B's having P2 at time t2, then whether A has R at time t1 depends on whether B will have P2 at time t2. Bernstein recognizes such forms of causation as unproblematic when the relation contains a temporal predicate or modifier, e.g., Jones becomes the penultimate president of the x club when the club disbands a month after Jones' death. But this exception opens the door wider than Bernstein can allow. Most open-ended comparative predicates contain temporal modifiers that constrain their range. Consider the relation "x is the tallest man." "Tallest" can be restricted to those who have lived so far or it can range timelessly over anything that ever existed. In the latter sense, whether Smith is the tallest man depends upon what happens after he dies. Only in the former sense is Smith's being the tallest independent of what happens after his death. Yet the latter is, if anything, less time-bound than the former. More importantly, the satisfaction of a post-mortem interest, like the truth of a prediction, does contain an implicit temporal predicate: just as whether my prediction that team A will win tomorrow is true depends upon what happens tomorrow, whether my interest in team A's winning tomorrow is satisfied depends on what happens tomorrow. If it is true now that team A will not win, then my prediction is false now and my interest in team A's winning is not satisfied now. It will be argued below that there are indeed reasons for holding that Jones' assertion on Tuesday that Team A will win tomorrow has a determinate truth value on Tuesday. The fact that Wolfgang's death makes Leopold's life worse is no more an instance of problematic backwards causation than is the fact that team A's losing makes my prediction false. I conclude, then, that a person's life can be better or worse depending on events that occur after his or her death.

Perhaps, however, some principled distinction may be drawn between departed objects and future objects. It is not at first clear what relevant moral factors would distinguish, non-arbitrarily, between departed and future objects in this context. Neither departed nor future objects are present now and both, at some time, are well defined, concrete sentient individuals.

However, while departed objects are now well defined, it may appear that future objects are not now well defined, however determinate they may be in the future. Ruth Macklin,[19] for instance, argues that even if there will be future generations, the class of members of future generations has no identifiable members now. Thus, suggests Macklin, future generations cannot have rights or be subjects of obligations until they actually exist. In contrast, the set of departed persons does have a specifiable set of members. Three points should be raised about this argument.

In what sense are future objects indeterminate? It is, of course, irrelevant to the present argument if future objects are indeterminate in the sense that we do not know who they will be. Macklin must mean that they are indeterminate in the sense that there is now no fact of the matter, knowable by us or not, about who they will be. Perhaps this claim seems plausible if indeterminism is true, since it is not yet causally determined who will be born (cf. Aristotle's sea battle).[20] However, even if we assume for the sake of argument that the future is causally undetermined, there are reasons for holding that statements about the future have a determinate truth value now: Jones' assertion on Tuesday that Team A will win tomorrow has a determinate truth value on Tuesday, even if whether team A will win is causally undetermined on Tuesday. Suppose Jones' statement is not true or false on Tuesday. The following day Team A indeed wins. Then the victory of team A on Wednesday causes Jones' statement on Tuesday to become true, a form of backwards causation. Moreover, suppose Jones says on Tuesday "either team A will win tomorrow or team A will not win tomorrow" (whether because B loses, no game is held, etc.). That statement must be true when Jones utters it, since any future outcome will render it true, that is, no matter what happens, one or the other disjunct will be true. Since it cannot possibly fail to become true either that team A wins tomorrow or that team A fails to win, it must be true now that either team A will win or team A will not win. But if neither "team A will win" nor "team A will not win" has a determinate truth value on Tuesday, then the truth value of an "or" statement is not a function of the truth value of the disjuncts. Similar points could be made about tautologies employing any of the other logical connectives (e.g., "if team A will win then team A will win").[21] Thus it is less puzzling to say that Jones' statement made on Tuesday is true on Tuesday if and only if Wednesday's events will in fact include A's winning. Thus "Withers will exist in the year 3000" has a determinate truth value now.[22]

If these arguments are compelling, then the statements "if we do x, we will violate an obligation to a person who will exist in the year 2500" and "if we do x, we will violate the rights of a person who will exist in the year 2500" have determine truth values now. Such statements, if true, are morally relevant in setting public policy: even if Macklin is correct that should we use all the world's oil we would not yet have violated anyone's rights, it is nonetheless wrong to do so, and for very much the same sorts of reasons that it is wrong to violate someone's rights. We can have duties toward future generations even if it is not certain that there will be future generations. As Edwin Delattre points out,[23] we have a duty to see if someone is inside a burning house we are passing (or at least a duty to call out a warning). Even if it turns out that no one was in fact inside, someone who simply walks on has violated a duty. It is clearly not permissible for me now to do something that will clearly, foreseeably, and directly result in your rights' being violated five minutes from now, or even in a year from now. Similarly, it is wrong for me to do something now that will insure that, two years from now, sixteen year old Sheila will be denied the opportunity to vote, even though she does not yet have the right to vote.[24]

Sheila, unlike future generations, is a currently existing person, but the case of Sheila helps make clear why future rights violations are to be avoided. Why is it wrong to act now so as to later deprive Sheila of the vote? The following argument certainly seems plausible:

1. The occurrence of a rights violation is a (morally) significantly undesirable event, else there seems little reason to respect rights.
2. Other things being equal, one should refrain from acting in ways that, foreseeably, will result in a (morally) significantly undesirable event.
3. Thus there is moral reason to avoid acting now in ways that will, foreseeably, bring about a rights violation in the future.

This argument also entails that there is moral reason to avoid acting now in ways that will, foreseeably, bring about a violation of the rights future generations will have. In general, it is hard to deny that:

P1. It is *prima facie* wrong (unjust) to do something now that clearly and foreseeably poses a clear and present danger of later resulting in an actual person's rights' being violated (that is, in an actual violation of an actual person's rights).

There is thus moral reason not to deplete the earth's non-renewable resources, and/or not to damage the environment irreversibly, etc.

Of course, in the case of Sheila, it is an identifiable person whose rights will be violated. Macklin's concern is that the class of future persons is not presently identifiable. Is this a crucial difference? Consider the following case. Suppose a million dollars are put in an escrow account in 2010. The money will be paid in ten years to whoever has accumulated the most points at the end of a contest. I steal the money from the escrow account right before the contest begins and hide the defalcation. The fact that the money is missing will not be discovered for another ten years. Have I violated no one's rights? It would seem that I have violated the rights of whoever eventually wins the contest. Of course, at present we have no idea who that will be. In fact, at present it is not even clear who the contestants will be. We don't yet know whose rights will be violated. But I have violated the winner's rights, whoever that will turn out to be.[25] The winner might even be someone who was has not yet been born. Suppose someone insists that I have not yet violated anyone's rights. Instead, I have merely acted in a way that guarantees that someone's rights will be violated. Now, even if we grant that, knowingly doing so is wrong in quite the same way and for quite the same reasons as is knowingly violating someone's rights, and I have quite the same sort of obligation to refrain from doing so. At most, then, Macklin's point would affect how we phrase the matter when speaking very strictly.

However, there is some reason for thinking that in depleting the world's oil resources we do now violate future persons' rights. After all, the winner of the contest may say, in the year 2020, that I violated her rights ten years ago, and her claim seems hard to deny. For instance, suppose the law imposes an "interest" penalty on rights violation: rights violators must pay $10 for each year that a rights violation remains unredressed. Can I justly insist that don't owe $100 because I did not violate anyone's rights until 2020 when the contest ended?

Of course, in the case of future generations, suggesting that we now violate future generations' rights by depleting the world's oil does appear to require that a person can have rights before being born. If, as Chapter 3 argues, rights are warrants, the assertion that a right can exist before the person who holds it is born is not implausible. A right, on this view, is a publicly sanctioned warrant for demanding, believing, or feeling something as one's due. Now suppose, for example, that we deplete the world's oil. Then a warrant currently exists for someone in 2300 to accuse us of injustice in depleting all the world's oil. Hence it can be said that the right exists in advance of the rightholder, for the warrant for a demand not to deplete all the world's oil exists before the person who holds that warrant does.

Either way, it is unjust to dispose of nuclear waste unsafely, create future overpopulation problems, etc., since these acts will probably lead, eventually, to the actual violation of actual persons' rights. Note that, if fetuses are merely possible or potential persons, P1) does not entail that abortion violates the rights of fetuses, since, if the fetus is aborted, there will be no actual person whose rights will actually be violated in the future. There is a real difference between an actual violation of an actual person's rights, even though it happens in the future, and something that would have happened to someone who would have but never did or will exist. In the latter case no actual harm or injustice ever occurs, while in the former case someone will actually suffer. This does seem a morally relevant feature.[26]

Macklin's second argument is that because future generations cannot have duties they cannot have rights. They will come to have duties just as they will come to have rights. But since they lack duties now, they also lack rights now. It is unclear, however, that having duties is a condition for possessing rights: rights without duties have been urged for children, animals, and ecosystems, for instance. John Ahrens suggests that only those who can have duties can have rights because "a primary function" of rights is to establish a standard of minimal treatment around which societies can organize.[27] Since future generations cannot understand and act in accordance with this standard, rights cannot be ascribed to them. There are, of course, other conceptions of the primary function of rights, but even if this is a primary function of rights, it does not follow that it is the only function of rights and (hence) a necessary condition for the ascription of rights. Moreover, future generations, if they exist, will be able to understand and act in accordance with that standard at the time our current actions affect them. To the extent that societies are ongoing, it is not clear why societies cannot be conceived as organizing around standards of minimal treatment that are inter-generational as well as intragenerational. (After all, future generations will have the same duties to the generations that succeed them.) Ahrens' argument could be construed as a version of the reciprocity argument: future generations cannot be viewed as having rights claims against us because they cannot be viewed as reciprocating parallel claims we might have on them. I suggest below that past generations may have rights claims against us, and so there may be some form of reciprocity from the future to the past.[28] Second, it is not clear that future genera-tions do not now have duties. It is at least arguable that they now have condi-tional and/or future-dated duties. Conditional duties are unproblematic for exist-ing persons. Suppose that I am offered the Presidency of the United States. I am deliberating whether to accept. At this moment I have the conditional duty of upholding the constitution if I accept. Future-dated duties are similarly unprob-lematic for existing persons: if I promise to take you to the zoo tomorrow, I now have a duty to take you tomorrow. That I have this duty now is manifest by the fact that I must now take whatever steps are necessary to be able to take you to the zoo tomorrow and refrain from actions that would prevent my doing so. Now suppose for the sake of argument that all children have a duty to support their parents when their parents turn 40. Then, it was true when I was 20 that a duty existed for whoever turned out to be my child to support me in 20 years: we can, it appears, be born into duties. Future generations can have duties in the sense that a duty now exists for them, whoever they will be.

Still, it does seem odd to say that someone who does not yet exist now has a duty. Is there a relevant difference between rights and duties that can explain this asymmetry? There is. Something that happens now can affect your future wel-fare. But you cannot perform a duty until you are born. So it seems more com-fortable to say that x's right was violated before x was born than it does to say x had a duty before he was born. I am not sure how much weight we should put on this feeling. When *Deuteronomy* proclaims that a given duty shall be "incumbent upon you and all of your descendents," the text is imposing a duty on future gen-erations: the text asserts that it is now incumbent upon whoever will be born to do certain things. That claim does not appear incoherent. If such a duty exists and I fail to fulfill it, one can correctly say that I have violated a duty that has existed for thousands of years. I haven't been violating it for countless years, of course, but the duty I violated existed before me.

C. Future People v. Merely Possible People

A second line of argument suggests that granting rights to future generations gives rights to merely possible persons and that intolerable conundrums result when merely possible persons are accorded rights. If, for example, the person who would be born if Mike raped Sheila has a right to life, then, it is argued, Mike violates that possible person's rights by refraining from raping Sheila. This argument is questionable in several respects, but it does appear that granting rights to merely possible persons has curious results. Sikora, for instance, suggests "that it is *prima facie* wrong to prevent the existence of anyone with reasonable prospects for happiness."[29] Sikora's principle appears to entail that it is *prima facie* wrong of me not to procreate whenever I can, provided the resulting child would have a reasonable prospect of happiness, lest I prevent the existence of that future child. But suppose I can produce six children with reasonable prospects for happiness. Then it is also *prima facie* wrong to have the sixth today, since doing so prevents the existence of the child who would have been born had I waited till tomorrow.[30] If, as Mary Anne Warren[31] and others suggest, rights and moral consideration are accorded only to those who will in fact exist, these conundrums are avoided. The person who would be born were Mike to rape Sheila will never actually exist, since Mike does not in fact rape Sheila. The child who would have been born had I waited is not due moral consideration and so it is not *prima facie* wrong to refrain from waiting.

For these and other reasons, I suggest that Warren is correct that the only ones who have genuine rights are actual persons, past, present and future (that is, those who, as a matter of fact, will exist). However, the issue becomes more complex when considering population policy or the obligation to ensure that there will be a future generation: these issues involve choices about who will be the set of future persons. Making such choices requires projecting, for each option, the set of persons who will become real if that option is chosen. These various outcomes may be rated and compared in a variety of ways. But morally evaluating projected futures is not the same as according genuine moral consideration. If I borrow ten dollars, I owe repayment to the actual person who in fact loaned me the money. If I choose to borrow from Jack, then Jack will be the rightholder. If I choose to borrow from Jill, then Jill will be the rightholder. When deciding from whom to borrow, I imaginatively project these two situations and compare their desirability (including their moral desirability). When I am occupied in making the choice, I don't know whether it is Jack or Jill who will be the actual rightholder, since that will be determined by the choice I am in the process of making. The hypothetical situation each will be in, were I to borrow the money from him or her, is a moral factor influencing my choice. Nonetheless, only the one from whom I actually borrow the money will have a right of repayment. A similar point applies to deliberating about choices that affect future persons (e.g., deciding whether to include in my will a trust fund for needy neonates). Suppose that some day in the medical future Sally, who is ovulating, will have only one chance to bring a baby to term. Genetic scanning of a type not currently available indicates Sally's current egg is capable of being fertilized but will die within 4 months of birth. Sally refrained from intercourse and later produced a healthy baby, baby A. Sally did not violate the rights of baby B, the baby who would have been born had Sally had intercourse. Nor, had she not waited and so given birth to baby B, would she have violated the rights of baby A. As it turns out, only A is a future person and only A has rights. But there are moral reasons for preferring the state of affairs in which it is A who has rights over the state of affairs in which it is B who has rights (that is, for preferring that it is A who is the actual future person and not B). Thus while Sally must consider merely possible persons in her deliberations, in doing so she is not giving genuine moral weight to the needs or interests of merely possible people. She is considering the moral desirability of the possible situation in which it is A who actually commands moral consideration versus the possible situation in which it is B who actually commands moral consideration, much like an artist with but one slab of marble must consider possible artworks when deciding which to make actual, a statue of Venus or a statue of Neptune.

In this sense, Sikora is correct. If human happiness is intrinsically good, then it is more morally desirable, other things being equal, to produce a state of affairs with ten happy people than with nine equally happy people,[32] and so, if we have some degree of obligation to promote the optimal good,[33] then we have some degree of obligation to promote the existence of potentially happy people, other things being equal.[34] It does not follow, however, that we would have an obligation to any particular possible person or are giving moral consideration to the interests of merely possible people. Rather, we are choosing to actualize the more morally desirable of two possible outcomes.

Thus Warren is correct that only future persons, and not merely possible persons, have rights or are due moral consideration, while Sikora is right that population planning must compare the desirability of actualizing one set of possible persons over another.

D. The Identity Problem and Future Generations

Another set of problems concerns how it is possible for us to harm future generations, since they owe their very existence to us. As Derek Parfit and Thomas Schwartz point out,[35] an interesting problem is raised by the fact that almost any change in our present actions would, over the course of 500 years, result in different people being born. Since it is but one sperm out of millions that fertilizes an egg, even a small change in conditions would result in a different sperm fertilizing the egg, thus resulting in someone with different DNA (and thus, presumably, a different person) being born. As Peter S. Wenz puts it, "if your parents had delayed even half an hour, to watch a TV show, for example, it is highly unlikely that the same one among the 20 to 60 million sperm in an ejaculation would have fertilized the ovum, and [as a result] you, your children, etc., would not exist."[36] After 500 years of causal interactions, it is unlikely that anyone born then has exactly the same DNA as anyone who would have been born had the original action not been performed 500 years earlier. Thus it could be argued that no act x of ours, done now, can harm Jones, born 500 years from now, unless x results in Jones' experiencing a fate worse than death, since, had we refrained from doing x, Jones would not have been born.

Thus Jones is better off for our performing x than he would have been had we refrained from doing x. Thus our performing x does not harm Jones.

This argument poses a problem for obligations to future generations if two assumptions are correct: 1) obligations center on refraining from causing harm, and 2) to harm someone by an action is to make that person worse off by the action than he or she would otherwise have been. There is good reason, however, to reject the conjunction of 1) and 2).

Suppose I both gratuitously promise to give you $10 and in fact give you only $8. By "gratuitously" I mean that my promise was not in exchange for something on your part nor prompted by any other obligation on my part, so that my obligation to give you $10 stems solely from my having promised to do so. In giving you only $8, I have failed to meet my obligations to you. However, I have not, as a rule, made you worse off than you would have been otherwise. Of course, it is possible that you acted in reliance upon my promise, that you were so upset or disappointed by my partial payment that you would have been better off had I never made the promise, etc. But consider an instance in which, in fact, you are better off by my promising to pay you $10 and paying you only $8 than you would have been had I not promised anything and not paid you anything (and would have violated no duty nor done anything wrong by not promising). I have not made you worse off than you would otherwise have been. Nonetheless, I have violated an obligation to you. This example suggests an alternative principle:

> P3) A (*prima facie*) violates an obligation to B if A's doing something he is not entitled to do leaves B worse off in a particular regard than A is entitled to leave B.

P3) readily explains how I have violated by obligation to you by paying you only $8: having $8 is worse than having $10, and, given my promise, I am not entitled to leave you with only $8.

Given P3), it may seem that we have a *prima facie* obligation not to deplete all the world's oil resources. Whatever a generation's "fair share" of the world's oil might be, taking all remaining oil, in the absence of special justifying circumstances,[37] obviously exceeds that limit. Precisely what constitutes taking too much oil depends upon which conception of justice, or, more specifically, "fair share" is correct. But no plausible notion of fair share would normally permit us to take all the current oil reserves. So it is not necessary, for present purposes, to specify which conception of justice is correct, since by any plausible general principles of fairness we are not entitled, absent special circumstances, to take all the world's oil resources.[38] If we deplete the earth's oil, therefore, in the absence of special justifying circumstances, we leave future generations worse off with respect to oil resources than we are entitled to leave them. Hence we have a *prima facie* obligation not to deplete the world's oil supply.

It might be argued, however, that even if Joe Smith in the year 4000 has zero oil resources to enjoy, he would still have zero had we not depleted the world's oil supply, since he would not exist. Hence he is not worse off than we are entitled to leave him. However, we are not entitled to leave anyone in the position of having no oil resources. P4) clarifies this point:

> P4) A (*prima facie*) violates an obligation to B if A's doing something he is not entitled to do leaves B worse off in a particular regard than A is entitled to leave anyone who might occupy the position that B in fact occupies.

Given P4), we violate an obligation to Joe Smith by depleting the world's oil resources, even though, had we not done so, Joe Smith would not have been born, since we are not entitled to leave the person who would have been born instead (and hence would occupy the position Joe Smith in fact occupies) with no oil.

Schwartz's formulation of the argument invokes the following premise: "If A's not doing something would wrong B, then, were A not to do that thing, B would lack some significant benefit he would have enjoyed (or could reasonably be expected to have enjoyed) had A done it" (p. 11). This ingenious formulation avoids the question of whether B would have been better off. Schwartz's point is that had we not depleted the world's oil supply, B would have enjoyed no benefit at all, since B would not exist. By contrast, when I pay Jones $5 instead of $10, he would have enjoyed a benefit had I paid him the extra $5.

One weak point in Schwartz's argument centers on the phrase "could reasonably be expected to have enjoyed." Consider a more familiar example of a type that sometimes arises in law. F, with malicious intent, shoots G, hitting him in the leg and knocking him backwards. To everyone's surprise, a platform suddenly falls from the adjacent building, hitting the spot G occupied a moment earlier. F deprived G of no benefit G would have enjoyed absent F's action: although F's action insures that G lacks the benefit of sound health, had F not fired, G would have been killed by the falling platform instead of being wounded by F's gun, and hence not enjoyed the benefit of sound health. Whether the case of F and G falsifies Schwartz's formulation, thus, depends upon whether G could reasonably be expected to have enjoyed sound health had F not fired. What is the relevant sort of reasonable expectation? Since we know that the platform fell, we have reasonable grounds for expecting that G would not have enjoyed sound health. Someone aware of the precise nature of the platform's precarious state could reasonably have anticipated the platform's falling, while F and G could not. In fact, we impute the reasonable expectation of sound health to G because falling platforms are not the sorts of circumstances we take account of in such cases. But in that sense it is not clear that future generations could not reasonably be expected to have enjoyed the benefits of oil had we not depleted the world's oil supply. What matters is that, absent special circumstances, F is not entitled to act in a way that insures that someone will be in the position of being wounded and none of those special circumstances (e.g., that F believed the platform would fall and that shooting G would save G's life) obtained. This insight forms the basis of P5):

> P5) A (*prima facie*) violates an obligation to B if A's doing something he is not entitled to do guarantees that B will not receive some good, G, when A

is not entitled to guarantee that whoever occupies B's position will not receive G.

For present purposes something weaker than P5) will serve. It is not necessary to claim that *all* deprivations of goods of the relevant type *prima facie* violate an obligation. It is enough that a certain kind of deprivation *can* serve as the basis of a violation of an obligation. Thus P5) can be dropped in favor of the weaker P6):

P6) The following can serve as the basis for A's violating an obligation to B: A's doing something, X, that A is not entitled to do, such that A's doing X guarantees that B will not receive some good, G, when A is not entitled to guarantee that whoever occupies B's position will not receive G.

If P6) is correct, then it appears that we can violate obligations to future generations by depleting the world's oil resources, since a) we are not entitled to do so by any plausible criteria of justice, b) by doing so we would guarantee that members of future generations will not receive some good (availability of oil resources), and c) we are not entitled to guarantee that whoever exists in the future will not receive that good.

The plausibility of P6) emerges when we consider Megan, who steals most of the money from a million dollar lottery, leaving only one thousand dollars. When the vault containing the lottery money is opened 16 years later, the theft is discovered. After a day's delay, a drawing is held for the remaining $1000. Bilbo wins. Years later he encounters Megan and charges her with violating his obligations to her. "Not at all," replies Megan. "Had I not stolen the money, the drawing would have been held a day earlier and, given the difference in circumstances, you would not have won. That is, while is its logically possible you would have won in either case, it is extraordinarily unlikely. So my defalcation did not deprive you of any benefit you would have received otherwise. In fact, you are a thousand dollars richer because of my theft. Moreover," continues Megan, "the ticket holders who would have lost had the lottery been held as scheduled were deprived of no benefit they would have enjoyed. So only the person who would have won had my theft not occurred can say I violated a duty to her." Of course, if that counterfactual is not well defined, if the question "who would have held the winning ticket had the theft not occurred?" lacks a well-defined answer, then no one can say Megan violated a duty to her. So, for the sake of argument, we will suppose that there is a clear answer: Charles is the person who purchased what would have been the winning ticket had the drawing been held as scheduled. Now suppose that Megan, as she emerged from stealing the money when the money had been in the vault 2 years, bumped into Charles, who had purchased a lottery ticket, intending it for his first born-child. As a result of bumping into Megan, Charles misses his bus. As soon as he arrives home he and his wife have sex and she becomes pregnant with their first child, Billy. Had Megan not stolen the money, bumping into Charles as a result and thus delaying his arrival home, it would not have been Billy who was born. Someone else, whom we will call Jilly, would have been Charles' first-born child. Then

Jilly is the person who would have won the lottery money had Megan not stolen it. Hence the only person who can claim to have been deprived of a benefit he or she would have had, absent Megan's theft, is Jilly. But Jilly has never existed-- she is a purely counterfactual person. Hence, Megan did not violate a duty to anyone by stealing the money.

This is clearly wrong. Megan has violated a duty to Bilbo (among others). P6) shows us why. Megan, by doing something she was not entitled to do, made whoever might come to win the lottery money worse off than she was entitled to make that person. So she has wronged whoever it is that, as a matter of fact, comes to win the lottery money. As a matter of fact, it is Bilbo who comes to win the lottery money. For this reason it seems plausible to say that Megan has violated a duty to Bilbo.[39] P6) encapsulates that intuition.

In short, P6) is both plausible and consistent with obligations to future generations. Thus P6) explains how is possible that we can violate an obligation to Hobart, who will be born 100 years from now, by depleting the world's oil reserves, despite the fact that, had we not done so, Hobart would not have been born. By taking more than our fair share of the world's oil, we guarantee that Hobart will not have the benefit of oil. We are not entitled to leave whoever will occupy Hobart's position without the benefit of oil. Since it is Hobart who in fact occupies that position, we can be said to have violated an obligation to Hobart.

E. The Obligation to Produce Future Generations

A final problem remains, however. It is to people who will actually exist that we owe moral consideration. But some actions are wrong precisely because they have the result that there will be no future generations. It may seem that we cannot explain this fact except by giving rights to potential future generations, that is, to the hypothetical persons who would have existed. The difficulty vanishes if there is an obligation to strive for the existence of future generations that is not owed to future generations. Consider the following:

P7) Each of us has a (collective) *prima facie* obligation to strive to insure that there will be future generations.

P7) is a collective obligation: it does not require, for example, that a fertile couple have children, so long as sufficient numbers of children are born, worldwide, to ensure the survival of the species, a condition that is clearly met at the present time. Of course, one must not be a freeloader: one must contribute reasonably to the totality of our collective obligations. But as long as all our collective obligations are met, people have considerable freedom in choosing which ones they will help meet. If there are, for example, collective obligations to advance knowledge, care for the sick, monitor human rights violations, and reduce world hunger, no one person need do all four, as long as all four are reasonably met, worldwide.

P7) need not be construed as deriving from the rights of the persons who would have existed. It may be, for example, be a duty owed to human achievement (or to the values underlying those achievements) to strive to insure that human achievement survives and flourishes. Some might claim that it is an obligation to God.

Several arguments support P7). Gregory Kavka[40] suggests that human life is intrinsically valuable because a) pleasure and/or b) certain experiences and/or c) the exercise of capacities and attainment of goals is intrinsically valuable. If any of these is intrinsically valuable and if we should, other things being equal, prefer the more valuable state of affairs and strive to produce it, then we have a *prima facie* reason to create future generations who will instantiate those valuable features. A parallel argument exists for almost any other feature of human life deemed intrinsically valuable.

Two other arguments for P7) deserve enumeration. They are independent, compatible arguments: each purports to provide one justification for P7). The first depends upon the argument given earlier that one can have obligations to departed persons. As Kavka points out, without future generations the collective enterprise of our species, our shared accomplishments, would end. One justification for P7) is an obligation owed to past generations, since, clearly, the continuation of the human species was a crucial project of theirs, and, arguably, a condition of the legacy (of knowledge, goods, etc.) that they have left us and which we have accepted. That is, we have a relationship to the work and projects of members of past generations that obligates us to be faithful executors of the legacy of human development. As Derr suggests, we owe concern for future generations to our ancestors whose concern for us made us what we are. Daniel Callahan suggests that "we owe to those coming after us at least what we ourselves were given by those who came before us"[41] and Avner de-Shalit writes "it is commonly argued that we have obligations to posterity because we have received certain goods from our predecessors in return for which we are virtually obligated and committed to maintain the chain."[42] While there is disagreement about whether accepting a benefit, in general, creates an obligation, in this case the benefit was attained at great cost by previous generations and conferred expressly with the expectation that it would be passed on to future generations, the expectation is a worthy one, to the extent that human life and human achievement have value (and hence to the extent that any human expectation is ever worthy), and the benefit accepted is of overwhelming importance (it fundamentally shapes the whole of one's life from birth to death). It would seem at least grossly ungrateful to make no effort to pass on the benefits for which thousands of generations have striven so mightily.

A second argument suggests that the collective obligation to ensure that there are future generations stems from a condition on human flourishing. One does not lead a good human life (flourish) unless one views oneself as part of a continuing and evolving human culture and community to which one ascribes some importance apart from oneself. Ernest Partridge[43] mentions a basic human need for "self-transcendence," a need persons have to identify with and further the well-being of communities, institutions, etc. that extend outside themselves and that they hope will flourish beyond their lifetimes. Several lines of thought support this conclusion. First, to lead a good human life one must have values, that is, things one deems of importance and worth quite apart from oneself. If I value learning, in this sense, then I think it is important that others learn, even if I will never know of their learning: to value learning, for example, is to believe that, if there are any beings whose light-line does not intersect mine while I am alive (and hence who can have no affect on me whatsoever), it is still (*ceteris paribus*) a good thing if they learn. So if I value learning, then it is important to me that future generations learn: I am morally invested in learning's continuing to occur after I die. As a philosopher, I value philosophical insight, so I care about, am morally invested in, philosophical insights that will occur after my death. If I do not, then I do not value philosophical insights—I might enjoy having them, but I do not value them in the sense under discussion, that is, regard them as of worth and importance quite apart from myself. In short, many of the values we regard as crucial ones entail a commitment to the flourishing of future generations. Moreover, human life is short and demanding. Pleasures are fleeting and hardships abound: life as an isolated radar blip on the screen of time does not seem satisfying. Much of the vast variety of potential human good cannot be realized by one person in a lifetime: it is through investment in others, in the joint human enterprise, that we can participate in these aspects of human good. It is hard to see how one can lead a truly satisfying and fulfilling life without viewing one's life as playing a part in an evolving project (or experiment or exploration or compilation of experiences) with a history greater than a lifetime. The argument, in other words is:

1)   Only those who have attitudes that commit them to the flourishing of future generations can flourish (lead good human lives).
2)   Hence either one is committed to the flourishing of future generations or one does not lead a good human life.
3)   We are obligated to strive to lead good human lives.
4)   Thus we are obligated to strive to commit ourselves to the flourishing of future generations.[44]

In short, P1), P6), and P7) appear to be plausible principles against which none of the objections considered in this paper succeed. P1) and P7) together mean that we have a *prima facie* collective duty to insure that there is a future generation and that the rights they will in fact have, in the future, will not be violated by what we do now. This seems to be enough to yield many of the results environmentalists seek when they speak of the rights of future generations, yet neither P1) nor P7) requires assigning rights now to persons who have not yet existed (although some additional reasons for so doing were mentioned), much less to potential persons who will never in fact exist. Similarly, P6) and P7), together with reasonable background assumptions (e.g., about what constitutes a fair share), seem adequate to establish that we bear significant obligations to future generations, such as not depleting the earth's oil reserves. The way is now clear to specify the content of those rights and obligations. The three obligations mentioned in Section A., as well as the arguments for P7), suggest the lines along which that task should proceed.

Notes to Chapter Eight

1 For instance, Richard and Val Routley, in "Nuclear Energy and Obligations to the Future," *Inquiry* 21, Summer, 1978, pp. 133-79, suggest that creating long-lived nuclear wastes that pose a possible danger to future generations is analogous to shipping toxic wastes on a passenger bus. If we have obligations only to contemporary and/or past generations then the analogy disappears. Of course, eco-centric views of environmental ethics can, without invoking obligations to future generations, require that we not despoil the planet. But such views do not address depleting such non-renewable resources as oil reserves deep underground, which are of interest primary to future generations of *Homo Sapiens* and their technologies.

2 De George, Richard T., "The Environment, Rights, and Future Generations," in Ernest Partridge, ed., *Responsibilities to Future Generations*, Buffalo: Prometheus Books, 1981, pp. 157-166; p. 159.

3 For a discussion of this problem, see Wenz, Peter S, *Environmental Ethics Today*, Oxford: Oxford University Press, 2001.

4 See Schlossberger, Eugene, *The Ethical Engineer*, Philadelphia: Temple University Press, 1993, for a discussion of the obligation to leave the world no worse than we found it.

5 We cannot, at present, be reasonably confident that there will ever be a safe, feasible method of dealing with large quantities of nuclear waste, much less that what we now do with nuclear wastes will not do significant harm in the future.

6 For a sensible stance on discounting the future, see Derr, Thomas Sieger, "The Obligation to the Future," in Partridge, ed., *op. cit.*, pp. 37-44, who urges moderate discounting of the future. De George, Richard T., *op cit.*, p. 163, similarly asserts that "we should use what we need, but we should keep our needs rational, avoid waste, and preserve the environment as best we can."

7 Whether future generations can have rights, and what those rights may be, are separate questions, despite some confusion about the connection. For instance, Annette Baier, in "The Rights of Past and Future Persons," pp. 171-183, in Ernest Partridge, ed., *op. cit.* p. 171, suggests that if future generations will have rights, they have a right of an equal share of what will be left, and that if they now have rights, they have an equal share of what is now left. In fact, however, we can quite intelligibly assert that future generations now have an equal right to what will be left or that they will come to have an equal right to what is now present. The difference in content is a function of what future generations have a right to, not whether they now have them or will come to have them.

8 For example, Martin Golding, in "Obligations to Future Generations," *Monist* 56 January 1972, reprinted in Louis Pojman, ed. *Environmental Ethics: Readings in Theory and Application* 1st ed., Boston: Jones and Bartlett Publishers, pp. 225-230, holds that members of my moral community are entitled to demand of me that I follow the social ideal, "the conception of the good life for man", p. 227. Moral communities may be formed by contract or by a social arrangement of mutual benefits. Moral communities may be formed from feelings of altruistic concern in which one acknowledges the other's good as good-to-me. It is in this third sense that future generations can be members of our moral community, i.e., that our conception of the good applies to them. Golding is skeptical that it does, especially with very distant generations. Golding is arguing for a conceptual

point that we cannot include future generations within the scope of our concern as well as a practical point that it is hard to predict what will harm future generations. Neither is convincing, since it is reasonably likely that future generations will share enough, at some very general level, of our conceptual framework that we would recognize them as moral agents and hence view them as worthy of concern, and, as Daniel Callahan (in "What Obligations Do We Have to Future Generations," Partridge, ed., *op. cit.*, pp. 73-88) and others point out, it is sufficiently likely to be the basis of reasonable action that, e.g., significant quantities of long-lived nuclear waste would be unwelcome and undesirable for future generations. See also Kavka, "The Futurity Problem," in Partidge, ed., *op. cit.*, pp. 109-122.

9 See Barry, Brian, "Circumstances of Justice and Future Generations," R. I. Sikora and Brian Barry, eds., *Obligations to Future Generations*, Philadelphia: Temple University Press, 1978; reissued Cambridge, England: White Horse Press, 1996, pp. 204-248, and de-Shalit, Avner, *Why Posterity Matters*, London and New York: Routledge Publication, 1995.

10 Feinberg, Joel, "The Rights of Animals and Unborn Generations," in *Rights, Justice, and the Bounds of Liberty*, Princeton, New Jersey: Princeton University Press, 1980, pp. 159-184.

11 The pleasure machine stimulates the brain to induce simulations of desirable subjective experiences, enabling one, for instance, to experience repeatedly the happiest moment of one's life. If the pleasure machine is defined correctly, life on a pleasure machine is more subjectively satisfying than real life, yet few would choose, for themselves, their children, and all of humanity, a life spent on a pleasure machine.

12 De George (*op. cit.*, p. 159) suggests that if the law were suddenly changed so that all estates became the property of the state, it would be more plausible to say that the rights of the heirs had been violated than the rights of the deceased. In fact it seems plausible to say the rights of both were violated: the heirs have an interest in receiving the money and the deceased has in interest in seeing to it that his wealth is enjoyed by, e.g., his son, and both interests have been set back. Will theories of rights make the case even stronger, for the state has arguably interfered with the sovereignty of the deceased over his worldly goods. The same point applies as well as the warrant theory, to the extent that the warrants involved are grounded, in whole or part, from testamentary sovereignty.

13 Feinberg, Joel, *op. cit.*, p. 174.

14 Pitcher, George, "The Misfortunes of the Dead," *American Philosophical Quarterly* 21:2, April 1984, pp. 183-188.

15 Bernstein, Mark H., *On Moral Considerability*, Oxford, New York: Oxford University Press, 1998.

16 There is a deeper sense in which both definitions may be argued to be circular, namely, that Leopold Mozart's identify must be presumed fully to understand the role of or importance of that particular set of causal contributions and/or the particular spatio-temporal sequence containing space m at time t and space q at time y. Space does not permit consideration of this issue.

17 Schlossberger, Eugene, *Moral Responsibility and Persons*, Philadelphia: Temple University Press, 1992.

18 Of course, were one to become convinced of the truth of solipsism, some painful experiences would no longer be painful, and hence we would lose some of what I am calling "solipsistic" interests. The point is not that one would continue to have those interests if one came to believe in the truth of solipsism, but rather that, for someone who is not a solipcist, the extent to which the interest is actually set back is unaffected by the actual truth or falsity of solipsism.

19 Macklin, Ruth, "Can Future Generations Correctly be Said to Have Rights?" in Partridge, ed., *op. cit.*, pp. 151-156; p.152.

20 There is some reason to think that physics will settle upon a conception of time according to which the past, present, and future of an observer are, in some ultimate sense, equally "real" and are timelessly co-realized, in which case, despite quantum indeterminacy, the future of an observer is as fully real (and definite) as the past of that observer. Since the objection at issue is more likely to be raised by someone who holds a classical view of time's arrow, the discussion here of that objection also employs the classical view.

21 The difficulty here is not merely the standard one for three-valued logics: the problem is that tomorrow the two disjuncts will each become fully true or fully false. In a three-valued logic, for instance, "team A will not win" can mean "either team A will win is false or N," where N is the third truth value. The truth value of "team A will win" is fully determinate between true, false, or N, and if it is N, it remains N. In the case of indeterminate futures, however, we know today that either "team A will win" will become fully true or "team A will win" will become fully false.

22 Of course, on some theories of reference, we cannot yet refer to Withers, and hence the sentence "Withers will exist in the year 3000" cannot be true or false because the term "Withers" lacks a reference. Nonetheless, it is now true or false that in the year 3000 someone will exist whose name (in 3000) will be "Withers."

23 Delattre, Edwin, "Rights, Responsibilities, and Future Persons, "*Ethics* 82:3," April 1972, pp. 254-258.

24 Of course, one might claim that it is wrong because doing so harms her now. Even if Sheila and I both know she will not live another year, she can, with some justification, claim that even now her present status in the society would be diminished, that her status as a full citizen would be impugned. But it would also be wrong to act so that she will be denied the vote two years from now, even if she will not learn of the problem until her 18th birthday.

25 Cf. Pletcher, Galen K., "The Rights of Future Generations" in Partridge ed., *op. cit.*, pp. 167-170; p. 168, who parses the right to a clean campsite of whoever will come next as: "For any x, if x is a person who wants to camp here, x has a right to a clean campsite." Avner de-Shalit (*op. cit.*) suggests Pletcher's example is disanalogous with future generations because those who will use the campsite already exist, p. 113. But such may not be the case: the campsite could lay unused for some years until used by someone conceived after I camped there.

26 It seems to provide the asymmetry James Sterba demands between rights of future generations and the right of the fetus to be born in *The Demands of Justice*, University of Notre Dame Press: 1980, and Sterba, James, "Abortion, Distant Peoples, and Future Generations," *The Journal of Philosophy*, 1980, pp. 424-440. Sterba does consider the reply

that bringing into existence a person who does not have a reasonable chance to lead a good life results in someone who can reproach me, while failing to bring into existence someone who would have such a chance does not result in someone who can reproach me. Sterba responds that the exact converse holds with respect to someone who can thank one. Thus any failure of reference hold equally in either case. But the relevant difference is not the voicing of thanks or reproach: it is the actual occurrence of an actual harm. Granted, if I do produce someone who has a good life, then an actual person experiences an actual good, but if I do not, then no actual person ever experiences the lack of an actual good. While I may be obligated to ensure that there will exist some people who experience some good, I am not obligated to strive to produce all possible people to experience all possible (deserved) goods in the same way I am obligated to strive to avoid producing the actual experience of actual (undeserved) harm.

27 Ahrens, John, *Preparing for the Future: An Essay on the Rights of Future Generations*, Bowling Green: Social Philosophy Policy Center, 1983, p. 14.

28 Alternatively, Ahrens' notion that rights are standards around which societies are organized could be viewed as an assertion that rights are purely contractual. Since we cannot contract with future generations, and rights are contractual, future generations cannot have rights claims against us. However, if the contracts upon which rights are purportedly based are hypothetical, there is no such impediment. This argument, therefore, depends on an actualist contract view of rights. Most modern contract theorists invoke hypothetical, not actual contracts, since the actualist view is prone to well-known difficulties, some of which are mentioned briefly in Chapter 1.

29 Sikora, R.I., "Is It Wrong to Prevent the Existence of Future Generations?" in Sikora and Barry eds., *op cit.*, pp. 112-166; p. 112.

30 Parfit, for example, suggests that if one plans to have only one child and if a child born at T2 would be happier than a child born at T1, one should have the child at T2. Following Parfit's suggestion would prevent the existence of a child with a reasonable prospect of happiness, and hence violate Sikora's principle.

31 Warren, Mary Anne, "Do Potential Persons Have Moral Rights?" in Sikora and Barry eds., *op. cit.*, pp. 14-30.

32 Of course, in an overpopulated world, other things are not equal.

33 This is not obviously true: while morality clearly demands some commitment to a future deemed better by our own standards of excellence, it is not clear that only the best will serve. In many ways, it is arguably true that good is good enough.

34 Mary Anne Warren's comment that morality exists to protect sentient beings does not adequately address this point. Certainly, if morality exists only to protect beings that are at some point actually sentient, then merely potential persons have no compelling moral status. Her claim, so construed, is plausible if, for instance, the goal is to prevent unhappiness rather than to promote good. Unhappiness for a merely potential but never actual person is unhappiness prevented, while failing to actualize a person who would be happy is good unpromoted. But it is unclear why the joint human project of collectively creating and sustaining a good world is not morality's concern.

35 Parfit, Derek, "Energy Policy and the Further Future: The Identity Problem," in Louis Pojman, ed., 2nd ed., *Environmental Ethics: Readings in Theory and Applications*, Bel-

mont, CA: Wadsworth, 1998, pp. 289-296; Schwartz, Thomas, "Obligations to Posterity," in R.I. Sikora and Brian Barry, eds. *op. cit.*, pp. 3-13.

36 Wenz, Peter S., *op. cit.*, p. 44.

37 For instance, we do not exceed our fair share by taking all remaining oil if we know the earth is about to be destroyed.

38 Obviously, to avoid circularity, the principle of fairness employed must not depend upon the notion of harm. For instance, the principle that each person should get an exactly equal share does not depend in any circular way upon the notion of harm.

39 Megan has wronged the lottery winner *de dicto*. Bilbo is the lottery winner *de re*. Since referential opacity does not apply, those two facts seem sufficient warrant to say that Megan wronged Bilbo.

40 Kavka, Gregory, "The Futurity Problem," in Partridge, ed. *op. cit.*, pp. 109-122.

41 Callahan, *op. cit.*, p. 77.

42 De-Shalit, Avner, *op. cit.*, p. 88.

43 Partridge, Ernest, "Why Care about the Future?" in Partridge, ed., *op. cit.*, pp. 203-220.

44 One refinement is necessary. In some special circumstances, having an attitude that normally commits one to the flourishing of future generations may not in fact require such a commitment. For example, the last living being in the universe, incapable of reproducing, is not obligated to commit itself to the flourishing of future generations, simply because there can be no future generations. It may nonetheless committed to giving its imprimatur to the existence of future generations and doing what it feasibly can to insure their existence, which, in this case, is nothing. This added complication is ignored in the argument given since, to the best of our knowledge, it is, in fact, feasible for human beings at the present time to strive to insure that there will be future generations.

Chapter 9:
The Right to Reproduce

Do we have a natural or moral right to reproduce, that is, do we have a right to create, in some fashion, children who carry some portion of our individual genetic code? If so, does that entail either that population control policies violate rights or that restrictions on reproductive technologies violate rights?

Two clarifications about these questions are necessary. First, the issue in this chapter is prescriptive rather than descriptive: at issue is which legal rights *should* exist, not which legal rights particular legal systems in fact recognize, and which moral rights should be recognized, not which moral rights particular societies widely accept. Thus the right to reproduce, in this chapter, refers to a prescriptive right, not a descriptive right. Second, the right to reproduce is quite different from the right to *refrain* from reproducing: a right to abortion on demand, for instance, would be an example of a right to refrain from reproducing, not a right to reproduce, while a right that the government not limit the number of children one may have would be an example of a right to reproduce, not a right to refrain from reproducing. The two are logically separate: there is no contradiction, for instance, in supporting abortion rights while denying that population control violates rights or in denying a right to abortion while holding that population control laws violate the right to reproduce. While rights to refrain from reproducing are controversial in the United States, some sort of right to reproduce appears to be widely accepted. However, the nature of that right and its application remain in dispute. Arguably, most people who appeal to the right to reproduce are not clear in their own minds what right, exactly, they are invoking.

This chapter deals with the nature of the right to reproduce and two important applications of that right: population control and the use of reproductive technologies such as cloning. I will argue that there is a weak liberty but not a natural right to reproduce. Eight possible reasons why individuals might want to reproduce (create children carrying some portion of their own genetic code) have some limited degree of legitimate weight. There are no compelling reasons to restrict specifically the appropriate usage of new reproductive technologies, although there may be compelling reasons to restrict all procreation, regardless of the method employed. This suggests that societies that do not restrict other forms of procreation should recognize a general permission to use new reproductive technologies and, further, that there is some, limited reason for others to support the use of those technologies and the choice to reproduce.

However, it is not a licit choice to encourage reproduction in the form of insisting upon an unrestricted right to reproduce at will and then allow the resulting infants to starve. The infant, after all, did not ask to be born and is in no wise responsible for its plight, while it seems plausible to suggest that, by knowingly insisting upon the cessation of governmental action that would have prevented the infant's suffering, we bear at least some responsibility for the infant's plight. Of course, some may object to generalizing the principle invoked by this argument. For example, it may appear to entail that a society that both recognizes an unrestricted right to bear arms and boasts a high rate of gun murders bears some responsibility for murders committed with guns and must make some sacrifice to assist victims and/or their families. It should be noted, however, that, provided the law of that society proscribes murder, the society has taken at least some steps to prevent the plight of those murdered by guns. Other controverted applications of the general principle might be similarly differentiable from reproduction in some relevant way. In any case, whatever the rationale, relatively few supporters of an unrestricted right to procreate would honestly insist that it is morally acceptable to tell others "go ahead and reproduce at will. If you cannot support your babies I will stand by and watch them starve to death."

Neonates require substantial amounts of resources and help requiring the time and labor of others. Neonates cannot feed themselves or produce their own food. Neonates must be provided shelter, protection from various harms, as well, perhaps, as contact, attention, and affection. All of this requires resources and a significant amount of time and labor on the part of someone other than the neonate. If this time, labor, and resources are not provided by the parents or by others, the neonate dies and/or suffers.

Unsupported pregnancies, thus, result either in infant suffering or in sacrifices on the part of others. By "unsupported" pregnancy I will mean cases where a woman is pregnant with a child she cannot, for financial, psychological, or circumstantial reasons, fully support, even with the contributions of the father, family members, and so forth, and there is no particular person or organization volunteering to take over care of the neonate. Thus a surrogate mother does not have an unsupported pregnancy—the support comes from the contracting family. If there are many people clamoring for an adoptive baby and the neonate is virtually certain to be adopted by one of them, the pregnancy is not unsupported. By definition, then, in the case of an unsupported pregnancy, not all the resources, time, and labor needed by the neonate are provided by the parents or others who freely chose to give it, and, hence, either the neonate dies and/or suffers or someone makes an unwilling sacrifice.[1] (Frequently, the need for such unwilling sacrifices does not end with infancy, since similar arguments might apply to ten year olds, so the total sacrifice imposed on others may continue to grow.) Often, much of the outside support takes the form of government subsidies, direct or direct, which are paid for by taxes. As a result, anyone who pays taxes must sacrifice whatever he or she would have done with that portion of his or her taxes. Perhaps a parent must work longer to make ends meet, thus being required to give up time with his own children. Perhaps the taxpayer must limit her purchases or live in a smaller home. But one way or another, taxpayers must make a sacrifice. Similarly, the costs of taxes on business are passed along to consumers, often through very indirect routes. The same is true of insurance. The cost to an insurance company of covering a procedure is distributed over everyone's premiums. If, for example, an employer pays 12 cents per employee more in health insurance as a result, the employer passes that cost on in some manner, by raising prices of its goods, firing employees, diminishing salaries, etc. If the employer raises the price of cloth used to make shirts, some part of the 12 cents come from the people who buy the shirts. If the shirt manufacturer cannot raise its prices because of market competition, it will downsize or diminish salaries or benefits, in which case some part of the 12 cents come from the employees of the shirt company, taxpayers who provide the funds for unemployment compensation for those downsized, and so forth. In short, requiring insurance coverage for or government subsidy of impecunious births or reproductive technologies amounts to requiring everyone to make some (perhaps very small) sacrifice to enable others to reproduce.

Thus, bringing to term an unsupported pregnancy either imposes obligations on other people or inflicts actual suffering on an actual person: either the rest of society, or some part of it, makes sacrifices to care for the baby, or the baby starves or is otherwise seriously harmed in some way. If we rule out as acceptable letting people bear children who are then allowed to starve or grow up severely malnourished, then, when Green lacks the means to support a child, Green's reproducing requires a sacrifice on my part. That is, for Green to reproduce, I must pay for the support of Green's child and/or the costs of procreation itself, which means, given finite resources, I must give up something I could otherwise have had. Thus, either people are not at liberty to reproduce at will or Green may impose upon us at will an obligation to make sacrifices to support Green's child.

This is a crucial point. An unrestricted right to reproduce at will brings with it an unrestricted right to impose sacrifices on others at will. I suggest below that the weak liberty to reproduce is not strong enough to impose a duty on others to make significant sacrifices to enable one to reproduce: the eight reasons have some weight, but not enough to impose such strong obligations on others. More-

over, environmental duties can create licit reasons for society to regulate reproduction. Thus it is within the legitimate discretion of societies to restrict reproduction in certain ways and for certain reasons.

The argument limned above appears to conflict with certain theological
views, since it appears to entail that Mother Teresa and others who support the
current, official Catholic position on birth control can be morally faulted: it is
morally unacceptable to demand that others not take simple steps, such as using
condoms, to prevent the birth of persons who will inevitably be born into misery
and starvation, whatever palliative measures one takes to comfort or assist some
small portion of the resulting starving children. While the Church does advocate
the alternative of abstinence for unmarried couples, it does not require abstinence of impecunious married couples and cannot easily do so, given its position
on the relationship between marriage, sex, and procreation. Demanding the deliberate and preventable causing of unnecessary suffering is morally invidious.
Of course, the Catholic position is that such death and misery is not unnecessary,
since it can be prevented only by violating God's will: God demands the suffering of millions of starving infants rather than the use of condoms. Showing that
such a cruelly demanding God does not exist is beyond the scope of this volume.
The argument in this chapter is that population control measures do not violate a
right to reproduce at will, whether or not they are impermissible because they
violate God's will. Since the Church does recognize a duty of charity, then, even
if the Church is correct, Green's reproducing does create an obligation on my
part to make a sacrifice. The issue, then, is whether this sacrifice is required because of Green's right to reproduce, rather than because of an obligation to conform to God's commands. True, if God commands Green to reproduce then
Green is warranted in reproducing, but the warrant is God's due, not Green's
due, and hence, given the account of rights in Chapter 3, it is a right of God's,
not of Green's. Thus population control would violate a right of God's, rather
than a right people have to reproduce at will. Of course, it might be argued that
Green holds a secondary warrant, that is, that Green's status as a child of God
warrants her in observing God's will, as her due. Nonetheless, much of the argument and many of the conclusions of this chapter remain even if the Catholic
position on birth control is correct. I will assume in the following discussion that
the Catholic position on birth control is not correct in order to draw some otherwise obvious conclusions from the argument. If I am wrong and the Catholic
position is indeed correct, then only those conclusions are affected.

A. The Right to Reproduce

If there is any sort of right to reproduce, what sort of right is it? Is there a
natural right to reproduce? Are there presumptive rights regarding reproduction?
If so, what, if any, entitlements, liberties, and permissions do they include?

I suggest that there is not a natural right to reproduce. If there is a natural right to reproduce, then, given the argument in Chapter 5, reproduction is not just an important interest but a precondition for P, the aspect of human existence that requires the use of force against persons to be justified. If reproduction is not a precondition for P, however important it may be to individuals, then there is no natural right to reproduce. Certainly, if human beings do not reproduce human life disappears within a generation, and so arguably there is a natural right for adequate provision for reproduction to occur within a society's boundaries. But "adequate provision" here means "adequate to sustain human life on this planet," a condition that has been globally met for thousands of years (and hence this particular natural right of reproduction will be ignored during the present discussion).[2] It does not mean adequate provision for each individual to reproduce, much less that each person is entitled to reproduce at will, since that is certainly not necessary, under present circumstances, to sustain human life. A natural right to reproduce at will would require that for every person, or at least many people, P is not feasible unless that person is free to reproduce at will. If P, as suggested earlier, is (roughly) the rational pursuit of a morally defensible conception of *eudaimonia*, then it would seem that the freedom to reproduce at will is not a precondition for P: no one can justifiably claim that a good human life is impossible without personally reproducing, much less reproducing as often as one desires. Some of the arguments provided in Chapter 8 suggest that it is an essential element of human flourishing to be involved in some significant way in the future of one's community, and hence in the fostering of future generations. Thus, arguably, there is a natural right to adequate provision for being personally involved in the fostering of future generations. However, genetic reproduction is only one way of satisfying this need. Teachers are personally involved in the promulgation of future generations. So, in quite a different way, are farmers who produce food for children. As long as there are copious opportunities for everyone to engage in this project in other ways, there is no natural right to genetic reproduction.

While there is no natural right to reproduce, there are some presumptive rights to reproduce. Presumptive rights are rights that legal systems ought to respect. While they do not lose legitimacy if they fail to do so, they are nonetheless flawed in that respect and ought to be changed. The presumption in favor of permissibility, argued for in Chapter 2, shows that individuals ought not to be forbidden to reproduce or use means of reproducing unless there is a good reason for forbidding them to do so. Thus, the law should restrict reproduction only in those ways and at such times that some strong reason dictates. It will be argued below that while there may be strong reasons for controlling population generally, there are not sound reasons for singling out for proscription new reproductive technologies as such. Thus access to new reproductive technologies as such should not be banned, but certain forms of general reproductive restrictions and bans for the purpose of population control are legitimate and laws restricting unsupported births, while perhaps inadvisable, do not violate reproductive rights.

Is there an objective (as opposed to merely positive) liberty to reproduce? Recall from Chapter 2 that a liberty is a permission calling for public support for fostering the conditions for exercising that permission. A liberty exists where there is strong reason to make fostering of the activity part of public policy, to regard it as a publicly sanctioned good, even at the cost of some sacrifice on the part of others. Thus a liberty to reproduce, since it expresses a commitment of public morality or legal policy to foster reproduction, must be grounded in some publicly recognized important interest in genetic reproduction as such, powerful enough to call, reasonably, for sacrifices on the part of others. Are there such legitimate and powerful social or individual interests in genetic reproduction— can the claim be *justified* that the interest in genetic reproduction is so strong and compelling that others should be called upon to make sacrifices on its behalf? Certainly there are significant numbers of people who regard genetic reproduction (as opposed to adoption) as of little consequence. However, for many, genetic reproduction has significant personal meaning. The reasons people give for this personal meaning vary, but they might include any of the following:

1) The experience of pregnancy is an important life experience.[3] More generally, Carson Strong mentions the value of participation in the creation of a child.[4]

2) Genetic reproduction is a form of personal survival and people have a socially and morally sanctioned impetus to ensure their personal survival (*vide* self-defense).

3) We are evolutionarily programmed, as, for example, the "selfish gene" theory suggests, to have, as one of our central life goals, the passing on of our genetic material. One reason we would object to being forbidden to reproduce genetically is that such a prohibition would shut us out of evolution, would exclude us from posterity in an important sense, since our genes, an important element of what makes one who one is, will have been eliminated from the pool of genes that is an important element of making future generations who they are. There are other ways, of course, in which one may contribute to the future, other ways in which who one is survives through one's effect on what comes after one (publishing, teaching, etc.). Moreover, even if an individual does not procreate, most of his or her genes will be passed on by others, since most of our genes are shared by others. But direct genetic contribution is not only one significant and element of contributing to the future of life on earth, it is irreplaceable in the sense that any other method contributes something quite different. More generally, reproduction preserves a way of life, both cultural (via upbringing) and biological. If preserving the genetic diversity contributed by the snail darter is morally important, why wouldn't similar considerations apply to genetic

differences more specific than species differences? Is it morally important to preserve racial characteristics--would the last Asian couple on earth have a special claim on reproduction? Individuals are, with rare exceptions, genetically unique combinations. At what level of specificity does the importance of genetic diversity cease to be a significant moral consideration?

4) Circumstantial reasons (that is, reasons that apply only to those in special circumstances). For example, Jews may feel that if they do not genetically reproduce, Hitler wins. Similarly, those with socially important special talents or abilities may feel a responsibility to pass them on. True, Einstein's child may not be a great physicist, but her chances of being able to make an important intellectual contribution of some sort are higher than average.

5) Theological tenets, e.g., the biblical injunction to be fruitful and multiply, may render attempting to reproduce a form of religious observance.

6) Genetic reproduction makes it much easier to engage fully in parenting, since the adoption of neonates may not be feasible for all people with reproductive inabilities.

7) There is psychological value to parenting someone who shares one's genetic inheritance (e.g., looks or thinks like you).

Carson Strong (*op. cit.*) offers an additional reason:

8) Genetic reproduction is an affirmation of mutual love: couples who produce together a child understand that process as affirming, encapsulating, expressing, and/or deepening their union.

This set of reasons collectively seems to support a weak liberty to reproduce. Some subset of these eight reasons seem, jointly, strong enough to justify some legitimate interest in genetic reproduction, and so individuals can show that their interest in genetic reproduction, if they have one, is a reasonable and significant interest. However, even the sum of all eight reasons does not appear strong enough to compel significant sacrifices on the part of others. For example, it seems hard to deny that the experience of pregnancy can be an important, fulfilling, enriching, and rewarding life experience and that, other things being equal, others should be inclined to look favorably upon those who wish to have that experience being able to have it. Yet it is not clear why Smith should be obligated to take six hours of time away from his children, and Smith's children obligated to sacrifice six hours of time with their father, in order to enable Jones to have the experience of pregnancy. Jones can have a rich, fulfilling, and rewarding life even if she never experiences pregnancy. No important social harm appears to result if some women are not able to experience pregnancy. The burden of proof rests on those who advocate a liberty, and, so far, to my knowledge, no convincing argument has been advanced that the eight reasons listed above (or any other reason) is sufficiently strong to demand significant sacrifices on the part of others. Thus the desire to engage in genetic reproduction merits some consideration on the part of society, but the consideration required is substantially less than the consideration required by central liberties such as speech.

Finally, some have held that there is an entitlement right to non-interference in reproducing. The onus is on one who claims an entitlement to provide justification for the purported warrant. In section C., several possible grounds for such an entitlement are considered and found wanting. Until a compelling justification for such an entitlement is presented, it is legitimate to assume that there is no entitlement to non-interference in reproduction.

B. Human Cloning and Reproductive Technology

A right to reproduce raises two sorts of questions about reproductive technologies. First, in which ways, if any, may governments properly restrict citizens from employing those technologies? Second, to what extent should societies support and assist individuals in using those technologies?

The Permission Right to Employ Reproductive Technology

The permission right defended here applies only to technically perfected methods of reproduction used to produce a child who will be reared by at least one of the persons who provided the DNA (the egg, the sperm, or the cloned cell). Some reproductive technologies are already comparable in safety to natural procreation as well as other comparable commonly accepted medical techniques. Others are rapidly approaching that point. Human cloning is not, at present, technically perfected: we are still far from the point at which human cloning can be achieved with a risk of harm roughly comparable to natural conception or the use of standard treatments to facilitate natural conception. However, no compelling reasons, at present, suggest that point cannot eventually be reached. Concerns about the safety of reproductive technologies are legitimate, but no different than concerns about the safety of any medical technology. Such concerns, thus, show only that reproductive technologies should be subject to the same sorts of safety and effectiveness controls as other medical technologies and may legitimately be regulated until they are technically perfected. Since the permission right defended here pertains to human cloning only when it reaches that point, the term "cloning" in this chapter will generally refer to technically perfected cloning. Similarly, cloning and other reproductive techniques may be employed for several purposes. The purpose most relevant to reproductive rights, and hence the purpose examined in this chapter, is producing a child who will be reared by at least one of the persons who provided the DNA, although some of the arguments given do apply as well to technologies for non-genetic reproduction, e.g., a couple contracting with a surrogate mother using her own egg and donor sperm. Other possible uses of cloning and other technologies constitute separate issues that will not be discussed here. (Arguments similar to the ones provided here can be constructed concerning laws forbidding researching or providing such technologies.)

The argument defended in this chapter, then, runs as follows:

1. There are no tenable good reasons for (specifically) legally forbidding people to employ technically perfected cloning techniques and other reproductive technologies for the purpose of having children they intend to rear themselves.

2. There exists a presumption in favor of permissibility: acts should be legally permissible unless a good reason exists for proscribing them.

3. Therefore the law should not specifically forbid people from employing technically perfected cloning techniques and other reproductive technologies for the purpose of having children they intend to rear themselves.

Since premise 2. was argued for in Chapter 2, all that remains is to establish premise 1. Since the burden of proof is on those who would deny a permission, it is sufficient to point out that no one has yet produced a tenable good reason for specifically forbidding the technically perfected use of cloning for the purpose of having children intended to be reared by oneself.

One class of arguments for banning reproductive technologies centers on legitimate concerns that are not truly pertinent to the present question. For instance, legitimate concerns about the use of animals in the testing and development process of cloning are no different in nature from such concerns about other areas of medical research. Obviously, if strong reasons can be given for restricting medical testing across the board, those restrictions would affect cloning research. They would not, however, pertain to cloning as such: they would merely place general limits on testing that would apply to cloning as well as any other research, so that issue will be put aside in this chapter.

Again, legitimate concerns may be raised about human harm done during the research, development, and testing periods. While this chapter focuses on technically perfected cloning, if the research needed to achieve technically perfected cloning requires great suffering on the part of "learning mistakes," that may constitute a legitimate reason to ban the research needed to produce technically perfected cloning. At present, there is no reason to think such disproportionate suffering is needed. The risk of unforeseen consequences exists in any medical research, especially research involving fetuses and neonates, who are often particularly vulnerable. In other areas, including research on pre-natal antiemetics to alleviate excess morning sickness, the response to that risk is to proceed cautiously, despite the fact that unforeseen tragedies actually resulted from the use of one such drug, thalidomide. Similarly, DES, in use from 1938-1971, was administered to supplement estrogen production. DES turned out to have widespread serious effects, particularly on women exposed to DES *in utero*. Yet research continues on medications to treat low estrogen levels. Thus, while it is legitimate to discuss the sorts of cautions and safeguards appropriate to cloning research as the research programs develop, there is no reason to think that cloning research should be singled out for outright banning.

Concerns about overpopulation can similarly be put aside in this section: such concerns, discussed later, apply equally well to natural birth. For instance, the "one child" rule would equally affect a couple considering cloning or natural reproduction for a second child, but not a childless couple striving for their first child, whether via cloning or natural reproduction. The present issue is not whether reproduction should be restricted across the board (e.g., allowing each family a single child), but whether reproductive technologies should be singled out for restriction.

Many of the remaining arguments against new reproductive technologies force one to question the sincerity of those who advance them. One large class of such arguments purports to show some egregious harm of the technology that, frequently, lacks the slightest vestige of empirical support, and/or is at most a minor harm, and, in many cases, equally true of other activities not similarly singled out for banning.[5] Whatever the justification for seeking to use reproductive technologies, the felt need that impels most users to bear the expense, trouble, and frequent disappointment of such technologies is sincerely and deeply felt. Something more than a trivial harm or wholly unsubstantiated speculation is needed to forbid them by law from taking steps to address one of their most deeply held desires. Most flagrant, perhaps, of these arguments is the oft-repeated claim that clones will be psychologically scarred by knowing that they are not genetically unique. There is of course not one scintilla of evidence for such a claim—it is a pure fabrication, based on no scientific study of any kind. There is, however, a strong reason to believe it is false. Identical twins are not genetically unique, yet if they scarred by the knowledge that they are not genetically unique, the effect is slight enough to have escaped notice over the centuries. Thus no minimally competent medical ethicist can honestly argue against cloning on the grounds that the offspring will be scarred by the knowledge they are not genetically unique.

Similar fabricated psychological harms have been claimed to result from virtually every form of reproductive technology, including, when first introduced, such low-level interventions as artificial insemination. Most of these hypothesized psychological harms of new reproductive technologies are at best slimly supported by evidence, and, in any case, would equally be true of adoption. Granted, Krimmel is correct that couples employing reproductive technologies foresee the differences from "normal" pregnancies, and so the case of children born of reproductive technologies differs from the case of children who lose a parent due to death or divorce.[6] In general, the fact that a harm occurs naturally is not an excuse for inducing it deliberately or foreseeably. The fact that many people are killed by automobiles in accidents is no justification for running over one's rival in love. However, death is a major harm on life's scale, not a minor one, and so we do generally intervene to prevent automotive deaths. By way of contrast, identical twins and adopted children live as long and happy lives as anyone else. Adoption or having only one parent is also often a foreseeable result when a 14 year old is allowed to carry her pregnancy to term, yet conservatives like Krimmel rarely demand immediate abortion (or legally mandated contraception). Again, Krimmel would no doubt oppose a law forbidding those with genetic diseases to reproduce, yet the obstacle of living with a major genetic disability beggars the disability of not knowing one of one's biological parent (e.g., the sperm donor). So a major precondition for intervening to prevent the postulated psychological harms of new reproductive technologies is not satisfied: the purported psychological harms produced by new reproductive technologies are not so grave as to justify intervention to prevent their natural occurrence.[7] In short, these relatively minor drawbacks on the scale of life's many hardships would justify restriction of reproduction only if we accept that reproduction should be limited to "ideal" cases, a restriction few if any opponents of reproductive technologies would accept. To single out the use of new reproductive technologies is hypocritical and inconsistent.

Some have objected to arguments focusing on the "harm" to offspring produced by new technologies on the grounds that one cannot be harmed by being born unless one's life after birth is not worth living. That is, the argument runs, whatever harms, psychological or physiological, a person suffers from the manner of his birth, without the use of those technologies the person would not have existed at all. The alternative, in other words, is non-existence. Hence, if the person's life is worth living at all, he is better off for his parents' having used those technologies. Hence he cannot be said to be harmed by their use. This argument bears some similarity to the "identity problem" discussed in Chapter 8 (that future persons cannot be said to be harmed by our harmful treatment of the environment, since, had we acted more responsibly, those people would not have existed). A similar argument is sometimes used to suggest that one does no wrong by knowingly bearing a child with severe birth defects or with genetic diseases almost invariably fatal during infancy. Thus the argument deserves a closer look, for it bears on several important issues.

Carson Strong, following Feinberg,[8] takes this view of harm, although Strong suggests one may be "wronged" if one is born without a reasonable chance of minimal development. To the objection that one cannot claim to have been wronged by an act that makes one better off than one would have been otherwise, Strong offers the example of someone who is given a life-saving transfusion against his will—such a person, Strong claims, is wronged, even though he is not harmed. This example does not answer the objection, though it may answer other objections. The person who refused the transfusion did in fact make a judgment that life is not worth living at the cost of, e.g., disobeying God's will: the patient made a judgment that living by violating God's will is a worse fate than dying in accordance with it. No such judgment can be imputed to a clone. So the two cases are relevantly disanalogous.

Nonetheless, the intuition behind Strong's claim can be captured without claiming that the baby is "harmed." There are only so many opportunities for life on earth. As noted in Chapter 8, while merely possible persons are not due moral consideration, ethics does sometimes require comparing which of two possible situations it is preferable to actualize. On these grounds, it is irresponsible to create a person whom one knows will experience severe and unusual suffering, thereby precluding a spot for the creation of a person who will have a rich and rewarding life. Thus it is irresponsible, on a crowded earth, to attempt to have a baby whom one knows will die in infancy or will live with lifelong severe pain, regardless of whether the baby can be said to be "harmed" or "wronged" by being born. Someone with cystic fibrosis suffers a great deal. We cannot assume that such a person would be better off never having been born—someone who lives to age 23 will suffer a good deal, but there are nonetheless rewards life can offer such a person. So she does suffer harms, but not necessarily overall harm, in the sense that she would be better off never having been born. Similarly, if she is grateful for her 23 years, it seems inappropriate to say she was wronged by being brought to term. Nonetheless, knowingly bringing such a fetus to term is irresponsible. Suppose only six places for higher education exist. Resources do not permit the creation of additional opportunities. Generally, it is not a wise and responsible choice to give a spot to someone who lacks the ability to absorb most of what is taught, but will learn a little of it, thereby denying someone else the chance to use the opportunity well and fully. The person denied a spot was not necessarily wronged, but the decision was not a responsible one. Similarly, if children born via cloning would suffer, simply by being a clone, to the extent that, for example, infants born with Tay Sachs disease suffer, it would be irresponsible to engage in human cloning, whether or not it would harm or wrong anyone or violate anyone's rights. However, to insist that the (wholly imagined) "harms" of being a product of technically perfected cloning are of this magnitude is, quite simply, absurd. Thus the arguments so far given against the use of new technologies on the basis of purely imagined "harms" to the offspring need not be taken seriously.

Several arguments suggest banning reproductive technologies because of some undesirable feature equally true of many activities the author would never consider banning. For instance, Hans O. Tiefel[9] argues that because the risk of harm in the wide sense is not conclusively known and conditions for informed consent of the offspring cannot be met, medical providers must refrain from offering such techniques as GIFT and IVF. This argument is repeated with embarrassing frequency. Yet as Richard Zaner points out, parents contemplating natural pregnancy are equally uncertain about which risks the offspring will run.[10]

R.G. Edwards[11] points out that the conditions for offspring's informed consent cannot be met when giving a pregnant woman acetaminaphen: virtually any intervention in pregnancy poses inconclusively known risks without an opportunity for informed consent of the offspring, a fact of which Tiefel, an experienced and widely published bioethicist, is surely aware. Indeed, if parents may not licitly make proxy decisions about medical risks, it is impermissible to give a lifesaving antibiotic to a six year old. Yet if a parent can licitly give proxy consent for a six year old, on what grounds can the parent not licitly give proxy consent in the case of IVF or cloning?

The argument that surrogate motherhood "reduces" women to baby making machines is puzzling. Leon Kass, for example, acknowledges that "if there is nothing wrong with foster pregnancy, what would be wrong with making a living at it?"[12] The answer, suggests Kass, is that "it is to deny the meaning and worth of one's body, to treat it as a mere incubator, divested of its human meaning" (p. 428). Bearing a child, singing opera, and driving nails are all things a person can choose to do with her body. When the Metropolitan Opera contracts with Karita Mattila to sing Salome they are not reducing her to a noise-making machine. To take an example closer to home, no one objects that a wet nurse is reducing herself to a milk-dispensing machine. A couple employing a wet nurse may be using her body to provide milk, but that does not mean they divest her body of its human meaning. When a construction company hires Sheila Smith to drive in nails, they are not reducing her to a nail-driving machine. They may be using Sheila Smith only to drive in nails, but they do so in a way that recognizes that she is a person performing this service, e.g., they obey safety regulations (we don't have safety regulations to protect hammers), give her reasonable breaks even if that doesn't serve the project (unlike letting a machine cool down), and they do so via a contract. The very existence of a contract reflects treating the surrogate mother as a person and not a machine. I don't have to contract with my hammer. Contracts are between persons (or constructive persons), with aims and wills, who are responsible for their decisions. Of course, some people object to surrogacy because they think surrogacy contracts fail to meet these conditions. Because some surrogate mothers are impecunious, they argue, the contract is coercive and not truly voluntary. If so, however, it is equally coercive to offer an impecunious person a job working in an automobile plant: the logic of that argument seems to entail that automobile plants are ethically free only to offer jobs to well-to-do job candidates, and must scrupulously screen out impecunious applicants. Bayles[13] points out that "because poor, uneducated women lack other opportunities to earn large amount of money" it doesn't follow that "they should also be denied this opportunity." (p. 25.) Some argue that surrogate mothers do not understand the emotional impact of surrendering the neonate they have carried to birth. This is a condescending argument. Undoubtedly, some do not. But the same is true of any kind of contract that might be made. People are, in general, responsible for their choices, and we don't, in general, take a legitimate choice away from everyone because some people might choose badly.[14] Perhaps Kass might object that, unlike surrogate motherhood, driving in nails requires some activity, some use of cognition. However, suppose I hire you to stand on pieces of wood as I am gluing them flat, so that you are being hired, more or less, as a portable weight. Is this practice immoral in the manner Kass suggests? Yet I am equally "reducing" you to a body divested of its human being—more so, since pregnancy requires some care on the part of the pregnant woman. The point of the example is to make evident how specious Kass' reasons are: we don't, in general, object to people using their bodies to make a living. It's your body, after all. Kass likens surrogate motherhood to prostitution. But Kass' arguments are just as specious when applied to prostitution. No one objects to using a picture of your foot for a sock advertisement, yet, in doing so, I am equally using your body as a mere body part for commercial ends. The real sources of the objections many people have to prostitution are: 1) the deception involved in pretending to be aroused, 2) a feeling that sex is intrinsically bad unless it is "purified" by certain conditions lacking in prostitution (such as marriage or mutual respect), and/or 3) disapproval of the milieu in which or conditions under which prostitution is often practiced. (Objections to using child prostitutes, taking advantage of desperate women, or using force to keep prostitutes in line would fall into this category.) None of these reasons applies to surrogate motherhood. There is no deception in surrogate motherhood. The milieu is markedly different from most forms of prostitution. And intercourse is not generally the method used to impregnate surrogate mothers. But in some people's minds, sex and reproduction are associated, and so their squeamish feeling about sex transfers to reproduction. As Laura Purdy puts it, "it is difficult to form a persuasive argument that goes beyond mere guilt by association."[15] This hardly seems a sufficient reason to outlaw a practice.

Some people object that the high cost of reproductive technologies means that they serve only the well-to-do. In one way, that is an argument in favor of permitting them. The high cost means that these technologies will be used only by a tiny fraction of the population. Hence new reproductive technologies are unlikely to have a significant effect on overpopulation. Every resource decision affects, in some way, everyone, but if only a few financially comfortable individuals employ new productive technologies, the cost of those technologies is not likely to amount to much when distributed over the population. Of course, someone might argue that if these technologies are not available to everyone, then they should be available to no one. This is a puzzling claim. One might, perhaps, argue that all worldwide wealth be evenly distributed, in which case there is no reason to ban new reproductive technologies, since either everyone or no one could afford it. It would appear that any plausible principle behind banning new reproductive technologies on these grounds would also require the banning not only of Mercedes and gourmet foods, but even home ownership of the *Encyclopedia Britannica* and perhaps the demolition of all homes or apartments more luxurious than the world median. In particular, it seems unintelligible to leave in place an unequal distribution of wealth and its use but ban one opportunity to employ it simply because not everyone can afford it.

A related objection is that it is obscene to spend huge sums of money to assist genetic reproduction for a few in an overpopulated world when so many are hungry or in dire poverty. This may be true, but the sum spent, nationwide, on reproductive assistance is meager compared to the sums spent on cosmetics, non-reconstructive plastic surgery, dandruff shampoos, and other "frivolous" amenities. It seems disingenuous to single out reproductive technology as "wasteful": using resources to achieve the good of genetic reproduction is certainly more defensible than is using resources to achieve shiny lips. Again, one might argue for a general policy of radically redistributing resources, a policy that applies to new reproductive technologies as a minor instance. But if people are free to spend their resources on bubble gum and sports cars, they should certainly be free to spend them on genetic reproduction.

Another set of arguments originates with one set of feminists (feminists as a group are split on the question of reproductive technologies). Susan Sherwin suggests that feminists ask how technologies such as IVF contribute to general patterns of women's oppression. "IVF," she avers, "is a practice which seems to reinforce sexist, classist, and often racist assumptions of our culture."[16] In addition, she gives ten reasons why reproductive technologies fail to increase women's autonomy. The medical establishment controls who is "worthy" of IVF. Women have little choice about the relevant consent forms. The protocols for IVF shift frequently, without much empirical support. The low success rate of IVF may not be known or understood by some women. IVF procedures may pose risks to the patient's long-term health. Women have little control over the disposition of surplus zygotes. Women's status in our society depends on fulfilling their purportedly natural role of childbirth. Technologies such as IVF might eventually make women superfluous. Capitalism and racism create a social understanding that children are "commodities whose value is derived from their possession of parental chromosomes" (p. 539). Finally, childraising is the only form of self-fulfillment available to many women in our society. For a response to the arguments that reproductive technologies are unsuccessful, unsafe, unkind, unnecessary, coercive, "unsisterly," unwise, and an attempt by men to wrest control of reproduction from women, see Michelle Stanworth.[17]

A final set of arguments are specious in that the purported harm or disadvantage is, on close examination, trivial. The argument that cloning produces too many parents, no parents, or turns a child's social grandfather into his biological father is also specious.[18] "Parent," in the sense of social parent, is unaffected by cloning, and it is only in a fairly technical and rather insignificant stipulative sense of "parent" that the clone's "parent" is missing or identical to the parent of the donor cell. Hence, in the only sense that these claims are true, they are of little or no moral importance. As Harris puts it "we do not normally criticize a grandmother when she takes on the mothering role for her orphaned grandchildren.... Why should we object when she 'creates' the grandchildren...?"[19] A similar point about the term "parent" serves to dismiss the Vatican's objection to reproductive techniques on the grounds that "it is through the secure and recognized relationship to his own parents that the child can discover his own identity and achieve his own proper human development."[20] Hilde Lindemann Nelson[21] argues that surrogacy is morally questionable because the responsibility one has when bringing a helpless infant in the world is too important to be done by proxy. Hence the surrogate mother acts wrongly. If Nelson's premise is true, however, then it is also irresponsible for any mother to give up an offspring for adoption. Perhaps Nelson's premise can be modified, e.g., it is morally undesirable to discharge such a responsibility by proxy and hence should be avoided whenever feasible. A surrogate mother can avoid this undesirable result simply by refusing to be a surrogate mother, while a pregnant early teenager's options are only abortion, adoption, or attempting to rear a child she feels inadequate to rear. However it is not clear why proxies are inherently so undesirable that couples should be forbidden to employ surrogacy, especially in cases where the proxies are far more committed and better equipped, psychologically and financially, to rear the child than the majority of natural parents. Many duties, both vital and minor, are best and most responsibly discharged through proxies. If proxies are morally undesirable, it can only be because of the uncertainty that the proxy will meet the responsibility adequately. When the likelihood of that occurring is less than it is with a non-proxy, the moral objection disappears. Imagine a parallel argument that surgery, with its life or death consequences for the child, is too important to be done by a proxy, and so a parent acts wrongly in turning his child over to a surgeon. In fact, since the surgeon is much better able to safeguard the child's welfare than the parent, it is irresponsible not to turn the child over to a proxy and, instead, either insist on performing the surgery oneself or deny the child the benefit of surgery. Of course, in this case the need for surgery is unavoidable, while the surrogate, by refusing to give life to the child in the first place, can avoid the situation in which a choice between biological mother and proxy mother must be made. But if it is morally acceptable for a woman who seems reasonably capable of motherhood to bear a child and raise it herself, given the risk that, despite appearances, she will not succeed in being a good mother, why is it morally unacceptable for that woman to bear a child to be raised by even more capable parents, with an even smaller risk that, despite appearances, they will not succeed in being good parents?

Krimmel objects to surrogate mother arrangements on the grounds that they treat creating a person as a means of gratifying others.[22] This, of course, is no more true than it is true that deciding to have a child by natural means is treating the creation of a person as a means of gratifying oneself: as Krimmel is no doubt aware, couples who strive to have children, whether through surrogacy or ordinary childbirth, do so for a wide variety of reasons, and there are no grounds, empirical or other, for thinking the motives of surrogate parents are different from the motives of other parents, except, perhaps, that the additional expense and difficulty of surrogacy might indicate that surrogate parents are more dedicated and committed. As John Harris points out, there is no evidence at all that people who use new reproductive techniques such as cloning to create their own children will fail to love them for themselves.[23] The Vatican has argued that artificial reproduction lacks the proper perfection of being the fruit of a conjugal act.[24] But even if true, this argument is puzzling—are prosthetic devices immoral and their use to be outlawed because walking with a cane lacks the proper perfection of normal walking? Normal walking may be preferable to walking with a cane, but, if the only way to walk is by employing a cane, must one refuse to walk? Similarly, natural conception may be preferable to technologically assisted procreation, but, if the only method of procreating is less preferable than natural conception, must one refuse to procreate? In both cases, the answer is "yes" only if the less preferable method is worse than abstinence. Walking with a cane is preferable to not walking at all. Is procreating via IVF truly worse than not procreating at all? Bayles points out that "...even if reproduction should occur only within a context of marital love, the point of that requirement is the nurturance of offspring....The argument confuses the biological act with the familial context" (p.15). The claim that IVF (for example) reduces infants to the fruit of scientific technology is equally specious—does employing an artificial bile duct reduce the patient to being an object of scientific technology? Yet in the latter case, a physical piece of the patient is artificial, while in IVF, the resulting neonate is 100% natural--only the technique of bringing sperm and ovum together is artificial. Equally unconvincing is the third claim, that reproductive technologies represent the improper domination of technology over the origin and destiny of human life. The "destiny" of a child is largely unaffected, in any important sense, by whether it was conceived by penile ejaculation or injection through a syringe. Saving a troubled pregnancy by placing on an IV a mother with severe morning sickness is also a technological intervention in birth. The smokescreen of verbiage in these cases fails to reveal any plausible principle behind these attacks on reproductive technologies.[25]

Hilary Putnam[26] suggests that treasuring diversity, the separateness and independence of other family members, is an essential part of the moral image of the family threatened by a future in which parents can select designer children. Undoubtedly, the reduction of human diversity to a small number of templates from which babies would be designed would be a significant loss, though it is hardly evident that permitting cloning research and the use of cloning by infertile couples would lead to such an outcome. Putnam himself says, on page 500, that such futures might result "very easily," without providing evidence for this somewhat dubious claim. But even in such a world it does not follow that parents will fail to appreciate and foster the thousand respects in which even genetically identical children will differ both from themselves and from their cell donors. If I have blue eyes, I can more or less guarantee that my children will have blue eyes by procreating with another blue-eyed person. This is hardly a reason for banning marriages between blue-eyed people. Nor, should I choose to marry for this reason, does it mean that I cannot accept the difference between my children and myself—a person is more than eye color. Genetically designed children, just like children today, will continue to "be a surprise" and to be "radically Other," (p. 500) and there is no reason to suppose parents will not continue to be as exasperated and delighted by that fact as they are today.

Leon Kass[27] employs these ideas more dogmatically. Without the slightest hint of evidence, Kass assumes that, because in ordinary procreation only half of one's genetic material is transmitted, parents who clone must fail to accept their finitude and the fact that others will replace them. Thus, insists Kass, parents of clones will, without exception, not only attempt to force the cloned child to be an exact personal replica and/or follow their own blueprint but succeed in the attempt. Kass does not even bother to couch this entirely fabricated attempt at predictive psychology in probabilistic terms: "despotism—the control of another through one's will—it will inevitably be," he proclaims on page 59, to the extent that, intones Kass, "it is not at all clear to what extent a clone will truly be a moral agent" (page 55). Again, it is hard to believe that a minimally competent bioethicist could sincerely make such sweeping, absolute, wildly implausible, and wholly unsupported claims.

Some have argued that surrogacy amounts to "selling babies" and is in that regard a form of or akin to slavery. The purported analogy is puzzling. If I sell you a plum, you can eat it or toss it in the garbage. Parents who adopt a surrogate baby go to jail if they toss the baby in the garbage—they are not contracting for "ownership" of the child. They are contracting for the opportunity to assume a responsibility; as Bayles says, "What is being bought and sold is not the child but the surrogate's services or the rights and responsibilities [that] constitute the parental role" (p. 25).

It is frequently averred that cloning is morally abhorrent because it separates sex from procreation.[28] Why that should be abhorrent remains wholly unclear. Sex may be the "normal" means of procreation, but it is unclear why morality should blench when those who cannot procreate in the normal way employ an alternative. Nutrition is normally effected by eating. Some pregnant women with intense morning sickness receive their nutrition via an IV at some point during their pregnancies. An IV separates nutrition from eating, yet it is not, on those grounds, objectionable in any way. The "natural end" of eating is nutrition, but, when someone cannot gain adequate nutrition by eating, no dictate of morality is violated by employing an alternative means. Why should sex and procreation be different?

Finally, it is often said that reproductive technologies amount to human beings "playing God" or going where they are "not meant" to go. As Lee M. Silver points out, "the real reason that people condemn cloning has nothing to do with technical feasibility, child psychology," etc. Rather, "the real reason derives from religious beliefs," namely "that man is venturing into places he does not belong."[29] "Meant" by whom or what, and how would we know this? When we give someone a life-saving antibiotic, we are "playing God" in the sense that we are deciding who will live. When we give drugs to correct a thyroid problem, we are making people grow taller. In short, we interfere with the natural order of death and development all the time. Thus vague statements about "playing God" or interfering with life will not serve. I have yet to see a detailed, plausible argument that squirting sperm into a vagina is radically different, in any morally important sense, from prescribing bed rest for a troubled pregnancy. Charges that cloning or other reproductive technologies change the very meaning of human life or fail to respect human dignity are implausible or left equally vague. In any important sense, human dignity and the meaning of human life have nothing to do with whether the cell from which a person developed formed in a uterus or in a laboratory. While there may be disagreement about the nature of human dignity and the meaning of human life, few would deny that it rests in qualities such as freedom, moral choice and commitment, the struggle to surmount obstacles, the appreciation of the manifold joys of life, intimacy, caring and concern, and so forth, and cloning does not affect even one of these in any significant way.

In sum, the industry churning out books, reports, and articles opposing reproductive technologies has failed to produce a pertinent, substantial reason for restricting technically perfected reproductive techniques used for the purpose of parenting. Widely anthologized bioethicists are reduced to specious dishonesty in opposing new reproductive technologies because, on the one hand, they feel the same strong superstitious shudder that led some to condemn Galileo's telescopic images as the work of the devil, and, on the other, they can find no reasonable arguments to support their heartfelt and sincere opposition. Leon Kass' oft-reprinted "The Wisdom of Repugnance," criticized above, contains a great deal of repugnance and very little wisdom. If this is unusually strong language for a philosophical work, it is because the arguments proposed by opponents of reproductive techniques are unusually bad: in few other areas of philosophy are such flimsy arguments widely repeated and reprinted. As Richard Lewontin puts it, "it is impossible to understand the incoherent and unpersuasive document produced by the National Bioethics Advisory Commission except as an attempt to rationalize a deep cultural prejudice."[30]

Of course, some give up the task of giving rational reasons, insisting both that they know by revelation that some reproductive techniques violate God's will and that the state should enforce God's will, or, alternatively, that their unsupported feeling of repugnance is sufficient reason to incarcerate people who attempt to pursue deeply rooted and reasonable life plans such as having children. Those who hold such a view will remain unconvinced not only by the arguments in this chapter but by any set of rational arguments. It should be noted, however, that their position appears to entail that the state should also prosecute women who perform in the theatre as well as anyone who stays home from

Church, has intercourse during a woman's menstrual period, becomes a Buddhist, or violates whatever Biblical or non-Biblical injunctions their individual sense of revelation indicates to be against God's will or whatever, for any reason whatsoever, moves them personally to repugnance. Given the range of things that significant numbers of members of various societies, at various times, have felt repugnant or ungodly (including educating women), this is a dangerous and distressing position. For most of us, at least, someone's feeling, unbuttressed by any rational argument, that something is personally repugnant or against God's will does not constitute good grounds for making it unlawful.

In sum, the arguments for a specific banning or restriction on the use of technically perfected reproductive technologies for the purpose of parenting by those who can afford them are, at best, extremely weak. Thus no such restrictions or bans should be imposed.

The Liberty to Use Reproductive Technologies

This conclusion is somewhat weaker than some proponents of cloning and other technologies might wish: it establishes a permission right, not a liberty. The distinction is an important one. A permission right to use new reproductive technologies merely implies that the law should not forbid access to them. A liberty to employ reproductive techniques such as cloning is much stronger. It entails that the conditions necessary for using such techniques are due consideration. Such a liberty grants some weight to requiring insurance to cover those procedures, for example, or for government to subsidize their use by the impecunious. It does not, of course, follow that citizens have an entitlement to subsidy—all that follows from a liberty is that the necessary conditions carry some weight, which must be balanced against other things. Nonetheless, if there is a liberty to employ new reproductive technologies, then there is at least one good reason to insist that insurance cover them. If there is merely a permission to employ them, no special consideration is due the conditions necessary for employing them: if there is a reason to insist that insurance cover those procedures, it must come from elsewhere. But any strongly plausible, directly moral reason[31] would most likely require widescale revamping of social institutions and mechanisms. For example, suppose a case can be made on the grounds of equality that opportunities for cloning not available to the impecunious should not be available to the rich. As noted above, whatever arguments ground such a claim would apply to much more than cloning. After all, if genetic reproduction is merely a permission, it is hard to see why someone would think inequality of opportunities for genetic reproduction in particular is intolerable unless inequality of opportunities for employing permissions generally is intolerable. It is unlikely that the institution of insurance, as we know it, would survive the redistribution this principle demands. To the extent, then, that current social institutions such as insurance coverage as we know it are licit at all, if genetic reproduction is merely a permission, no strong moral reason exists to require insurance to cover cloning.

A liberty, it was noted earlier, requires a public commitment to the exercise of a permission strong enough to justify calling for sacrifices on the part of others. Requiring insurances to cover procedures or direct government subsidy of them amounts, for reasons mentioned earlier, to requiring people to make sacrifices in order to enable others to pursue their interest in genetic reproduction. The eight reasons earlier do not seem strong enough to justify such a demand: genetic reproduction is at most a weak liberty. Thus, while there is some reason for societies to choose to subsidize the availability of these technologies, it remains within the reasonable discretion of the society whether or not to do so.

C. Population Control and Unsupported Births

Overpopulation is a serious problem globally and among the most pressing of problems in some parts of the world. There is an extensive literature detailing and debating the extent of the problem, now and over the foreseeable future, as well as possible solutions to the problem. The primary question of this section is: "if overpopulation is indeed a serious problem in a given region, would laws regulating reproduction (e.g., restricting couples to a single child) violate a right to reproduce?" For the purpose of discussion I am assuming the laws in question are not objectionable on other grounds, in the following sense. A law restricting African-American couples to a single child but permitting so-called "Caucasian" couples to have unlimited numbers of children would be objectionable on grounds of discrimination, even if there is no right to reproduce of any kind. There is no right to jaywalk, but a law permitting only "Caucasians" to jaywalk would be objectionable. A law imposing capital punishment on couples who have two children would normally be objectionable because of the severity of the punishment, even if there is no right to reproduce. There is no right to jaywalk, but a law calling for the beheading of jaywalkers would be objectionable. Reproduction enters only tangentially into the wrongness of discriminatory or overly harsh methods of population control, that is, the wrongness of those laws concern not reproduction as such but the singling out of a minority group or the imposing of too harsh a punishment, and that objectionable element could simply be removed from the law (e.g., the law could impose a fine instead of imposing capital punishment and the law could limit all couples to the same number of children regardless of race). Similarly, it was argued earlier that population control legislation that forbids reproduction assisted by technology but permits unlimited "natural" reproduction is objectionable. Thus, in the following discussion, reference to population control laws will mean laws that do not single out special groups or means of reproduction, do not impose unduly harsh punishments, do not unduly and unnecessarily invade privacy, etc. A related issue concerns laws restricting "unsupported birth," that is, producing a child that neither the parents nor some other freely assenting individual or group is able and willing to support, either for financial or psychological or circumstantial reasons. (Recall that a pregnancy is not unsupported if the resulting neonate is virtually certain to be willingly adopted and that support in the case of surrogate mothers comes from the contracting family.) Again, the present discussion pertains only to laws restricting unsupported birth that are not objectionable on other grounds (e.g., by singling out a particular ethnicity).

If laws restricting population or unsupported pregnancies violate a right to reproduce, it is because they violate either a liberty to reproduce, the permission to reproduce discussed earlier, or an entitlement to reproduce, that is, an entitlement to non-interference in reproducing. The liberty to reproduce, it has already been argued, is too weak to justify demanding significant sacrifices on the part of others. The ensuing discussion shows that both overpopulation and supported births do require significant sacrifices on the part of others. Hence population control legislation and laws regulating unsupported births do not violate a liberty to reproduce. Would laws restricting reproduction for the purpose of population control violate the presumption in favor of permitting reproduction? The argument for the presumption in favor of permissibility shows only that reproduction should not be legally restricted without a good reason. If it can be shown that controlling population in overpopulated regions is a good reason, then the presumption in favor of permissibility does not apply. All that is required to address this concern, then, is showing that controlling population in overpopulated areas is a good reason for restricting reproduction. It would not, of course, follow that reproduction *should* be restricted: good reasons for restricting reproduction must be balanced against good reasons for not doing so. The presence of a good reason merely negates the presumption in favor of permissibility. It does not, by itself, establish what should be done. Since the discussion below will present a good reason, the presumption in favor of permitting reproduction does not apply to restrictions for the purpose of controlling population. Similarly, it will be shown that there is at least some good reason for regulating unsupported births, although it will be suggested that, in the United States today, such regulation would be bad public policy. Finally, an entitlement right to non-interference in reproduction requires justification: the onus is upon one who claims such a right to provide grounds for such a warrant. Various possible grounds for such a warrant will be considered and found to be untenable.

Thus, it will be concluded, some laws restricting reproduction for the purpose of population control and some laws regulating unsupported births do not violate the right to reproduce.

Why would anyone assert an entitlement right to reproduce? Perhaps the most powerful and widely felt motivation for asserting a right to reproduce is the sense that whether and how often one reproduces is no one else's business. This sense takes several forms. A woman's body is hers to use as she wishes, and hence it is solely her choice whether or not to reproduce. To insist otherwise is to claim sovereignty over another's body, a form of slavery. Family size primarily affects the family and should be each family's decision, not the decision of others. What conceivable grounds could others have to tell you how many children to have? Whatever form the feeling takes, it is a feeling that reproduction is the exclusive concern of the person or couple who reproduces.

Essential to understanding the ethics of reproduction is realizing that this is simply not true. As noted earlier, an entitlement to reproduce at will entails that each person has the right to require others to make sacrifices whenever she chooses to reproduce. Such a right would give each person the arbitrary power to take various things away from others an indefinite number of times at his or her whim or caprice. Conversely, if you do not have the right to require others to make sacrifices anytime you choose to reproduce, then you do not have an entitlement to unsupported births and, in an overpopulated region, you do not have an entitlement to have as many offspring as you wish.

Thus the argument that reproduction is "no one else's business" fails. Rights over one's body are generally limited by the impact one's body has on others. My right to move my finger does not extend to moving it on the trigger of a loaded gun pointed at my neighbor. If I chose to move my body through a forest, that does not by itself obligate you to spend your day clearing a path for me. In the case of an unsupported pregnancy, then, a woman's right over her body does not automatically extend to giving birth, since, unless an acceptable alternative is permitting the birth and simply allowing the baby to die or suffer from malnourishment and grow up malformed, etc., her having the child obligates me to spend my time and resources on caring for her child for the next 18 years.[32] The question, then, is whether an individual's ability to reproduce at will is sufficiently important, morally or consequentially, to obligate others to make significant sacrifices against their will. The burden of proof is on the person demanding those sacrifices of others, and no sufficiently strong argument has been advanced plausibly justifying such a demand. Indeed, it is not clear on what grounds you could legitimately demand from me those sacrifices, as your due, simply because you wish to reproduce. Perhaps I have some obligation to make sacrifices to keep you from dying. But losing any of the goods mentioned above as reasons for a legitimate interest in reproduction does not seem so dire a catastrophe that one may reasonably demand that others disrupt the pursuit of their own goals to prevent it. The psychological value of my extra time with my children has as legitimate a claim on social consideration as the psychological value of your bond with someone who bears your genes. And, after all, it is my time that is at issue. Thus it seems reasonable to say that I, my projects, my spouse, and my children are not hostage to anyone who feels like reproducing.

It may prove helpful here to consider the difference between an unrestricted welfare right (W1) and a welfare right for those who cannot find work (W2). W1 would entail that anyone who simply did not feel like working is entitled to impose an obligation on others to support him, an obligation imposable at will, as the result of a person's choice not to work. The obligation imposed by W2, by contrast, is not imposable at will: the recipient of welfare must make a good-faith effort to obtain work. His inability to find work is not a choice of his and it is a result of others' use of land, natural resources, etc. Thus, in the case of W2, the welfare recipient's need for support is an involuntary result of the use of (and benefit from) resources by those who must bear the obligation, and so it may reasonably be argued to be their responsibility. For good reason, then, most people are comfortable with W2 but balk at W1: you are not entitled, most people feel, to impose on me the sacrifices needed to support you because you choose not to work. An unrestricted right to reproduce, however, is like W1, not W2. It is imposable at will by a voluntary choice to have a baby. The recipient's being pregnant is not the result of any action on the part of those who must make the sacrifice, and so it is not their responsibility in the sense that W2 is. Moreover, an unrestricted right to reproduce is an open-ended obligation the recipient can impose on others as often as she wants. It seems reasonable, then, to say that you are not entitled to impose on me, as often as you like, the sacrifices needed to support your child simply because you choose to have a baby.

So you are not warranted in claiming that my sacrificing extra time with my children is your due.[33] If I (and others) do not make those sacrifices, then the prospective parents have no resultant right to carry through a pregnancy at the cost of starvation, malnutrition, disease, and so forth, borne not by the parents but by the baby. That is, the parents are not overall warranted in doing so. I am warranted in refusing to assume the obligation of caring for their baby. And others are warranted in saying that it is irresponsible to inflict such suffering when the suffering can be prevented by the use of a condom.

Justine C. Burley considers the application of Dworkin's egalitarianism to reproduction.[34] Dworkin[35] suggests that if B would prefer the resources A has to his own, and if the difference in their resources is not due to choices or preferences of theirs, then B is due compensation—other people, in other words, are required to make sacrifices to ameliorate B's deficiencies in resources. Now, if this principle is correct, then, other things being equal, I may have an obligation to make sacrifices to compensate someone who wishes to have an unsupported pregnancy, since her resources for reproduction are less than mine.[36] But why should Dworkin's principle be correct? Perhaps because A has an "unfair" advantage over B. However, there are two quite different senses of "unfair advantage." A might have an unmerited advantage over B. If A and B both buy lottery tickets and A wins, A's winning was not earned. So A's advantage is unmerited: the difference in A's and B's situation is not mandated by fairness. A might also have a dishonorable advantage over B, an advantage resulting from a sharp, improper, or dishonorable practice such as cheating (e.g., secretly violating agreed upon rules). If A wins a round of the card game War because A draws a king and B draws a jack, A's winning is unmerited but not dishonorable: A did not "earn" drawing a king (it is simply a matter of "luck") but his advantage over B was not dishonorably obtained. If A wins because he secretly substitutes a king stashed up his sleeve for the ten he drew, his winning is dishonorable. While I may owe it to others to refrain from employing a dishonorable advantage, do I owe it to others to make sacrifices to erase an unmerited advantage? Dworkin draws a distinction to deal with the card game—he distinguishes between option chance and brute chance. Buying a winning lottery ticket is an option chance, while having one's crops destroyed by hail is a brute chance. Only the latter deserves compensation. However, it is not clear why a farmer in Bolivia must eat less because hail destroyed some portion of the crops of a farmer in Peoria. True, the advantage of the farmer in Bolivia is unmerited, but it is not dishonorable. Notice that Dworkin's principle is different from a humanitarian duty to aid the starving. The Perorian farmer need not be starving at all, but quite comfortable. All that matters, for Dworkin's principle, is that the Bolivian farmer has more, in the relevant sense, and it is not clear why the Bolvian farmer's projects should be hostage to another's minor inconvenience.

Some suggest that since, in the United States, African-Americans are disproportionately poor, restricting reproduction of the impecunious amounts to genocide. This is a strange argument in several ways. If "genocide" means the systematic attempt to eradicate a population based on ethnicity, broadly understood, it is a fatuous claim: such restrictions stand no chance of eradicating the population of African-Americans. If "genocide" means widespread killing of individuals based solely on their ethnicity, it is also fatuous, since such reproductive restrictions would be neither killing nor based on ethnicity. One can, of course, stipulate that by "genocide" one will mean anything one wants, but then the fact that something counts as "genocide," in this stipulative sense, has no moral force.[37] Of course, if, as seems undeniable, there are structural inequalities in the US about access to means, there is some unfairness about restricting reproduction on the basis of means, just as there is some unfairness about apportioning anything on the basis of means, from Mercedes ownership to education. The solution is not to pick one example and eliminate means as a consideration, but to address the structural inequalities. For example, suppose all blue-eyed people are herded into ghettos and permitted only a few crumbs of bread a day. As a result, few blue-eyed people are strong enough to be dock loaders. The solution is not to continue the ghettos and restricted food allotments but hire as dock loaders large number of blue-eyed persons who are too weak to do their jobs. Even the most ardent supporters of affirmative action would advocate, instead, eliminating the food restrictions. Of course, some case might be made if hiring blue-eyed people would give them a salary sufficient to purchase food so that they can become qualified dock loaders. This may be an inefficient solution, compared to eliminating the food restrictions, but if it is the best available, it has some merit. However, having unlimited numbers of extra babies will do nothing to rescue a welfare mother from poverty.

Overpopulation similarly imposes sacrifices on others. Some would argue that overpopulation improperly harms other animals, ecosystems, nature, or the earth, something we are not entitled to do because it is intrinsically wrong and/or because doing so harms other human beings, including future generations. The environmental argument, then, is that in overpopulated regions people do not have a right to reproduce at will because doing so wrongs others (other persons, other animals, and/or whole ecosystems) via the harm done to the environment, and/or because there are duties to the environment that are violated by giving birth in that situation. Since an extensive literature on this subject already exists, I will focus on the social harms of overpopulation rather than the environmental harms.

By "overpopulated region" I will mean a region in which, normally, there are insufficient resources, indigenously or via trade, to support the entire population in a minimally acceptable way, when reducing the population would normally make it possible to do so. Several points about this rough definition require explication. What is "minimally acceptable" is partly a matter of culture and circumstances (see the discussion of "adequate provision" in Chapter 5). What level of health care is minimally acceptable, for example, depends in part upon available medical technology. Some cultures may have unreasonably high standards of minimal acceptability and others may have unreasonably low standards, but there are certainly many clear cases in which there are insufficient resources to provide what most people in the region reasonably and justifiably consider an appropriate minimum. Few cultures if any think of dying from starvation as acceptable, for instance. I say "normally" for several reasons. First, special, rare, and temporary circumstances should not make a region "overpopulated," e.g., five hundred year high flood levels may mean that for a period an ordinarily prosperous region cannot maintain its population acceptably. Conversely, temporary extreme measures may stave off widespread famine, but if such measures are not sustainable and widespread famine is inevitable, then the existence of the temporary extreme measures does not rescue a region from being overpopulated. Finally, I wish to rule out various sorts of peculiar circumstances, such as aliens threatening to unleash horrible plagues if the population of a region drops below its current level, so that reducing the population would not permit supporting the population in a minimally acceptable way, although normally, absent the alien threat, reducing the population would make it possible to support everyone in a minimally acceptable way. The definition of "overpopulated region" does not refer to distribution of resources within a region: arguably, in the United States many individuals live below a minimally acceptable level, but this is a result of distribution rather than population level and total resources. The United States is (arguably) not overpopulated in the sense that the food, water, minerals, and other natural resources available within the boundaries of the United States are sufficient to maintain adequately a population of 270 million persons. Poverty in the United States is not, currently, the result of overpopulation within the United States. However, a region may be said to be over-populated if maintaining that number of persons in that region requires others in other regions to live less than minimally acceptable lives, a condition that would be ameliorated by reducing the population. If 100,000 people can live on Mount Olympus only because a million persons in the flatlands must surrender all the food they grow to the denizens of Mount Olympus, then Mount Olympus is overpopulated, since the flatlanders would avoid starvation were the population of Mount Olympus only 2000. On the other hand, while the denizens of Mount Olympus act wrongly if they impose slavery on the flatlanders not in order to survive but in order to maintain a lavish lifestyle, that does not make Mount Olympus overpopulated: a less lavish lifestyle without a decrease in population is a morally acceptable (even mandatory) solution. Similarly, it has been argued that the lavish lifestyles of many Americans requires poverty in other regions, but, if so, that makes America greedy, not overpopulated: a less lavish lifestyle without a decrease in population is a morally acceptable solution.

The impact of a region's being overpopulated upon those who live in the region is dramatic. People suffer from overpopulation in a diffuse network of ways, some direct and some indirect, some dramatic and some subtle, some overwhelming and some merely inconvenient. The list of consequences, from the life-threatening to the minor nuisance, is endless. Competition in such a region is fiercer, opportunities harder to come by. For many, hunger is a constant companion. Lack of adequate childhood nutrition has significant results in adult life. If educational resources are less available because of diminished resources and if children in large numbers leave school early to help support their struggling families, the electorate in a democracy will be less educated and, presumably, the quality of government will decline. Lines are longer, as there are more people to be served and fewer resources for serving them. Moreover, overpopulation makes more difficult the long climb upward from poverty, just as poverty makes population control more difficult. For instance, in a wealthy society, people with small families can make adequate provision for old age. There may be adequate social security, incomes may be sufficient for retirement saving, and the incomes of two children are frequently sufficient to support a parent. In a poor society, frequently none of this is true. Without social security or the ability to save for old age, the elderly are dependent upon children or other family members. When each child is barely subsisting, each child can contribute perhaps a tenth of the cost of supporting his or her elderly parents. Moreover, since medical care and nutrition are less available in poor countries, childhood mortality rates are higher: a couple with two children may find that neither survives to adulthood. Thus people need ten or more children to be able to survive old age. The children themselves need to rely upon large numbers of siblings and other relatives to assist with sickness, loss of income, etc., since they cannot save for such contingencies, government assistance is limited, and family members can each contribute only a small amount. Thus parents who have only two children jeopardize their children's ability to survive. Since this is just one of many such effects, overpopulation pressures those in the region to have larger families. Controlling population and improving education, social security, economic opportunity, and medical care go hand-in-hand: it is difficult in developing nations to do one without the other. Thus overpopulated societies have powerful and legitimate reasons for controlling population, and, in overpopulated regions, those who reproduce copiously thereby impose hardships and sacrifices on others.

In overpopulated regions, then, whether a couple has four babies is other people's business: a woman's right over her body does not automatically mean she is free to reproduce at will. The question is whether an individual's ability to reproduce at will is sufficiently important, morally or consequentially, to obligate others in an overpopulated region to undergo significant hardships against their will, that is, whether a couple's reproducing at will outweighs the pressing need of others in the region to control population. The burden of proof is on the person demanding those sacrifices and hardships of others, and no sufficiently strong argument has been advanced plausibly justifying such a demand.

The argument so far has been cast in terms of overpopulated regions, rather than world population as such. Given current conditions, the global obligation to control human population is best handled regionally, society by society. In other words, each legal system covering a more or less sovereign domain must take adequate steps to insure that its population remains within the resources of the region it governs. While worldwide population is a legitimate global concern, human social structures are still sufficiently local that geography matters. If, as seems likely, the world becomes increasingly a single community, economically and politically, this will change. At the moment, however, the most effective and reasonable way to control global population is for each society to insure that its population remains within the economic and environmental constraints of its territory, that is, that it can support its current population by employing its current economic resources in a manner that is environmentally responsible. Japan's population remains within Japan's economic resources because Japan uses more of the world's natural resources than it produces and because Japan's per capita use of resources is significantly greater than the global per capita use. Thus Japan can support a higher population density than Madagascar.

Some might object to the principle of regional control on the grounds that it is unfair that Japan has greater access to world resources than Madagascar. However, questions of global equity about the use of world resources are best addressed as a separate issue. Population policy should reflect world resource allocation policy. Perhaps considerations of global equity require a change in the relative access of Japan and Madagascar to global resources. The principle of regional control insures that if Japan's and Madagascar's relative access to world resources changes, so should their population policies. But it makes no sense to insist that Japan and Madagascar attain the same population density while leaving intact Japan's much greater access to world resources. So the principle of regional control neither affirms nor denies that the existing allocation of global resources is morally acceptable.

In addition, as noted, negative effects of overpopulation are human as well as environmental. With regard to human or social negative effects, standards of living may legitimately vary. Within certain limits, trade-offs between a higher standard of living and greater population and/or reproductive freedom may be made: that is a local (regional) decision. This is true of environmental damage to a much lesser extent, both because environmental consequences do not remain local and because human beings have general environmental obligations. When the six dwellers of a village decide to give up having dessert in order to add a seventh villager, they act within their legitimate realm of discretion. When they decide to dump toxic wastes, they pollute the water supply of neighboring villages and, arguably, fail to meet their environmental obligations, neither of which lies within their realm of legitimate discretion. So, within the limits of environmental and social responsibility, regional societies should be allowed to make their own choices about population size.

I conclude, then, that restricting unsupported pregnancy or reproduction in overpopulated regions doesn't violate the right to reproduce. It is a further question, of course, whether reproduction *should* be restricted in these ways.

It is bad public policy, at this time, to pass legislation within the United States restricting unsupported pregnancy. There are not 40 million impoverished children born in the US every year. The cost to each taxpayer is small enough that that sacrifice is worth avoiding the negative consequences of a policy of means-tested reproduction regulation. Since the costs of supporting impecunious babies are sometimes hidden, it is hard to assign a clear figure to the total cost. How much does one extra baby contribute to the cost of the school system, the sanitary disposal system, wear and tear on roads, etc.? Moreover, in some cases, these costs are more of an investment than a disbursement. During childhood, the impecuniously born and their parents may not contribute significantly to the network of institutions and activities that support them. However, impecuniously born infants can grow up to be highly productive members of society, more than reimbursing society for those costs by their contributions as adults. In addition, maintaining any mechanism for regulating impecunious births also imposes some costs. Some of those costs, such as the salaries of those who enforce the regulations, are easily identified. Others are amorphous. Thus it is possible only to guess at the savings to each currently existing U.S. citizen of imposing means-based reproductive regulations. A plausible guess is that the total savings would amount to less than five dollars a year per person. Such a small financial gain does not seem to justify the various negative effects of legally restricting reproduction. Arguably, saving five dollars a year is not a strong enough reason to override the presumption in favor of permissibility, particularly given the strength of the desire to reproduce felt by a significant number of individuals. In other circumstances, where the relative cost of permitting unsupported births is much greater, legislation restricting unsupported births could be defensible.

In short, given current conditions in the United States, the best policy appears to be to refrain from imposing means-based restrictions on reproduction. On the other hand, there are good reasons to provide disincentives for having babies one cannot afford. Such babies, as a rule, are disadvantaged in several important respects. Thus we should institute policies that humanely and non-invasively discourage unsupported reproduction. Advertising and education are examples of relatively unobtrusive and inexpensive attempts. However, any such policies must be carefully considered. Some school systems attempt to make their students more aware of the real costs of reproduction in an attempt to foster responsible attitudes toward reproduction. Such programs, when they are carefully considered, limited, and flexible, may be genuinely useful. Unfortunately, school systems are already overburdened with the charge of instilling attitudes and experiences that should be provided by parents and peers. It may be reasonable to ask our schools to perform these functions if they have time and resources left over after doing their primary job. When schools nationally are unsuccessfully struggling to teach reading, history, critical thinking, and other core educational matters, such demands are counterproductive and unreasonable. Moreover, school programs for the purpose of instilling particular attitudes tend to be distorted by politics, the incompetence of educational institutions, and the general problems inherent in "canned" programs. They are often ill conceived.

Thus educational and publicity initiatives should be undertaken gingerly, with great care. The ultimate source of education about attitudes must be participation in a real community, including families, peers, books, television, activities, and social institutions, including schools. Asking television and school teachers to do the task alone is destructive and ineffective. Granted, many parents have abandoned their role. Nonetheless, fostering and supporting genuine parenting may be a better approach than asking schools to do more and more of the job of parenting. Here it must be remembered that parenting involves more than the nuclear family. Parenting is working with and guiding a child through the stages of living a life. To an important extent, parenting depends on the parent. But it also depends on the world through which the child moves, something over which individual parents have limited control. A parent may restrict the television shows his child watches. He has no control over the TV shows that his child's classmate watches, and peer attitude is a brute fact of life. There is no easy fix. Nonetheless, advertising and school programs can, properly done, play a small but significant role, particularly when supported by broader social initiatives, many of which are non-governmental.

Population control measures in overpopulated areas must be holistically and carefully conceived. Such programs should be responsive to local conditions, attitudes, and customs: no generic template is applicable across the globe. The need for population control in some regions is urgent and imperative. Target populations depend partly on societal choices about what level of life quality and risk is an appropriate trade off for reproductive freedom. Programs generally should seek a satisfactory network of mutually reinforcing means. In some cases, a single direct measure, such as limiting all individuals to one child each,[38] is the only workable measure, but to the extent feasible population programs should avoid quick fixes and seek holistic methods of approaching target populations. Appropriate means for a region depend upon such factors as the extent and urgency of the problem, local circumstances, customs, and attitudes, and special problems of equity facing the region. In some cases programs are most effective and humane when working in partnership with religious, social, and political organizations. In some cases any effective program requires "taking on" a powerful religious organization that unremittingly opposes any form of restricting the number of births. In general, programs should strive, to the extent feasible, to have the greatest overall effect on population while being as unobtrusive as feasible. All of these conflicting *desiderata* must be weighed and balanced for a particular region at a particular time.

D. Restricting Reproduction in the Case of Genetic Disease or Incompetent Parents

The discussion so far serves to clarify a variety of other issues concerning reproductive rights, such as restricting reproduction of mentally incompetent parents or giving birth to severely deformed neonates. Two reasons may be proposed as sufficient to override the presumption in favor of permissibility: society's unwillingness to make sacrifices to support such offspring and the future suffering of such offspring. Both reasons, it was argued earlier, have some weight. In most cases, offspring will require some form of social support, thus requiring some sacrifice on the part of persons not volunteering to make those sacrifices. There is some reason to think that giving one of the limited slots for human life on earth to a severely deformed neonate is not a responsible decision. But, of course, reasons supporting a policy must be weighed against reasons for opposing that policy. The above arguments serve to show that whether it is permissible or advisable to restrict reproduction in these cases depends upon the result of weighing those two reasons against the costs, moral and practical, of restrictive measures. Those costs can be considerable. State implementation of such restrictions must employ either rigidly defined criteria, discretion on the part of an individual, or some combination of general criteria and discretion. Rigid criteria for unsuitable births inevitably produce injustices and absurdities, as they preclude the use of common sense and compassion. Allowing individual state representatives to make entirely discretionary decisions grants such persons too much power and invites abuse. Any such program, whether criteria-based or discretionary, curtails the liberties of citizens and fosters discontent. Such programs would require an extensive bureaucracy and produce frequent court challenges.

One common objection to such measures is that they violate either the parents' right to reproduce or a woman's right over her own body. Section C. argued that the right to reproduce and the mother's right to the use of her body do not extend this far—people are not generally warranted in reproducing, as their due, when reproducing imposes significant and involuntary sacrifices of certain sorts on others. Nonetheless forbidding a person to reproduce is a significant incursion that would require a strong justification. So again, this objection amounts to asking whether the two justifications for restriction are sufficiently weighty in a given society.

Another common objection is that such restrictions are improper forms of discrimination. However, if either of the two justifications mentioned above are licit, then the discrimination involved is not improper. It is permissible to discriminate between individuals when the discrimination is based on a defensible and pertinent reason. For example, it is a perfectly licit form of "discrimination" not to entrust the safety of a nuclear reactor to someone who is incapable of performing the requisite tasks. Thus it is an improper form of discrimination to prevent those with genetic diseases or the incompetent from reproducing only if there is no strong, defensible, and pertinent reason for doing so. Hence this objection is really another way of asking whether either of the two justifications mentioned above is tenable.

Another objection is sometimes phrased along these lines: "who is to say which lives are worth living? Can we really say that the life of someone with a severe genetic abnormality is not worth living?" Note first that this objection applies only to one of the justifications for restriction—regardless of the "worth" of the life lived by those born with severe abnormalities, costs are generally imposed on others. Moreover, the justification for restriction at which the objection is directed does not assert that any particular life is not worth living. It does not deny that those born with severe birth defects can often lead rich and rewarding lives. It asserts rather that there are a limited number of slots for human life, that those born with severe birth defects will foreseeably undergo severe hardships that others will most likely not undergo, and that it is, absent other overriding considerations, irresponsible and cruel knowingly and intentionally to create someone who will undergo that suffering instead of someone who will not. To do so is intentionally to create avoidable, severe suffering, and avoiding severe suffering is a major moral desideratum. In a given case, other factors may mitigate or override the moral importance of avoiding severe suffering, but it remains an important moral reason affecting moral deliberation.[39] Thus it provides a strong (though perhaps not decisive) reason for restricting reproduction.

Two further objections to both justifications immediately come to mind. First, would not the same reasoning apply to other foreseeable hardships in addition to birth defects? The answer is that it does: it is *prima facie* irresponsible knowingly and intentionally to have a child one knows will suffer severe hardships that most others will not suffer. A couple's knowledge that, if they decide to reproduce, their child will suffer severe hardships that others will not provides a strong reason (to be weighed against other pertinent factors) for them to refrain from reproducing. However, there are good policy reasons for the state to refrain from attempting to regulate many such cases. A determination in the case of some birth defects is relatively objective, is relatively unlikely to be mistaken, and is relatively non-intrusive to make, at least in comparison with, for example, the state's deciding that a child will be hated instead of loved by its family of origin or that the child will suffer severely from some form of strong social stigma or that the child is likely to impose other sorts of costs. A law forbidding parents from giving birth to "unloved" offspring would be, at best, dismal policy, and its implementation might well violate a variety of (non-reproductive) rights. Thus, although the same reason applies, there are good reasons for not restricting reproduction for such prospective hardships or costs. Second, would the same argument suggest that responsibility requires producing only ideal children? That is, why stop with extreme hardship? Is it not more responsible to give the limited number of slots on earth to only the babies most likely to be happy? Classical utilitarianism does seem to imply that it is wrong to produce, collectively, any but the set of optimally happiness-producing babies, to the extent that the project of doing so does not, as a process or policy, reduce happiness. But the argument does not depend upon invoking classical utilitarianism: it makes the much more limited claim that, when one has a choice, it is *prima facie* better to refrain from creating avoidable severe suffering. Isn't it also *prima facie* better to refrain from creating avoidable minor suffering? Yes, it is. But the degree of certainty as well as the relative weight of that consideration diminishes with the degree of suffering involved, and, as the suffering becomes more trivial, other considerations easily swamp this one. It is not defensible policy to invoke the weight and cost of the law and take away reproductive decisions from individuals to avoid prospective minor sufferings and prospective minor costs. Thus there are good reasons to draw the line at severe birth defects almost certain to create severe suffering and significant costs.

In sum, whether to restrict reproduction in cases of severe birth defect is determined by weighing, for a given society, the force of avoiding social and financial costs to others and suffering for the prospective baby against the costs, moral, personal, and practical, of doing so. Given the costs of restriction and the relatively small burden imposed on the general citizenry by severe birth defects in the United States and Europe at the present time, state restriction of such births in the United States and Europe would be inadvisable.

E. Policy Summary

New reproductive technologies should be permitted, subject to the same safety controls and standards used for all medical technologies. Although a society that legally proscribes some such technologies does not rise to the level of violating natural rights, it acts wrongly in so doing. Societies in overpopulated regions that institute equitable and humane mechanisms for controlling their populations do not violate rights and are responding legitimately to pressing environmental and standard of living concerns. Population control programs should be holistic and tailored to the particular region. While restricting unsupported births and pregnancies predictably resulting in severe birth defects does not, *per se*, violate rights, no legislation restricting unsupported births or pregnancies predictably resulting in severe birth defects should be passed in the United States or Europe at the present time. Educational and advertising initiatives to foster responsible reproduction may play a useful role when implemented carefully and thoughtfully and supported by broader, non-governmental initiatives.

Notes to Chapter Nine

1 Of course if there are enough individuals who will willingly make those sacrifices, either by volunteering or freely contributing to a fund that employs caregivers, then no births are unsupported. "Willingly" here, of course, does not include those who feel that, because unsupported pregnancy is not in fact restricted, they have no choice, as their only other option is watching the baby die. It includes, rather, just those who willingly sacrifice in order to permit unrestricted reproduction.

2 In other words, in this chapter I am assuming, for the purpose of discussion, that the human population on earth or the number of individuals able or willing to have children is not so drastically reduced as to imperil human survival. Should that ever happen, several of the arguments in this chapter would be affected.

3 This reason does not apply, of course, to techniques in which the person engaging in the activity does not experience pregnancy.

4 Strong, Carson, "Cloning and Infertility," *Cambridge Quarterly of Healthcare Ethics* 7:2, 1998, pp. 279-93.

5 For additional discussion of such arguments see Pence, Gregory E., "Will Cloning Harm People?" in Gregory E. Pence, ed., *Flesh of My Flesh: The Ethics of Cloning Humans*, London, Boulder, New York, Oxford: Rowman and Littlefield, 1998, pp.115-128.

6 Krimmel, Herbert T., "The Case Against Surrogate Parenting," *Hastings Center Report* 13 #5, October 1983, reprinted in Rem B. Edwards and Glenn C. Graber, eds., *Bioethics*, Harcourt Brace Publishers, 1988, pp. 658-664.

7 Note also that forbidding the use of new reproductive technologies differs from legally preventing pregnant women from smoking or drinking. In the former case, unlike the latter, the cost of preventing the purported harm is the nonexistence of the person who would be harmed.

8 Feinberg, Joel, "Wrongful Life and the Counterfactual Element in Harming," *Social Philosophy and Policy* 41, 1987, pp. 145-78.

9 Tiefel, H.O., "Human in Vitro Fertilization: a Conservative View," *Journal of the American Medical Association* 247, 1982, pp. 3235-3242

10 Zaner, Richard, "A Criticism of Moral Conservatism's View of In Vitro Fertilization," *Perspectives in Biology and Medicine*, 27 n.2, 1984, pp. 201-212.

11 Edwards, R.G., "Fertilization of Human Eggs in Vitro: Morals, Ethics, and the Law," *Quarterly Review of Biology* v. 40 n.3, 1974, pp. 3-26.

12 Kass, Leon, "Making Babies Revisited," *Public Interest* 54, Winter 1979, pp. 44-51, reprinted in Ronald Munson, ed., *Intervention and Reflection* 3rd Edition, Belmont, CA: Wadsworth, 1988, pp. 426-430; p. 427.

13 Bayles, Michael D., *Reproductive Ethics*, Englewood Cliffs: Prentice Hall, 1984.

14 I suspect some readers might say "only a man would say that. Men cannot understand the unique bond between a mother and her baby." This kind of gender stereotyping is invidious. When my children were born, I would have given my life for them. But, equally, I would not have contracted to give them away for adoption. Other people may feel differently. I personally would have a hard time selling my paintings at any price.

But it would be fatuous to insist that, because I feel this way, it should be illegal for artists to sell their paintings. Perhaps it is true that most women are genetically inclined to feel some attachment to their babies. But not every woman does, the strength of that feeling varies, and people are entitled to make decisions at the expense of a strong feeling.

15 Purdy, Laura M., "Surrogate Mothering: Exploitation or Empowerment?", *Bioethics* 3, January 1989, pp. 18-34, reprinted in Tom Beauchamp and LeRoy Walters, eds., *Contemporary Issues in Bioethics* 5th ed., Belmont, CA: Wadsworth, 1990, pp. 666-674; p. 668.

16 Sherwin, Susan, "Feminist Ethics and In Vitro Fertilization" in Marsha Hansen and Kai Nielsen, eds., *Science, Morality, and Feminist Theory*, Calgary: University of Calgary Press, 1987, pp. 265-284, reprinted in Wanda Teays and Laura Purdy, eds. *Bioethics, Justice, and Health Care*, Belmont CA: Wadsworth, 2001, pp. 537-542, p. 541.

17 Stanworth, Michelle, "Birth Pangs: Conceptive Technologies and the Threat to Motherhood," in Marianne Hirsch and Evelyn Fox Keller, eds. *Conflicts in Feminism*, New York: Routledge, 1990, reprinted, in Teays and Purdy, *op. cit.*, pp. 549-554.

18 Cf. *Cloning Human Beings: Report and Recommendations of the National Bioethics Advisory Committee*, Rockville, MD: The Commission, June 1997. Similarly, John M. Haas, in testimony delivered before the Senate Subcommittee on Health and Public Safety on June 17, 1997, claimed that cloned children would be denied the nurture of parents, since those raising the clone would, in this technical sense, be siblings.

19 Harris, John, "Rights and Reproductive Choice," in John Harris and Soren Holm eds., *The Future of Human Reproduction*, Oxford: Oxford University Press, 1998, pp. 5-37; p. 9.

20.*Instruction on Respect for Human Life in Its Origin and on the Dignity of Procreation* issued by the Congregation for the Doctrine of the Faith February 22 1987.

21 Nelson, Hilde Lindemann, "Dethroning Choice: Analogy, Personhood, and the New Reproductive Technologies," *Journal of Law, Medicine, and Ethics* 23, 2, 1995, pp. 129-35; reprinted in Teays and Purdy, *op. cit.*

22 Krimmel, Herbert, "Surrogate Mother Arrangements from the Perspective of the Child," *Logos* 9, 1988, pp. 97-112, reprinted in Teays and Purdy, *op cit.*, pp. 566-577.

23 Harris, John, "Why Not Clone?" in Justine Burley, ed. *The Genetic Revolution and Human Rights: The Oxford Amnesty Lectures,* Oxford University Press, 1998.

24 "Instructions on Respect for Human Life in Its Origin and on the Dignity of Procreation: Replies to Certain Questions of the Day" issued by the Congregation for the Doctrine of the Faith, February 22, 1987, reprinted in Richard Hull, ed., *Ethical Issues in the New Reproductive Technologies*, Belmont, CA: Wadsworth, 1990, pp. 21-39.

25 See also "Ethical Considerations of the New Reproductive Technologies," Ethics Committee of the American Fertility Society, approved September 1987, reprinted in Hull, ed., pp. 40-48.

26 Putnam, Hilary, "Cloning People," in Justine Burley ed. *The Genetic Revolution and Human Rights: The Oxford Amnesty Lectures,* Oxford University Press, 1998, reprinted in part as "Against Cloning People," in Raziel Abelson and Marie-Louise Friquegnon,

eds., *Ethics for Modern Life*, Boston, New York: Bedford St. Martin's Press, 2003, pp. 494-500.

27 Kass, Leon"The Wisdom of Repugnance: Why We Should Ban the Cloning of Human," *New Republic* 2, June 1997, pp. 17-26, reprinted in *Ethical Issues in Human Cloning* Michael C. Brannigan, ed., New York, London: Seven Bridges Books, 2001, pp. 43-68.

28 See, for instance, Meilaender, Gilbert, "Begetting and Cloning," *First Things* 74, June/July 1997, reprinted in part in Paul A. Winters, ed., *Cloning*, San Diego: Greenhaven Press, 1998, pp. 21-25.

29 Silver, Lee. M., "Cloning, Ethics, and Religion," *Cambridge Quarterly of Healthcare Ethics*, v. 7. n. 2, 1998, pp. 168-172, reprinted in Teays and Purdy, *op cit.*, pp. 656-660; p. 659.

30 Lewontin, Richard, "The Confusion Over Cloning," *New York Review of Books* 1997, reprinted in Glenn McGee, ed., *The Human Cloning Debate*, Berkeley, CA: Berkeley Hills Books, 1998, pp. 125-140; p. 128.

31 It could be argued, for instance, that insurance companies that cover cloning gain a business advantage and that companies are morally required to maximize shareholder value. The phrase "directly moral" is intended to exclude arguments of this sort.

32 Abortion (terminating pregnancy) and carrying unsupported pregnancy to term both involve the use of a woman's body and the needs of another biological entity of some sort (the fetus in one case and the neonate in the other). However, unless the fetus is a full person who will endure suffering if aborted and the neonate is both not a person and painlessly euthanized before it becomes one, the two cases differ markedly in a crucial respect. Bringing to term an unsupported pregnancy either imposes obligations on other people or inflicts actual suffering on an actual person: either the rest of society, or some part of it, makes sacrifices to care for the baby, or the baby starves or is otherwise seriously harmed in some way. Aborting a fetus, by contrast, entails neither.

33 If the only true fulfillment for women were making babies, then denying a poor woman the chance to make babies would be denying that woman her humanity. That might plausibly require some sacrifices on the part of others. Fortunately, few are so benighted nowadays as to insist that a woman's humanity depends upon making babies.

34 Burley, Justine C., "The Price of Eggs: Who Should Bear the Cost of Fertility Treatments?" in John Harris and Soren Holm, eds. *The Future of Human Reproduction*, Oxford: Oxford University Press, 1998, pp. 127-149.

35 Dworkin, Ronald, "The Foundations of Liberal Equality," in S. Darwall, ed., *Equal Freedom*, Ann Arbor: University of Michigan Press, 1995, pp. 190-306.

36 Dworkin's principle applies, of course, to the totality of resources, not just ability to support a baby, and does not apply to differences resulting from choices or preferences, such as being lazy. However, in this world there are clearly overall differences of means over and above any that can be traced to choices or preferences, and inability to support a pregnancy generally follows this overall difference.

37 For example, one can define as "genocide" any measure whose effect, regardless of its intention, is, taken by itself, to reduce the relative numbers of one ethnicity versus an-

other. However, it is not clear that there is anything morally objectionable about "genocide," so defined. In fact, on this definition, given the birth rates in the United States, a policy of unregulated reproduction counts as "genocide" against so-called Caucasians, but that is not a legitimate reason for objecting to unregulated reproduction.

38 I say "limiting all individuals to one child each," rather than "limiting all couples to two children," because some people remarry, as a result of divorce or death of a spouse. For instance, I have two children with my ex-wife and one with my wife (neither of whom has other children), for a total of three children for three adults, just under the replacement rate (since some children will not live to reproductive age). This approach does require childless couples to decide whose "ticket" to use when having their first child, but it is, overall, the fairest way to calculate.

39 For example, in a highly racially prejudiced society, it could be argued that the offspring of parents of differing races will suffer as a result of racial prejudice. Taking a stand against such prejudices by refusing to bow to them may override this concern.

Chapter 10:
Group Rights, Loyalty, and Affirmative Action

Group Rights have proven controversial not only in their own right but because they bear importantly on hotly debated topics such as affirmative action, a people's right to self-determination, and the cultural rights of minorities. Jacob T. Levy[1] points out that group rights claims may be claims to a wide range of different things: exemptions from laws, special assistance (e.g. multilingual ballots), self-governance, external and internal rules restricting group members' autonomy from the group (e.g., laws restricting the use of English in Quebec), legal recognition of traditional rules (e.g., aboriginal land rights), representation in government (e.g., party list ethnic quotas), and/or symbolic acknowledgements (e.g., national holidays). At least one such claim might apply to virtually any social or political issue, including medical ethics, school curricula, drawing of electoral districts, corporate downsizing policies, and tort law. Group rights also raise issues about the nature of loyalty and group identification. Deeply divisive issues about patriotism, standing by one's mate, and identity politics are all affected and illuminated by a thorough analysis of group rights. Chapter 10 contains a detailed analysis of the nature of group rights, substantive conclusions about loyalty and affirmative action, and a look at some particular issues, such as the right of self-determination.

A. The Nature of Group Rights, Individualism, and Universality

Group rights, some have held, violate two important moral claims: the individualist thesis and the principle of universality. Close examination of these claims reveals the nature of group rights.

Individualism

At its broadest level, the individualist thesis claims that all civic and social relationships reduce to individual ones. At issue in this chapter is a more specific thesis—all rights are rights of individuals, and so, if there are any group rights, they can be nothing but aggregates of the individual rights held by members of the group. Three views of group rights respond to this claim. View 1) denies the individualist thesis: some rights belong to groups: a group, as such, is the possessor of the right. On this view, the right (if it exists) of the Quebecois to street signs in French is a right possessed by Quebecois as a group, as a collective entity. As Kymlicka puts it[2], this view asserts that communities have rights independent of and perhaps conflicting with those of the individuals that compose them. For example, groups may have rights intended to protect cultural practices from internal dissent. View 2) affirms the individualist thesis: rights belong only to individuals as individuals. The term "group right" is just shorthand for the aggregate of rights of the individual members of the group. On this view, the right of African-Americans to equal access to mortgage loans is just the right of each person, including each African-American, to equal access to mortgage loans. View 3) modifies the individualist thesis: some rights of individuals, which may be called "group-oriented rights," center on group-oriented interests. Group-oriented rights, unlike the rights advocated by 1), are rights of individuals, but, unlike the rights advocated by 2), are possessed by individuals as members of a group, because of their interest in the group as such. More specifically, x is a group-oriented interest of A when x is in A's interest only because it benefits a group and x benefits A specifically because A has an interest in the group as a group, and not merely because the groups' benefiting helps bring about some benefit to A whose value does not include within its content the group's flourishing as a group. For example, if all blue-eyed people have a right to a million dollars, I benefit because I have blue eyes. But I have no investment in the fates of other blue-eyed people—I would benefit equally if I alone had a right to a million dollars. Of course, there may be other particular blue-eyed individuals in whom I have an interest, e.g., my children, but again, my interest in their receiving a million dollars exists because they are my children, not because they are blue-eyed. Similarly, if I sell refrigerators to Native Americans, a financial benefit to Native Americans benefits me in that my customers can buy more refrigerators. But the value of the benefit to me, increased profit, does not include as part of its content the flourishing of Native Americans as a group. My interest is in the money, not in the flourishing of Native Americans as such, and other methods of obtaining that money are "fungible," in the sense that I am relatively indifferent about whether I receive an extra $10,000 (fully adjusted for tax differences and so forth) through increased sales or by winning a lottery. To qualify as a group-oriented interest, a measure that benefits the group must benefit me not just consequentially, but also because I have a concern for the group as a group: concern for the group as such must be part of the content, and not merely the extension, of my concern. On this view, the right of Jews in 1946 to a Jewish state is a right possessed by individual Jews because of their interest in the Jewish people as a group. Kymlicka identifies as "special rights" the rights that are owed to individuals as members of a particular community—they are community-specific rights of individuals. Kymlicka's "special rights" could belong to either category 2) or group 3). Special rights that are specific forms of general individual rights could belong to category 2). If, for example, everyone has a permission right to speak his or her first language, then Spanish speakers have a special right to speak Spanish in Kymlicka's sense (it is a right owed to individual Spanish speakers as Spanish speakers) but it is not, in any deep sense, a group-oriented right. The right of Jews in 1946 to the establishment of a Jewish state is also a special right, in the sense that it is a right owned by particular Jews as members of a community, but it falls in category 3), as it is a right that centers on the interest in a group as a group.

If a group itself is the holder of rights, as view 1) suggests, then groups must be entities of some sort in their own right. View 1), in other words, requires that a group either be a genuine ontological item (a real piece of the world's furniture) or some sort of object of thought (e.g., a virtual object, an artificial object, or a fiction). Both views of groups find adherents among those who argue for category 1) rights.

Some have argued that group rights cannot be understood as functions of individual rights because groups are in some sense ontologically prior to or independent of individuals. Group membership, it has been claimed, "defines one's very identity."[3] F. W. Maitland regarded groups as genuine persons with a will distinct from that of its members, and hence entitled to independent rights.[4] It is certainly true both that one's sense of who one is as a person incorporates, in some important ways, various sorts of group memberships and that group dynamics are complex and can sometimes be usefully described in terms of "group psychology," but neither fact requires the problematic claims that groups are literally persons (see the remarks below concerning Dennett and the intentional stance) or that groups are ontologically independent of the individuals who compose them. Since a detailed treatment of groups as genuine entities would require a separate treatise, a few remarks concerning the difficulties with such views must suffice. First, groups are generally indeterminate in ways that individuals are not. Contrast the Armenian painter Minas Avetisian with the Armenian people. While there may be some interesting and difficult ontological questions about Minas Avetisian's identity, we can generally talk about him without disputing what counts as Minas Avetisian. Defining peoples, however, is a problematic business. What constitutes a people? Are left-handed residents of Munster, Indiana a "people" entitled to collective self-determination? Does someone who is one eighth Armenian count as a member of the group *Armenians*? If the group is held to be an actual entity possessing rights, these questions must be answered definitively and non-arbitrarily. A genuine entity is what it is, and is governed by ontological truth. If the group definition serves merely to identify rightholders, it can be a social or legal fiction. A legal or social fiction, since it is just a useful fiction, may reflect convenience, historical convention, etc. Of course, if the right is to be properly grounded, the fiction cannot be wholly arbitrary, that is, it must be a justifiable fiction. Ease of administration is one consideration that may partly justify a fiction. In contrast, ease of administration does not determine metaphysical truth. Genuine objects are what they are independently of arbitrary restrictions for the purpose of administrative convenience. Morever, if both Minas Avetisian and the Armenian people are genuine entities, then more than one entity can exist in the same spatio-temporal location. How can this fact be accounted for? Aristotle proposed one sort of answer. A thing, for Aristotle, is so much matter going together over time fulfilling functions characteristic of a substantial form with a final cause. A car, for instance, is so much metal, plastic, etc. functioning over time to provide transportation in a characteristically automotive way, exhibiting functions such as movement, directional control, etc., in the way automobiles (as opposed to airplanes) characteristically do. A part of a thing, such as a liver, exists only potentially, in that the human being of which it is a part can cease to function as a human being and become a heap of organs such as a liver, but, while the human being is alive, the liver exists not as a liver as such but as the matter of a human being. A social organist may be tempted to give this sort of answer, but it will not serve, for several reasons. Minas Avetisian is independent in a way that a liver cell is not. Liver cells function in a living body only in conjunction with heart cells and lung cells: if the heart stops pumping, the liver cells die. Moreover, a liver cell does not have a will, moral standards, feelings, and attitudes of its own.[5] It is difficult to support the claim that while the Armenian people exist actually, Minas Avetisian exists only potentially, particularly with respect to the sorts of properties that are relevant to rights. Some groups, such as small tribes, may appear to exhibit an organic unity of this sort, with each individual contributing collectively to joint functions such as rearing young and gathering food, so that each individual's survival literally depends upon the success of the other community members. However, most of the groups for which rights are claimed, such as women and African-Americans, do not exhibit that sort of organic unity: despite the rhetoric of sisterhood, the ability to eat of a woman in Idaho does not, generally, depend on the ability of another woman in Ankorage to gather food. Moreover, liver cells do not covet the oxygen supply of brain cells the way individuals within a tribe may covet their fellow tribe members' wealth or status or spouse. If the Aristotelian model is not employed, then some other analysis of the ontological relation of individuals and groups must replace it. No one has yet succeeded in proposing a satisfactory alternative.

It is worth mentioning as well that if groups are genuine ontological entities with rights then groups would also seem to be bearers of blame. If a constituent part of a corporation, such as a subdivision of IBM, commits a wrong, then the corporation has committed a wrong. Similarly, I am a whole composed of various parts including my finger and my foot. If I murder someone by pressing my finger on the trigger of a gun, I cannot complain that it is unjust to put my foot in jail for the misdeeds of my finger. The organic view seems to entail that groups bear responsibility for every wrong done by any one of its constituent parts. If the group of women is an organic entity of which each woman is a part, then, it would seem, if one part of the group has committed a wrong, the group has committed a wrong, and one woman may not complain if she is incarcerated for the (private) murder committed by a different woman, any more than other subdivisions of IBM can complain when IBM is fined for the misdeeds of a different subdivision. The organic view, then, seems to justify incarcerating Gloria Steinem for Medea's murder of her children.

A more subtle form of argument runs that because, it is asserted, groups are not reducible to the individuals that compose them, group rights are not reducible to the rights of the individuals that compose them. This argument leaves open the question of whether groups are genuine entities or virtual objects. For instance, Carol C. Gould,[6] who holds that groups are constructed objects, suggests that groups rights are rights of individuals in the group to self-development, which appears to be a category 2) right. However, while Gould avers that group rights are "derived from the rights of the constituent individuals," she insists that "group rights are not reducible to or identifiable with the distributive rights of each individual to the conditions for his or her own cultural development" but are "rights of...those who constitute the group collectively" (p. 48). Part of her rationale for this stance is the claim discussed below, that individuals cannot exercise this right in isolation. A further reason she might be tempted to hold this view is her claim that while groups are individuals in relation, they are not, she says, "reducible to the individuals distributively, taken apart from these relations" (p. 45). However, it does not follow from the purported fact that the group itself is not reducible to the individuals apart from their relations that group rights are not reducible to the rights of the individuals in the group, since the individuals are in fact in relation and their individual rights may be relational. A motor may not be the same as the parts of the motor apart from their relationship to other parts, but the spatial extension of the motor is reducible to the spatial extension of its parts, since the latter, jointly, already reflects the parts' spatial relationships to one another. There is nothing incoherent about Chandras Kukathas' assertion that "While groups or cultures or communities may have a character or nature which is not reducible to the nature of the individuals who inhabit them, their moral claims have weight only to the extent that this bears on the lives of actual individuals."[7] Thus the mere fact, if it is a fact, that groups are not reducible to individuals apart from their social relationship does not entail that group rights are not reducible to individual rights.

Some have argued for category 1) rights along these lines: because some kinds of things can be exercised or realized only collectively and not individually,[8] rights to those things must be held by the collection and not by the individual members of the collection. For instance, Vernon Van Dyke[9] cites the General Conference of Unesco's assertion[10] that all peoples have a right to preserve their culture. Since individuals cannot preserve a culture alone, says van Dyke, "it makes sense to speak of a right to preserve a culture only if the right is attributed to the cultural group as a whole" (p. 186). Van Dyke mounts a similar argument concerning religious freedom: "it is not the right of an individual to go into a closet and worship alone. It is a communal right..." (p. 186). However, even if a right is a right to a collective good, the question of who *holds* a right and the question of what the right is *to* are separate questions. If you promise to dance with me, I have a promissory right to our dancing together, a cooperative activity I cannot perform alone. Nonetheless, it is I as an individual who holds that right, not the two of us as a group. (For instance, only I can waive the right, and I can do so acting unilaterally.) Morever, the right of the group to preserve its culture might be construed as the permission right or liberty of each member of the group to engage in concerted action to preserve the culture, or as entitlements of non-interference each member of the group possesses concerning his or her engaging in concerted efforts to preserve the culture. Consider rights of assembly. My right to march, after all, is my right to engage with others in a collective march. Such a right to march is an individual right each citizen has. That right cannot be a right of the group of marchers as a group, since it precedes and indeed protects the formation of the group as a group. Thus the fact that a right cannot be exercised in isolation and the fact that the right is a right to collective good, activity, or outcome do not themselves entail that the right is not a right of individuals.

Denise Reaume[11] presents a special version of this argument. Following Raz, Reaume holds that a right is an interest sufficient to warrant a duty. Because an individual's interest in a collective good cannot be sufficient to impose duties on others, the right must be held by the group: it is not for the individual's sake, says Reaume, that the duty is imposed, but "for the sake of all, considered as a group" (p. 121). The argument depends on two points: the insufficiency of the individual's interest in imposing a duty and for whose sake the duty is imposed. First, it is not clear why the fact that something is a good only if enjoyed collectively cannot mean duties to protect that good are imposed for the sake of the individuals who enjoy the collective good—why cannot a duty be imposed for the sake of Mary, and the sake of Joe, and the sake of Tabbetha, each of whom has an interest in participating collectively, jointly, and publicly in a collective good? Relevantly, Jeremy Waldron[12] argues that the value of communal goods, such as conviviality, depends essentially upon co-enjoyment, just as the pleasure of hearing the "Liebestod" in *Tristan* is not just a momentary experience: it derives in part from context, from the four hours that preceded it. Hence, says

Waldron, the value of a communal good cannot be the sum of what each individual receives from it. "Welsh people, for example," writes Waldron, "do not benefit as individuals from the preservation of their language" since that enjoyment's "nature and value make sense only on the assumption that others are enjoying and participating in it too" (p. 358). While Waldron is correct that the value of a communal good to an individual depends essentially upon co-enjoyment, it does not follow that the value of that good cannot be the sum of the value to each individual who enjoys it. When Jim and Jane dance to a CD in an otherwise empty room, part of Jim's own enjoyment of the dance is Jane's enjoying it as well, but it doesn't follow that the value of the dance is something over and above the value it has to Jim and Jane. Co-enjoyment is not a free-standing value independent of, over and above, the value of a communal good to each given individual who participates in the good, just as the value of the cohesive experience of Tristan is not something over and above the sum of the value of each moment of the experience, precisely because, as Waldron says, the value of the cohesive experience is an ineradicable constituent of each moment's enjoyment. Hence the importance of co-enjoyment is already included in the value of the dance to Jim and Jane individually. Thus summing the value of the dance to Jim and Jane does capture the importance of co-enjoyment. Waldron ultimately concludes from this that, because rights fundamentally stem from affirming the importance of the individual, there cannot be rights to communal goods. Even if Waldron is right that rights stem from affirming the importance of the individual, it does not follow that there cannot be rights to communal goods: rights to communal goods can be seen as affirming the importance of co-enjoyed goods to each individual who participates in the good. Second, while Mary's interest, taken singly, may not be sufficient to impose a duty, that is equally true of many non-group rights. Zoning laws also protect summations of individual interests. My interest in less traffic on my street may be insufficient, by itself, to impose a duty on a store to locate in a different neighborhood, but the collective interests of all my neighbors are sufficient to impose this duty. Conversely, as noted in Chapter 3, an interest can be sufficient to impose a duty without constituting a right. See also note 31 below.

At least one set of rights does seem to be a set of genuinely joint rights, but those rights are, of practical necessity, held only by extremely small groups. When the students of Fairweather University name the school mascot by ballot, they are, in a sense, exercising jointly the right to name the mascot. However, this joint right merely amounts to the rights of each individual student to vote, taken together. Even if the students must vote whether to determine the name by ballot or leave it to the Provost to name the mascot, the joint right of the students to name the mascot amounts to the summation of each student's right to vote on that matter. This joint or collective or group right, then, is a right of type 2) or type 3), not of type 1): it is, like the right of shareholders to choose a board of directors, a derivative right (see below). If Carruther's will merely assigns

$10,000 for the purchase of a mascot for Fairweather University to be named by the students, Carruther's will merely promises that a right will be forthcoming, the exact nature of which will be determined by the executor of the will, and once the executor makes that determination (e.g., that the students will select the name by ballot), the actual right conferred is the summation of a set of individual rights. However, in other cases, no specific mechanism for exercising the right is spelled out: how the right is to be exercised is genuinely left for the rightholders to decide between themselves. Menudos' will leaves seven million dollars to begin a charitable foundation, the name of which shall be chosen by his children. Krasnitz's will stipulates that his ex-wife shall receive an annuity, the amount of which is to be determined by his children. Menudos' three children jointly hold the right to name the foundation: it is a right they must exercise together and co-operatively, as a threesome, and the will stipulates no mechanism for their doing so. It is up to the children to decide whether to vote on the name, negotiate, grant each child a veto power over any proposed name, and so forth. Krasnitz's two children jointly hold the right to determine the amount of their former step-mother's annuity, a right they must exercise together as a duo, and the will de-scribes no method or mechanism for doing so. What makes these genuinely joint rights, and not merely the result or sum of the rights of the individual children, is that the rightholders must determine together how the joint right emerges from the contributions of the individuals who hold it jointly, and, once again, no mechanism is spelled out for making that second-order decision. Menudos' will does more than promise that some right will be conferred whose nature will be determined by the executor: it confers upon the three children, as a group, the right to determine how the right to name the foundation will be exercised. In practice, such genuinely joint rights can be feasibly held only by very small groups. Two or three children can decide together the mechanism by which a jointly held right will be exercised (as well as how to make that decision). Fifty thousand persons, in practice, cannot. Thus, if such jointly held rights are genu-ine group rights of type 1), they are not the sorts of rights, such as affirmative action rights to group compensation for discrimination or a people's right to self-determination, over which friends and foes of group rights have argued. This sort of group right, then, will be ignored in the ensuing discussion.

It may seem obvious that at least one sort of group possesses rights, since corporations, universities, and nation states possess numerous legal rights. While some insist that corporate rights are actually rights of individuals (such as stock-holders), it has proven difficult, for reasons bruited below, to reduce corporate rights to rights of individual shareholders, employees, or executives. It might seem, then, that some group rights belong to groups as such, namely those held by corporations, universities, and nation states. George Rainbolt, for example, gives "Georgia State University has a right to $325 from Ed" as an example of a claim asserting "that certain groups have rights" and "The Hopi have a right that the United States meet its treaty obligations" as an example of a group being the object of a right claim.[13] Carl Wellman distinguishes between two kinds of groups, namely groups such as corporations that are structured by rules and groups lacking normative structures, such as women and left-handed taxidermists.[14] Jeremy Waldron avers that we already grant rights to groups, since we grant rights to corporations.[15] James Nickle cites International Amnesty USA as an example of a group.[16] James Sterba cites, as an example of a group right, the right of a political party to use contributed funds.[17] Vernon van Dyke[18] claims both that "groups exist in the same sense that corporations do" and that "the sovereign state is the most obvious illustration of a collective entity with rights." It is unclear from this passage whether van Dyke is counting sovereign states as groups, but, in any case, while the citizens of a sovereign state might constitute a group, the state itself is an organizational entity, not a group entity.

Organizations are not groups: whatever the ontological status of organizational entities such as corporations, Georgia State University, and The United States of America may prove to be, they are not, it will be argued, groups of people. Since the error of identifying organizations as groups is widely prevalent and plays a significant role in much discussion of group rights, carefully correcting this error is a matter of some importance.

The mistake of identifying organizations as groups arises because organizations generally have a base, that is, a group of people involved, in the proper way, in the administration and functioning of the organization.[19] In common parlance we often fail to distinguish between an organization and its base: speaking loosely, we often refer to individuals who belong to an organization's base as "part" of the organization. However, the base of an organization, which is a group, is not identical to or a proper part of the organization itself. To see this, consider a true group, such as the seventeen farmers who maintain a levy. That group is just those seventeen persons: a group, after all, is just a collection or aggregate of individuals.[20] Over time, by implicit understanding, some farmers may take charge of certain aspects of levy maintenance. Groups of people, then, may have certain well-defined common purposes and the interactions of their members may display a certain amount of structure. However, if those farmers decide to form an organization, the Levy Maintenance Organization, with by-laws and dues and monthly meetings, the Levy Maintenance Organization (LMO), however closely bound to the group of farmers who constitute its membership, is not a group but an organization. After all, the very same group of farmers could, if they chose, form a rival organization, the Rival Levy Maintenance Organization (RLMO). The LMO might play the RLMO in a yearly soccer game, where membership in the soccer team rotates between the seventeen farmers who are the members of both organizations. The LMO might borrow $10 from the RLMO, and hence have a right to be repaid by the RLMO. Although both organizations have exactly the same purpose and membership and are founded and continued by the same group of farmers, acting as a group, the LMO and the RLMO are not identical—they are distinct organizations. Since whatever would make the LMO identical to its base applies equally to the RLMO (and vice versa), if one is identical to its base, so is the other. The base of the LMO is identical to the base of the RLMO (the same seventeen farmers). Thus, since the LMO and RLMO are not identical to each other, it follows that neither the LMO nor the RLMO is identical to its base--identity, after all, is transitive. Thus neither the LMO nor the RLMO is identical to the group of seventeen farmers.

It is worth noting as well that trust funds have legal rights, but trust funds are not groups of people. In fact, an organization can have no members yet continue to exist as an organization with rights (e.g. when the last members of a registered organization, which is governed by formal by-laws and possesses an organizational bank account, die in an automobile accident). This is possible because organizations are social structures, arrangements, and while arrangements are established by and made between persons, the arrangements themselves are not people or groups of people. In some cases, in fact, the rights of the organization may conflict with the rights of part or even all of its base.[21] Thus an organizational entity such as the University of Chicago is not identical to the collection of students, faculty, administrators, etc. who constitute the "university community," however closely tied to the University of Chicago those groups might be.

How is it possible for organizational entities to have rights that are not rights of the base of the organization? Organizational entities are virtual objects. Virtual objects have virtual properties; virtual objects are constructs that can be described as having properties when speaking within the world of the construct. Thus we can say that Godzilla, a fictional object, is radioactive. The ultimate ontological analysis of the facts that make true the assertion that Godzilla is radioactive averts to genuine objects, such as the writers of the films. Corporations have virtual rights, just as Barney, another virtual object, has the virtual right not to be shot by Baby Bop; when speaking within the fictional world of Barney, we can correctly assert that Barney has this right. Barney's virtual rights have little force in the non-virtual world. However, virtual properties always reflect some non-virtual reality. The virtual properties of a character in a computer game, such as *Pajama Sam*, reflect, among other things, the actual states of the physical computer. As Dennett points out when discussing the intentional stance, this does not mean the virtual object is, in any simple sense, reducible to those actual states.[22] Pajama Sam's curiosity, because it is a feature of the operation of the program as a whole and not any particular subroutine or piece of code, does not correspond in any simple way to particular hardware states on one computer, and may be equally realized by totally different states in two different computer systems. Pajama Sam and his curiosity are not elements of what is ultimately real. Every true statement about Pajama Sam corresponds, in some very complicated way, to a vast network of statements about vast numbers of subatomic particles over stretches of time. Nonetheless, Pajama Sam and his curiosity are not reducible in any straightforward, simple way to what is ultimately real. (A parallel point is made by Donald Davidson about the anomalism of the mental.)[23] Similar points can be made about organizational entities. What force in non-virtual reality a virtual property has depends upon what non-virtual facts the virtual world reflects. A virtual particle in quantum mechanics can have non-virtual consequences (as in, for example, Stephen Hawking's theory of black hole radiation) because virtual particles reflect the real quantum potentiality of spacetime. The virtual world of organizations reflects morally and legally significant needs of and relationships between actual people, and hence the virtual rights of corporations are legitimately given legal standing.

Thus, while the rights of corporations, governments, and universities ultimately derive from morally salient features of individuals, they do not necessarily reduce in any straightforward way to rights of individuals: the rights of organizational entities are virtual warrants of virtual entities, grounded in morally salient features of actual individuals, that are legitimately given moral and legal force. They are thus not group rights.

Could a similar strategy be employed for groups? As Thomas W. Simon puts the question, "if we confer rights on federal units and corporations, why not on groups?"[24] Using the analysis proposed above for organizational entities, could the totality of women be regarded as a virtual entity with virtual rights legitimately accorded legal or moral standing? I suggest not. Organizational rights require both sufficiently well-defined structures within the virtual world to make rights meaningful and appropriate moral grounding in the needs, aims, and so forth of actual people. Groups, as a rule, lack both. As James Nickle argues, "groups often lack effective agency and clear identity."[25] Since organizations and their rights vary greatly, a few examples must suffice. Nickle points out that when a family, a group, is asked to care for an incapacitated relative, it is unclear who is to be included in making the decision. Which of these should have a voice in the decision: parents, children, spouses of children, cousins, siblings of the patient and/or their spouses? Even when the family agrees upon who will participate in making the decision, Nickle says, "their discussions and attempts to organize themselves often fail" to produce a decision recognized by all decision makers as the authoritative family decision (p. 237). By contrast, when the state of Hawaii, an organizational entity, makes a decision for an incapacitated citizen, the law specifies a procedure for making the decision and indicates relatively clearly who will play what role in that procedure. Georgia State University can have a right to $325 from Ed Smith because Georgia State University has a well-defined mechanism for contracting: there is an institutional structure that indicates which individuals in which circumstances are entitled to enter the institution into which sorts of contracts. There is no such mechanism for women as a group—women as a group cannot contract with anyone. An organization purporting to represent women can form contracts, of course, but the rights and obligations of the contract are held by the organization, not by women as a group, however much the organization insists it represents the group. An organization such as IBM or the American Philosophical Association may have a right to speech, that is, a right to broadcast organizational messages without censorship, because some mechanism exists for distinguishing organizational speech from the speech of individuals who happen to belong to the organization. For example, in some organizations, official pronouncements must be approved by a majority of the membership. There is no such mechanism for distinguishing between the speech of women as a group and individual women. In fact, the LMO and RLMO could, in principle, take opposite organizational stands on some issue, though both organizations' membership is exactly the same group of farmers. The LMO and the RLMO can speak as organizations, but the group of farmers cannot speak as a group, even though each farmer in the group can speak as an individual. Every farmer in the group can sign a statement or petition, but the petition still is a speech act of each farmer, not of the group itself. After all, if one farmer refuses to sign, the petition is the speech act of 16 of the 17 farmers and not a speech act of the farmer who refused to sign. By contrast, an official statement by the LMO is a speech act of the LMO, even if some of the membership voted against the statement. Some organizational rights are morally or legally grounded, in part, because they serve to protect the legitimate projects of individual members of the base who are free to resign from the organization if they do wish to participate in the project, and hence can be held to approve the project. No such moral grounding is available for a group such as women. Of course, one can arbitrarily define rules for what counts as a group action, e.g., one can stipulate that whatever Andrea Dworkin says in print counts as the speech of women as a group. The arbitrariness of this stipulation, however, undermines the moral grounding that would give moral weight to the non-virtual reality this stipulation reflects. Examples are not proof, but they suggest the lines along which specific claims that a particular group has a particular virtual right might be shown untenable: groups as virtual objects either lack the determinate structures needed for rights or possess that structure in ways (such as through arbitrary stipulation) that undermine the moral grounding required for rights.

For these reasons, it appears that groups as such cannot hold rights in the way that corporations, nation states, universities, and other organizational entities hold rights.

This is not merely a technical distinction requiring only that those who advocate group rights for ethnic minorities restate their claim. The difference between organizational rights and group-oriented rights of individuals is substantially significant. Americans of Italian descent are a group. The Association of Italian-Americans (AIA) and the Organization of Italian-Americans (OIA) are organizations. The claim that (the group of) Italian-Americans have certain cultural rights cannot be restated as the claim that the AIA or the OIA has those rights. Neither the AIA or the OIA is morally justified in claiming to speak for the group of Italian Americans. The moral grounding for the warrants claimed for the group of Italian-Americans does not ground those warrants for either the AIA or the OIA. Suppose it is claimed, for instance, that for reasons of self-esteem, pride of heritage, and so forth, Italian-Americans have a right that the contributions of Italian-Americans to American history be highlighted in school history curricula. Those reasons do not apply to granting that right to the AIA. Rather, those grounds suggest that each individual American of Italian descent has a right, grounded in his or her individual interest, that Italian-American contributions be highlighted in school curricula. Thus, if such a right exists, it is a right not of type 1) but of type 2) or 3).

The importance of this distinction lies in the fact that the logic of group-oriented rights of individuals differs from the logic of corporate rights and rights of type 1). For example, it is often objected to the compensatory justice argument supporting affirmative action that not every woman has suffered substantially from sexism. The issue of group compensation is complex and will receive more detailed treatment below. Note, however, that were the right of compensation held by women as a group, rather by individual women, this objection would be specious. For IBM to be owed compensation, it is not necessary that every stockholder (or employee or other member of the corporation's base) suffered harm, nor even that every division of IBM suffered harm: the right of compensation belongs to IBM, not to its stockholders or divisions. Hence it is sufficient that IBM was harmed (even if it is the stockholders or divisions that ultimately benefit from compensation), and IBM is harmed when any subdivision of IBM is harmed. However, if it is not women as a group that holds the right of compensation but individual women, then only women who were personally harmed or treated unjustly can justly claim a right to compensation. Thus defenders of the compensatory justice argument must answer the objection. Since many supporters of the compensatory justice argument already treat the right to compensation as a right of individuals, such ways are familiar, e.g., claiming that all women have in fact suffered significantly from sexism and arguing that the law may legitimately use an approximating fiction in compensating those who have been harmed. (Sterba, for instance, suggests that using SAT scores in college admission decisions is also an approximating fiction, since SAT scores are at best approximate predictors of academic performance.) The point here is that the fact that the right of compensation is held by individual women rather than by women as a group affects the logic of the debate. Similarly, it is coherent to say that establishing a homeland for living Jews who did not undergo the Holocaust counts as compensation to (many) Holocaust victims, while it would not make sense to compensate me for the money stolen from you. This is because, when money was stolen from you, giving me a comparable sum does not advance the interest of the person from whom the money was stolen, while most Jews who perished in the Holocaust did have an interest in seeing to it that Jews as a group continue to survive, and that interest is (partly) met by establishing a Jewish homeland that protects other Jews *qua* Jew, that is, in instantiating their Jewishness as such.

Thus establishing the state of Israel does advance the actual interests of many of those who actually perished in the Holocaust. Some Jews who perished in the Holocaust and some Jews alive today may have no such subjective interest. It is an interesting question whether those Jews have the right to a Jewish homeland but choose not to exercise their right or whether they do not have the right to a Jewish homeland, but, since the right to a Jewish homeland is a distributed right and the majority of Jews do feel such a subjective interest, the cumulative strength of the remaining vector warrants is not significantly affected.[26] In the case of ethnic groups claiming a right of self-determination, many of the arguments in the literature invoke analogies between the autonomy rights of an individual (such as an individual's right to self-determination) and the autonomy rights of groups such as "the Kurds." Such arguments are not sustainable if it is not the Kurds as a group that holds rights but individual Kurds with diverse and amorphous views. Whether or not the group-oriented interests of individual Kurds grounds a right held by each member of the group to a Kurdish state, arguments for that position are different and more complex.

Of course, it might be objected that group rights of type 1), as opposed to speech rights and contractual rights, are of a sort that does not require structure. Consider the claim that women as a group have a right to proportional representation in the legislature, meaning, for example, that if 49% of the population is female, 49% of legislators must be female. The only structure required by such a right is a mechanism for determining who is a woman and who is not. Thus holding that women as a group constitute a virtual object all of whose virtual rights are of this nature appears to circumvent the problem. However, what non-virtual reality could ground such a warrant? If there were a distinctive "woman's viewpoint" that all women and only women held, perhaps that non-virtual reality could ground such a right. Again, it might be held that (all) women have a set of common interests that in some significant way conflict, directly or indirectly, with interests of (all) men, and that, as a minority of voters in a "winner take all" electoral system, those interests would not be represented without such a right. Some perception of this sort, that members of certain groups have common interests or viewpoints or needs, provides the rationale for those constitutions that require specific percentages of representation for linguistic or ethnic groups or that have reserved certain offices for linguistic or ethnic minorities.[27] Reasons against this view in the case of women appear elsewhere, but even if a group does have a common interest or viewpoint, there is no need to invoke a virtual group entity. That rationale for group-proportional representation could equally be captured by claiming that each voter has a vector warrant to be represented by someone of the same gender or who speaks the same primary language, a claim that equally captures the idea that in some crucial respect only a woman can represent a woman and only a French-speaker can represent a French-speaker, coupled with a general theory of what constitutes "adequate" representation. One version of democratic theory holds that, in general, the weight of a perceived interest's sway on political decisions should reflect the number of people who hold that perceived interest (as opposed to whether it is or is not the majority view), and so, in the most central respects, the representational body should reflect the spectrum of those represented. At issue is the general question of whether "all or nothing" allotments (such as a state's electoral vote in U.S. Presidential elections) or proportional allotment is the appropriate form of adequate representation. Given the sorts of compromises legislative or regulative bodies routinely reach, the difference is often pragmatically significant. For instance, in a town almost evenly divided between those who favor commercialization of the town and those who favor retaining its residential character, the town's zoning board, on this view, should not consist entirely of commercialization enthusiasts, even if those who favor commercialization constitute a slim majority. It seems odd to insist that opponents of commercialization are a group entity that collectively bears a right to proportional representation. Rather, the claims being made are that each individual has a right to adequate representation and that a zoning board composed entirely of commercialization enthusiasts does not adequately represent the electorate. At most, then, talk of group representation is loose and convenient shorthand for saying that each person should have adequate representation for his or her interests or stances, including, perhaps, group-oriented interests such as interests in collective or participatory goods, where representation counts as adequate only when it reflects the proportion of voters who share that interest or stance. By way of contrast, there is no similar clear and simple adequate rephrasing of a corporation's or a government's right to contract.

Significantly, these considerations do not count against the claim that groups can be a virtual object insofar as they enter into an individual person's interests. While the fact that Jews as a group have no mechanism for differentiating a speech act of Jews as a group entity from speech acts of individual Jews poses a severe conceptual problem for attributing a right of speech to Jews as a group, the same fact poses no conceptual problem for the claim that Schwartz has an interest in the flourishing of Jews. Similarly, the moral grounding in non-virtual reality needed to justify the importance of an interest in something is different from the moral grounding in non-virtual reality needed to justify ascribing a right to that thing. I can have a morally justifiable interest in the Grand Canyon even though the Grand Canyon does not have rights. Thus neither of the two general features of groups that count against groups having virtual rights is an impediment to groups being the subject of an individual's interest. Jones can have an interest in the flourishing of the group of farmers even if the group of farmers is not an entity with rights.

Thus there is at least some strong reason to think that groups are neither part of the world's furniture nor constructed or artificial entities of a sort that would ground the group's possessing rights. If so, groups cannot themselves be the possessors of rights: although it may be legitimately convenient to speak of a group as possessing a right, it is, in fact, the individuals within the group who are, strictly speaking, the possessors of the right. Before reaching this conclusion, however, several further reasons for attributing rights to groups as such must be addressed.

First, some rights may seem intelligible only as the right of a group as such. For example, Carl Wellman writes "although any individual Croatian could emigrate from Yugoslavia, only collectively could Croatians secede and form an independent nation-state. If there really is any right to secession, it is presumably a group right."[28] James A. Graff suggests that while women's right to equal pay for equal work is equivalent to the right of each individual woman to equal pay for equal work (category 2), the right of a people to self-determination is different—it is not equivalent to the right of each member of the group.[29] If such a right existed, Graff suggests, it would belong to category 1). Graff himself does not support such a right. Nonetheless, those who urge such a right are making an intelligible claim. The relevant question at this point in the discussion is not whether their claim is true or false, but how best to understand their claim.

Why do Wellman, Graff, and others think the right of self-determination cannot be reduced to a set of individual rights? It might seem, after all, that each member of the group could have a right to the existence of a democratically governed state within the group's traditional territory such that a majority of that state's citizens are members of the group, in which case the right to self-determination would belong to category 2.[30] One objection to that analysis is that some members of the group may have no interest in such a state. On the interest theory of right, those members of the group would appear to have no right. There are several methods of circumventing this problem for the interest theory, e.g., insisting that everyone in the group does have such an interest, whether acknowledged or not, but each of these solutions strike many as implausible or objectionable. Similarly, the fact that no individual can waive this right presents a problem for the will theory: only the group as a whole can waive the right of self-determination, hence the right must belong to the group, not each individual. Will theorists do talk of individuals exercising a right collectively, but, when some individual members of the group dissent, it is not always clear what this can mean for a will theorist if the right does not belong to the group as a group. Some group rights can readily be reduced to will theory rights of each individual in the group. For instance, the right of shareholders of a corporation to fidelity on the part of corporate officers is owed individually to each shareholder. An individual shareholder can indeed waive that right, in which case the corporate officer does not have a duty of fidelity to that particular shareholder, although, in general, the corporate officer's duties to other shareholders will equally benefit the shareholder who waived his right. We can call such a right a "distributed right." The force or importance of a distributed right is the sum of the force of each individual right, which is generally greater than the force of any one of its constituents. This feature may prove problematic for those who hold that rights are absolute, but it is not problematic for the warrant theory: each individual has a vector warrant, and the sum of all the relevant vector warrants weighs more heavily than any one of those vector warrants does in determining resultant rights.[31]

The right of the shareholders to choose a board of directors is slightly different: it is the resultant of each shareholder's having a right to vote for a board of directors.[32] In this case, the sum of a collection of individual rights create or constitute a different right that is reducible to that collection of individual rights: the right of shareholders to choose a board can be reduced to the right of each shareholder to vote for a board. We can call such rights, following Wellman,[33] "derivative rights." Neither case presents a problem for the will theory. However, when groups are ill-defined or are conceptualizable independently of their memberships, neither sort of reduction appears to be available, since both derivative and distributed rights are comprised of a clearly defined set of individual rights. In any case, the problem does not arise on the warrant view: the claim is just that each person in the group is warranted in demanding such a state, regardless of whether she wishes to employ the warrant or whether the existence of such a state is to her benefit.

The possibility of dissenters also presents a more profound problem for this analysis, namely, that self-determination means a people assenting to their political situation, and what they assent to may not be a democratic state in which they constitute a majority. On the warrant view, then, the right of a people to self-determination can be construed as a warrant held by each member of the group to demand, as his or her due, that the group not be subject to a political regime to which a preponderance of members of the group does not assent.[34] Thus claiming that peoples have a right to self-determination need not entail granting a right to a metaphysical entity such as "the Armenian people." Since, as we have seen, there are significant problems with treating the Armenian people as a genuine entity or as a virtual entity with rights, it is more plausible to claim that the right of a people to self-determination, if such a right exists, is a warrant held by various individuals, who may or may not desire to employ the warrant, grounded in the general interests most individual group members have in the group (loosely defined) as a continuing group, that members of the group not be subject to a political regime to which a preponderance of group members do not assent.

Thomas Simon provides another interesting example: "The collective right to the common heritage of humanity, found in treaties and commentaries on the international law of the sea, provides a challenging example of a collective right."[35] This right would appear to be a distributed right: each member of the group of *Homo Sapiens* has a right to the common heritage of humanity.

Second, some have worried that ascribing rights only to individuals must result in a particular form of liberalism that denigrates the importance and value of culture, reducing individuals to, using John Gray's phrase, "merely persons, right-bearing (and, doubtless also, gender-neutral) ciphers."[36] If view 3) is correct, however, individuals can possess powerful warrants about their group-oriented and culture-oriented interests. Adopting view 3) in no way entails denigrating the claims of culture; the strength and nature of those claims remains a subject of substantial investigation and is not determined by deciding whether rights are possessed by individuals or groups as such.[37] Thus the pragmatic argument, that construing group rights as rights of individuals vitiates group rights and/or the protection of cultural interests, does not hold against view 3).

Another argument that group rights must be owned collectively derives from H.L.A. Hart's "Choice Theory of Rights,"[38] later disavowed by Hart. Choice Theory insists that to have a right is to be in control of a duty, that is, to be able either to demand or waive the performance of the duty. Waldron (*op. cit.*) points out that no individual member of the group can waive the performance of the duty. Hence, suggests Waldron, group rights are incompatible with Choice Theory. However, if groups as such are the holders of group rights, the group collectively may waive or demand the performance of the duty. Hence, if Choice Theory is correct, group rights must be owned collectively by the group and not by the individual members of the group. However, as Waldron points out, Choice Theory is not a popular theory of rights: ample reasons, apart from the issue of group rights, including reasons that swayed Hart himself, exist for rejecting Choice Theory.

These arguments suggest that there exist no category 1) group rights: there is no ultimate entity, African-Americans, that possesses a full-blown right. View 1) is incorrect.[39] Some rights we loosely describe as "group rights" belong to category 2). In addition, I suggest, there is an important distinction to be drawn between group-oriented and individual-oriented rights: View 3), I suggest, is correct about an important set of rights. Some rights can be understood only in terms of essential interests that center on goals for a group or institution. For example, many Jews share a vital interest in seeing to it that the way of life consisting of Jewish cultural, religious, historical, and traditional practices, attitudes, etc. continues to flourish on this earth. Notice that this interest is not an interest in the flourishing of any particular person. Indeed, the interest may be met even if every living Jew converts to Buddhism and a new set of converts to Judaism carry on the tradition. It is an interest fundamentally based on an ideal for a group, independently of the individuals who happen to be members of the group. Thus I would argue that, after World War II, Jews had certain kinds of claims against the rest of the world, based on the historical and persistent world-wide threat of Anti-Semitism and the vital, legitimate interest many Jews share in seeing that the Jewish people survives as a people. In this sense, the right to a homeland is a group-based right of Jews. (Note that as an American citizen who does not wish to immigrate to Israel, I already have a homeland, namely the United States, so my general and individual right to having a homeland is already secured without the existence of Israel.) Put another way, each Jew was warranted in demanding as his or her due that the rest of the world accede to and perhaps facilitate the establishment of a Jewish homeland. Thus each individual Jew had a (vector) right to the establishment of a Jewish homeland. This group-based right is a right each Jew individually possesses, but it is a right focused on the goal of a group as a group.

Group rights, then, are rights that individuals have by virtue of a particular loyalty pertaining to their group, that is, because they have particular warrants regarding their legitimate interests in and commitments to a group as such. Not all group loyalties create rights—warrants, after all, are based on warranting features, and loyalties can be morally evaluated. Group rights do violate a strong form of individualism that claims all rights and interests pertain solely to individuals *qua* individuals, but group rights do not violate weak individualism, which claims only that the ultimate possessors of rights are individuals.

Universalism

Individualism is not the only stumbling block to group rights. Some object that group rights violate universalism and equality: group rights, they hold, deny that everyone has the same rights and that everyone should be treated equally. For many, universalism of this sort, that everyone has the same rights and should be treated equally, is at the heart of the notion of rights and of ethics itself. To deny universalism appears to deny, for example, that all people are of equal worth and concern, a principle disputed by some but held by Dworkin to be a self-evident fundamental tenet of morality that forms the basis of political and legal philosophy.[40] As Carl Cohen puts it, "that equals should be treated equally is a fundamental principle of morality."[41] To deny universalism may appear to deny the principle that like cases be treated alike, a foundational principle of Kantian ethics that Kant, along with many others, regarded as the defining principle of all moral thinking.

Do group rights violate universalism? In one sense, it is clearly false that everyone has the same rights. If you borrow ten dollars from me, I have a right to ten dollars from you that Wilfred, who never loaned you money, lacks. Similarly, Carl Cohen points out that "the poor or the elderly or the disabled may have special needs,"[42] and to say that African-Americans have a special right other groups lack need not be to deny that like cases be treated alike, but rather to assert that, in some particular respect, the case of an African-American and the case of a white Irish Catholic are not like cases. Group rights need not deny that all people are of equal worth—group rights might be considered necessary to safeguard the equal worth of all persons. Carole Pateman takes this approach[43]. The Permanent Court of International Justice saw group rights as an application of the universal right of equality: group rights seek to insure that minorities are fully the equal of the majority and hence have an equal opportunity to preserve and practice the customs and institutions that distinguish them. Since different groups have different cultures and needs, this general, universal right would result in different groups possessing different more specific rights.[44] When affirmative action is viewed as compensation for past wrongs, group rights to preference in hiring are understood as applications of a universal right of compensation. Nonetheless, there is an important difference between some group rights, such as affirmative action rights, and the right to be repaid a loan. My right to $10 is different from Wilfred's because of something I myself did and which Wilfred is equally free to do. By contrast, an affirmative action right for women confers some right on Susie that Wilfred lacks that is not dependent upon anything Susie did and which Wilfred is barred by nature from ever acquiring (leaving aside the status of sex change operations). A right to food stamps for those with incomes below $10,000 and a right to elevator signs in Braille may not benefit wealthy, sighted Wilbert, but Wilbert is not biologically incapable of becoming vision impaired or poor, and so such rights increase Wilbert's security, however unlikely it may be he will ever need to exercise them. Wilbert, however, is biologically barred from ever being eligible to exercise affirmative action rights for women. In this respect, group rights seem to violate universalism. Technically, every group right can be expressed as a circumstantial instance of a universal right. An affirmative action right for women is "universal" in the sense that everyone has the right to the preference his or her sex is accorded. That Wilfred also has this right is not likely to afford him much comfort. Universalists are sometimes sarcastically accused of offering everyone, beggar and Lord alike, the right to sleep under London Bridge. Wilfred is likely to voice parallel sarcasm about this universal right.

Nonetheless, when Wilfred and Wilhelmina are differently situated, the fact that Wilfred can never be situated as Wilhemina is does not by itself entail that a difference in rights violates universalism. Suppose the law gives infants born without a bile duct the right to a state-financed surgical implantation of an artificial duct. Wilfred can never be an infant born without a bile duct. Nonetheless, the law does not violate universalism: the law grants every infant a right to a natural or artificial bile duct, and Wilfred should simply be glad he can never be an infant in need of an artificial one. Similarly, it might be argued, Wilfred should simply be glad he can never experience the discrimination experienced by women. However, in this respect affirmative action rights differ from rights of the fully sightless and infants born without bile ducts. Everyone who is fully sightless cannot read printed signs, and so every member of the group of fully sightless persons has a need to have otherwise unforeseeable severe dangers indicated in some way other than printed signs, just as every infant born without a bile duct needs an artificial duct. These needs follow directly and immediately from the interest in surviving that is normally among the overriding interests of every person in every group. The need applies compellingly to every member of the group, and the need is genuinely universal in some very direct and immediate way. By contrast, Jill, a possessor of a Harvard education, a daughter of a Supreme Court justice and the CEO of a major multinational corporation (both of whom are Harvard alumnae who have made substantial donations), and a personal acquaintance since childhood of numerous Senators, publishers, movie producers, and corporate CEOs, needs less workplace assistance than does Joe, a typical son of a janitor in rural West Virginia. In the world of work, Jill is remarkably more privileged than Joe. Similarly, not all people of Native American extraction possess a subjective interest in the perpetuation of Native American traditions—in terms of felt concern, an anthropologist may have considerably more interest in the perpetuation of those traditions than does a Manhattan insurance executive, whose great-great- grandparents lived on a reservation, who may feel no connection to or interest in traditional Blackfoot ways. Thus, if those of Blackfoot ancestry possess group cultural rights or women possess affirmative action rights, those rights differ in an important way from the rights of the fully sightless to have otherwise unforeseeable severe dangers marked in some way other than by printed signs and the rights of infants born without bile ducts to artificial replacements.

What these and other examples bring out is that group right claims make certain kinds of assumptions. Which specific assumptions are being made depends on the specific group right claimed and the argument used to support it. Some arguments for special rights, in Kymlicka's sense, are applications of general principles. Consider the argument for equality, as Kymlicka formulates it. Minority cultures, it is argued, are disadvantaged in the cultural marketplace—they are vulnerable to economic, political, and cultural pressure. Thus, the argument goes, special rights are needed to alleviate this inequality and restore equality. "Our language and culture provide the context within which we make choices," suggests Kymlicka, and so "loss of cultural membership...is a profound harm that reduces one's very ability to make meaningful choices."[45] Some minority groups, he suggests, need special rights to support the cultural resources that are the foundation of leading a good life.[46] But what of an individual who wishes to assimilate? Does such a person have an interest in the preservation of his inherited culture and language, regardless of his subjective preferences? Is the choice to assimilate necessarily irrational, wrong, or self-negating? Kymlicka himself insists that group rights for cultural minorities must respect individual rights of group members, including those who dissent from group practices. Others disagree. This question engenders emotionally laden disputes.

Consider the compensatory justice argument for affirmative action for women (discussed further in section D.). The argument claims that because many women were victims of discrimination in the past, an undeniable fact, and many women continue to experience workplace discrimination, another undeniable fact, compensation is due for these wrongs, and affirmative action is an acceptable or required form of compensation. If, as some argue and others deny, the beneficiary of the program (Susan) has not (or may not have) sustained the wrong, then assisting Susan in getting a job constitutes compensation to Miriam for being unfairly denied a job only to the extent that Miriam can be held to have an interest in the flourishing of all women in the job market. After all, while you cannot compensate me for breaking my vase by giving some other blue-eyed person a vase, you can compensate me by giving my heirs the vase, since I have an interest in the welfare of my heirs. This particular form of the compensatory justice argument, then, must presume that Miriam has an interest in women in general, while I have no interest in blue-eyed people in general. It is certainly true that many persons have an interest in the flourishing of a group to which they belong. As Leslie Green puts it, "some of our most urgent interests lie…in collective goods….Individuals have interests as members of a certain social group, in collective goods that serve their interests as members."[47] However, many women do not feel special concern for other women. Thus the argument in question must ascribe to each woman, independently of her actual felt preferences and viewpoints, an objective interest in women as women. This amounts to claiming that gender solidarity is an essential element of flourishing: you flourish to the extent that your gender flourishes, no matter how much or how little you feel concern about gender or think of yourself in terms of your gender. To the extent that you lack this concern or self-conception, you are wrong or misguided. Similarly, some arguments for cultural rights presume that if your ancestors were Spanish, you have an objective interest in the flourishing of Spanish culture and the flourishing of other persons of Hispanic origin, because that is an essential element of your flourishing. While many arguments for various group rights make no such claims, including many versions of the compensatory justice argument, those that do affirm this sort of "identity politics" are perceived by many as posing a threat to many conceptions of rights, equality, and morality.

On the other hand, we have seen that some of the interests some people have can only be understood as interests in a group. Most Jews have a strong interest in the continuation of the Jewish people as a people, and that interest can morally ground a right (provide just grounds for a warrant). It is at least conceivable that someone could argue convincingly that a sufficient number of women and African-Americans who suffered discrimination in the past had a parallel interest in the liberation of future women and African-Americans, whoever they happened to be, and thus that affirmative action programs do compensate those individuals for the injustice they suffered. At the very least, this would be an argument that needs legitimately to be discussed. The issue of loyalty and particularist bonds requires close examination.

B. Loyalty and Particularist Bonds

Group rights grounded in group-oriented interests are based on particularist bonds. By a particularist bond I mean a special concern for or higher prioritization of commitments to a collection of persons based on some shared, non-universal feature reflecting a general, non-instrumental loyalty to those who share that feature because they share that feature. To be a particularist bond, the reason for the special concern must not be merely a straightforward application of a general rule or value that is independent of a general loyalty to one's kind. For example, if Smith has created one ounce of a new cure for a lethal disease and cannot generate any more for at least 24 hours, and if Irma and Wilma will both die of the disease unless they receive an ounce of the cure within 24 hours, Smith responds to the pull of a particularist bond if he gives the medication to Irma instead of Wilma precisely because Irma is Smith's wife. Smith and Irma share the feature of being members of a particular marriage. Only two people in the world share that feature. Smith gives a higher priority to Irma's need than to Wilma's solely because he and Irma share that feature. By contrast, if Smith (who has small children) gives the medication to Irma because she has small children and Wilma does not, but Smith's decision is based on the principle of utility or some other general rule that is not a loyalty-to-kind rule, then Smith is not responding to a particularist bond. True, he prioritizes Irma's needs because she has small children, a non-universal feature that he and Irma share, but his prioritization is not based on the fact that he and Irma *share* that feature. It is based, rather, on the quite general principle of maximizing overall utility. If Smith and Irma share a rare blood type and Smith gives Irma the medication solely in order that she be alive to donate blood to him should he ever need it, his decision is based not on loyalty to those who have that blood type but on a general rule of maximizing his own utility, where Irma's having the same blood type is only instrumentally of interest to Smith.

It seems fairly clear that at least some particularist bonds are morally compelling while others are morally disfavored. If my closest friend and a total stranger both want to talk to me immediately, with equal urgency, about a personal problem of equal severity, where both equally have no one else with whom to talk, and so forth, clearly I do something amiss if I choose to give my attention to the total stranger instead of my closest friend. The fact that he is my closest friend surely entitles him to some priority over a stranger when everything else is exactly equal. A world without any personal relationships would be insupportable to human beings, given how we are constituted, and personal relationships, where they exist, demand at least *ceteris paribus* prioritization in discretionary contexts. It seems equally clear that some particularist bonds are morally disfavored. If I am a judge deciding a legal case, I am duty bound to eschew favoritism. If the plaintiff's case and the defendant's case are equally sound and I rule in favor of the plaintiff because she and I are both Jewish, I have violated my duties as a judge. (Acting as presiding judge is, in this respect, a nondiscretionary context.) In some cases, then, expressing particularist bonds violates obligations and violates rights. Other instances of particularist bonds are morally unsavory. If Talcott establishes a scholarship, with her own money, with the proviso that the money never go to a Jew or an African-American (that is, Talcott prioritizes, out of loyalty, the category of non-Jews or non-African-Americans), Talcott may or may not be within her rights, but her decision carries moral disfavor—it would be a moral improvement if she changed my mind about this restriction.

In short, every expression of loyalty discriminates in the sense of displaying unequal concern. To be loyal to the right is to discriminate against the wrong. To give greater priority to my children's needs is to give lesser priority to the needs of those who are not my children. To be loyal to women is to give lesser weight to the flourishing of men. To be loyal to white males is to give lesser weight to the flourishing of women and non-whites. The examples above show that some kinds of discrimination are legitimate and others are not. Since rights are legally or morally grounded warrants, the issue of which group-oriented interests give rise to group rights of type 3) cannot be discussed without investigating the ethics of loyalty. We must determine which sorts of group-oriented interests and which sorts of particularist bonds of loyalty are morally supportable. When is loyalty a virtue and when a vice? More specifically, what are legitimate *grounds* of loyalty and what are legitimate *expressions* of loyalty?

In assessing the claims of various particularist bonds, it is useful to organize them into seven related categories. Individuals may feel the pull of special bonds of the following sort:

1. *Typological bonds*:
An individual may feel a particularist bond to others who share a common characteristic solely because it is a shared characteristic. Most commonly, typological bonds are expressed by commitment to a socially defined group possessing a common property such as race[48] and gender. The property involved may be natural or socially constructed, but in either case the importance of the property is, to a large extent, socially defined. Gender is not a trivial feature, since procreation is an important function in any enduring society, but the ways in which gender defines groups in our society go well beyond biology. In my son's school, kindergarten students waiting to enter class were required to form two lines, one for boys and one for girls. That practice had no basis in biological function. The practice encouraged students to think of themselves not as tall or short, happy or sad, but as boys or girls. Typological bonds exhibit and result from this kind of social encouragement toward self-classification.

2. *Bonds of legitimate social responsibilities* (e.g., parental, spousal, professional):
Societies recognize various relationships that carry special responsibility. The nature and content of these relationships may vary between societies. Virtually all societies recognize special bonds pertaining to child rearing, but in some societies it may be a group, institution, or persons other than a father and/or mother who bear responsibility for a child's welfare and rearing. When social recognition of a relationship of special responsibility is morally defensible, that relationship constitutes a particularist bond exerting legitimate moral pull.

It seems undeniable that some patterns of social responsibilities calling for particularist bonds are legitimate (morally defensible). Attending to the continuity of human culture by rearing a next generation is a central task of human beings. The absence of a reasonably healthy, educated, and flourishing next generation entails that many of the central labors and struggles of many members of all previous generations come to naught: it entails, for instance, the disappearance of the results of the work of generations of scientists, theologians, writers, painters, and philosophers. Human offspring cannot fend for themselves at birth. If no one feeds a neonate, it dies. Moreover, human beings can survive in reasonable numbers only in social groups. (A lone *Homo Sapiens* is easy prey for a saber-toothed tiger, while a group of club-wielding *Homo Sapiens* is not.) The survival of a flourishing next generation, then, requires that older persons assume responsibility for those too young to function and survive within the group. The age of independence, that is, the age at which substantial numbers of human beings can begin to function fully within a social group, ranges, depending upon the way of life and circumstances of the group, from age 4 to post-adolescence. (In most U.S. jurisdictions, children may legally drop out of high school at age 16 but may not legally drink alcohol until age 21.) Thus societies must contain some arrangement for the care of those below the age of independence in that society. Many such arrangements are possible. The literature, academic and popular, on child rearing contains many parochial and conflicting assertions about what children need, backed by flawed research, but it does seem clear that any satisfactory system of child care will be relatively stable and include some significant individual relationships. Virtually every major study, as well as the experience of most people who deal with children, gives reason to believe that for large numbers of children to function in a social context in a way that preserves the knowledge base of human culture, large numbers of those children need to have experienced some significant degree of stability in their care and to have experienced significant individual relationships. I am not asserting that every child raised in an institution with a different caretaker every day will turn out badly, but only that for the next generation of the group to turn out well as a whole, large numbers of them must have experienced these two things in some form. Moreover, many forms of significant stability and individual relationships can take place in the context of a group—group rearing of children can be satisfactory as long as adequate opportunity for individual relationships within the system is provided. Nonetheless, it follows from these requirements that not every member of a large social group can have equal responsibility for the needs and interests of every child. Thus societies are justified in recognizing some system of assigning to a subset of the society's individuals special responsibilities for a subset of the society's children. Obviously, many possible systems of child rearing meet this description. Among these different systems numbers the nuclear family, a system that has seemed to work reasonably satisfactorily reasonably often. Thus a society's recognizing a system of nuclear families, supplemented, as needed or desired, by other arrangements, is justifiable, absent some argument showing that systems of nuclear families have important morally undesirable properties that other systems lack. Assuming no such argument is forthcoming, a person who lives in a society recognizing the bonds of nuclear families is justified in giving special consideration to the needs and interests of other members of his or her nuclear family. Of course, other societies might also be justified in recognizing very different systems of child care. Those societies, however, would also recognize particularist bonds between some caretakers or groups of caretakers and particular children. Individuals living in those societies would be justified in responding to those particularist bonds. So particularist bonds of some sort between a set of caretakers and a child are justifiable.

Fiduciary relationships can be justified in a similar way. While many methods of attending to the health, education, and other interests of persons may succeed, no system is satisfactory for a large and complex society that does not recognize some form of particularist bond. Investment advisors cannot have no more concern for the interests of their clients than they do for any other investor. While societies may not need investment advisors, societies do have a diverse range of needs and interests satisfied by a diverse range of methods. Any satisfactory overall system for any large society must include at least some special responsibilities. In a large society, it is not feasible for all physicians to give their attention equally to all sick patients. George Fletcher,[49] disagreeing with a paper by Charles Fried,[50] characterizes professional loyalties as relationships of contract. However, while fiduciary relationships are often formed via a contract, they need not originate through contract. A court may appoint an attorney to an indigent client, for instance. More importantly, even when a fiduciary relationship is formed through an explicit contract, the content of the contract adverts to notions of loyalty that go well beyond the promissory notion of contract. While no formal distinction between fiduciary and contractual duties may be tenable, at the core of fiduciary relationships is a broad general duty to serve the interests of the beneficiary that is encapsulated in a broad moral conception of fidelity. At the core of contractual duties is the promissory force of explicit or implicit agreement to particular provisions, within the context of a socially recognized understanding of what such an agreement is to include (which may or may not coincide with the contractor's actual intentions). While some special responsibilities may be primarily promissory (Hilbert has a special responsibility to water Jameson's lawn twice a day because Hilbert contracted with Jameson to do so in exchange for a fee), many special responsibilities, even if formed via a contract, include a broader notion of loyalty to someone's interests. If Garber contracts with Lee to be "pure of heart," then Garber's contractual duty of self-obligation includes whatever duties are implicit in the moral concept of purity of heart, and those duties of purity of heart are not primarily promissory in nature. Similarly, the contractual duties of an attorney include whatever duties are implicit in the moral concept of fiduciary relationships, and that concept is not primarily promissory. Thus the category of fiduciary bonds reflects loyalties that are not fully explained by the concept of promise as such. Fletcher is entitled, if he wishes, to draw a distinction between bonds that are formed by contract and bonds that are formed by common history (though it is perhaps misleading to call the former "divergent"—they are divergent only in the sense that they diverge from his account.) Nonetheless (and Fletcher does not deny this), fiduciary and family bonds both differ importantly from purely promissory obligations.

3. *Bonds of team loyalty to those engaged in a common project*:
Loyalty may exist between members of a group of individuals who are mutually engaged (recognize themselves as co-participants) in some activity, in the broadest sense of activity, seeking to instantiate or realize some loosely or strictly defined set of goals, end-states, or values that those engaged in the activity believe to be important and worthy. Individuals engaged in that activity might feel, toward others engaged in the activity, special concerns relevant to the activity. For example, historical preservationists may legitimately feel a special moral pull to support, in relevant ways, the participation of other historical preservationists in morally defensible preservation projects. (*Cf.* the argument for this sort of team loyalty in Chapter 7.)

4. *Bonds of commitment to a shared way of life or shared set of values*:
To the extent that a way of life is a project with goals and a commitment to instantiating a shared set of values, bonds of commitment to a shared way of life or shared set of values are instances of team loyalty. However, there may be more to a shared way of life than goal-realizing activities and more to a shared set of values than seeking to instantiate them. Members of Shaker communities, for example, certainly view themselves as living out a common project, but there may be more to the bonds they feel than the project itself. Out of bonds of team loyalty may grow social bonds that are in some sense a further ground for loyalty.

5. *Bonds of commitment to a shared history*:
Particularist bonds may center on the fact of a shared history rather than either the goal-centered activity, if any, generating the history or the shared way of life or shared of values, if any, implicit in the history. Senses in which two people may have a shared history, as such, include:
  a)   both witnessed a single event (or series of single events), e.g., those on the ground who saw the Hindenburg catch fire,
  b)   both witnessed or experienced similar kinds of events or different events that are part of a single larger event (e.g., a survivor of Auschwitz and a survivor of Treblinka),

   c)   both have an historical relationship to something that can be presumed
        to exert some causal influence over time (e.g., their grandfathers were
        both pupils of Nadia Boulanger),
   d)   both have a history of social interaction, that is, they are players in the
        story of each other's lives.
George Fletcher identifies such bonds as the moral ground of loyalty.
6. *Frontier bonds*: In the face of a hostile social or natural environment, a group
of individuals may need to form bonds of mutual dependence in order to survive
hardship. Such bonds generally involve bonds from other categories, for instance, loyalty to a common purpose (surviving as Jews in the Warsaw ghetto) or
socially defined responsibilities (barn raisings). However the element of coming
together for support in the face of a common severe and specific danger is worth
separate mention.

7. *Bonds resulting from acts of commitment*:
Individuals sometimes commit themselves to special concern for another person
or group of persons. A promise made to a dying friend to take care of his son
Jamal constitutes a commitment to show special concern for Jamal.
      These categories frequently overlap. Fiduciary obligations often originate in
an act of commitment, although some social responsibilities may be involuntary
and some voluntary acts of commitment may fall in none of the six other categories. Two African-American soldiers fighting in France during World War II
may have the special responsibilities of fellow soldiers, the loyalty due those
engaged in the common project of winning the war, the shared way of life of the
army, the shared history of experiencing D-Day, bonds of mutual assistance in
the face of common danger, and the common property of being African-
American. Since socially defined groups may be based on anything, they may
also be based on any of the other categories. But even when a socially defined
group is based on participation in a common project, there is still a distinction to
be made between particularist bonds based on participation in the common project, as such, and particularist bonds based on belonging to the same socially
defined group, as such—a given environmentalist may feel both sorts of pulls
toward other environmentalists. Thus it remains useful to inquire, about a given
persons' special concern for environmentalists, what part of or which aspect of
or how much of the strength of that special concern is based on loyalty to the
environmentalist project as such and what part of or which aspect of or how
much of the strength of that special concern is based on the fact that both fall
under a socially defined category.
      Two sources of the strength of an interest-protecting claim are the moral
importance of the interest and the extent of the need. Bonds of social responsibility and team loyalty can create morally compelling group-oriented interests.
When the practice of social responsibility involved and the common project or
moral ideal involved, respectively, are morally defensible, urgent needs in sup-

port of those interests can create warrants for various demands, beliefs, practices, and so forth that belong to warrant-holders as their due, in recognition of their status as, for instance, morally evaluative project pursuers (in the case of team loyalty) or family member (in the case of bonds of social responsibility).

Type 7. bonds are perhaps the most familiar in ethical thinking. Since, other things being equal, one should keep one's commitments, the presence of a type 7. bond is *prima facie* a legitimate reason for special concern. However, not all commitments are morally equal. The status of evil promises (e.g., promising to kill an innocent person) has vexed ethicists for years. The moral grounds for making the act of commitment that originates type 7. bonds is thus an important element in evaluating the moral strength and importance of type 7. bonds.

Typological bonds, unlike bonds of common commitment to an ideal, do not reflect value-based interests. If I desire the flourishing of all blue-eyed people simply because they, like me, have blue eyes, then my group-oriented interest is not the outcome of or a manifestation of some general value—my loyalty is based only on a (non-moral) typology. By contrast, if I desire the continuation of X culture because of the moral genius of its way of life, my group-oriented interest is value-based—it is based on the general value of exemplifying good ways of human life, or, more generally, on a commitment to human goodness and the values constitutive of that goodness. If part of what I find so special about X culture is that it displays a unique form of concern for feelings, my group-oriented interest in the continuation of X culture is a reflection, in part, of the general value I place on concern for feelings.

Of course I need not be a member of a group to have an interest in its flourishing. If I am specially taken by the nobility of the Shaker way of life, I may have a significant interest in averting threats to the continued existence of Shaker communities even though I myself am not a Shaker. Yet it seems odd to say that my rights are violated by laws that threaten the continued existence of Shaker communities. Similarly, it seems odd to say that a law imposing real estate taxes on the X tribe, thus forcing tribe members to eschew their traditions of subsistence farming in order to generate cash to pay the taxes, violates the rights of an anthropologist studying the X tribe, though the law significantly sets back a very important interest of the anthropologist.[51] The anthropologist and the admirer of Shaker life both have strong and legitimate reasons for opposing legislation that threaten, respectively, the continued existence of the X tribe and Shaker communities, but their reasons do not include a violation of their own rights, since neither can claim for himself a relevant status requiring recognition as his due that the law fails to recognize. By way of contrast, members of the X tribe can argue that the moral value and importance of X tribe's way of life justifies their insistence that interfering with their participation in that life fails to recognize appropriately their status as evaluative seekers of good lives.

The psychological strength of typological bonds, even when arbitrarily constructed with no social history, is supported both by common sense and research.

The question at issue, however, is not the felt strength of such bonds nor their typical affect on human conduct, but the strength of the moral warrants, if any, such felt bonds create.

Mere typological bonds do not generally create morally compelling interests. On what grounds would, for instance, shared race or shared gender alone suffice to make worthy a commitment to those who share it over those who do not? The mere fact that Jones and Smith share a common characteristic, which Williams lacks, provides no compelling justification, by itself, for Jones to display special concern for Smith and not Williams. While the nature of the characteristic itself can provide such grounds, the bare fact that it is shared cannot. If the characteristic is honesty, for instance, Jones may be justified in showing special concern for honest people because of his loyalty to the moral importance of honesty. In that case, Jones' loyalty is to honesty because of its moral superiority over dishonesty: it is the value of honesty over dishonesty that justifies Jones' special concern, not the mere fact that Jones and Smith share a characteristic. Jones and her daughter may share the characteristic of belonging to the Jones family, a characteristic Williams lacks, but that justifies Jones' special concern for her daughter only because of the value of the bond of social responsibility that belonging to a family entails in our society.

Put another way, one aspect of loyalty is having a greater intrinsic stake in the flourishing of the thing to which one is loyal than in the flourishing of other things. An intrinsic stake is not just a consequential stake, as when I have a stake in your winning the lottery because, if you win, you will be able to repay me the money you owe me. An intrinsic stake in x's flourishing means that, to a large or small extent, x's flourishing is a part of my own, in the sense that I have adopted the welfare of x as part of my life project, as one of the things to which, as such, I am committed, and so, to a trivial or great extent, the success of my life must be judged, in part, by the extent to which x flourishes. If I am loyal to the idea of equality, then whether my life is going well or not depends, to some extent, upon the extent to which equality is realized or becoming more fully realized. If I am loyal to you, and your life is going badly, then, to that extent, my life is going badly. Someone for whom this is not true at all with respect to x cannot be said to be loyal to x. Loyalty, then, always encapsulates a moral judgment. Normally, loyalty to x (partly) results from or expresses the judgment that x is somehow worthy of one's greater commitment to its flourishing because either the special intrinsic worthiness of x itself or some aspect of one's relationship to x (e.g., promises one made concerning x) makes that preferential commitment to x a worthy one. Intrinsic loyalty to other women, then, expresses one of two judgments. It may express the judgment that the possession of an extra x chromosome makes someone intrinsically more worthy of flourishing (that all women are somehow more worthy of flourishing than men). While some have argued for some form of this thesis (e.g., that males advert to a different and inferior ethics from females), innumerable counterexamples prove that such claims are at best statistical generalizations, which cannot support intrinsic loyalty. (Recall that if one's loyalty is to those who display an "ethic of care," then a rule-following woman is not included in the scope of one's loyalty while a man displaying an ethic of care is included.) Alternatively, it may express the judgment that one's relation to other women justifies preferential commitment to flourishing. For example, some have sought to ground preferential commitment in self-identification. Some people's sense of self may indeed be partly constituted by their possession of typological features such as gender, but, unless the identification is value-based and the value involved is morally defensible, it is not clear what moral demands such an arbitrary (even if widely shared) self-identification makes on others, what status worthy of public recognition remains unrecognized, or why such an identification justifies preferential commitment (see the discussion of Fletcher, below).[52]

In short, sharing a common characteristic creates a morally compelling interest only when (and only because) sharing that characteristic falls under one of the other categories. Do loyalty to other women and other African-Americans fall under one of the other categories? There is no common moral project of women as women and African-Americans as African-Americans. Certainly the struggle against oppression and prejudice is a profoundly important project, but it is not a project limited to women or African-Americans, nor is it a project in which all women or African-Americans participate. There is a significant difference between a commitment to erase discrimination against women or solidarity with those working toward the common goal of ending oppression and a commitment to women as such: the former is ultimately commitment to an ideal or project (and to those, of whatever race or gender, who are committed to that ideal or project), while the latter is a commitment to the flourishing of each woman over and above non-women, regardless of her individual merit or the extent to which she has personally suffered from or is working to end discrimination. Thus, while a feminist may compellingly feel team loyalty to others in the woman's movement, that team is not identical to women as a group: it includes a significant number of men and excludes a significant number of women. Similarly, loyalty to other women as such differs from a merely instrumental commitment to assisting women in various particular situations, e.g., preferring that a particular women be promoted over a man because the promotion of that woman will help inspire victims of discrimination to succeed.

Again, loyalty to the cause of preserving various elements of African-American culture or Judaism differ, respectively, from intrinsic loyalty to African-Americans or Jews *qua* African-Americans or Jews. These differences become important when discussing group rights and affirmative action. Some forms of the claim that affirmative action assistance for Susan compensates Miriam require that women have intrinsic loyalty to other women *qua* women, while arguments for affirmative action as an effective means of ameliorating discrimination do not. The argument for a Jewish right to a Jewish homeland does not require that Jews feel loyalty to other Jews as such, but rather to the continuation of Judaism. While such loyalty to the continuation of Judaism may justify support for Israel, it does not support a preference for hiring fellow Jews. Similarly, arguments for supporting projects to preserve and commemorate the Harlem Renaissance do not require that African-Americans feel loyalty to other African-Americans as such. In any case, while some speak glibly of "Black culture," African-Americans are not a culturally homogenous group: there is no reasonably well-defined coherent set of cultural practices, moral outlooks, ways of life, and so forth that are characteristic of African-Americans as a group.[53] As Iris Marion Young, a supporter of group representation rights, puts it, "differences of race and class cut across gender, differences of gender and ethnicity cut across religion, and so on. Individual members of a gender or racial group have life histories that often make them very different people with very different interests and outlooks."[54] To deny this is to be blinded by stereotypes to the empirically manifest diversity of ways of life of individual African-Americans, from a physician to a gang member, from African-Americans residing in Scarsdale and African-Americans residing in Harlem, and so on. "African-American life in America" is not a single story, but a fabulously diverse array of very different stories.

Finally, if there is a socially defined practice of "looking after one's race" or "looking after one's gender" it is not generally morally defensible. The moral rationale for such a practice would be either a) the moral importance of typological bonds, which has already been addressed, or b) frontier bonds in the face of racism and sexism. Frontier bonds, in contemporary America, are plausible in specific contexts (female co-workers within a particularly sexist company), but the experiences and situations of all women and all African-Americans within the United States are too diverse and amorphous to create genuine frontier bonds. Ann Cudd suggests that involuntary groups share the same set of social constraints, e.g., stereotypes.[55] Do the presence of such constraints in contemporary America create the conditions for frontier bonds?[56] Frontier bonds emerge in the face of severe and clearly recognizable dangers that confront everyone in the group. In contemporary America, stereotypes, perceptual prejudice, and other forms of racism and sexism remain an urgent matter for social action, but they present a more amorphous, ambiguous, and heteronymous pattern of obstacles than, for instance, a drought does to a frontier settlement of farmers, who face the same dangers equally and together. Conditions for a frontier bond are more clearly met by an African-American and a Jew in a small, poorly educated southern town than by an African-American sharecropper in Texas and an African-American physician's son at Harvard. These remarks are in no way meant to belittle the importance or urgency of addressing racism in the United States. Indeed, the subtlety and diversity of racism is part of what makes racism so intractable. There is no simple magic bullet that will slay racism. The instantiation of racism in the United States today, evil and powerful as it is, does not create the specific conditions requisite for a frontier bond between all African-Americans across the United States. In many ways, racism would be an easier foe if it did.

Thus if women and African-Americans have morally compelling interests in the flourishing of (all) other women as women and (all) other African-Americans as African-Americans, it must be because of bonds of shared history.

Do bonds of shared history also exert a compelling moral claim? That is, can shared history serve as the morally justifiable special relationship to the object of one's loyalty? The question is an important one. Bonds of shared history rank among the primary plausible rationales for considering patriotism a virtue. Many who argue for the importance of group membership in politics and school curricula base their assertions on the perception that group membership largely constitutes identity, a perception based largely upon shared history. Since a married couple shares a history, however bad their marriage may be, those who oppose divorce may justify their opposition by invoking bonds of shared history. If shared history creates compelling moral bonds, the consequences reach far beyond group rights.

The foremost proponent of shared history as the legitimate ground of loyalty is George P. Fletcher. Fletcher's intriguing and important work raises two major, interrelated issues that deserve detailed treatment. Fletcher argues that Jones' history and culture are part of what he is, part of what makes him the person he is, and so for Jones to deny his culture and history is for Jones to deny his very self. "In acting loyally," Fletcher says, "the self acts in harmony with its personal history. One recognizes who one is. Actions of standing by one's friends, family, nation, or people reveal that identity. The self sees in its action precisely what history requires it to do."[57] This argument, closely related to the view, mentioned earlier, that group membership partially defines the individual, merits close scrutiny. Second, Fletcher argues that loyalty is not an autonomous choice. Josiah Royce, for instance, suggests that loyalty consists in the voluntary submission of one's "natural desires" to a cause.[58] Gerald Dworkin points out that loyalty in this sense is autonomous:[59] if Royce is correct, one is free to choose one's loyalties. Of course, in this context, a "moral choice" may not be a choice in the way one chooses vanilla over chocolate ice cream from a menu. There may be no explicit act of choosing at all and one may feel, like Martin Luther, that one cannot choose otherwise. Moral choice, in this context, means the holding of one evaluative stance over another, based on or reflecting one's values, principles, and moral attitudes. One holds those values, principles, and moral attitudes because they seem to one to be correct. In that sense, they are involuntarily held: one cannot simply choose to have a principle appear to oneself to be correct, just as I cannot simply decide to believe in the traditional Christian God. After all, that decision will not cause me, in any simple or direct way, genuinely to see the world as a place run by a supreme being with particular attributes, however much I mouth the appropriate tenets to others or to myself. I can, of course, act in various ways that are causally likely to bring about a new belief or perspective. Some of these ways we might call "external." For example, if I want to believe in the Christian God I can spend all my time with evangelical Baptists. Other methods we might call "internal." I can choose whether or not to subject my perspective to certain sorts of inquiries and define limits to those inquiries. If I believe in God, I can decide whether or not to examine the argument from evil and whether or not to read certain authors. (I can't, obviously, read everything—what governs my choices about reading material?) I can choose whether to strive for the stance of a partisan or the stance of an objective seeker of truth. Nonetheless, to believe in God, the arguments I choose to read, whatever stance I adopt toward reading them, must actually convince me, and that is something I cannot simply choose. So, in an important sense, believing or not believing in God and holding or not holding a certain value are not autonomous choices. But they are choices in which autonomy plays a major role: they are not autonomy-free choices. In particular, one's values, principles, and moral attitudes, are, presumably, at least partly subject to change as a result of rational reflection. In any case, one important sense of "choosing" something is conferring one's imprimatur upon it.[60] In some sense, then, moral attitudes are "chosen" in a sense that one's history is not chosen. It is in this sense of "moral choice" that, it will be argued, loyalty involves moral choice.[61] Fletcher, following Ladd[62], argues against Royce's view by pointing out that if some general property P, were the ground of loyalty, then we would switch our loyalties the moment we discovered something else that is more P.[63] Since that sort of fickleness is antithetical to loyalty, no general property P can be the ground of loyalty (pp. 7-8). Only shared history, argues Fletcher, grounds the sort of stable fidelity characteristic of the virtue of loyalty. Others hold that loyalty cannot be based on a general property P (and cannot be a moral choice in the sense described above) because loyalty is an irrational emotion and not (the result of) a reflective judgment.

Is loyalty is an irrational emotion? Is Fletcher's argument that no general (morally important) property can be the ground of loyalty sound? At question is not just whether loyalty is autonomously chosen, but whether bonds of loyalty are grounded in moral evaluation of the object of loyalty (and not merely one's historical or emotional relationship to that object). The issue is a crucial one, for if a bond of loyalty is grounded in a moral evaluation of the object of loyalty, and that moral evaluation is faulty, then the resulting loyalty is morally suspect. Thus Jones' loyalty to her country can be impugned if the moral evaluations of her country, on the basis of which her loyalty is given, are faulty. By contrast, if loyalty is due to any country to which one has historical bonds,[64] then moral evaluation of that country's actions, way of life, political system, and so forth are irrelevant to the bond of loyalty, and so Jones' loyalty to her country cannot be impugned on the grounds that Jones' moral evaluation of her country is faulty. Of course, Fletcher holds that obligations of loyalty to one's country must be balanced against one's own conscience. Nonetheless, the obligation of loyalty to country, *per se*, is not, for Fletcher, based on moral evaluation. For Fletcher, while Jones may be faulted for placing loyalty to country above overriding moral imperatives, she may not be faulted for feeling loyalty to an evil society and giving that loyalty moral weight. Similarly, if loyalty is an irrational feeling one happens to have or not have, then moral evaluation of the object of loyalty is irrelevant: one simply feels loyalty or one doesn't. Hence Jones' loyalty to her country could not be impugned on the grounds that her moral evaluation of her country is faulty. The issue, then, goes to the heart of the nature of loyalty and the morality of loyalty.

Fletcher's argument is that if some general property, P, were the ground of loyalty, then we would switch our loyalties the moment we discovered something else that is more P. This argument overlooks the fact that there are several different grounds of loyalty. Loyalty must constitute something more than merely a pro stance toward P. But P may be the reason or ground for making a commitment, and a commitment, once made, has some pull of its own. In other words, my loyalty to X may stem from a commitment I made to X, and that commitment may have been based on P. And while my loyalty to X is more than a pro attitude toward P, if some threshold degree of P-ness is not maintained, the reason for the commitment of loyalty disappears and, in most cases, the commitment comes to an end.

Suppose a Martian came to our planet. He studies all of earth's nations and decides to become a citizen of Sweden because of its liberal laws. On Fletcher's view, the Martian cannot have "loyalty" to Sweden, except in the "divergent" sense of contractual loyalty, since the Martian lacks significant shared history with the people or territory of Sweden. But the point here is not just that the Martian has *pledged* his loyalty, but that he has pledged his *loyalty*. He has thrown in his lot with Sweden, lack of history notwithstanding. Henceforth he sees himself as a Swede. Fletcher is correct that I cannot simply choose to be loyal to, for example England, however much I admire it and wish it well. But I can, despite a lack of history, make a commitment and change my life accordingly, so that my loyalty is linked to my future history, to the life on which I am embarking. Self-definition is importantly prospective as well as retrospective.

Fletcher himself recognizes two stages of membership in a group: entry and identification (p. 34). One must enter the community in some formal or informal way and one must identify oneself as a member of the community, come to see membership in the group as part of one's sense of oneself. While one may find oneself included in a group by birth, Royceans would deny that entry in a group without autonomous assent entails binding moral demands of loyalty. Fletcher avers that the second stage, identification, is required for true loyalty and necessarily requires considerable time, since, for Fletcher, the basis of identification is shared history. French soldiers, Fletcher avers, who fought in the American Revolution out of a moral sense that the colonists should win did not evidence "loyalty." Why not? Because the newly self-declared Republic did not constitute their historical self. In this, Fletcher is both right and wrong. In every important ordinary sense of loyalty, at least some of those French soldiers were loyal to the revolution: they were, after all, deeply committed to its success, non-instrumentally, as a personal goal, and were willing to risk life and limb in dedicating all their efforts to it. An overnight convert to an evangelical religious group might think of himself primarily as a member of that group almost immediately. Granted, if the conversion does not last, he might later think of his membership in that group as a passing phase of little interest to his life story—in this sense, Fletcher is correct about identification over the long haul. Nonetheless, while his ardor lasts, he feels intense loyalty to the group, and if he remains a committed member of the group until his death, he will date his loyalty to the group as commencing from the time he joined the group, not some years later. Similarly, the Martian will date his loyalty to Sweden from the time he made his commitment. His loyalty, no doubt, will grow and deepen over the years, but it did not come into being only after many years of shared history with other Swedish residents.

In any case, one day after the Martian pledges his loyalty to Sweden, Norway adopts yet more liberal laws. Would a highly ethical Martian respond by renouncing his Swedish citizenship and becoming a citizen of Norway? Of course not—he has made a commitment to Sweden that he is obligated to honor. That commitment was made on the basis of Sweden's liberal laws, but, once made, it is a commitment to Sweden, not just to whichever country boasts the most liberal laws. Of course, on the other hand, if Sweden becomes a harshly repressive country, over a long span of time, hopelessly unresponsive to all of the Martian's efforts at liberalizing reform, our Martian may justifiably consider renouncing his Swedish citizenship and emigrating.

Similarly, suppose I marry A for reasons P. Then I meet B, who satisfies P more than does A, so that, had I known B before I became involved with A, I would have married B instead of A. I do not immediately divorce A and marry B because marriage involves significant commitments that have an integrity of their own. Sharing history certainly deepens ties with one's spouse. One would not feel quite the same sense of loyalty to a spouse who was forcibly abducted by aliens immediately after one's marriage and whom one had not seen for 20 years. But such ties, in their most potent form, develop not from shared history alone but from something more, namely, building a life together as a team. Fletcher appears to conflate common history with "common purpose" and "equal partner in a common cause" (p. 21), as if the former entailed the latter two. Partnership in a common cause, category 3), involves moral choice and continuing moral commitment in a way that that mere common history, category 5), need not. The difference is critical to Fletcher's conclusion that loyalty is not a matter of autonomous choice. In any case, in addition to the general moral implications of making commitments, marital loyalty is grounded in the vision to which one subscribes of what a marriage should be. "Loyalty to one's man" (or one's woman) means different things to different people. For some who feel it, it is informed by one of several competing normative conceptions of marriage or relationships. Some people feel that spousal loyalty, regardless of the attributes of the spouse, is a duty to God. Others adopt a promissory model of marital loyalty: by exchanging marriage vows, this view holds, one commits oneself, for better or worse, to certain standards of loyalty, and so that commitment cannot be abrogated even when the other party fails to honor it. Notice that shared history plays little role in either of those normative conceptions: to those who hold them, loyalty springs from the act of marriage, and is due even if the spouse decamps immediately after the wedding (providing the marriage is not annulled). For other normative conceptions of relationship loyalty, shared history might play an important role. The point, however, is that to the extent that loyalty to one's man or woman stems from a normative conception of relationships, it is a Roycean moral commitment. For others, loyalty to one's man or women may be driven primarily by desire or fear. Someone might feel loyalty to his woman because he feels he needs someone to love fiercely in this way and does not want to give up having a passionate attachment. He might be unwilling to give up the excitement she provides, despite the high cost. "Standing by one's man" may be driven by expediency or by perceived duties to third parties (children, for example). Normative conceptions of relationships and desire often come together, as when a particular woman's self-esteem is largely bound up with her conception of herself as someone who does not complain, or who pleases others, or who is steadfast and stoic. To reduce all such loyalties to moral burdens of shared history is to be blind to the complexity and diversity of human worldviews, the variety of multi-leveled stories to be told about how different people think, act, feel, and realize their lives. Of course, Fletcher might be suggesting that, despite this psychological diversity, the moral justification of such loyalty is shared history: loyalty of this sort is morally justified by shared history. Other psychological sources for loyalty may exist, Fletcher might say, but they do not ground, morally warrant, loyalty to one's man. This claim seems somewhat implausible. If a normative conception of a relationship demanding loyalty is correct, then surely it morally warrants loyalty. So, if Fletcher wishes to make this claim, he must argue that all such normative conceptions (except those based on the duties of shared experience) are incorrect. Fletcher, of course, does not make such arguments. Alternatively, Fletcher might claim that the sorts of commitments, sacrifices, and special concern displayed by a woman who stands by her man do not constitute "loyalty" unless they spring from duties of shared history—they are something else, "shloyalty," perhaps, or a "divergent" form of loyalty. It is not clear what purpose such a linguistic game would serve.

In many cultures one chooses a spouse, but not one's family. Nonetheless, loyalty to family also frequently stems from a moral conception of family. Different families parse this moral conception of family loyalty differently, but, not infrequently, it covers distant relatives with whom one shares no significant history other than the family relationship itself. The New York Karkoskas have had no dealings with the Polish Karkoskas for three generations, yet, when Piotr Karkoska arrives in New York from Poland, Joey of the New York Karkoskas takes him in and supports him because "he's family." What history do Piotr and Joey Karkoska share? Their ancestors four generations ago, long since dead, none of whom was personally acquainted with either Piotr or Joey, may have shared history. Does this suffice to attribute the force of Joey's loyalty to Piotr to shared history?

Fletcher further argues that Roycean loyalty misses the tragic aspect of conflicts of loyalty. Fletcher cites the example of Lee, who was opposed to slavery and cherished the Union but chose to serve the South from loyalty to kith and kin. If loyalty is simply a matter of choice, Fletcher avers, Lee need not feel the agony his situation provokes. In fact, however, Lee's commitment to kith and kin reflected, presumably, his moral outlook, not merely shared history. Presumably, Lee chose to side with kith and kin not solely because they were his kith and kin, but because Lee found something worthy and good in kith, kin, and the Southern way of life that motivated his choice. It is not just that they shared something, but that they shared something that Lee, rightly or wrongly, found good and worthy. If we imagine, instead, that Lee regarded kith and kin as scoundrels living an evil life and the Southern way of life as thoroughly reprehensible, Lee's choice becomes weak instead of tragic. Fletcher's picture of Lee's conflict as one between shared history and principle also misses the tragic dimension of Lee's choice.

This response raises a second, related argument against loyalty as moral choice. "Loyalty is an emotion," many will say, "and emotions aren't rational. Loyalty is thus not a matter of rational moral choice, but of having feelings." This is both true and false—emotions are as rational or irrational as the people who have them. I am not claiming that people feel loyalty as a result of a deliberative process—some do and some do not. I am claiming that people's loyalties, however arrived at, express and reflect their moral attitudes, which may be neither explicit nor self-aware. I am also not claiming that people have fully consistent moral attitudes—conflicting moral attitudes are often the source of much emotional turmoil. It is certainly possible for someone to say "I hate X and think X is evil, but X is my country/friend/church and I am loyal to it/her." But that, too, is a moral choice (perhaps a wrong one), reflecting a set of moral attitudes.

Consider an instance of loyalty that may seem to be prototypically about feeling and not about choice and moral attitudes—the loyalty of a parent to a child as it exists in our society. Parental loyalty has two components, which are not psychologically separable in that they grow together over the course of the parent-child relationship. A parent may love his child impersonally, simply because she is his child, and a parent may love his child personally, as a response to the unique individual she is. In all but the most extreme of cases, some element of each is present. I love my son because he is my son, and that love will endure no matter what he does. I love him intensely at the moment of his birth, when, as far as I am able to see, the only significant thing separating him from other babies is that he is my son. (Insofar as neonates have unique personalities, feelings, perceptions, etc., whatever at that moment separates him from other persons as persons is not yet visible to me.) But, as he grows, I also love my son because of who he is--I love him as a unique individual, and that love changes and grows and shifts as my son changes and grows and shifts. To the extent that my love for my son is a response to the particular person he is, it will grow with his growth as a person. It is possible to love someone as a child or parent and dislike her as a person. It is possible to love a child or parent as a person but not as a child or as a parent. Normally, and ideally, both elements are present. Both loves, and their interaction, are properly guided by ethical considerations. Ideally, one's emotional responses as a parent reflect those norms. When they do not, one hopes, those ethical considerations reshape how one's emotional responses are expressed in one's conduct.

My impersonal love for my children reflects, to some degree, my attitudes about parenthood, and since those attitudes have normative dimensions, my love reflects my moral choices. Suppose I discover that 12 years ago a sperm sample of mine was stolen from a clinic's office and used to impregnate a stranger. In some sense, the resulting child, Alicia, is my child. Do I feel the same impersonal loyalty to Alicia as I do to Rachel, the child I have reared since infancy? Is whether I do or not wholly unrelated to my normative conception of biological parenthood? That is, if I see biological parenthood as normatively implying responsibility for the needs of the child, and if I also feel the loyalty of impersonal love toward Alicia, is it merely a co-incidence that my emotion fits my normative outlook? And is not adopting a normative conception of biological parenthood a moral choice, that is, an assent to, acceptance of, one set of normative views from among alternatives? So I am not wholly passive with regard to my loyalty to Alicia—it does not come over me like measles. The same is true of personal love. Personal love is a response to the particular nature of the person one believes the other person to be. If my son's act of kindness to his sister warms my heart, does this not reflect my evaluative stance on kindness, the moral value I place on kindness? Or is it merely a co-incidence that the things that most strongly evoke my personal love for someone tend to correspond, in some important way, directly or indirectly, to what I value, think good? The matter is complicated, of course, by the facts that people are often not explicitly aware of their evaluative stance, that people's evaluative stances are sometimes inconsistent, and that traits or features of a person may be associatively rather than logically linked to one's evaluative stance (e.g., Joan's hair smells like my grandmother's, my grandmother is kind, and I value kindness, so the smell of Joan's hair evokes the pro-attitudes I bear toward kindness). So personal love need not dovetail precisely with explicit moral attitudes. But one's personal loves are deeply shaped by and reflect, in some important if complex way, one's evaluative stance upon the world. Thus feeling loyalty to a child deeply involves moral choice.[65]

Moral choice also affects the way a given loyalty is felt and expressed. For example, my impersonal love for my three children as my children may be equal. But personal love shifts as the person changes, and since no two people are identical, one never loves one's children equally. One loves each child in his or her own way, and there is no simple "common currency" of love that can be equally apportioned. Which love exerts a stronger pull on my heart at any given moment varies and shifts with each subphase of their development, with what each needs from me and my personal inclination to give it, and even with the passing occasion that gives each a chance to shine. But part of my duty of loyalty from the impersonal love I have for my children as my children is not to favor the child whom, at the moment, I like better. Suppose I have three cookies. Ideally, the burning personal love I feel for my youngest child at this moment does not prompt me to give the youngest child all three cookies, nor, a day or a year later, would the burning personal love I feel for my oldest child prompt me to give all the cookies to him. If it does, however, it is to be hoped that the moral importance of treating my children fairly would bring me to evaluate my impulse to give all the cookies to one child as an impulse upon which I will not act. Moreover, while the simple realization that I ought not to favor one child may not magically eliminate my impulse to give all the cookies to one child, thinking through the moral implications of parenthood, over time, that is, living through parenthood in a morally self-aware way, does affect my inclinations. This is just one example. In short, the idea that parental love is irrational and beyond moral considerations applies only to bad parents.

Sports loyalty appears to be a paradigm case of purely emotional attachments possibly founded on shared history. Loyalty to one's man might derive from a normative conception of marriage, but sports loyalty for most fans cannot plausibly be said to derive from a normative conception of fandom—Cubs fans do not root for the Cubs out of a moral duty to be fans. Nor do fans generally take an Aristotelian stance toward their team, that is, they do not generally root for a team because it possesses virtues that demand affection. Fan loyalty might be influenced, in some ways, by general ethical considerations. Jackie Robinson, already retired by the time I became aware of baseball, was a major reason the Dodgers captured my childhood heart. But fan loyalty is not an expression of principle. One can pick a team to root for during any sporting event, but one cannot simply adopt the kind of deep-seated loyalty some teams evoke in some fans, the deep seated passion about the team, the sense that, in some way, the team is oneself, its losses are one's own losses. That has to grow over time, in part because it expresses one's sense of rootedness. But is there a magic line between picking a team to root for in a game one doesn't care all that much about and the deep identification of the lifelong Cub fan with her team? Is it not a continuum, with new elements growing in some complex way along the continuum, not, as Fletcher's view seems to suggest, a metamorphosis based on totally different things? That is, if loyalty is based solely on shared history, and if there is no shared history at all in picking a team in a single game, then whatever one feels cannot be loyalty, and so must be totally different from what one feels for the baseball team one has grown up viewing and rooting for. Fletcher might point out that history develops, and loyalty deepens as the history unfolds. Hence it is easy to switch sides at the beginning of a game between two unknown teams, harder to do so near the end of the game, when one has shared hopes with the team for two hours. But other things besides shared history can create a sense of stake in the team's fortune. If Joe spends 10 minutes before the game arguing publicly and vociferously with his arch-rival in life about who is going to win, he will not find it easy to switch loyalties. My point is that many things, of which shared history is just one, can create a sense of stake in a team's fortunes. One can even arbitrarily adopt a stake, as a kind of game, to make the contest more interesting—most people do this when witnessing a sporting event if they have no other stake in the contest. Viewed dispassionately as two sets of people hitting a ball, a sporting event seems pointless—certainly not exciting. Only when one personalizes the contest, makes a win my win and a loss my loss, can one begin to get truly excited about a man hitting a ball of string with a stick. In a sense, for most people, the experience of watching a game demands having a stake in the outcome, and so, one way or another, we manufacture a stake in the outcome. But it is playing at having a stake, and that is what makes the tension pleasurable—we know, really, that our team winning or losing will not affect our lives in any genuine way. Even for the most loyal Cub fan, losing the pennant to the Dodgers is not like losing one's job. Even the disappointment is relished because it is play disappointment, like the disappointment one feels when the hero of a movie loses in the movie. To be moved by the heroine's plight, common wisdom goes, you have to care about the heroine. The more you care about the heroine, according to common wisdom, the more touched you will be by her story. Do we care about a nonexistent heroine of a novel? We do and we don't. We enter a fictional world and care about that world—but as fiction. We know it is not real. It is a kind of play concern we feel. Sports, ultimately, is a form of fiction. The more we care about a team, the more exciting the game is. We enter a fictional world and care about that world, about the game's outcome—but as fiction.

That is why anything can be impressed to give us a stake in the game: it is not a genuine stake but a fictional stake. The sense of going through a lot with the heroine of a story increases our sense of stake in her story, heightens the immediacy of the fictional world. The sense of shared history with a sporting teams similarly heightens the immediacy of the fictional world of the game. But, in both cases, it is neither necessary nor sufficient. Other things may make me care about the heroine—for example, if I have been in a similar psychological spot. Other things may make me care about the team's winning. Conversely, I can experience a lot with the heroine and still not care much about her fate if the experience is tedious, if I feel she is just getting what she deserves, and so forth. I can grow up next to Yankee stadium and hear endless talk from friends and newscasters about the Yankees' doings and prospects and yet not care one whit whether the Yankees win, without my lack of concern about the Yankee's standings being a moral failing of any sort.

In sum, while sports loyalty seems, for the most part, to lack the elements of Roycean loyalty, that is in part because sports loyalty is, in essence, play loyalty, a fiction, a game we enter into with ourselves. Part of its appeal may be that it serves as a substitute for genuine loyalty. Someone may be unable or unwilling to realize the difficult and demanding aspects of marital loyalty, loyalty to friends, etc. Sports loyalty is a relatively easy way to have the experience of loyalty. It may be difficult and demanding to feel part of a genuine community, particularly in America. But it is relatively easy to belong to the "community" of Cubs fans. What makes sports loyalty play loyalty is largely that it does not raise the complex moral questions of genuine loyalty, raise the complex emotional and personal demands of genuine loyalty, or have much impact upon the ordinary course of our lives, as genuine loyalty invariably does.

Nonetheless, Fletcherians will insist, one's history, one's country, race, gender, and so forth are ineradicable constituents of who one is. If Gilliam was raised Catholic, then, regardless of his current moral assessment of Catholicism, Catholicism is part of what Gillian is, and hence to deny loyalty to Catholicism is to deny his very self. In this sense, Fletcher claims, loyalty is independent of automous moral choice.

Fletcher is correct that there is an important link between loyalty and self-definition. However, history is only one aspect of self-definition. As we have seen, self-definition can be prospective and not just retrospective. In addition, the way in which one's history enters into one's self-definition depends on how one comes to see that history. In particular, it is always a moral choice to view an historical connection as a ground for loyalty. The self is defined by beliefs, values, attitudes, and propensities to perceive as well as by history and relationships. My beliefs and attitudes will come in important ways to shape and define my relationships and their retrospective meaning, just as my relationships help provide a life framework in terms of which I make sense of ideas. Aristotle points out that we are rational animals and that we are social animals, and neither can be understood without the other. We are social as thinking beings, and we think as social beings. It is a complex relationship, dynamic and interactive. One or the other may largely dominate one aspect of a local portion of life, so that it is sometimes only a little misleading to say one is being rational or historical about a given thing. It is only slightly misleading to speak of Modus Ponens as a form of logic independent of histories: in many important ways, it is. Other times it is wholly wrongheaded to pick one or the other as "dominant," because they cannot be understood apart from each other. As Jean-Paul Sartre famously pointed out, choice is never irrelevant to self-definition. I can't change the fact that I was born in New Jersey. As Sartre would point out, I can change what that fact means, how I see it, its import and significance. Of course, as mentioned before, there is an involuntary aspect of belief. I cannot simply decide to see my New Jersey birth in a certain way. Nevertheless, how we view an historical connection reflects and is shaped by our attitudes and values, and so whether a given historical connection engenders loyalty, emnity, or some other stance always involves moral choice in the relevant sense. Part of loyalty is commitment, and commitment is always, to some degree, a matter of moral choice, in the sense that to be committed is always, ultimately, to assent to that commitment and assent to what that commitment implies about the moral issues raised by being committed in that way. My history is my history, but what I make of that history, how it enters into my sense of myself, can be good or bad, morally acceptable or unacceptable. The answer to Fletcher's question, "need we act loyally toward the groups and individuals that have entered into our sense of who we are?" (p. 16) surely depends upon how they have entered into that sense.

That Gillian was raised as a Catholic is certainly one important part of who he is about which he may have had little choice. But the way in which having been raised Catholic defines him can vary greatly from other Catholics. He might embrace Catholicism, lose interest in Catholicism, or reject Catholicism. He may see himself as a dissident Catholic embarrassed by the Church and feel some commitment to its reform or even dissolution. He may see himself as a non-Catholic who views Catholicism as the enemy from whose clutches he fortunately escaped. In short, the mere fact that the Catholic Church has in some important way defined who Gillian is does not mean that he owes it loyalty—he may, in fact, owe it enmity for precisely that reason. Suppose, then, that Gillian's views have changed considerably since childhood. (Whether Gillian's views are correct or not is not relevant to the present point.) Gillian has come to see various elements of Catholic theology and Church practice as pernicious. He thinks that fundamental and underlying tenets of Catholicism, constitutive of the Church's core approach to human life, are the views that human beings are by nature shameful and that this life is of little importance, serving primarily as a kind of gateway or passage to the afterlife. He sees several more specific views he attributes to the Church as embedded in this fundamental approach, namely the Church's stance, as he interprets it, on sex, birth control, and end of life issues. He thinks the Church's view of sexuality is harmful and, in particular, views it as having caused him much needless suffering in the past and in the present. He thinks the Church's view of birth control is cruel and inhuman, responsible for starvation and hunger in many parts of the world, and a reflection of what he thinks is the Church's cavalier attitude toward human suffering. Similarly, he sees the Church's insistence on prolonging the life of terminally ill patients in pain or distress as a form of cruelty rooted in the sense that human beings deserve to suffer. So Gillian, whether rightly or wrongly, sees the Church as evil and as having seriously harmed and wronged him. He sees certain tenets and practices of the Church as the source of much that is wrong in his life, in the past and the present. He views those tenets and practices as central to what the Church stands for. Is loyalty to the Church morally appropriate for Gillian, given his views? Would Gillian be acting morally if he sincerely held those views but remained staunchly loyal to the Church? Would Gillian be acting morally if, although those views represent his best and most objective effort to reach truth, he renounced them, not out of a genuine sense that they are not true, but because voicing them and acting on would not be showing loyalty to the Church? Of course, if Gillian's views about the Church are incorrect, he should change his views because they are incorrect (not because they are disloyal). If his views are in fact correct, and he changes his views out of loyalty to the Church, is he acting morally?

Similarly, A German citizen who grew up under Nazism is morally flawed for embracing Nazism in later life, because the way in which Nazism forms his sense of self, if he has morally defensible attitudes, do not warrant loyalty. Fletcher recognizes that "we could hardly insist on total commitment—regardless of the evil that might follow—to friends, family, community, or country." (p. 151). For Fletcher, "loyalties generally lead people to suspend judgment about right and wrong" and "defer to the judgment of the other" (p. 36). He regards this problem, however, as defining the limits of loyalty: "the recurrent problem is working out the limits of this loyalty" (p. 36), a problem he tries to solve through the concept of "higher" and "lower" loyalties. However, this problem reaches through to the very basis of loyalty itself. The German citizen's rejection of Nazism is not a conflict of legitimate loyalty to Nazism versus loyalty to either humanity or the "true" Germany, but a recognition that Nazism warrants emnity rather than loyalty, a recognition that Nazism deserves no loyalty at all.

Fletcher is of course correct that the German's Nazi upbringing is part of what makes him the person he is, just as Gillian's Catholic upbringing is part of what makes him the person he is. What is not clear is why Gillian cannot define himself as an ex-Catholic ("recovering Catholic" is the phrase one sometimes encounters). More generally, why cannot one define oneself as a person who changed from being x to being y? If Smith has been blind since birth, then his blindness is an important part of who he is and what made him the person he is, but does it follow that he denies his very self if, at age 30, he opts for surgery to restore his vision? That he was blind certainly affects the way he will view life after he is able to see. Does that mean he is morally obligated to remain blind? Is he disloyal if he opts for the surgery? Is he disloyal if he wishes he had been born sighted instead? The mere fact that something is part of one's history and will forever influence, in some important way or other, one's outlook, does not itself entail that one is disloyal, irrational, unethical, or denying one's nature if one decides to change one's way of life. If an Afghan villager grew up hearing nothing but indigenous music, hears a Beethoven symphony at age 30, begins studying violin, and devotes the remainder of life to performing European music, is he disloyal? Is a European disloyal who devotes his life to Afghan music? Hispanic culture is a rich and profound culture, but if a different cultural milieu better suits Hidalgo's individual needs and aspirations, must we regard it as a moral fault if Hildalgo wholeheartedly enters into that cultural milieu? Of course, if there is no good reason for him to change, then perhaps Hidalgo's decision is suspect. But there may be all sorts of legitimate reasons for a given individual to wish to change. Cultures and ways of life vary, as do individuals. Each has many virtues. A different way of life may suit a given person better than the one in which one was raised. Consider the following argument: either some cultures and ways of life are, overall, better than others, or they are all equally good. If some are better, why is it wrong to choose a better one? If they are all equally good, then why should one not be free to choose between them? Moreover, while a sense of cultural rootedness is *prima facie* a good thing, it is not the sole or overriding human good. Even if it were, why is it obligatory to feel rooted in one's culture of origin and not another? A sense of belonging to the culture of one's childhood (as opposed to the culture of one's adulthood) may be a benefit, but it is surely not the only or overwhelmingly most important benefit.

Thus Fletcher is off the mark when he writes: "To love myself, I must respect and cherish those aspects of myself that are bound up with others. Thus by the mere fact of my biography I incur obligations toward others, which I group under the general heading of loyalty (p. 16)." To love oneself is not to affirm uncritically that everything that was ever a part of one's history is worthy. Self-love can equally require repudiating aspects or elements of one's past that are morally unworthy. The recovered alcoholic need not "respect and cherish" her former drunkenness in order to love herself, and, speaking specifically of social bonds, a rehabilitated bank robber need not respect and cherish his former alliances in crime in order to be said to love himself.

In short, conceptions of self both involve the making of moral evaluations and are themselves subject to moral evaluation. The mere fact of shared history neither determines a person's self-definition nor justifies the one he or she has. Hence the argument from self-definition does not show that shared history, *per se*, justifies bonds of special concern.

In sum, then, bonds of special concern, that is, loyalty, may create warrants when they reflect commitment to a set of shared values, legitimate acts of commitment, bonds of legitimate social responsibilities, and legitimate bonds of team loyalty and moral community. Bonds of special concern based solely on shared history or shared typology, *per se*, do not create legitimate warrants.

Does it follow, then, that someone who shows special concern for Jones over Smith on the basis of a purely typological bond violates Smith's rights? Do we have a right not to be discriminated against?

C. The Right to Non-Discrimination

If there is a right not to be discriminated against, it is not a natural right. No one can reasonably claim that unjustified discrimination, as such, renders the rational pursuit of P infeasible. Particular instances of discrimination, such as slavery, may violate natural rights, but they do so by violating some other right (e.g., basic autonomy rights). However, governmental discrimination on the basis of race, gender, religion, and so forth does violate presumptive rights. Ashmed is warranted, both by U.S. law and by our (legitimate) public morality, in demanding, as his due, that if Booth is hiring an Assistant Professor of Chemistry for a state university, Booth refrain from hiring Kirk instead of Ashmed solely because Kirk is a fellow Pentecostalist.[66] Membership in the Pentecostalist movement may or may not be a legitimate ground of loyalty, but Booth is not entitled to express that loyalty by using the trust a state institution places in him to give preference to the interests of Pentecostalists over non-Pentecostalists. Ashmed and Kirk both pay taxes that fund the position Booth is filling, and it is wrong for the state to take Ashmed's money and use it in a way that discriminates against him because of his religion. Since Booth, in hiring, is acting for the state, for Booth to give preference to a Pentecostalist, as such, is for the state to do so: it amounts to a state declaration that non-Pentecostalists are not as worthy of state concern as Pentescostalists are. Booth's doing so violates Ashmed's rights under U.S. law and provides legitimate grounds for a suit (Ashmed is warranted in demanding compensation or redress). Our public morality justifiably sanctions Ashmed's demand that Booth refrain from employing the power of his public position to deprive Ashmed of that job for that reason.[67]

In the public sphere, then, there is a presumptive but not a natural right not to be discriminated against on the basis of gender, religion, race, etc. Is the private sphere different? Lisa Newton suggests that the ideal of equality of citizenship, which she understands as including equality before the law and that all citizens possess the same rights, guarantees, and protections, is a fundament of political justice. Any form of discrimination (including affirmative action), she avers, "violates the public equality which defines citizenship and destroys the rule of law."[68] However, there is an important difference between equality before the law, equal treatment by the law, and laws requiring equal treatment outside the arena of the law itself (e.g., in hiring). Equality before the law requires only that the law applies equally to all. If the law holds that noblemen may whip but not kill serfs at will while serfs may not strike noblemen, the law does not treat serfs and noblemen equally, but the law, such as it is, applies equally to all (no nobleman is above the law). Equal treatment by the law requires that the law itself treat all persons equally. Owen Fiss points out that judicial treatment of the 14th Amendment has shifted in just this way, from "equal protection of the law," the original wording, to "the protection of equal laws."[69] Of course, laws that incarcerated felons and innocent persons equally would be unjust: some forms of unequal treatment are not only licit but required. A more precise form of the principle avers that any form of unequal treatment by the law must be both justifiable and universalizable: if the law treats differently those in category X from those not in category X, then everyone in category X must be treated equally and it must be justifiable to treat those in category X differently from those not in category X in that particular way. Laws requiring equal treatment go further: they require not just that the law and its representatives not discriminate, but that others not acting in the name of the law, such as private employers or businesses open to the public, treat everyone equally (in the sense described above). Thus, for example, a law that says employers may hire entirely at will, and hence does not mandate equal treatment by employers, nonetheless treats all job applicants equally—it offers no protection to anyone. Conversely, a law that requires employers to eschew discrimination in hiring but permits blue-eyed persons to recover double damages mandates equal treatment in one respect but does not treat everyone equally. Thus equal treatment by the law and legally mandated equal treatment are quite different. The rule of law certainly requires that the law apply equally to all. While there is some debate concerning whether the rule of law requires equal treatment by the law, a society that scrupulously enforces the abovementioned law regarding serfs and noblemen, however unjust the laws, does seem to be ruled by law. In any case, a society in which the law treats all equally but whose laws do not mandate equal treatment by employers doesn't thereby fail to instantiate the rule of law; whether or not laws ought to mandate equal treatment, the lack of such laws does not eliminate the rule of law. Thus the claim that any form of discrimination violates the rule of law seems false—it appears to confuse the equal application of the law to all (or perhaps equal treatment by the law) with laws requiring equal treatment. This is important because affirmative action in private contexts does not violate either the principle that the law must apply equally to all or the principle of equal treatment by the law, although there are questions about how much state involvement renders a context public. (In *Moose Lodge*,[70] for instance, the issue was whether granting a state liquor license to a private club that practiced discrimination counted as denying equal treatment by the law.) Does affirmative action by a public hirer, such as a government agency or a public school, violate the principle of equal treatment? The courts have held that the 14th Amendment applies to any state action, including policies of public high schools, although it is arguable that unequal treatment by a high school dress code is not unequal treatment by the law. In any case, whether affirmative action required by law violates the principle of equal treatment has been the subject of much debate. If the compensatory justice argument entirely succeeds, for instance, then affirmative action conforms to the principle of equal treatment, since the law equally offers compensation to everyone who deserves compensation. That is, the argument goes, it is justifiable to treat differently those who deserve compensation from those who do not, and everyone in the category of those who deserve compensation is treated equally.[71] In short, it is only the principle that the law must mandate equal treatment that can be invoked across the board against all affirmative action programs, and, even then, it must be carefully argued that affirmative action indeed constitutes illicit unequal treatment. Since the absence of laws mandating equal treatment does not undermine or violate the rule of law, Newton cannot argue that all forms of affirmative action violate the rule of law. Perhaps Newton's use of the phrase "rule of law" was unfortunate. Perhaps Newton meant to assert that all three principles are basic requirements of political justice. But such a claim requires further argument. Interestingly, Aristotle, to whom Newton attributes the ideal of equal citizenship she is invoking, did not include legally mandated equal treatment in private contexts in his conception of political justice.

Ronald Dworkin[72] suggests that the right of equal treatment means only equal concern in formulating policy, and hence policies that place some at a disadvantage (such as affirmative action) are justifiable if the overall gain to the community exceeds the overall loss and any other policy to accomplish roughly the same gain would place someone at a comparable or greater disadvantage. Dworkin considers the objection that this principle might also justify segregation. His response is to distinguish between external and internal preferences. Internal preferences are preferences based on one's own personal enjoyment of certain goods, while external preferences pertain to how goods are assigned to others. Dworkin cites as an external preference a desire that a municipal fund be used to build a swimming pool rather than a dance hall on the grounds that dancing is immoral. According to Dworkin, only internal preferences should count, since including external preferences in policy calculations amounts to double voting. There are two major problems with this response, ingenious as it is. First, the distinction between internal and external preferences cannot be rigorously maintained. A preference for winning a race is at once an internal preference that I personally enjoy the good of winning and an external preference that everyone else not enjoy that good—the two are logically inseparable. More generally, an external preference on the part of a white attorney that African-Americans not practice law is also an internal preference to enjoy the (perceived) good of practicing in a "racially pure" profession. Preferring that the city not build an "immoral" dance hall is an internal preference for personally enjoying the good of living in a moral community. This is a problem for Dworkin because he attempts to employ the distinction to draw a sharp line. That is, we often employ nonrigorous distinctions. A woman may say she is attracted to bald men without being able to specify exactly what counts as "bald." Many distinctions are invoked in this very volume that cannot be rigorously drawn. However, such vagueness is unacceptable in a concept used to draw a sharp line, especially when the line is supposed to be formal one: the point of Dworkin's distinction is that it is intended to be neutral between those with different value frames, and so Dworkin cannot advert to value frameworks such as "common sense." For example, if the legislature passes a statue forbidding bald men from purchasing land, the law, in the form of judicial interpretation, regulatory language, or statuatory language, must specify precisely what counts as baldness and what does not. Since Dworkin is drawing a sharp line between preferences that may count and preferences that may not count, he must specify precisely what counts as an internal preference and what counts as an external preference. Since Dworkin's distinction is meant to provide a rationale, the distinction cannot be arbitrarily drawn. Since Dworkin's distinction is meant to be neutral, troublesome cases must be resolved without resorting to contested value judgments. The problem is that no non-arbitrary, neutral, sharp distinction between internal and external preferences can be drawn. Second, it is not clear why only internal preferences should count. Why should only my pleasure in swimming count and not my moral abhorrence of dancing? The former is trivial while the latter is deeply held, deeply meaningful and important to me, and supported by my deepest convictions and concerns. Satisfying the latter preference has a much more profound and important effect on my life than satisfying the former. To the extent that preference satisfaction per se is the goal of public policy, public policy is much better served by satisfying the latter than the former. What sense does it make, then, to say that law and public policy should be exclusively concerned with satisfying my trivial preference and not my deep and profound preference?

In any case, even if we grant Dworkin his distinction between internal and external preference satisfaction, it would appear that such a broad utilitarian principle would justify enslaving some for the collectively greater benefit of others, measured purely in terms of internal preference satisfaction, if slavery is the only way to obtain that benefit. Perhaps Dworkin means to say that while such a policy of enslavement would not violate the principle of equal treatment, it is wrong for some other reason, R. If so, Dworkin would need to show that R does not apply equally to affirmative action programs. Thus Dworkin would need to identify R and demonstrate its lack of application to affirmative action.

Dworkin adds that the argument for segregation is purely utilitarian while the argument for affirmative action is both utilitarian and ideal (it brings us closer to an ideal society). This argument begs the question in one important sense: critics of affirmative action argue that racial or gender discrimination of any sort is an injustice, and hence affirmative action by nature brings us further away from an ideal society. The question then becomes whether the purported injustice of affirmative action is greater or less than the purported injustices affirmative action is intended to address, which is precisely the question with which we began. Dworkin is correct in distinguishing between reasons pertaining to utility and reasons pertaining to justice and other moral ideals apart from utility. One set of arguments does center on the beneficial or harmful effects of affirmative action while a second set of arguments center on the justice or injustice of affirmative action, and it is the second set that Dworkin is addressing. Hence it is precisely whether affirmative action brings us closer to justice that is at issue.

For Judith Jarvis Thomson, the distinction between private and public goods is a crucial one. Thomson suggests[73] that, in the case of public benefits, all members of the public are equal owners of the benefit, and so have an equal right to the benefit (perhaps in the form of an equal opportunity to obtain the benefit). Some legitimate grounds exist, she claims, for overriding this right, e.g., the gratitude owed to veterans. Absent such grounds, however, a hiring officer for a state institution violates the rights of non-Pentecostalists if he gives priority in his hiring to Pentecostalists. The issue for affirmative action in the public sphere, then, is whether the grounds for affirmative action programs justify overriding this *prima facie* right. By contrast, suppose Smith has an apple by some process that makes it purely his own, e.g., the apple grew on a scarcely populated planet abundant with applies and Smith scratched the back of a visitor from that planet who gave it to him in gratitude. Smith gives the apple to Jones instead of Cavalli simply because Cavalli is of Italian descent and Smith dislikes Italians and believes they are dishonest. Does Smith act injustly? Thomson suggests that I have a right to dispose of a benefit I own in any way I like, so long as I do not give needless offense, I make no promises, explicit or implicit, that give others an equal right to or chance of gaining that benefit, and my doing so violates no duties to third parties. Some reasons for disposing of the benefit (such as Smith's) may be irrational or wrong, but actions reflecting those reasons violate no one's rights. Presumably, Thomson's claim is based on the purported sovereignty one holds over purely private goods. Thomson does not blankly deny that other considerations may make demands on the employment of that sovereignty. Pressing needs (as opposed to mere benefits) might impose limits on our sovereignty over purely private good, although Thomsom avers "I suspect the same holds true of things people do actually need" (p. 25) and argues for one instance of sovereignty over private goods outweighing others' urgent needs in her famous paper on abortion.[74] Moreover, in *The Realm of Rights*[75] Thomson suggests that rights center on trespass and harm. Am I improperly harmed if you dispose of something I need? Still, there is at least some reason to think needs can make obligatory demands on private goods. If an invariably lethal extraterrestrial virus threatens all human life and I possess, through some process that makes it purely mine, a cure, do I do no one an injustice if I refuse to sell or give my cure to any African-American and require anyone purchasing my cure to sign a contract forbidding the sale or donation of the cure to any African-American? Perhaps Thomson would maintain I do no injustice, but that claim requires argument: it is at least initially plausible to claim that one does an injustice by acting in that way. And if needs can make demands on sovereignty over private good, why can't benefits? A thoroughgoing defense of Thomson's claim would require either establishing a pre-eminent sovereignty over private goods with well-defined exceptions, if any there are, or an argument establishing clear limits to right claims that exclude rights to private benefits.

I wish to suggest that while, in some sense, Smith had a right to do what he did, he acted wrongly and ought not to have done it (as Thomson acknowledges). Smith also, in some sense, wronged Cavalli (which Thomson denies), though no redress or compensation is due. How can this be?

You are warranted in demanding, as your due, that others not treat you adversely merely because of your ethnic origin or unfairly assign negative traits to you based only on your ethnic origin, except in special circumstances that might justify such actions or thoughts. For example, Michaels is lost on a lonely corner of the city. He sees two people about to enter their cars, in opposite directions. Michaels can accost only one of them—by the time he has done so, the other will be gone. No one else is nearby. Michaels must make a snap judgment about which of the two people is more likely to be of genuine help. Since he has no genuine information upon which to base his judgment, he is justified in using purely statistical information. For example, if he knows that 43% of women but only 24% of men ignore requests for help from strangers, he is justified in accosting the man instead of the woman. He should realize, of course, that the woman might be extremely helpful and the man surly, but he has no way to know this. Assigning a negative trait to the woman in this instance wrongs no one—Michaels acts rationally, he has no special duty to ask someone for directions, he believes not that the woman will be unhelpful but merely that the probability that he will receive the help he needs is higher if he asks the man than if he asks the woman, given the limited information he has, and he is happy to revise that judgment in the light of any forthcoming relevant information. In other words, when we lack genuine information and have no special duties regarding a decision, it is not wrong to employ statistical information of whatever sort we have. If Michaels, by way of contrast, is awarding a state scholarship funded by tax dollars, he may have a special duty not to employ that kind of statistical information in making his decision. Similarly, police use of racial profiling is open to challenge on the grounds police have a special duty not to employ that kind of statistical information when deciding whom to subject to questioning and detention.

Why are we warranted in making that demand? For several reasons, I think.

1. People are obligated to participate, in some manner and to some reasonable degree, in the moral enterprise, that is, in the joint project of making this a morally good world.

2. A wrongs B when they are teammates in the moral enterprise and A treats B in a manner inconsistent with the manner in which teammates in an enterprise should treat each other, all things considered.

3. Absent other overriding circumstances or concerns, treating a teammate in a manner that ultimately undermines or is in blatant opposition to the goals of the team is treating a teammate in a manner inconsistent with the manner in which teammates in an enterprise should treat each other.

4. Therefore A wrongs B when they are teammates in the moral enterprise and, absent other overriding circumstances or concerns, A treats B in a manner that ultimately undermines or is in blatant opposition to the goals of the team.

5. Treating someone adversely merely because of her ethnic origin, race, gender, etc., or unfairly assign negative traits to her based only on her ethnic origin, race, gender, etc., except in special circumstances that might justify such actions or thoughts, is treating someone in a manner that ultimately undermines or is in blatant opposition to the goals of the moral enterprise.

6. Thus A wrongs B when they are teammates in the moral enterprise and A treats B adversely merely because of her ethnic origin, race, gender, etc., or unfairly assigns negative traits to B based only on her ethnic origin, race, gender, etc., except in special circumstances that might justify such actions or thoughts.

7. When someone, C, is obligated to do x and, were C to do x, C would owe you y, C wrongs you if C denies you y.

8. Therefore A wrongs B when A treats B adversely merely because of her ethnic origin, race, gender, etc., or unfairly assigns negative traits to B based only on her ethnic origin, race, gender, etc., except in special circumstances that might justify such actions or thoughts.

For these reasons, then, Smith has wronged Cavalli. However, as noted in Chapter 1, there are at least two ways in which my having a right that you violate may not entail that I have grounds for redress against you. First, my right might be a vector but not a resultant right (it may be overridden). Your right to silence may be overridden by my right to talk. Second, violating your right in that way might be within my legitimate purview. You do not have a resultant right to my silence, but you do have a resultant right to my not being rude. Thus, when my right to talk overrides your right to silence, I have not, overall, wronged you. I have, overall, wronged you when I am gratuitously rude, although I am immune to redress: my decision to violate your resultant right to courtesy is morally un-dressable and your right is morally unenforceable. When Smith gives his apple to Jones, he wrongs Cavalli, but, because it is purely his apple, it is within his purview to wrong Cavalli in that way. Smith is warranted in claiming immunity from redress, though not from negative judgment.

In this sense, then, Thomson is right in distinguishing public from private benefits. I have a moral right not to be discriminated against. But your discriminating against me in distributing a private benefit is (at least sometimes) morally unredressable, while, other things being equal, your discriminating against me in distributing a public benefit is morally redressable. She is also correct that other things are not always equal—there could be, in some circumstances, grounds for giving preference in distributing a public benefit on the basis of race, gender, etc. that either justify the preference or render it morally unredressable. What such grounds would be, of course, is a matter for further argument. For example, if the police use statistically based racial profiling in the absence of any other information when pursuing their inquiries, they might marginally increase efficiency—using statistical information in the absence of any other information marginally increases the probability of success. Whether these are legitimate grounds for unequally distributing the benefit of avoiding the stress and inconvenience of police detainment and questioning is a matter for further argument. If affirmative action in state hiring does, in fact, provide socially useful role models and hence has some success in prompting African-Americans to become qualified for desirable jobs, whether that social benefit constitutes legitimate grounds for unequally distributing the benefit of a public job is a matter for further argument.

A further complication is that some goods are neither fully private nor fully public. U.S. law, for instance, regards a job as a quasi-public good and matrimony as, in most respects, fully private. Hence hiring is included in the scope of anti-discrimination laws and regulations while deciding whom to marry is not. Elsewhere I've argued that, because society provides "opportunity capital" for every business venture, society is a part owner of every business venture.[76] If that argument is sound, then much of what Thomson considers "purely private" is, while private, not "purely" private. To the extent that such goods are private, the wrong of discrimination concerning them is *prima facie* non-redressable, while, to the extent that such goods are public, the wrong of discrimination concerning them is *prima facie* redressable. The realm of the quasi-private, then, constitutes a gray area within which the extent to which the wrong of discrimination is redressable must be weighed on a case-by-case basis. A corporation's tendency to prefer subcontracting with white-owned engineering firms differs from a travelers' tendency to select Asian porters in an airport.

In general, then, discrimination by anyone on the basis of race, gender, etc. is a prima facie moral wrong. There is reason, thus, for opposition to discrimination to be part of public policy, and hence some justification for a liberty from discrimination. There is also a presumption in favor of permissibility for individuals to dispose of private goods as they see fit. Hence, to the chagrin of both liberals and conservatives, laws regarding the disposal of private goods should result from weighing, in particular instances, whether the legitimate policy goal of opposing such discrimination is strong enough to outweigh the presumption in favor of permissibility. Conversely, to the extent that affirmative action discriminates, particular affirmative action measures should be evaluated by weighing the particular benefits and rationale for the measure against the general public policy goal of opposing discrimination. No general principle, in other words, either restricts or demands, across the board, affirmative action or permitting the discriminatory disposal of private goods: each case must be carefully weighed.

D. Group Compensation

Issues of group compensation arise in several ways. Famously, compensation or reparation provides one oft-invoked argument supporting affirmative action. Many women were, undeniably, victims of discrimination in the past. Just as undeniably, many women continue to experience workplace discrimination. The compensatory justice argument claims that compensation is due for these wrongs and that affirmative action for those women is an acceptable or required form of compensation. Reparations to Jews for the Holocaust may take the form of specific payments to individuals for their personal sufferings. Such cases do not constitute true group compensation, even though all the individuals compensated are members of a particular group. However, in some instances individuals cannot be identified, as is the case with some of the Swiss Bank money deposited by the Nazis, and hence compensation must be somehow distributed among members of the group. It has also been argued that the establishment of a Jewish homeland in Israel was required by compensatory justice. Other groups have made similar claims. Understanding such cases requires a closer look at the notion of compensation.

Reparation or compensation involves five elements. The notion of reparation is least problematic when all five elements are perspicuously present. In paradigmatic cases of reparation there is 1) a clearly appropriate remedy for 2) a clearly demarcated harm to 3) a clearly demarcated set of harmed individuals. The harm is 4) clearly assignable by a clearly delineated appropriate process to 5) a clearly demarcated set of responsible individuals. The appropriateness of a remedy in turn depends upon four factors. The remedy should be commensurate to the harm. If Jones breaks Smith's vase, requiring Jones to pay Smith a million times the value of the vase he broke is not a commensurate remedy. The remedy should be fitting: requiring Jones to replace the vase is a fitting remedy while requiring Jones to have sex with Smith is not. The remedy should be directed toward the individuals who were harmed. Finally, the remedy should be provided by or at the expense of the set of responsible individuals. In the case of Jones breaking Smith's case by throwing a stone at the vase, the loss of the vase is the harm suffered by Smith, assignable by a clear process to Jones, who is the responsible party, and requiring Jones to reimburse Smith for the value of the vase is commensurate, fitting, and compensates the harmed party at the expense of the responsible party.

In paradigmatic cases the notion of reparation is reasonably clear and its moral importance widely accepted. Not all cases in which reparation might be justifiably demanded are paradigm cases. In certain cases of libel, for instance, an individual may be clearly harmed by the libel without being able to specify precisely the exact nature of the harm, as the effects of libel are sometimes subtle and amorphous and libels can sometimes aggravate harms they did not cause by themselves. In such cases, the notion of reparation may be applied even though one element is present in a less than fully perspicuous manner. Nonetheless, libel is more problematic than breaking a vase, as is evidenced by the arguments that may be encountered in the courtroom pertaining to determining the degree of harm of a particular libel. Compensation for psychological harm, even for something as palpable as physical pain from a burn injury, has proven controversial in tort law, and while few would assert that physical pain deserves no compensation at all, allowable sorts of distress has become a bitter battleground. Distress is a real harm but an amorphous one, and the more amorphous the harm the less plausibly the notion of compensation can be applied. In general, the further from the paradigmatic case the concept of reparation is stretched, the more problematic it becomes. There is no clear line beyond which the concept of reparation cannot be applied, given that all five elements are present in some fashion, however unperspicuously. Nonetheless, some cases, such as libel, are clearly close enough to the paradigm to require compensation, although some aspects of the case may be more difficult to resolve or determine than is generally the case with more paradigmatic cases. In other cases, it is just as clear that applying the notion of reparation would stretch the concept of reparation too far. There are clear cases at either extreme even if there is no sharp boundary dividing the ground between them. To the discomfort of those who like sharp answers, the ground between the extremes is extensive indeed.

In the case of general affirmative action programs as compensation, the five elements are typically present in a less than perspicuous fashion. Much discussion has centered on whether affirmative action compensates the wrong persons at the expense of those who have not done the wrong. Affirmative action programs for undergraduate study programs typically come at the expense of white male high school students who, it is averred, have never been in a position to discriminate in the workplace. Thus using such affirmative action programs as compensation is akin, the argument goes, to compensating you for the vase I broke by requiring a stranger to pay you for the vase. You may be owed compensation from me, but not from the stranger. Some, such as Judith Jarvis Thomson, reply that the white male high school student benefited from years of racism and sexism, even should he not have practiced racism and sexism himself, and hence it is not unjust that he should incur a loss in order to compensate a victim of racism or sexism. Robert Fullinwinder and John Rowan suggest that receiving an involuntary benefit due another is not grounds for compensating the injured party: compensation is due, they suggest, from the party denying the benefit, not the one who received it.[77] Considerable debate surrounds the question of whether receiving an involuntary benefit confers obligations, but, in any case, some receive with skepticism the claim that a teenage son of a latrine cleaner in rural Tennessee received much benefit from the long history of racism in the United States. Gertrude Ezorksy points out that while the history of racism has benefited some whites, it has hurt others. "On the whole, some white workers have lost and some have gained from racism" she writes. "But to disentangle the two groups," she suggests, "is a practical impossibility...."[78] While it is clear that racism and sexism have opened extra opportunities for some white males, as Sterba notes, inequality in America exists as well between white males, with the result that many white males were also excluded from using those extra opportunities, and hence cannot be said to have benefited from them. An alternative argument is that, just as tort courts sometimes exact compensation from those who can best afford to remedy the injury, whites can best afford to bear the costs of compensation. However, courts do not require General Motors to compensate my neighbor for the vase I break simply because General Motors can afford to do so. Rather, the reasoning in tort cases seems to be that a corporation or individual voluntarily engaged in a risk-posing enterprise from which the corporation or individual expected to benefit and thus can be reasonably required to assume the risk posed by the enterprise as a cost of engaging in the enterprise. It is unclear that a similar argument can be reasonably applied to 18 year old white applicants for entry level jobs. In any case, as Rowan and others point out, it is far from clear that all those applicants can afford to bear the costs, as the range of white male applicants may include impoverished sons of alchoholic transients who have been routinely beaten and abused. In short, for many affirmative action programs, it is difficult to specify a responsible party, to whom the wrong is clearly assignable, who is providing the remedy: in many cases, this element is unperspicuously present. The degree to which it is present varies from case to case. Consider the difference between these two arguments:

A. The X Corporation has recently engaged in specific discriminatory hiring policies against women and hence the X Corporation should be required to take specific and appropriate extra measures to increase the number of women it employs.

B. Women have been discriminated against in various ways by various individuals at various times and places, and hence the X Corporation should be required to take specific and appropriate extra measures to increase the number of women it employs.

In case A., there is a clearly demarcated responsible individual, the X Corporation, and the remedy sought is provided by the responsible individual. It may also come at the expense of a job applicant who was not party to the X Corporation's discriminatory practices, but this is frequently the case. If Garcia recovers from Rivera for sexual harassment, Rivera's six year old son, who was not party to the harassment, may suffer as a result, e.g., by being required to leave a private school for which Rivera can no longer afford tuition. Thomson generalizes this response: the job for which the white applicant competes, she avers, is not his, but the community's (in the case of a public employer). He is deprived, she says, of his chance for equal consideration by the community in order that the community can make reparations. In case B. there is no clearly identified party and the remedy is provided by a party, the X Corporation, against which no claim of specific discrimination has been established. Thus case A. is closer to the paradigm in this respect than is case B., and so, in at least one important respect, the application of the notion of reparations is less problematic in case A. than in case B.

Of course, if groups were metaphysical entities capable of bearing blame for the misdeeds of their parts, the problem disappears. As noted earlier, if I am sentenced to prison for punching someone in the nose, I cannot argue that it is unjust to punish my feet for the misdeeds of my fist. Similarly, it might be argued, whites discriminated against African-Americans, and hence the teenage white applicant cannot argue that it is unjust to require him to pay compensation for what some other white did. The arguments found in this chapter, it will be assumed, are sufficient to dispel this approach. In any case, few would accept other applications of this principle. As pointed out earlier, were women as a group a metaphysical entity capable of bearing blame for the misdeeds of its parts, then an employer would be justified in firing Sheila because another female worker is perennially late for work.

It is frequently argued that affirmative action programs typically do not benefit those who have been most wronged by sexism and racism, and in particular does not benefit those who were denied jobs in the past because of sexism and racism.[79] As Robert Simon puts it, there is something suspect about saying that "compensation is owed collectively to a group [but] only a special sort of group member is eligible to receive it...."[80] More generally, some have argued that if reparation via affirmative action is required by previous discrimination it must also be required by all past wrongs. Michael E. Levin, for instance, argues that discrimination is a wrong, but no different from other wrongs and not as great a wrong as murder, and hence, were the compensatory justice argument sound, preferential hiring for offspring of murdered persons would be a requirement of justice.[81] Bernard R. Boxill correctly points out that a person who has lost one leg deserves compensation regardless of whether someone who lost two legs deserves compensation more and that the fact that someone has overcome an injury does not entail that compensation for the injury is not due. Thus affirmative action could be a legitimate means of reparation if it compensates those who suffered wrongs, even if it does not compensate others who suffered even greater wrongs.[82] James W. Nickel suggests that even if affirmative action is imperfect, it is preferable to a policy of color-blindness in that at least some who deserve compensation will be compensated.[83] Nonetheless, it does seem improper for a society to engage in a widespread policy of reparation for one arbitrarily selected sort of wrong and ignore other sorts that are equally or more wrong. (Recall the earlier discussion of equal treatment.) Moreover, if the argument is that affirmative action is a requirement of justice, then the extension of the reasoning to all wrongs may be used as a form of *reductio ad absurdum*:

were the compensatory justice argument for affirmative action correct, the argument goes, then justice would require preferential hiring for all vic-
tims/descendents of any injustice. Since that is absurd, the argument runs, the
compensatory justice argument for affirmative action is not correct. Thus it is
worth pointing out two things. First, there are some important differences between the history of discrimination in America against African-Americans in
particular and other sorts of wrongs. While the son of a murdered father suffered
from a wrong, the wrong was not an officially sanctioned wrong written into law
over an extended period of time. Arguably, then, the United States government,
and more generally the United States as a political entity, owes something to
African-Americans it does not owe to the son of a murdered father. Of course,
the United States government performed many wrongs during the course of its
history, such as killing thousands of Filipinos in conquering the Philippines after
the Spanish-American war. Nonetheless, with the possible exception of its treatment of Native Americans, for whom affirmative action rights are also often
claimed, none of the other wrongs committed by the United States were as extensive, long-lasting, and deeply entrenched in law. It is not one law or one action
that is at issue, but a wide variety of laws, judicial judgments, regulatory decisions, and actions over a very long period of time. Moreover, the effects of this
discrimination have been particularly pervasive because they were officially and
pervasively exercised against an entire cohesive community for many generations, and hence created an environment, a culture, in which generations grew
up. As George Sher points out, the effect of such multigenerational, community-
wide financial and psychological harms is to deprive many of the opportunity to
compete on equal terms.[84] In some sense, then, discrimination in the United
States against African-Americans and Native Americans does occupy a special
position, both because of its character as officially entrenched doctrine explicitly
and pervasively present in law over a long period of time and because of the
practical pervasiveness of its effects. (Some argue that a parallel point applies to
women.) Second, it is undeniable that, as Boxill, Thomson, Sterba, and many
others point out, virtually every African-American and American woman has
suffered to some extent from racism and sexism. Cohen (*op. cit.*, p. 27) is correct
that while many African-Americans are poor, others are rich and powerful.
Nonetheless, rich and powerful African-Americans are not wholly insulated from
racial prejudice. Perceptual bias, the tendency of many individuals to be more
ready to perceive a group member as displaying a certain property, is widespread
in American society. While perceptual bias and its effects may be more severe
for a ghetto youth than a Supreme Court justice, every woman and every African-American has experienced it to some degree. Moreover, every African-
American would undeniably be in a different position had the practice of slavery
never occurred, although it is impossible in practice to say, for any given individual, what that position would be. Interestingly, for reasons akin to the identity
problem discussed in Chapter 8, Christopher Morris[85] argues that no African-

American alive today would exist had slavery never been practiced. It is highly unlikely, given all the changes that the absence of slavery would entail, that the very same sperms would have fertilized the very same ova, and hence, had slavery not occurred, different persons would have been born instead of the ones who populate the world today. Thus, it could be argued, no one alive today can claim to have been harmed by slavery (although, if the argument in Chapter 8 is correct, they may claim to be wronged by slavery). More importantly, the concept of reparations for distant, widespread, and sweeping harms is highly problematic because it is virtually impossible to determine, for any individual, the *status quo ante*. No doubt I would be in a different position than I am today had the Romans not expelled the Jews from Israel in 72 A.D., but I cannot recover damages from the Italian government. Of course, slavery and subsequent discriminatory practice are more proximate in time and their current day effects more palpable in the lives of many African-Americans, but the intractable difficulty remains of tracing back causes and constructing a counterfactual history of what would have happened without those wrongs. Thus this particular sort of harm to current day African-Americans, generations after the fact, though real, is too amorphous for the concept of reparation to be reasonably applied. Boxill suggests that even privileged African-Africans might suffer at the realization that they might be next. He contrasts this situation with that of an American Jew safe in Scarsdale during the Holocaust who, avers Boxill, knows it is unlikely that he himself will die in a gas chamber. Equally, however, it is unlikely that a child of Clarence Thomas will face the grinding poverty of the inner city ghetto or be disadvantaged over the general population in his or her search for a job. Conversely, if Boxill means to suggest that a Scarsdale Jew in 1944 could feel total confidence that anti-Semitic violence can never befall him, he is sadly mistaken. (Boxill appears also to neglect the fact that most American Jews lost relatives to the Holocaust.) In any case, the harms of racism suffered by rich and powerful African-Americans are real but largely too amorphous to be perspicuous candidates for reparation. It would be fatuous to say that an African-American supermodel born of wealthy parents feels no effects of racism, but equally implausible to say that her personal suffering from racism outweighs the suffering from prejudice and unequal opportunity felt by a white, impoverished, overweight, physically unattractive son or daughter of a latrine cleaner in rural Tennessee. In any case, the supermodel is certainly advantaged in the job market over the latrine cleaner's son. The point is that while the element of harm is undeniably present for all African-Americans, some harms to some African-Americans are clearly specifiable and demarcated in a way that permits the concept of reparation to be comfortably applied (e.g., losing a promotion to a less qualified white co-worker), others are harmed in amorphous ways that, while real and important, do not lend themselves to compensation, at least in the form of individually specific remedies such as affirmative action.

Perhaps it could be argued that the law should employ approximating fictions similar to those used in setting driving and voting ages. That is, it might be granted that compensation is due not to women or African-Americans in general but to each particular individual who has suffered gender or racial discrimination, just as the right to drive is properly earned by being mature enough to drive, not by turning 17. Nonetheless, it may be argued, legal policies should employ the approximating fictions that all and only those over 17 are mature enough to drive and that all and only women have been unfairly deprived of jobs due to gender discrimination, since it would be impractical and intrusive for the law to attempt to make judgments about each individual concerning her actual level of maturity or actual experience of discrimination. The plausibility of this argument depends upon the nature of the affirmative action program being reviewed. Approximating fictions are most defensible when a) an important need is involved, b) the consequence of being unfairly excluded by the fiction is minor, c) making the actual judgment is impossible and/or the social, moral, and financial costs of not using a fiction are prohibitive, and d) the approximation is a very good one (or the best available) in the circumstances.[86] In the case of driving, for instance, the ability to drive is important, the cost of allowing large numbers of immature drivers on the road is high (significant numbers of deaths and serious injuries), the cost of having to wait a year or two are relatively minor, making the actual judgment for each individual is infeasible, and the vast majority of 17 year olds are capable of driving. The less well these conditions are met, the less defensible an approximating fiction becomes. Owen Fiss, describing the court's approach to the 14th Amendment (of which he himself is critical), points out that when criteria are intrinsically suspect (such as race) and/or the rights involved are fundamental, criteria of selection must show a very tight fit (approximating fictions must come very close), the state end must be legitimate and compelling, and there must be no reasonable alternative method producing a tighter fit, except when the measure is part of a "step-by-step" reform lessening discrimination from what it previously was.[87] Different affirmative action programs meet these criteria to different extents. For example, beneficiaries of an affirmative action program for an unskilled entry-position job for residents of Harlem more closely approximates those who have suffered clear harms from discrimination than does an affirmative action program for women with Ph.D.'s from top universities (as when a research university hires an Assistant Professor in philosophy). Once again, this argument cannot be used across the board for all affirmative action programs but requires case-by-case weighing of the relevant factors.

Thomson suggests that compensation effected by affirmative action programs for women and African-Americans is analogous to gratitude expressed by hiring preferences for veterans. While gratitude and reparation are not identical, says Thomson, "to fail, at the very least, to make what counts as public apology to all, and to take positive steps to show that it is sincerely meant, is, if not injustice, then anyway a fault at least as serious as ingratitude" (p. 38). Thomson is certainly correct, but the issue is whether affirmative action is the appropriate means for doing so. (George Sher, for instance, suggests that outright payments would be more appropriate and better targeted.[88]) There is a significant disanalogy between hiring preferences for veterans and for members of groups that suffered discrimination. Every veteran gave to his or her country something specific, typically two or more years of service, from which every job applicant benefits. In the case of veterans, then, the corresponding elements of providing a benefit (rather than suffering a harm) and receiving the benefit (rather than responsibility for the harm) are perspicuously present. The appropriate conclusion is not that Thomson is wrong, but rather that compensation through affirmative action is more of a stretch than is gratitude expressed by hiring preferences for veterans.

In sum, for some beneficiaries of some affirmative action programs, the element of harm seems unperspicuously present. It thus becomes significant that merely typological loyalty to women or African-Americans as such is not morally justifiable. If it were, then an African-American who suffered a clearly identifiable harm, such as being refused a job on account of race, could be compensated by giving preference in hiring to a different African-American. That is, since there are undeniably African-Americans, such as Jones, who were specifically harmed in clearly demarcated ways by racial discrimination, giving preference in hiring to Smith would compensate Jones (not Smith) for that wrong by advancing Jones' interest in the flourishing of African-Americans. Thus, if merely typological bonds were morally justifiable, the element of harm would be perspicuously present whichever African-American is benefited by an affirmative action program, since it is not necessarily the person hired who is being compensated. It could be argued that, as long as Jones felt the relevant typological bond, Jones can be compensated by giving preference to Smith, whether or not Jones' felt bond is morally defensible. In general, however, we do not hold that compensation in the form of advancing a morally objectionable interest is appropriate, much less a requirement of justice. If A breaks B's vase and B is rabidly anti-Semitic, requiring A to publish an anti-Semitic tract is not an appropriate form of compensation. After all, it was an instance of typological bonding that created the harm to Jones in the first place. Similarly, since merely typological bonds are not morally justifiable, one cannot compensate Cohen, a victim of the Holocaust, by giving preference in hiring to Levi, although one can (partially) compensate Cohen by establishing or supporting a Jewish homeland, provided Cohen had (like most Jewish Holocaust victims) a legitimate, significant interest in the survival of the Jewish people as a people.

In sum, group compensation requires weighing, in each individual case, the extent to which the proposed form of compensation diverges from the paradigm against the moral importance and urgency of effecting compensation.

E. Applications: Affirmative Action and the Right of Self-Determination

In many ways, the conclusions to be drawn from the preceding discussion will please no one. Magic bullets that decide social issues involving group rights do not exist. Instead, each claim must be individually weighed. By way of illustration, brief discussions of affirmative action and the right to self-determination follow.

Affirmative Action

In one sense it is impossible to have a simple position on affirmative action, since there is a wide range of possible affirmative action programs that raise different issues and are justified or held objectionable for different reasons. A partial list of types of affirmative action program on behalf of any group G, which can be mixed and matched in various combinations, follows:

Type 1: Making a special effort to recruit candidates from group G. Colleges that send recruiters to predominantly Hispanic-surnamed high schools in an effort to increase the number of applications from Hispanic-surnamed students are engaging in Type 1 affirmative action. Type 1 is the original form of affirmative action in U.S. law.[89]

Type 2: Giving preference, among a set of otherwise equally qualified candidates, to a member of group G. In type 2 programs, institutions select the most qualified candidate. When two candidates are in other respects equally qualified, one of whom belongs to group G and one of whom does not, the candidate belonging to group G is selected. Thus Type 2 affirmative action has effect only when the competing candidates are otherwise equally qualified.

Type 3: Using an unequal scale in determining qualifications. A law school that added ten percent to the LSAT score of each woman applicant and then accepted students purely on the basis of their adjusted LSAT scores would be employing Type 3 affirmative action.

Type 4: Quotas, which can be employed either as goals or as restrictions. (Quotas are generally employed with the restriction that minimal qualifications must be met.) Most commonly, quotas are employed as goals, as when an institution makes some significant efforts to bring it about that at least 20% of admitted students belong to group G. A corporation that required at least 40% of all new hires to be women would be employing Type 4 affirmative action as a restriction.

Type 5: Restricting hiring or admissions to members of group G: those who are not members of group G need not apply.

Type 1 programs have few strong opponents while most proponents of affirmative action are uncomfortable with most type 5 programs. Since programs of types 3 and 4 are more common, and so tend to generate the most controversy, the ensuing discussion will focus on them.

Arguments for and against affirmative action are generally divided by philosophers into two categories. Some arguments focus on rights and justice, while others focus on the beneficial or harmful effects of affirmative action programs.[90]

The two most commonly discussed arguments focusing on rights and justice are the compensatory justice argument supporting affirmative action and the argument against affirmative action that affirmative action discriminates against non-members of the preferred group. The argument above suggests that neither of these two arguments is decisive. The concept of reparations cannot generally be perspicuously employed for broad, across the board affirmative action programs. On the other hand, particular examples of narrowly focused affirmative action programs may come closer to the paradigm of reparations. Thus the compensatory justice argument cannot be employed as a definitive justification of affirmative action across the board. Rather, one must examine, on a program-by-program basis, the extent to which the notion of reparation can be perspicuously applied. The answer will be a matter of degree rather than a simple "yes" or "no." The argument that affirmative action discriminates similarly cannot be used to show that affirmative action is impermissible across the board. Whatever discrimination against non-minorities affirmative action programs create is generally non-redressable in the private sphere and must be balanced against legitimate social goals in the public and quasi-public spheres. Thus affirmative action programs cannot be ruled out across the board as legitimate policy on the grounds that they discriminate against those outside the preferenced group.

As a result, affirmative action programs must be evaluated on a case-by-case basis, weighing the justness of that particular program and its effectiveness in advancing legitimate and worthwhile social goals against the potential harms and injustices of that particular program. Making that evaluation about a particular program requires, in addition to evaluating the requirements of justice, examining in detail how each of the potential harms and benefits of affirmative action programs might come into play in the operation of that particular program. An extensive literature reviews those potential benefits and harms. Below is a brief, partial list, intended merely to give the flavor of the sorts of considerations that must be carefully weighed.

Affirmative action is said to provide role models, thus promoting an increase in future qualified candidates as well as increasing general pride, self-confidence, and motivation. Affirmative action programs are claimed to promote diversity. Corporations, universities, and governments are said to flourish when informed by diverse perspectives. While it is sexist to assume there is a "woman's point of view," since individual women differ in their views as widely as do men, there are certain kinds of experiences undergone by many women and few men, and input by those who have undergone those experiences may certainly be fruitful. (See also note 54.) Affirmative action is said both to change attitudes and enforce stereotypes. On one hand, it is increasingly hard to maintain that "women don't have what it takes to be good lawyers" when, as a result of affirmative action, seeing a highly effective female lawyer in action is a daily experience. On the other hand, if the result of affirmative action is that significant numbers of less qualified members of group G are hired or admitted, it is argued, it is likely that the lowest performing segment will have a disproportionately high number of members of group G, thus reinforcing negative stereotypes about group G. (See Murray, *op. cit.*, for a more detailed analysis of this point.) For similar reasons, affirmative action is claimed to lower the level of performance by admitting less qualified applications. Affirmative action programs lead to greater equality of distribution and help eliminate or mitigate institutional inequalities. Affirmative action is held to reinforce thinking in terms of gender or race and promotes racial or gender polarization. Affirmative action is charged with lowering the incentive to improve education for minorities by offering an alternative, less qualified "track." Since minority candidates may be discouraged from applying and qualification measurements, whether quantitative or subjective, may be biased against minorities, affirmative action can offset the effects of bias, especially perceptual bias.

Thomas Hill raises another important ethical dimension of the issue by drawing attention to the messages sent by affirmative action programs. Hill correctly points out that while the message sent by a program is not morally determinative, it is a morally significant feature of social policies. After pointing out shortcomings of messages inherent in both the reparative and purely utilitarian justifications of affirmative action, Hill suggests that affirmative action should deplore the wrongs of the past and "affirm a commitment to promote mutual trust and respect in the future."[91] Affirmative action, suggests Hill, should be understood as "an opportunity and a responsibility offered neither as charity nor as entitlement" but as "a special effort to welcome and encourage" full participation (pp. 209-210). Narrowly focused, flexible, and well-thought out affirmative actions that balance the full range of relevant factors (such as the multifaceted outreach program cited by Hill or a diverse and flexible combination of efforts to increase the number of Hispanic police officers in a predominantly Hispanic precinct) are better suited to sending this message than are rigid or across-the board programs, such as a large multinational corporation requiring that at least 30% of new hires be women.

In general, the best response to the lingering effects of racism and sexism, as many have urged, is a broad-ranging network of efforts to alleviate remaining vast disadvantages in education, housing, social environment, as well as more subtle forms of discrimination such as perceptual bias. Carefully planned and limited affirmative action programs may well play an important role in that process. In addition, such broad-scale initiatives take considerable time, and carefully planned affirmative action programs may help ameliorate disparities while those more comprehensive efforts are being implemented and effecting change.

In sum, affirmative action should be used carefully as a tool in particular situations in which it is likely to have beneficial consequences. The motivations for and methods of implementing affirmative action programs vary widely. Some affirmative action programs are initiated merely as a defensive measure against potential discrimination suits or to qualify for federal programs. Some originate in a vague but powerful sense that "we should do something" about racism and sexism. Some programs have narrowly focused and appropriate goals, such as increasing the number of Hispanic police officers on the street in heavily Hispanic neighborhoods, where (often justified) community distrust of police officers constitutes a major bar to good policing. Not surprisingly, then, affirmative action programs range from wrongheaded to highly useful. Too often, affirmative action programs are broad-scale, heavy-handed, and ill-conceived, but while many affirmative action programs are justly subject to criticism, blanket condemnation of affirmative action ignores the important good accomplished by narrowly focused and thoughtfully conceived affirmative action programs.

Thus politicians who proclaim themselves "for" or "against" affirmative action are misguided. Narrowly-focused affirmative action programs intelligently designed to accomplish, efficiently, specific, worthwhile goals are good public policy and should be supported. Affirmative action programs that lack these features should be modified or abandoned.

The Right to Self-determination

The argument above, if successful, shows that it is false that each "people" is a group that, as a group, possesses a right to self-determination. Any legitimate state must respect the natural rights of everyone. Jordan must respect the natural rights of Jews and Israel must respect the natural rights of Palestinians. But neither the Jewish people nor the Palestinian people possess a right, as a people, to a homeland. On the other hand, individual Jews could have vector rights concerning their group-oriented interest in a Jewish state whose sum may be weighty enough to create a resultant right to a Jewish state. Thus neither proponents nor opponents of the right of self-determination can win a general victory. There is no general right of self-determination every group possesses, but members of particular groups can successfully argue for resultant rights to a particular homeland. Each case must be weighed and argued individually, and, although some general factors can be articulated in advance, such as the importance and value of joint practices that would be extremely difficult to realize within a larger state, the relevant factors, circumstantial, historical, moral, and legal, will differ from case to case. The fact that Jews have historically and persistently been severely persecuted in states in which they constituted a minority while others have stood by idly permitting this persecution, shutting their borders to refugees trying to escape with their lives, certainly counts toward the need for a Jewish state. Relevant also is the strength and value of Judaism and Jewish tradition in the lives of Jews and the repeated, right-violating efforts of others in many places and at many times to undermine it. The facts that Jews have regarded Israel as their homeland for thousands of years and, on the other hand, that a Jewish state must result in the displacement of non-Jews from long-held homes are also relevant, as are a host of other factors. Different factors may be relevant to assessing the claims of individual Basques to a right to a separate Basque state. The complexity of the moral arguments in each case, drawing upon an open-ended field of considerations, cannot be avoided. The price of this complexity is that it rules out simple solutions. The virtue is that it promotes understanding, helping to devillify opponents. Moreover, because overridden vector rights still retain some force, something is still due those who are the losers of the moral weighing. If Jews do have a resultant right to a homeland, Palestinians who suffer from its implementation nonetheless have some vector warrants and are due important forms of consideration, a fact that is often overlooked in the debates on such questions.

Finally, while diverse bonds such as family, local community, culture, and so forth are of deep importance in human life, so is the broader, universalist bond of all moral agents, and, beyond that, the interconnectedness of all that exists. Emphasis on universality tends to homogenize, depersonalize, and rob us of the rich diversity life affords. Emphasis on particularity tends to become oppressive and parochial. A great society is like a great poem. Great poems are rich in striking details that work cohesively together to create a unity that is at once simple and complex. Similarly, the ultimate hope is for a richly and flexibly federated world society, fostering complex and multi-tiered bonds of special concern and responsive to animals and the environment. Such a world sometimes seems depressingly far from our reach, but cherishing that vision can moderate the harsher demands of universalism and parochialism, improving life now for those of us who stumble hesitantly and hopefully toward a better future.

Notes to Chapter Ten

1 Levy, Jacob T., "Classifying Cultural Rights," in Ian Shapiro and Will Kymlicka, eds., *Ethnicity and Group Rights: Nomos XXXIX*, New York and London: New York University Press, 1997, pp. 22-68.

2 Kymlicka, Will, "Individual and Community Rights," in Judith Baker, ed., *Group Rights*, Toronto, Buffalo, London: University of Toronto Press, 1994, pp. 17-33.

3 Young, Iris Marion, "Polity and Group Difference: A Critique of the Ideal of Universal Citizenship," *Ethics* 99, 1989, p. 260, as quoted in Stapleton, Julia, *Introduction to Group Rights: Perspectives since 1900*, Bristol: Thoemmes Press, 1995, xxxi. However, Young says specifically, in "Deferring Group Representation," in Shapiro and Kymlicka, eds., *op. cit.*, pp. 349-376; p. 365, that "it is a mistake to think that structural positioning forms the identity of persons."

4 See H.A.L. Fisher, ed., *The Collected Papers of Frederick William Maitland*, Three Volumes, Cambridge: Williams and Norgate, 1911.

5 A liver cell might, of course, be said to have a "good" of its own and even "purposes," in the sense of goal-oriented directedness in function, of its own, and although, ultimately, its "good" and "purpose" are dependent upon the good and purpose of the whole organism, a social organicist would claim the same is true of the good and purposes of an individual person in a community. The analogy breaks down, however, at a certain point; individual persons within a society are not fungible in the way that liver cells are.

6 Gould, Carol C., "Group Rights and Social Ontology," in Christine Sistare, Larry May, and Leslie Francis, eds., *Groups and Group Rights*, Lawrence, Kansas: University of Kansas Press, 2001, pp. 43-57.

7 Kukathas, Chandran, "Are there any Cultural Rights?" *Political Theory* 20:1 1992, pp. 105-139, reprinted in Stapleton, ed., *op. cit.*, pp. 258-298; pp. 267-268.

8 See, for example, Taylor, Charles, "Irreducibly Social Goods," in Geoffrey Brennan and Cliff Walsh, ed., *Rationality, Individualism and Public Policy*, Canberra: Australian National University Press, 1990, pp. 45-63.

9 Van Dyke, Vernon, in "Collective Entities and Moral Rights: Problems in Liberal-Democratic Thought," *Journal of Politics* 44:1, 1982, pp. 21-40, reprinted in Stapleton, ed., *op. cit.*, pp. 180-200.

10 17/C/Res.4.111., 15 November 1972.

11 Reaume, Denise, "The Group Right to Linguistic Security: Whose Right, What Duties," in Baker, ed., *op. cit.*, pp. 118-141

12 Waldron, Jeremy, *Liberal Rights: Collected Papers 1981-1991*, Cambridge: Cambridge University Press, 1993.

13 Rainbolt, George, "What Are Group Rights," in Sistare, May, and Francis, eds., *op. cit.*, pp. 71-81; 71. It should be noted that both these claims can be true: 1) The Hopi Nation (an organizational entity) has a right that the United States meet its treaty obligations" and 2) each individual member of the Hopi has the right that the United States meet its treaty obligations.

14 Wellman, Carl, "Alternatives for a Theory of Group Rights," in Sistare, May, and Francis, eds., *op. cit.*, pp. 17-42.

15 Waldron, Jeremy, *op. cit.*

16 Nickle, James W., "Group Agency and Group Rights," in Shapiro and Kymlicka, eds., *op. cit.*, pp. 235-256.

17 Cohen, Carl and Sterba, James P., *Affirmative Action and Racial Preference: A Debate*, New York: Oxford, 2003.

18 Van Dyke, Vernon, *op. cit.*, *p.* 181 and p. 183.

19 Just what "the proper way" means is an interesting and difficult question: recipients of a charity's aid are not part of the charity's base, while students are part of the base of a university.

20 Thomas W. Pogge, in "Group Rights and Ethnicity," in Shapiro and Kymlicka, eds., *op. cit.*, pp. 187-221; p. 187, avers that the term "'group' stands for any set of persons who are identified with this set: viewed as belonging together." Pogge is roughly right: strictly speaking, a group is not a set, which is a mathematical entity, but the members of the set.

21 See also May, Larry, *The Morality of Groups*, Notre Dame: University of Notre Dame Press, 1987.

22 Dennett, Daniel, *Brainstorms: Philosophical Essays on Mind and Psychology*, Montgomery, Vermont: Bradford Books, 1978, as well as much of his later work.

23 Davidson, Donald, "Mental Events," in *Essays on Actions and Events*, Oxford: Clarendon Press, 1980, pp. 207-25.

24 Simon, Thomas W., "Rights, Wrongs, and Culture," in Sistare, May, and Francis, eds., *op. cit.*, pp. 96-114; p. 99.

25 Nickle, James W., *op. cit.*, 235. Nickle denies that groups altogether lack identity and agency. However, the items in the list of sample groups with relatively clear identities and effective agency that Nickle provides on page 238 are all organizations and not groups.

26 The distinction nonetheless can have practical import when a group right is violated. For instance, one can be entitled to compensation for the violation of a right one chose not to exercise. If you illegally took steps to prevent me from entering a public park I can be compensated even if I never chose to try to enter the park. Suppose, then, that a Jewish homeland had not been established. If those Jews who lacked a subjective interest in the continuation of the Jewish people as a people did not have a right to a Jewish homeland, they would not be entitled to compensation, while they would have a vector right to compensation if they possessed the right but chose not to exercise it. Since, arguably, the grounds supporting the relevant vector right exists regardless of the subjective interests of individual Jews, I would urge that Jews with no such subjective interest nonetheless hold a vector warrant. I will generally assume the correctness of this conclusion in the way I phrase things below, but, if I am mistaken about this, the relevant passages can be rephrased without changing the basic points being made.

27 Van Dyke, *op. cit.*, cites Belgium as an example.

28 Wellman, Carl, *op. cit.*, p. 17.

29 Graff, James A., "Human Rights, Peoples, and the Right of Self-Determination," in Baker, ed., *op. cit.*, pp. 186-214.

30 For instance, Yael Tamir, in *Liberal Nationalism*, Princeton: Princeton University Press, 1993, analyzes the right of self-determination in terms of each individual's right to practice his or her own culture.

31 See also Rainbolt's discussion (*op. cit.*) of an example provided by Joseph Raz in *The Morality of Freedom*, New York: Oxford, 1986, namely, that the interest of one individual in a homeland for a people is insufficient to justify the large network of duties on the parts of many individuals that a people's right to a homeland imposes, while the collective interests of all the individuals comprising the people may be sufficient. (Raz himself holds that collective rights are convenient ways of talking about individual rights to protect interests in collective goods.) Rainbolt points out that rights are often granted to protect the interests of individuals besides the right-holder.

32 Note that while a corporation itself is an organizational entity and not a group, the group of shareholders of a corporation is a group of persons, not an organizational entity, even though membership in the group is defined via an organizational entity: the group of shareholders forms part of the base of the organization.

33 Wellman, Carl, *op. cit.*, p. 22.

34 What this means, of course, is subject to debate. "Assent" may mean "express consent" or merely "absence of profound dissent." One interpretation is that assent must be expressed through a vote. Another is that leaders who are viewed by a majority as legitimate leaders assent or do not voice profound dissent. The term "preponderance" may be construed as a majority of members, a plurality of members, the view of the most vocal and committed members, etc.

35 Simon, Thomas W., *op. cit.*, p. 112.

36 Gray, John, *Liberalism: Essays in Political Philosophy*, London and New York: Routledge, 1989, p. 234.

37 See also Kukathas, Chandran, "Are There any Cultural Rights?" *op. cit.*, for a different set of arguments that a liberal system of individual rights is compatible with concern for "the cultural health of minority cultures", p. 261.

38 Hart, H.L.A., "Are There Any Natural Rights," *Philosophical Review* LXIV 2, April 1955, pp. 175-191.

39 For answers to further arguments in favor of category one rights, See Rainbolt, *op. cit.*, and Hartney, Michael, "Some Confusions Concerning Collective Rights," *Canadian Journal of Law and Jurisprudence* 4, 1991, pp. 293-314.

40 See, for instance, Dworkin, Ronald, *Sovereign Virtue*, Cambridge, MA: Harvard University Press, 2000, and *Taking Rights Seriously*, Cambridge, MA: Harvard University Press, 1977.

41 Cohen, Carl and Sterba, James P., *op. cit.*, p. 23.

42 Cohen, Carl, *ibid.*

43 Pateman, Carole, "Democracy, Freedom, and Special Rights," in David Boucher and Paul Kelly eds., *Social Justice from Hume to Walzer*, London and New York: Routledge, 1998, p. 215-231.

44 *Minority Schools in Albania*, 1935 P.C.I.J. (Ser.A/B/) No. 64, cited in Anaya, S. James, "On Justifying Special Ethnic Group Rights: Comments on Pogge," in Shapiro & Kymlicka eds., *op. cit.*, pp. 222-231.

45 Kymlicka, Will, *op. cit.*, p. 25.

46 David West, in "Beyond Social Justice and Social Democracy: Positive Freedom and Cultural Wants," in Boucher and Kelly eds., *op cit.*, pp. 232-252, suggests that "cultural rights" safeguard the right to have "authentic" wants free from the "distorting" influence of culture.

47 Green, Leslie, "Internal Minorities and Their Rights," in Baker, ed., *op. cit.*, pp. 100-117; p. 103 and p. 104. Green avers that "x has a right only if x has an interest sufficiently important to warrant holding others to be under some duties to respect or promote that interest", p. 102.

48 It is controversial whether there is any such thing as "race," that is, whether a) the standard racial categories constitute a clear division of human morphology, b) if so, whether that categorization reflects significant biological differences and/or c) reflects important genetic or ancestral lines. While I would be inclined to answer "mostly no" to all three questions, space does not permit discussion of this issue.

49 Fletcher, George, *Loyalty: An Essay on the Morality of Relationships*, New York, Oxford: Oxford University Press, 1993.

50 Fried, Charles, "The Lawyer as Friend: The Moral Foundations of the Lawyer-Client Relation," 85 *Yale Law Journal* 1060, 1061, 1976.

51 This case provides another interesting problematic third-party beneficiary case for the interest theory of rights.

52 Perhaps some might argue for a right to self-identification. But it is hard to imagine a compelling argument that tax law must be amended to accommodate Jones' arbitrary preference to see himself as a blue-eyed person more than as a tall person: if such a right exists, it is a right to think as one likes, not a warrant for demanding sacrifices of others.

53 See also Rowan, John, *Conflicts of Rights*, Boulder, CO: Westview, 1999, esp. p. 110.

54 Young, Iris Marion, "Deferring Group Representation," *op. cit.*, p. 350. Young claims that what women, for example, have in common is a social experience based on their social positioning. However, the content and effect of being "positioned as a woman" varies greatly in different subcultures, classes, families, workplaces, and so on. Thus either women do not share a single "social perspective" or, if that perspective is understood as what is common to all women's experience despite this diversity, then social perspective has little content. Young herself recognizes on page 368 that individual women's perspectives are as diverse as their interests. She deals with this by distinguishing between shared "background and perspective" and particular interpretations or content. The point, however, is that the background perspective of being a woman could be vastly different for a given coal miner's daughter in rural West Virginia who married another coal miner at age 17 and a given daughter of members of a commune in Cam-

bridge, Massachusetts. Even the public culture of the United States does not speak with a univocal voice. Social expectations of the sort Young describes certainly exist, but they are not, to use Young's term, "univocal." The reality is that there exists a variety of fragmented, conflicting, and overlapping social expectations, some vague and some specific, some informal and some reflected in rules of some sort. For any given aspect of this complex network of social understandings, the commonality of experience of women in America forms a rough bell curve, and an individual woman may find herself at a different point in the curve for each aspect. While this fact does not support the claim that women must be represented by women, it does support the more general, merely statistical claim that affirmative action tends to generate greater diversity.

55 Cudd, Ann, "Nonvoluntary Social Groups," in Sistare, May, and Francis, eds., *op. cit.*, pp. 58-70.

56 Cudd herself does not make this claim.

57 Fletcher, George, *op. cit.*, p. 25.

58 Royce, Josiah, *The Philosophy of Loyalty*, New York: Macmillan, 1908, p. 21.

59 Dworkin, Gerald, *The Theory and Practice of Autonomy*, Cambridge: Cambridge University Press, 1988.

60 Cf. Schlossberger, Eugene, *Moral Responsibility and Persons*, Philadelphia: Temple University Press, 1992.

61 If Fletcher in fact meant something different by "moral choice" when denying that loyalty is a choice, his arguments nonetheless can be discussed as applying to moral choice in the sense limned above, although, in that case, defects of the arguments may not reflect upon Fletcher himself.

62 Ladd, John, "Loyalty," *Encyclopedia of Philosophy* 5, 1967, pp. 97-98.

63 Of course, the argument leaves open the possibility that loyalty is autonomously chosen on some basis other than a general property. The kind of choice that interests Royce and Dworkin, however, is principled choice, which, presumably, would be based on some general property.

64 It should be noted that Fletcher recognizes that individuals may have different historical bonds to several countries and discusses possibly conflicting claims of nativity, upbringing, and citizenship.

65 For further discussion of this issue, see Schlossberger, Eugene, *Moral Responsibility and Persons, op. cit.*

66 The term "because" here expresses the motivating reason. Suppose that, because Kirk attends Booth's Church, he has become well acquainted with her mesmerizing public speaking abilities. In that case, Kirk's being a fellow Pentecostalist is a causal factor explaining Booth's decision, but not the motivating reason—the motivating reason is Kirk's public speaking skill.

67 It should be noted, however, that the importance of addressing discrimination must be weighed against the value of discretion and qualitative judgments. Discretion and judgment always poses the possible danger of discrimination. Discrimination may be explicit or perceptual—an employer may show preference for, for example, another male either because he acts out of loyalty to his gender or because he is prone, perhaps without

knowing it, to view males and females differently. While explicit discrimination is less pervasive than in the past, perceptual discrimination still pervades the workplace and the legal system.

Legal systems, thus, must always balance the value of discretion and judgment against the danger of abuse. If a sentencing judge must decide whether to impose a three or five year sentence upon a convicted felon, the danger exists that the judge will tend to impose longer sentences upon African-Americans than upon others. This danger is mitigated by a strict schedule of sentences for specifically defined crimes. However, legislators drawing up such a schedule cannot possibly detail every relevant factor that will ever arise and deal with it in a reasonable way. Thus such schedules, wholly unresponsive to any features of the case not specifically detailed by the schedule, can lead to substantial unfairness. A simple clerical error can result in the same long prison sentence as deliberate and invidious fraud. Thus sentencing procedures must attempt to balance the need for the use of discretion and judgment in interpretation against the danger of discriminatory sentencing practices.

Because our legal system is so sensitive to discrimination, legal practice, and as a result, social practice, has become increasingly dominated by schedules. A tenure committee that awards tenure on the basis of quality of publications risks losing a lawsuit, while a tenure committee that awards tenure on the sheer number of publications is fairly well-protected, since quality is a discretionary judgment while number, by and large, is not. A tenure committee that awards tenure on the basis of a careful judgment of the quality of teaching risks losing a lawsuit, while a tenure committee that awards tenure on the basis of the numerical mean of student evaluations is protected, because judgments of quality are discretionary while numerical means, by and large, are not. A professor who gives careful thought to the legitimacy of a reason for missing class risks losing a lawsuit, while a professor who fails every student who misses four classes, for whatever reason, is better protected. Businesses that promote according to a rigid schedule based on quarterly bottom line are better protected than businesses that promote on a careful consideration of how well an employee has handled the situation in which he or she finds herself.

This feature of present law works against the recommendation for affirmative action advocated in this chapter. A rigid affirmative action program is easier to document than more flexible and balanced programs and a broad-scale program is better protection from court scrutiny than narrowly-defined programs. Institutions must find a workable compromise between legal practicality and what is ethical and sensible. A more enlightened judicial view of the matter would improve the range of feasible compromises. Such a change would also ameliorate the conflict between discrimination law and an increasing tendency for the law to adopt the principle of *respondat superior*. Employers are increasingly being held liable when employees act improperly without the knowledge or consent of the employer. But employers who use their subjective sense of who is trustworthy when hiring or monitoring employees risk losing discrimination lawsuits. Thus one court insists that it is the employer who has the best opportunity to hire trustworthy employees and monitor their activities while another court effectively prevents the employer from doing so.

A better and more sensitive balance is needed between the legitimate need to address discrimination and the legitimate need to make qualitative judgments.

68 Newton, Lisa H. "Can Reverse Discrimination Be Justified," *Ethics* 83 4, 1973, pp. 308-312, reprinted in Raziel Abelson and Marie-Louise Friquegnon, eds., *Ethics for Modern Life* 4th ed., New York: St. Martin's Press, 1991, pp. 271-275; p. 273.

69 Fiss, Owen M., "Groups and the Equal Protection Clause," *Philosophy and Public Affairs* 5:2, Winter 1976, reprinted in Marshall Cohen, Thomas Nagel, and Thomas Scanlon, eds., *Equality and Preferential Treatment*, Princeton: Princeton, 1977, pp. 84-154.

70 *Moose Lodge No. 107 v. Iris*, 407 U.S. 163, 1972.

71 Relevant to this particular argument, however, is the claim, discussed below, that affirmative action programs fail to compensate those who deserve it most.

72 Dworkin, Ronald, "The DeFunis Case," *The New York Review of Books* 23:1 February 5, 1976.

73 Unless otherwise specified, references to Thomson in this chapter refer to Thomson, Judith Jarvis, "Preferential Hiring," *Philosophy and Public Affairs* v. 2 no. 4, Summer 1973, reprinted in Cohen, Nagel, and Scanlon, eds., *op. cit.*, pp. 19-39.

74 Thomson, Judith Jarvis, "A Defense of Abortion," *Philosophy and Public Affairs* 1, 1971, pp. 47-66.

75 Thomson, Judith Jarvis, *The Realm of Rights*, Cambridge, MA: Harvard University Press, 1990.

76 Schlossberger, Eugene, "A New Model of Business: Dual-Investor Theory," *Business Ethics Quarterly* 4, Fall 1994, pp. 459-474.

77 Fullinwinder, Robert, "Preferential Hiring and Compensation," *Social Theory and Practice* 3, 1975, pp. 16-17 and Rowan, John, *op. cit.*

78 Ezorksy, Gertrude, *Racism and Justice: The Case for Affirmative Action*, Cornell University Press, 1991, reprinted in Raziel Ableson and Marie-Louise Friquegnon, eds., *Ethics for Modern Life* 6th ed., Boston: St. Martin's Press, 2003, pp. 440-447; p. 446.

79 See, for instance, Wilson, William J., *The Truly Disadvantaged*, Chicago: University of Chicago Press, 1987, cited in Rowan, *op. cit.*

80 Simon, Robert T., "Preferential Hiring: A Reply to Judith Jarvis Thomson," *Philosophy and Public Affairs* 3, 1974, reprinted in Cohen et al. eds., *op. cit.*, pp. 40-48; p. 43.

81 Levin, Michael E., "Is Racial Discrimination Special?" *Journal of Value Inquiry* 15 3, 1981, pp. 225-234.

82 Boxill, Bernard R., *Blacks and Social Justice*, rev. ed., Roman and Littlefield, 1992.

83 Nickel, James W, "Should Reparations Be to Individuals or to Groups," in Barry R. Gross, ed., *Reverse Discrimination*, Buffalo: Prometheus Books, 1977, pp. 315-316.

84 Sher, George, "Justifying Reverse Discrimination in Employment," *Philosophy and Public Affairs* 4 2, Winter 1975, reprinted in Cohen, Nagel, and Scanlon eds., *op. cit.*, pp. 49-62.

85 Morris, Christopher, "Existential Limits to the Rectification of Past Wrongs," *American Philosophical Quarterly* 21, 1984, pp. 175-82.

86 For example, many colleges would no doubt reply to Sterba that while grades and SAT scores are at best approximating fictions of future academic performance, they are

the best feasible measure available. Whether this claim is correct remains a matter of considerable controversy, but, for most institutions that base admissions on grades and SAT scores, belief in the truth of claim does constitute the rationale for the practice. As Sterba notes, even universities with the most relative resources cannot feasibly mount a "comprehensive evaluation of each applicant's qualifications", p. 257. By contrast, rough measures of disadvantage, such as family income, can readily be obtained. Sterba insists that, given the pervasiveness of racism, rarely do affirmative action programs benefit applicants who do not deserve compensation. As noted elsewhere in this chapter, the degree to which this claim is correct varies with the particular program.

87 Fiss, *op. cit.*

88 Sher, George, *op. cit.*

89 See Murray, Charles, "Affirmative Racism," *The New Republic,* 1964, reprinted in Ableson and Friquegnon, eds., 6th edition, *op. cit.*, pp. 430-439.

90 John Rowan, *op. cit.*, suggests that the central question about affirmative action for the interest theory of rights is whether there is a legitimate interest, possessed by all members of the preferenced group, that is both effectively served by affirmative action and not overridden by any other considerations. Rowan's question is certainly pertinent, since an interest of this sort could be the basis of a warrant. Of course, even on the interest theory, the mere fact that C has an interest does not, by itself, create a duty on the part of D to advance that interest: the interest must further be shown to be a compelling one, in the sense that it is sufficient to create a duty. Moreover, if the warrant theory is correct, there are other forms of warrant besides compelling interest. Hence a negative answer to Rowan's question is not definitive if, as Chapter 3 argues, the warrant theory is correct.

91 Hill, Thomas E. Jr., *Autonomy and Self-Respect*, Cambridge and New York: Cambridge University Press, 1991, p. 207.

Index

Ahrens, John, 223-224, 237n
Amoralism, 49-50
Autonomy, 37-40
Baier, Annette, 234n
Baker, C. Edwin, 163, 168-170, 176-
177, 190n
Barry, Brian, 235n
Bayles, Michael, 251, 255, 256
Benditt, Theodore, 20-22, 83-84, 85
Bentham, Jeremy, 1, 93-94, 127, 134-
135, 157n
Bernstein, Mark, 218-220
Bok, Sissela, 196
Bosanquet, Richard, 155n
Boxill, Bernard, 333, 334, 335
Brandt, Richard, 107n
Burley, Justine, 262
Callahan, Daniel, 231, 235n
Carr, Albert, 211n
Cavell, Stanley, 148
Cohen, Carl, 295, 334
Community, 44, 51
Contract Theories, 41-46
Cudd, Ann, 308, 347n
Delattre, Edward, 221
Davidson, Donald, 287
Dennett, Daniel, 286
Derr, Thomas S., 231, 234n
De-Shalit, Avner, 231, 232n, 236n
Devlin, Lord Patrick, 34, 147
Discretion v. rules, 347-348n
Dworkin, Gerald, 309
Dworkin, Ronald, 34, 39, 71, 112, 262-
263, 275n, 295, 324-325, 347n
Edwards, R.G., 251
Ellin, James S., 195
Ethics of care, 50-51, 143
Ezorsky, Gertrude, 331
Feinberg, Joel, 53n, 61, 70, 78, 107n,
124n, 157n, 216-217, 249
Fishkin, James, 25
Fiss, Owen, 322, 336
Fletcher, Joseph, 46
Fletcher, George, 302-303, 304, 309-
321, 347n
Frey, R.G., 157n
Fried, Charles, 84, 159n, 302
Fullwinder, Robert, 331

Future, truth value of statements about,
221, 236n
George, Richard T. de, 213, 234n, 235n
Gewirth, Alan, 47-49, 133, 156n
Gilligan, Carol, 50, 143
Golding, Martin, 234-235n
Gould, Carol, 281
Graff, James, 292
Gray, John, 293
Green, Leslie, 298, 346n
Grice, Russell, 115
Haas, John, 274n
Harming the dead, 216-220
Harris, John, 253, 255
Hart, H.L.A., 84, 90, 119, 126n, 157n,
294
Hartney, Michael, 345n
Hill, Thomas Jr., 38, 196, 340
Hobbes, Thomas, 136, 152, 156n
Hohfeld, Wesley, 4, 31, 56, 64n, 77,
80, 110, 121
Holland, Tom, 167
Jenkins, Iredell, 1, 50, 70, 78
Kant, Immanuel, 139, 148, 198-199
Kass, Leon, 251-252, 256, 257
Kavka, Gregory, 231, 235
Korsgaard, Chirstine M., 210n
Kramer, Matthew, 69, 87, 89, 90, 93,
94-5, 99, 117, 123n, 124n
Krimmel, Herbert, 248-249, 254
Kukathas, Chandras, 281, 345n
Kymlicka, Will, 278, 279, 297
Ladd, John, 310
Langlois, Anthony, 34, 141-142
Lewontin, Richard, 257
Levi, Edward H., 108, 112
Levin, Michael, 333
Levy, Jacob, 277
Lippke, Richard, 53n
Locke, John, 32, 136, 142, 153, 159n
Lomasky, Loren, 46, 49, 54n, 155n
Lombardi, Louis, 158n
Lyons, David, 94-95
McCloskey, H.J., 72
MacCormick, Neil, 125-126n
MacDonald, Margaret, 157n
MacIntrye, Alasdair, 1, 148
McMahon, Christopher, 204

Mabbott, J.B., 135
Machon, Tibor, 157n
Mackie, J. L., 157n
Macklin, Ruth, 220-224
Maitland, F.W., 279
Marx, Karl, 141
May, Larry, 344n
Meilaender, Gilbert, 275
Mill, John Stuart, 139, 146, 148, 163
Morris, Christopher, 334
Murray, Charles, 340, 350n
Nelson, Hilde Lindemann, 254
Newton, Lisa, 322-324
Nickle, James, 285, 287, 333, 344n
Nozick, Robert, 36-37
Obligations to the dead, 216-220
O'Neil (State v.), 112
Organizations v. groups, 284-289
Parfit, Derek, 226, 237n
Partridge, Ernest, 231
Pateman, Carole, 295
Pence, Gregory, 273n
Pitcher, George, 218-219
Pletcher, Galen, 236n
Pogge, Thomas, 344n
Positivism, legal, 52n
Posner, Richard, 155n
Prince (Regina v.), 26, 112
Purdy, Laura, 252
Putnam, Hilary, 255-256
Rainbolt, George, 108, 284, 343n, 345n
Ramsey, Paul, 1
Rawls, John, 36-37, 41-45, 139-140
Raz, Joseph, 33-34, 35, 94, 99, 115, 282, 345n
Reaume, Denise, 282
Rights: as morally basic, 45-46;
    discretionary/non-discretionary,
    26; epistemological 31, 79-80,
    120; holistic approach to, 2-3,
    177-178; implicit (legal), 27-28; in
    personam, 22-23; in rem, 22-23;
    moral, 23-25, 194; natural, 28-29;
    need theory, 46-49; positive and
    negative, 32-33, 36, 56;
    presumptive, 28-29, 129-130;
    prima facie, 20-22; proclamative,
    76-77, 113, 120; redressable/non-
    redressable, 26-27, 328; regulative
    ideals, 29-30; resultant, 20-22;

social, 25-26; to call oneself a
    poet, 30-31, 77-78, 111, 120-121;
    to life, 2, 133; to privacy, 147-
    150; to property, 150-153; to vote,
    29-30; vector, 20-22; to die, 60-62
Rocheleau, Jordy, 61
Ross, William, 52n
Routley, Richard, 234n
Routley, Val, 234n
Rowan, John, 34, 53n, 157n, 164-165,
    190n, 331, 332, 346n, 350n
Royce, Josiah, 309, 310, 311, 313, 314,
    318, 347n
Russell, Bruce, 155n
Sandel, Michael, 44
Sartre, Jean Paul, 318
Scanlon, Tim, 42-45
Schlossberger, Eugene: *Moral
    Responsibility and Persons*, 39,
    50, 126n, 137, 174, 219, 347n;
    The Ethical Engineer, 40, 104,
    234n; *Environmental Ethics: An
    Aristotelian Approach*, 50, 53n; *A
    New Model of Business*, 159n
Schwartz, Thomas, 226, 228
Self-regarding/world-oriented interests,
    33-34
Sher, George, 334, 337
Sherwin, Susan, 253
Shue, Henry, 157n
Sikora, R.I., 225-226
Silver, Lee M., 256-257
Simmonds, N.E., 104
Simmons, A. John, 210
Simon, Robert, 333
Simon, Thomas, 287, 293
Stanworth, Michelle, 253
Steiner, Hillel, 67, 84, 89, 92, 96, 124n
Sterba, James, 236-237n, 285, 289,
    332, 334, 349-350n
Strong, Carson, 244, 245, 249-250
Sullivan (N.Y. Times v.), 4, 59, 164
Sullivan, William, 147
Sumner, L., 155n, 156-157n
Talbott William J., 129
Taylor, Charles, 148, 343n
Tamir, Yael, 345n
Thomson, Judith Jarvis, 24, 53n, 57-58,
    60, 114, 126n, 155n, 326-329,
    331, 332, 334, 336-337

Tiefel, Hans, 250-251
Universal declaration of human rights,
     9, 127-128
Utility, 39-40
Van Dyke, Vernon, 282, 285, 347n
Van Wyck, Robert N., 210n
Vlastos, Gregory, 156n
Waldron, Jeremy, 156n, 282-283, 285,
     294
Walzer, Michael, 148
Warrant: defined, 72
Warren, Mary Ann, 225-226, 237n
Wasserstrom, Richard, 155n, 157n
Wellman, Carl, 22, 106n, 123n, 126n,
     285, 292, 293
Wellman, Christopher Heath, 156n
Wenz, Peter, 226, 234n
West, David, 346n
White, Alan, 88
Wilson, William, 349n
Young, Iris Marion, 308, 343n, 346-
     347n
Zaner, Richard, 250

About the Author

Eugene Schlossberger (Ph.D. University of Chicago, 1978), Associate Professor of Philosophy at Purdue University Calumet, is the author of two previous books, *Moral Responsibility and Persons* and *The Ethical Engineer*. His numerous articles and reviews on a range of philosophical topics, including ethical theory, business and engineering ethics, political philosophy, family therapy, the logic of counterfactuals, Wittgenstein, Aristotle, and Peirce, have appeared in various journals including *Mind, Analysis, Philosophical Studies, Ethics, Journal of Marital and Family Therapy, Science and Engineering Ethics*, and *Business Ethics Quarterly*. He also publishes poetry and composes operas.